A Handlist of the Manuscripts in the Institute of Ethiopian Studies, Volume One

ETHIOPIC MANUSCRIPT IMAGING PROJECT

Ethiopic Manuscripts, Texts, and Studies

The series Ethiopic Manuscripts, Texts, and Studies offers, in the first place, catalogues of the Ethiopic Manuscript Imaging Project whose purpose it is to digitize and catalogue collections of Ethiopic manuscripts in North America and around the world. Beyond this, though, the series offers a venue for monographs, revised dissertations, and texts that explore the rich historical, literary, and artistic traditions of Ethiopia and the Ethiopian Orthodox Church.

The series has particular interest in Ethiopic manuscripts and the scribal practices in evidence within them. This includes analytical studies of particular manuscripts or particular scribal practices and illuminations. Moreover, the interest extends to synthetic studies that explore the developments of scribal and artistic practice across time or those that probe the interconnections between common elements in manuscripts, scribal practices, scribal education, and community ideology.

Series Editor
Steve Delamarter

A Handlist of the Manuscripts in the Institute of Ethiopian Studies, Volume One: The Gǝ'ǝz and Amharic Materials of the Ethiopian Orthodox Tradition

Demeke Berhane,
qäsis Melaku Terefe, Steve Delamarter,
Jeremy R. Brown, and Jacopo Gnisci

Edited by
Steve Delamarter, Jacopo Gnisci, and Jeremy R. Brown

◆PICKWICK *Publications* · Eugene, Oregon

A HANDLIST OF THE MANUSCRIPTS IN THE INSTITUTE OF ETHIOPIAN STUDIES, VOLUME ONE
The Gəʿəz and Amharic Materials of the Ethiopian Orthodox Tradition

Ethiopic Manuscripts, Texts, and Studies 19

Copyright © 2025 Wipf and Stock Publishers. All rights reserved. Except for brief quotations in critical publications or reviews, no part of this book may be reproduced in any manner without prior written permission from the publisher. Write: Permissions, Wipf and Stock Publishers, 199 W. 8th Ave., Suite 3, Eugene, OR 97401.

Pickwick Publications
An Imprint of Wipf and Stock Publishers
199 W. 8th Ave., Suite 3
Eugene, OR 97401

www.wipfandstock.com

PAPERBACK ISBN: 978-1-6667-8553-1
HARDCOVER ISBN: 978-1-6667-8554-8
EBOOK ISBN: 978-1-6667-8555-5

Cataloguing-in-Publication data:

Names: Berhane, Demeke, author; Terefe, Melaku, author; Delamarter, Steve, author; Brown, Jeremy R., author; Gnisci, Jacopo, author; Delamarter, Steve, editor; Gnisci, Jacopo, editor; Brown, Jeremy R., editor.

Title: A handlist of the manuscripts in the Institute of Ethiopian Studies, volume one : the Gəʿəz and Amharic materials of the Ethiopian Orthodox tradition / by Demeke Berhane, Melaku Terefe, Steve Delamarter, Jeremy R. Brown, and Jacopo Gnisci ; edited by Steve Delamarter, Jacopo Gnisci, and Jeremy R. Brown.

Description: Eugene, OR: Cascade Books, 2025. | Ethiopic Manuscripts, Texts, and Studies 19. | Includes bibliographical references and indexes.

Identifiers: ISBN 978-1-6667-8553-1 (paperback). | ISBN 978-1-6667-8554-8 (hardcover). | ISBN 978-1-6667-8555-5 (ebook).

Subjects: LSCH: Manuscripts—Ethiopic—Catalogs. | Codicology. | Scribes—Ethiopian. | Scribes—Africa.

Classification: BS4.5 B45 2025 (print). | BS4.5 (ebook).

VERSION NUMBER 05/19/25

Photos in the preface taken by and courtesy of Steve Delamarter, director Ethiopic Manuscript Imaging Project.

Photos courtesy of Ethiopic Manuscript Imaging Project (Steve Delamarter, director).

Contents

Series Foreword / vii
Table of Plates / ix
Preface / xi
    by Steve Delamarter
The History of the Collection at the IES / xli
    by Demeke Berhane
Introduction to the Handlist / li
    by Steve Delamarter and Jacopo Gnisci
The Digitization of the Materials in the Manuscripts
    and Archives Department of the IES / liii
    by Jeremy R. Brown
The Urgent Need for Digitizing and Cataloging Ethiopic Manuscripts / lix
    by *qäsis* Melaku Terefe
Illuminated Ethiopic Manuscripts at the IES / lxi
    by Jacopo Gnisci
List of Abbreviations / lxv

Catalogue of the Manuscripts / 1

List of Manuscripts by IES Shelf Mark / 263
IES Manuscripts Microfilmed in the EMML Project / 277
List of Dated or Datable Codices / 281
List of Undated Codices / 287
List of Dates of the Magic Scrolls / 291
Plates / 293
Index of Major Works in the Codices / 315
Index of Miniatures / 329
Index of Names and Places in the Codices / 337
Index of Names of Owners in the Magic Scrolls / 341

Series Foreword

The series *Ethiopic Manuscripts, Texts, and Studies* offers, in the first place, catalogues of the Ethiopic Manuscript Imaging Project whose purpose it is to digitize and catalogue collections of Ethiopic manuscripts in North America and around the world. Beyond this, though, the series offers a venue for monographs, revised dissertations, and texts that explore the rich historical, literary, and artistic traditions of Ethiopia and the Ethiopian Orthodox Church.

    The series has particular interest in Ethiopic manuscripts and the scribal practices in evidence within them. This includes analytical studies of particular manuscripts or particular scribal practices and illuminations. Moreover, the interest extends to synthetic studies that explore the developments of scribal and artistic practice across time or those that probe the interconnections between common elements in manuscripts, scribal practices, scribal education, and community ideology.

Steve Delamarter, series editor

Table of Plates

Plate 1. IES 4, ff. iv v(erso)-1r	293
Plate 2. IES 7, ff. 34v-35r	294
Plate 3. IES 7, ff. 48v-49r	294
Plate 4. IES 7, ff. 49v-50r	295
Plate 5. IES 7, ff. 50v-51r	295
Plate 6. IES 7, ff. 16v-17r	296
Plate 7. IES 73, front cover	296
Plate 8. IES 73, back cover	297
Plate 9. IES 73, ff. ii v(erso)-1r	297
Plate 10. IES 73, ff. 109v-110r	298
Plate 11. IES 74, ff. i v(erso)-1r	298
Plate 12. IES 74, ff. 124v-125r	299
Plate 13. IES 34, inside front cover-1r	299
Plate 14. IES 34, ff. 226v-inside back cover	300
Plate 15. IES 103, ff. iv v(erso)-1r	300
Plate 16. IES 103, ff. 26v-27r	301
Plate 17. IES 103, ff. 67v-68r	301
Plate 18. IES 105, f. 6r	302
Plate 19. IES 105, f. 5v	302
Plate 20. IES 242, ff. 2v-3r	303
Plate 21. IES 242, ff. 3v-4r	303
Plate 22. IES 242, ff. 75v-76r	304
Plate 23. IES 242, f. 161r	304
Plate 24. IES 722, ff. 74v-75r	305
Plate 25. IES 721, ff. 2v-3r	305
Plate 26. IES 721, ff. 85v-86r	306

Plate 27. IES 721, ff. 174v-175r	306
Plate 28. IES 723, ff. ii v(erso)-1r	307
Plate 29. IES 723, ff. 6v-7r	307
Plate 30. IES 679, f. 1r	308
Plate 31. IES 679, spine	308
Plate 32. IES 496, ff. 14v-15r	309
Plate 33. IES 496, f. 43v	309
Plate 34. IES 496, f. 43v	310
Plate 35. IES 496, f. 43v	310
Plate 36. IES 496, ff. 70v-71r	311
Plate 37. IES 496, f. 70v	311
Plate 38. IES 496, f. 71r	312
Plate 39. IES 496, f. 102r	312
Plate 40. IES 496, f. 89v	313
Plate 41. IES 496, f. 89v	313
Plate 42. IES 496, f. 89v	314

Preface

Steve Delamarter

This is now the second volume catalogue to be published on the holdings at the Institute of Ethiopian Studies (IES). The actual second volume, though first to be published, was *A Handlist of the Manuscripts of the Institute of Ethiopian Studies, Volume Two: The Arabic Materials of the Ethiopian Islamic Tradition*.[1]

The story of the digitization of the collection of manuscripts at the IES in 2010 and the eventual cataloguing of that collection in the subsequent years is a long and complex one. It is bound up with a series of people and initiatives that had begun six years earlier and was to play out for another dozen years after 2010 in order to reach the point of the publication of the volume you have here. It is not possible to understand what happened in 2010 nor today in 2023 without a review of the people and processes that have taken place across these years.

One of the best outcomes of my first trip to Ethiopia in 2004 was the relationship I developed with the community at the Institute of Ethiopian Studies and with the IES director, Dr. Elizabeth W. Giorgis, and with the director of the Manuscripts and Archives Department, *ato* Demeke Berhane. Dr. Elizabeth oversaw my application for affiliation

---

1. Alessandro Gori, *A Handlist of the Manuscripts in the Institute of Ethiopian Studies, II: The Arabic Materials of the Ethiopian Islamic Tradition*, with contributions from Anne Regourd, Jeremy R. Brown, and Steve Delamarter, and a foreword by Demeke Berhane. Ethiopic Manuscripts, Texts, and Studies Series 20 (Eugene, OR: Pickwick Publications, 2014).

with the IES as a researcher. Demeke checked out manuscripts to me (I remember, especially, IES 1081, a copy of the Lectionary for Passion Week, ግብረ ሕማማት). My time in Ethiopia began on the 13th of April, 2004 and ended on May 4 when I returned to my home in Portland, OR. In the first week I became familiar with the IES and using its collection. I also looked for everything I could find on Ethiopian scribes and their practices. For the following weeks, I and my translator, Daniel Alemu a member of the Jerusalem Ethiopian Orthodox community, travelled to various monasteries in Ethiopia to locate and interview scribes.

I had met Daniel in Jerusalem where I had spent the previous six months on sabbatical. I stayed at the Tantur Ecumenical Institute overlooking Bethlehem. The director, Father Michael McGarry introduced me to Dr. Kirsten Stoffregen-Pedersen, a Brigettine sister from Denmark, living in close relationship with the Ethiopian community. She was known popularly in Jerusalem as Sister Abraham.

Seeing that I had no experience in the Middle East, Dr. Kirsten took me under her wing, and helped me to meet several leaders in Jerusalem. When she found out about my plans to go to Ethiopia, she introduced me to the Ethiopian community there in Jerusalem and to Daniel Alemu, a young man of remarkable linguistic capability, and well along in his college education. He had grown up in Jerusalem, the son of an Ethiopian with roots in Wollo and an Arabic Christian mother from the Old City. Daniel had never been to Ethiopia to see the country nor to meet his father's family. I invited him to join me on the trip to Ethiopia as a translator. In truth, Daniel was more than a translator. He became a fellow researcher on the trip.

Figure 1: View from Tantur towards Bethlehem (the wall was built during the time I was in Israel) (left); Kirsten Stoffregen-Pedersen (center); Holy Saturday at the Ethiopian site at the Church of the Holy Sepulcher (right)

I was interested in learning about the social location of scribes in Ethiopia and the nature of their roles in relation to the Ethiopian Orthodox Tewahedo church. I had studied carefully the works of Emanuel Tov[2] on Qumran Scribal Practices and the works of Shemaryahu Talmon[3] on

---

2. His magnum opus on the subject is *Scribal Practices and Approaches Reflected in the Texts Found in the Judean Desert* (Leiden: Brill, 2004). But Tov had published a host of smaller works leading up to that book. These include: "Correction Procedures in the Texts from the Judean Desert," in *The Provo International Conference on the Dead Sea Scrolls: Technological Innovations, New Texts, and Reformulated Issues*, edited by Donald W. Parry and Eugene Ulrich, STDJ 30 (Leiden: Brill, 1999), 232-63; "The Textual Base of Corrections in the Biblical Texts Found in Qumran," in *The Dead Sea Scrolls—Forty Years of Research*, edited by D. Dimant and U. Rappaport (Leiden: Brill, 1992), 299-314; "The Dimensions of the Qumran Scrolls," *DSD* 5 (1998): 69-91; "Scribal Practices Reflected in the Texts from the Judaean Desert," in *The Dead Sea Scrolls after Fifty Years: A Comprehensive Assessment*, edited by Peter W. Flint and James C. VanderKam, 2 vols. (Leiden: Brill, 1998), 1:403-29; "The Scribes of the Texts found in the Judean Desert," in *The Quest for Context and Meaning: Studies in Biblical Intertextuality in Honor of James A. Sanders*, edited by Craig A. Evans and Shemaryahu Talmon (Leiden: Brill, 1997), 131-52; "Scribal Markings in the Texts from the Judean Desert," in *Current Research and Technological Developments on the Dead Sea Scrolls: Conference on the Texts from the Judean Desert, Jerusalem, 30 April 1995*, edited by Donald W. Parry and Stephen D. Ricks, STDJ 20 (Leiden: Brill, 1996), 41-77; "Scribal Practices and Physical Aspects of the Dead Sea Scrolls," in *The Bible as Book: The Manuscript Tradition*, edited by John L. Sharpe III and Kimberly Van Kampen (London: The British Library, 1998), 9-33; "Sense Divisions in the Qumran Texts, the Masoretic Text, and Ancient Translations of the Bible," in *The Interpretation of the Bible: The International Symposium in Slovenia*, edited by Joze Krasovec, JSOT Supplement Series 289 (Sheffield: Sheffield Academic, 1998), 121-46; "Special Layout of Poetical Units in the Texts from the Judean Desert," in *Give Ear to My Words: Psalms and Other Poetry in and around the Hebrew Bible: Essays in Honour of Professor N. A. van Uchelen*, edited by Janet Dyk et al. (Amsterdam: Societas Hebraica Amstelodamensis, 1996), 115-28; "The Socio-Religious Background of the Paleo-Hebrew Biblical Texts Found at Qumran," in *Geschichte—Tradition—Reflexion: Festschrift für Martin Hengel zum 70. Geburtstag* (Tübingen: Mohr Siebeck, 1996), 333-74; "Scribal Practices Reflected in the Paleo-Hebrew Texts from the Judean Desert," *Scripta Classica Israelica* 15 (1996): 268-73.

3. Of Talmon's significant scholarly output, I have focused particularly on "The Transmission History of the Text of the Hebrew Bible in the Light of Biblical Manuscripts from Qumran and Other Sites in the Judean Desert," in *The Dead Sea Scrolls: Fifty Years after Their Discovery. Proceedings of the Jerusalem Congress, July 20-25, 1997*, edited by Lawrence H. Schiffman et al. (Jerusalem: Israel Exploration Society in cooperation with The Shrine of the Book, Israel Museum, 2000), 40-50; "Anti-Lunar-Calendar Polemics in Covenanters' Writings," in *Das Ende der Tage und die Gegenwart Des Heils: Begegnungen mit dem Neuen Testament und Seiner Umwelt Festschrift Für Heinz-Wolfgang Kuhn Zum 65. Geburtstag*, edited by Michael Becker and Wolfgang Fenske (Leiden: Brill, 1999), 29-40; "Calendar Controversy in Ancient Judaism: The Case of the 'Community of the Renewed Covenant,'" in *The Provo International Conference on the Dead Sea Scrolls: Technological Innovations, New Texts, and Reformulated Issues*, edited by Donald W. Parry and Eugene Ulrich, Studies on the Texts of the Desert of Judah 30 (Leiden: Brill, 1999), 379-95; "The Essential 'Community of the Renewed

the sociology of the community at Qumran. I met with both while in Jerusalem and talked about my plans for research in Ethiopia.

Figure 2: Shemaryahu Talmon (left); Emanuel Tov (right)

With the help of a professor of sociology at Portland State University, I had developed a set of interview questions I planned to ask of Ethiopian

Covenant': How Should Qumran Studies Proceed?," in *Geschichte—Tradition—Reflexion: Festschrift Für Martin Hengel Zum 70. Geburtstag. Band I Judentum*, edited by Peter Schäfer (Tübingen: Mohr Siebeck, 1996), 323–52; "The Community of the Renewed Covenant: Between Judaism and Christianity," in *The Community of the Renewed Covenant: The Notre Dame Symposium on the Dead Sea Scrolls*, edited by Eugene Ulrich and James VanderKam (Notre Dame: University of Notre Dame Press, 1994), 3–26; "The Internal Diversification of Judaism in the Early Second Temple Period," in *Jewish Civilization in the Hellenistic-Roman Period*, edited by Shemaryahu Talmon, Journal for the Study of the Pseudepigreapha, Supplement Series 10 (Sheffield: Sheffield Academic, 1991), 16–43; "Oral Tradition and Written Transmission, or the Heard and the Seen Word in Judaism of the Second Temple Period," in *Jesus and the Oral Gospel Tradition*, edited by Henry Wansbrough, Journal for the Study of the New Testament, Supplement Series 64 (Sheffield: Sheffield Academic, 1991), 121–58; "Between the Bible and the Mishnah: Qumran from Within," in *Jewish Civilization in the Hellenistic-Roman Period*, edited by Shemaryahu Talmon, Journal for the Study of the Pseudepigrapha, Supplement Series 10 (Sheffield: Sheffield Academic, 1991), 214–57; "The Emergence of Jewish Sectarianism in the Early Second Temple Period," in *Ancient Israelite Religion: Essays in Honor of Frank Moore Cross*, edited by Patrick D. Miller, Paul D. Hanson and S. Dean McBride (Philadelphia: Fortress, 1987), 587–616; "Waiting for the Messiah: The Spiritual Universe of the Qumran Covenanters," in *Judaisms and Their Messiahs at the Turn of the Christian Era*, edited by Jacob Neusner, William Scott Green, and Ernest S. Frerichs (Cambridge: Cambridge University Press, 1987), 111–38; "Types of Messianic Expectation at the Turn of the Era," in *King, Cult, and Calendar in Ancient Israel: Collected Studies* (Jerusalem: Magnes, 1986), 202–24; "The Old Testament Text," in *Qumran and the History of the Biblical Text*, edited by Frank Moore Cross and Shemaryahu Talmon (Cambridge: Harvard University Press, 1975), 1–41; "The New Covenanters of Qumran," *Scientific American* 225 (1971): 73–81; "The Calendar Reckoning of the Sect from the Judean Desert," *Scripta Hierosolymitana* 4 (1958): 162–99.

scribes. These questions focused on their educational processes, the roles they played in the church, their tools and practices as scribes, and the economic engines that sustained their lives and livelihoods. Daniel and I headed for Ethiopia where I established the affiliation with the IES and we settled into a series of trips and interviews with scribes around the country.

Figure 3: Director Elizabeth Giyorgis with Daniel Alemu (left); a scribal school in Iste, South Gondar (right)

On the 22nd of April, 2004, not long before I was to go home, Daniel and I made a trip north from Addis to the site of the important monastery at Däbrä Libanos. While there, a man approached me with some manuscripts to sell. I was surprised at his offer and told him that I had not come to take anything away. He pressed me saying that he had debts to pay and needed the money in order to do so. The guide provided by the monastery said that these were the property of the man and it was legal for him to sell them. I knew that this was part of the story. But I also knew it was illegal to remove anything from the country without first receiving authorization from either the IES or the National Museum. In the end, I bought two, a Gospel of John and an oddly-shaped manuscript containing a work on the Blessed Virgin Mary. On the drive back to Addis, I called Demeke and asked to meet with him to know what to do.

Demeke had been working at the IES since September 1986. Taddese Tamrat, the second director of the IES had identified several promising young people in Ethiopia and sent them to various countries for degrees and training. The plan was that they would return to Ethiopia and contribute to the development of country. Demeke had been sent to Italy for a program of study in Archives, Paleography, and Diplomatics (the study of documents). After two years he received an MA degree. When he returned to Addis Ababa, the IES's third director, Taddese Beyene was in place. Taddese gave Demeke a mandate to establish the Archives center in the IES.

Figure 4: Mandate from Taddese Beyene to establish the Archives Department at the IES (left), Demeke Berhane, founding director of the Archives and Manuscripts department (center); Delamarter's Visiting Scholars Identity Card (right)

Demeke and I met the next day after our return from Däbrä Libanos, and he authorized the Gospel of John to go, but said that the other should not leave the country. Together he and I digitized the manuscript—the first I had ever done—and I donated it to the IES. His fingers and my fingers in the pictures of an Ethiopian manuscript became something of a foreshadowing of things to come. I gave the Gospel of John to Daniel to give as a gift to his father in Jerusalem.

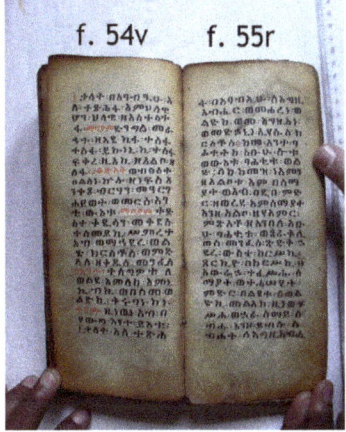 

Figure 5: Manuscript acquired at Dabra Libanon (left); acknowledgement of receipt from the IES (right)

By the time I left Ethiopia, Demeke and I had become friends and in the next few years we made plans to meet and work together. I had begun to locate and digitize manuscripts in North America and had formed the Ethiopic Manuscript Imaging Project (EMIP). Colleagues at the Hill Museum and Manuscripts Library (HMML) were particularly helpful in getting me oriented to some of the technical and photographic techniques and practices necessary to document manuscripts.

In June of 2005, Demeke and I met in England and toured holding institutions with Ethiopian manuscripts. We went to the John Rylands Library in Manchester, the University Library in Cambridge, the British Library in London, and the Bodleian Libraries in Oxford.

Figure 6: June 2005 at the John Rylands Library of the University of Manchester (left); with Prof. George Brooke (right)

In each location we were warmly received. In Manchester, we stayed with Professor George Brooke, editor of the *Journal of Semitic Studies*, and Demeke spoke with him about the possibility of one day publishing a catalogue of the IES collection of Ethiopian manuscripts.

In London, the curators of the Ethiopian manuscripts at the British Library were extremely hospitable. They prepared tours for us into the stacks where the manuscripts were actually housed and into the conservation lab where manuscripts were cleaned and repaired.

Figure 7: British Library—in the stacks (left), in the conservation lab (right)

At each of these institutions we were given manuscripts that had been recently acquired and were as yet uncatalogued. Demeke and I prepared entries for eventual publication in *A Catalogue of Previously Uncatalogued Ethiopic Manuscripts in England*.[4]

In conjunction with these visits, Demeke was asked to address the London chapter of the Anglo-Ethiopian society. One of the members had volunteered to host Demeke for the evenings we were in London. In the course of our conversations with him we discovered that not long before he had acquired several items from Maqdala at an auction at Maggs Brothers. He had, in fact, spotted the lot and realized that it contained not only three manuscripts, but also a tabot from a church in Ethiopia. Being himself a convert of the EOTC, he knew the sacred value of the items and bought them. Within weeks he took the tabot back to Addis and delivered it to the Patriarch's compound with some fanfare. Richard Pankhurst and others brought attention to the plight of Ethiopian artifacts abroad and praised the generosity of this act of MacLennan. *Abuna* Paulos himself

---

4. Steve Delamarter and Demeke Berhane, *A Catalogue of Previously Uncatalogued Ethiopic Manuscripts in England*, Journal of Semitic Studies, Supplement 21 (Oxford: Oxford University Press, 2007).

met with MacLennan and presented him with a printed copy of the work known as *Faith of the Fathers* in which he inscribed a notation of appreciation. MacLennan retained the manuscripts in London and allowed us to digitize them late into one of the evenings we were there.

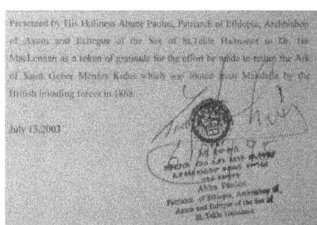

Figure 8: Dr. Ian MacLennan and Anne Parsons at the Anglo-Ethiopian Society Meeting in London (left); inscription from Abuna Paulos to Dr. MacLennan (center); Psalter taken at Maqdala (right)

In June of 2006, Demeke, Daniel Alemu, Roger Rundell (my assistant at the time), and I met in Collegeville, Minnesota, to spend a couple of weeks with Professor Getatchew Haile on manuscript studies and cataloguing of the manuscripts we were digitizing in North America. These had reached several hundred manuscripts by 2007. Early on, Professor Getatchew had volunteered that he would produce catalogue entries for all the manuscripts I located and digitized in North America. But, soon I knew I had to release him from that promise. He never asked to be released, but I could see that the task was already becoming much larger than either of us first anticipated. Further, there were very few persons in North America qualified to catalogue Ethiopian manuscripts. A new generation needed to be raised up and I was looking for candidates.[5]

---

5. Getatchew was the primary cataloguer for *Catalogue of the Ethiopic Manuscripts Imaging Project, Volume 1: Codices 1–105, Magic Scrolls 1–134*, Ethiopic Manuscripts, Texts, and Studies Series 1 (Eugene, OR: Pickwick Publications, 2009), and played a substantial role in the next volume as well. In 2007, at the 16th International Conference of Ethiopian Studies in Trondheim, Getatchew introduced me to Veronika Six, and she agreed to work on entries for the magic scrolls 135–284 in the second volume. The entries for the codices (EMIP 106–200) were the product of collaboration with Getatchew, in which he produced entries of the content, which were reviewed and modified slightly with the help of *qäsis* Melaku, and Jeremy and I added codicological information and other notes.

Figure 9: Demeke Berhane and Daniel Alemu with Father Columba Stewart at HMML (left), Daniel, Demeke, Wayne Torborg (director of digital collections at HMML), and Roger Rundell (right)

By the end of 2007, it had become evident to me that the holdings of Ethiopian manuscripts in North America were, perhaps, more extensive than was yet known. I set out, like others before me,[6] to get an idea of locations and demographics of the major collections in North America. In March of 2008, I made a trip to UCLA to learn more about their collection of Ethiopian manuscripts. Wolf Leslau had come to UCLA in 1955 and in 1958 had founded the university's department of Near Eastern and African languages. He had left his personal collection of manuscripts to the library. Emperor Haile Selassie had come to UCLA on April 24, 1967 and given a sumptuous Four Gospels manuscript to the library.[7] Richard and Rita Pankhurst had come there in March of 2005 to inspect the collection of manuscripts. I met Wendy Belcher who was a faculty member at the time, and also *qäsis* Melaku Terefe who was an Ethiopian Orthodox priest at Saint Mary's Ethiopian Orthodox Church in Los Angeles. I learned that he had grown up around manuscripts in Ethiopia in the home of a learned Ethiopian scholar. Indeed, Melaku had taken in a vast knowledge of the tradition and of its writings. In a very short

---

6. Such inventories had been made to varying degrees of completeness by Richard Pankhurst in a couple of similarly titled articles about "Five Thousand Ethiopian Manuscripts Abroad, and the International Community," by Robert Beylot and Maxime Rodinson in *Répertoire des Bibliothèques et des Catalogues de Manuscrits Éthiopians* (Paris: Brepols, 1995), and in the "Inventory of Libraries and Catalogues of Ethiopian Manuscripts" on the *Ménestrel* website.

7. On May 27, 1954, Selassie had made a visit to McGill University and donated a bilingual (Ge'ez and Amharic) Four Gospels of similar quality there. It can be seen at https://archive.org/details/McGillLibrary-rbsc_arba-tu-wangel-MS-Ethiopian-3-item1-20001. McGill conferred a doctorate degree on Selassie.

time, he and I had become fast friends and began to correspond regarding manuscripts and their contents.

Figure 10: (clockwise from top left)—Young Research Library at UCLA; Emperor Haile Selassie's gift to UCLA; qäsis Melaku in the stacks; Genie Guerard, Rita and Richard Pankhurst, and Wendy Belcher inspecting the manuscripts (Photo of Guerard, the Pankhursts, and Belcher together was taken by Octavio Olvera and is reproduced with permission from UCLA Library Special Collections)

In May of 2008, I made trips to three other leading collections of Ethiopian manuscripts in North America. The first was at Duke University in Durham, North Carolina, with about 110 items in their collection. I was curious to see Ethiopian ms 32, a nineteenth-century four Gospels manuscript acquired at a Sotheby's auction, December 6, 1988, in London.

xxii   *Preface*

*Figure 11: Ethiopian Manuscript 32, Four Gospels (left);
and a view of Duke University (right)*

From there I went to Washington, DC and inspected the collection of Ethiopian manuscripts at the Library of Congress (LOC). I had met *ato* Fentahun Teruneh (Reference Specialist, African Section, African & Middle Eastern Division of the LOC) at the 16th International Conference of Ethiopian Studies in Trondheim and he had invited me to come anytime to see the Africa and Middle East Reading Room. The Thomas Leiper Kane collection had been recently acquired by the LOC and was not yet catalogued. They also asked for a presentation about my work and I told them about Ethiopian Psalters, based on the one hundred and ten we had already digitized in North America.

*Figure 12: Entrance to the Library of Congress Rare Books Room (left); Fentahun
Tiruneh (center); making a presentation on Psalters (right)*

Fentahun also told me that the Howard University School of Divinity also had a large collection that was not yet widely known. He and I made arrangements to go together to Howard and see what was there. What we discovered was the Andre Tweed Collection of 151 codices and seventy-eight scrolls of spiritual healing. Henry Ferry and Alice Ogden-Bellis, two of the faculty at Howard, gave us a tour of the collection, much of which was on display under glass museum covers.

Figure 13: Items from the Andre Tweed Collection (left); Alice Ogden-Bellis and Henry Ferry (center); the cover page for the digitized manuscript collection (right)

Eventually, in June 2012, Jeremy R. Brown, Alice Bellis, and I digitized the entire collection in a project of 23,481 shots and with the support of the Association of Theological Schools (ATS). During the same trip, we digitized the collection of manuscripts at Catholic University of America and at Haverford College. And since 2022, in a collaboration with Dr. Ralph Lee of Cambridge, UK, and supported by the Ogden-Bellises, the Tweed images have all been uploaded to the Hiob Ludolf Centre for Eritrean and Ethiopian Studies' hypercatalogue website called Beta maṣāḥǝft in Hamburg, Germany, along with substantial metadata.

Meanwhile, in my correspondence with Demeke, he and I began to talk about the possibility of offering a digitization workshop at the IES for employees at the IES and several other institutions in Addis. I contacted Mr. Wayne Torborg, director of digital collections at Hill Museum and Manuscripts Library, and he and I developed a plan for facilitating the workshop in Addis.

In June of 2008, on my way to Addis for this workshop, Jeremy R. Brown, my new assistant, and I went first to Nairobi, Kenya. We had digitized Ethiopian manuscripts from people in North America with reports they had acquired them in Nairobi. Our plan was to set up a "catch and release" operation with dealers in the Maasai markets. Jeremy was to run this program in Nairobi while I went to Addis for the workshop. He was to make arrangements to rent or borrow the manuscripts just long enough to digitize them, then return them to the owners. The very first day we were there, we did, indeed, find a half dozen manuscripts in the markets, made our arrangements with the owners, and digitized them. The next day I headed for Addis.

As the workshop was getting underway, Demeke and I began to talk about the IES collection and the need for digitization as part of their manuscript security strategy. Together we toured the IES and inspected the storage and conditions of the manuscripts. I took pictures of water stains in some of the store rooms, and of scorch marks near the splice of a set of electrical wires. Off-site backups of digital images of the collection seemed like a very good idea. Demeke spoke with director Elizabeth who authorized a small pilot project to learn what would be entailed in such an undertaking. I set up a digitization station in Demeke's office and we started the work.

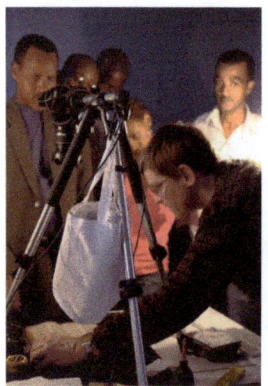 

Figure 14: First digitization workshop at the IES. Wayne Torborg, demonstrating techniques (left), Steve Delamarter working with a group outside when the power failed (right [photo courtesy of Wayne Torborg, Hill Museum & Manuscript Library; used by permission]).

At the same time, I received word from Jeremy that things in Nairobi were not as they first appeared. The Maasai markets were open each day in a different part of the city. People had reported buying manuscripts in various locations. But when Jeremy went to the locations in the next days, he discovered that the same set of manuscripts were travelling from place to place. There was no great supply of manuscripts available. I called him over to Addis and we set up a second digitization station and he joined me in the pilot project for the IES. During the workshop sessions, I was helping Wayne facilitate. Before and after, Jeremy and I were shooting manuscripts.

Figure 15: Delamarter and Demeke, pilot project at the IES (left [photo courtesy of Wayne Torborg, Hill Museum & Manuscript Library; used by permission]); a digitization demonstration with Yaqob Taddese at the Patriarch's Library (right)

By the time the week was out, we had been able to digitize some 169 manuscripts (119 codices and fifty magic scrolls) in 39,914 shots. The pilot project produced good results and was favorably received. Yaqob Taddese, another participant in the digitization workshop, worked at the Patriarch's library just a few blocks away from the IES. He and the authorities at the library invited us down to their offices and we conducted a brief demonstration of the digitization process on one manuscript in their collection.

Later that year, Demeke contacted me about a need at the IES. The Rev. Dr. Vreg Nersessian had contacted the IES from his post in the British Library as curator of the Christian Middle East Section. He brought to their attention the Endangered Archives Programme (EAP) and encouraged the IES to apply. After a first proposal was reviewed, the EAP suggested that the IES engage a consultant who might be able to assist with the finalization of a successful proposal. Demeke contacted me and we began working together to formulate a plan.

By August 2008, I was convinced that *qäsis* Melaku was the perfect person to take up the work of cataloguing manuscripts. He and Jeremy R. Brown and I went back to Collegeville to work for a week with Professor Getatchew Haile on manuscript cataloguing. Getatchew and his wife, Meseret, extended generous hospitality both in the research room and at the meal table.

Figure 16: qäsis Melaku Terefe before the Great Sanctuary at HMML (left), cataloguing with Getatchew and Delamarter (right [photo courtesy of Wayne Torborg, Hill Museum & Manuscript Library; used by permission])

In November of 2008, as chair of the Society of Biblical Literature's section on the Textual Criticism of the Hebrew Bible, I convened a session on the nine largest collections of Ethiopian manuscripts in North America and invited various scholars to contribute a report. Lucas van Rampay reported on the Duke collection, Wendy Belcher on the Princeton collection, Father Columba Stewart on the holdings at the Hill Museum and Manuscripts library, Fentahun Teruneh on the Library of Congress collection, Alice Ogden on the Tweed collection, Melaku Terefe on the UCLA collection, and myself on the private collections of manuscripts held by various individuals, specifically, the Marwicks in Williams, Oregon, Eliza Bennett in Denver, Colorado, Mohammad Alwan in Belmont, Massachusetts, and Gerald and Barbara Weiner in Highland Park, Illinois. All of the latter were previously unknown.

Our meeting began with a review of Pankhurst's estimate of the number of manuscripts in the United States: "slightly over 400 mss. No less than 325 are in the Princeton University Libraries. Smaller collections are in four libraries in New York, with a total of 17 mss; and at the Free Library in Philadelphia, with 13. Yale has nine." By the end of the session, we had established the whereabouts of 2,017 just in the nine collections we had covered. Nevertheless, in terms of impact on the textual criticism of the Bible, North America had little to offer with the possible exception of manuscripts of the modern textus receptus of the Ethiopic Four Gospels. This conclusion drove home the point that the richest materials for such studies were to be found in a few European libraries, but primarily in Ethiopia at institutions like the Institute of Ethiopian Studies.

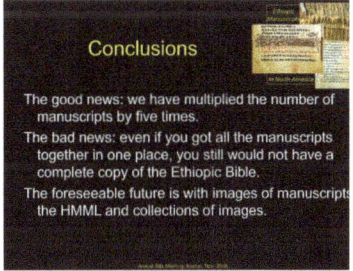 

Figure 17: Presenters at the 2008 Annual Society of Biblical Literature—VanRampay, Belcher, Stewart, Fentahun, Ogden-Bellis, Melaku, and Delamarter

In December of 2008 and January of 2009, Jeremy R. Brown, Erik Young, and I came back to the IES to continue the pilot project begun there. We wanted to test the adequacy of the digitization stations which had been built for use in the North American context would work well in Ethiopia. *Ato* Kaleab Demeke, joined us to run a fourth station. We were invited to the Theological College in Addis to provide a brief workshop on manuscript digitization and to show members of the community there what was involved in such work.

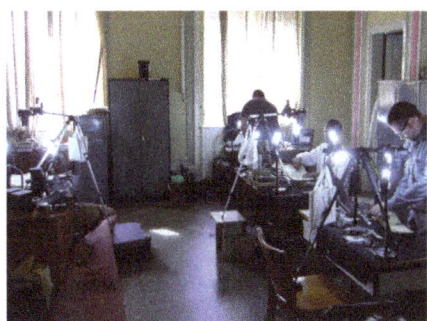 

Figure 18: Four station pilot project at the IES with Demeke Berhane, Steve Delamarter, Jeremy R. Brown, Erik Young, and Kaleab Demeke (left); and digitization presentation at the Holy Trinity Theological College (right)

During this time we were able to complete just over another one thousand manuscripts in the IES collection. We used the opportunity to refine the workflow for managing the shooting, making backups, and capturing metadata for the manuscripts. With this experience we finalized a proposal to the EAP, submitted in February 2009. We described the specific outcomes of the project in this way:

> We will digitise 3,391 items in the IES collection at the IES, requiring ca. 399,799 shots and 4.533 terabytes of storage space for each set of RAW and JPG images. From these, a set of PDF files will be produced in the United States for the IES and made accessible to users on two work stations in the IES reading room. In addition, a set of TIFFs (requiring about 13.5 terabytes) will be produced in the United States for the British Library (along with a set of the PDF files). Complete metadata will be entered into a spread sheet. A master and backup set will be kept at different locations in Addis Ababa; a deep backup set will be deposited at the Hill Museum and Manuscript Library in Collegeville, Minnesota, USA; a master set of TIFFs will be deposited at the British Library. In addition to this work of digitisation, 1,500 of the most fragile codices will be secured in archival quality boxes.

Demeke and Delamarter would work together as co-directors. The proposal was accepted and given the project number EAP 286.

I returned to Addis Ababa in July of 2009. The purpose of this trip was to finalize some of the details of the upcoming project at the IES, as well as to conduct two further digitization projects in Addis. Dr. Loren Bliese, a former president at Mekane Yesus Seminary had introduced us to the leaders of the institution who invited us to digitize the collection. *Ato* Kaleab stepped in once more to assist in that work. We worked with head librarian *ato* Mehret'ab Bereke. It required some 6,798 shots to digitize the fifty-four manuscripts. This project, as well as a larger project to digitize nearly two hundred manuscripts at the Capuchin Franciscan Theological Center in Asko, gave us further experience in the workflow of a larger digitization project. A full catalogue[8] of the Mekene Yesus collection was eventually published along with a plates volume on Ethiopian Scribal Practices.[9]

---

8. Melaku Terefe, Steve Delamarter, and Jeremy R. Brown, *Catalogue of the Ethiopic Manuscript Imaging Project: Volume 7, Codices 601–651, The Meseret Sebhat Le-Ab Collection of Mekane Yesus Seminary, Addis Ababa*, Ethiopic Manuscripts, Texts, and Studies Series, 13 (Eugene, OR: Pickwick Publications, 2011).

9. Steve Delamarter, Marilyn Heldman, Jeremy R. Brown, and Sara Vulgan, *Ethiopian Scribal Practice 7: Plates for the Catalogue of the Ethiopic Manuscript Imaging Project*

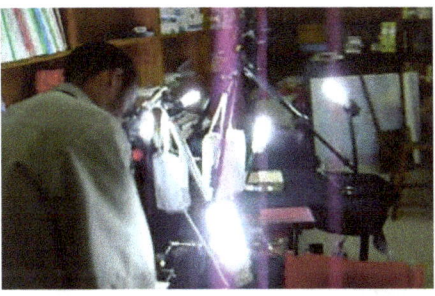

Figure 19: (clockwise from top left) Digitization of the collection at Mekane Yesus Library by Kaleab and Delamarter; with Rev. Dr. Daniel Assefa planning for the digitization of the collection at the Capuchin-Franciscan monastery in Asko; working out processes for the digitization of microfilms; and meeting with University President Eshete and director Elizabeth about the EAP project

At the IES we worked out letters of understanding between EMIP and the IES about the backup services that HMML would supply for the ongoing storage of the images produced by the project and regarding the servicing of scholars of the materials. Further, we wanted to gain some experience with adequate methods of making the images of IES manuscripts available for scholars to consult. Toward that end, EMIP loaded 1,276 pdfs with full sets of images of the manuscripts shot to this point at the IES as well as a spreadsheet with initial metadata regarding each manuscript. These were loaned to the IES for the six months between July 2009 and the commencement of the major digitization work set to begin

---

(Eugene, OR: Pickwick Publications, 2014). Earlier, *qäsis* Melaku and I had produced a similar volume in conjunction with the first of the EMIP catalogues: *Ethiopian Scribal Practice 1: Plates for the Catalogue of the Ethiopic Manuscript Imaging Project*, Ethiopic Manuscripts, Texts, and Studies Series 2 (Eugene, OR: Pickwick Publications, 2009).

in January of 2010. Our goals were set forth in the letter of understanding when the two reader stations were loaned:

> The intent is that these reading stations and the Handlists would be 1) located permanently and not removed from the Manuscripts Reading Room; 2) that they would be continuously available to users whenever the IES is open. The third copy of the Handlist is for archival purposes. This initiative is related to our mutual pursuit and implementation of the British Library Endangered Collections grant. One element of that proposal has us creating just such stations for users and placing on them all the sets of images of the 3,000 remaining manuscripts which are yet-to-be digitized. These stations are preliminary steps toward that goal. It gives us an opportunity to test out the concepts, the technology and the patterns of use, between now and when the British Library EAP grant is implemented. At that time, we will address any problems of technology or use that have been identified, and we will reload the reading stations with all of the new materials and they will become the property of the IES (paid for by the Endangered Collections grant). Until that time they remain the property of EMIP and on loan at the IES for the uses stated above.

By now it was well into 2009 and we began to prepare in earnest for the work of the EAP 286 project at the IES in Addis. Our plan was to be there January through June of 2010. So, in the months leading up to this, Jeremy and I acquired the equipment necessary for a four-to-seven-station digitization project at the IES. Four of the stations would be paid for within the EAP project budget, and remain with the IES. The remainder were resources from the EMIP project. It took weeks to assemble all of the items for each station and to pack everything. We worked with a cardboard-box manufacturer in Portland, OR, to design and produce a couple thousand box covers with acid free linings. These were in an array of sizes to accommodate the manuscripts of various dimensions.

One of the positive outcomes of the collaborations in 2008 to identify the whereabouts of Ethiopian manuscripts in North America, was that, by September 2009, Mr. Weiner donated several hundred of his manuscripts to UCLA, making the collection there the largest in North America for a brief time.

I returned to Addis once more from 1 to 5 November, 2009, to attend the 17th International Conference of Ethiopian Studies, held at the Akaki Campus of Addis Ababa University. In addition to presenting a paper at the conference, the main goal I needed to accomplish was to move forward in lining up digitizers for training and working on the project. The EAP guidelines were very clear about the desire for outcomes to include transfer of knowledge to those working in the communities served by the projects. For this reason, I had been working to identify candidates with two connections: the EOTC and the IES Philology department. I was able to find three good candidates who were deacons or priests in the EOTC and also MA students in the Philology department. After clearing it with director Elizabeth, I met with the three and we made an agreement. The three were Hailemariam Aleyew, Makonnen Desta, and Sileshi Kebede. With these final arrangements completed, I returned home to pack up the remaining equipment to bring to Ethiopia.

Figure 20: (From left to right) Hailemariam Aleyew, Sileshi Kebede, Makonnen Desta, and Alessandro Gori

At the Conference at the Akaki Campus, I was assigned a roommate in the dorm housing. It turned out to be none other than Alessandro Gori, accomplished scholar of languages and Arabic literature. Within a couple of years he was awarded a grant to run a very substantial project on Islam in the Horn of Africa (IslHornAfr), which catalogued hundreds of Arabic manuscripts from Ethiopia. I was astonished at the good fortune of meeting Professor Gori and learning of his expertise. Within a day or two we had begun to talk about the need for someone to catalogue the Arabic items in the IES holdings. Alessandro was amenable and went on to lead the preparation of that volume.

The work of EAP 286 began with a digitization workshop for the three men we had hired for the project along with ten others: Kemal Abdulwehab, Abreham Adugna, Bedru Adem, Samuel Ayehu, Mehamed Hakim, Abebech Shiferaw, Emabet Mehari, Hiwot Samuel, Addisalem Birhanu, and Tsige Mamo. Kaleab Demeke also joined the training, in part, to give assistance to others from the wealth of experience he had gained. The training lasted from December 28, 2009, until January 1, 2010, and ended with a final exam, including a written section and a hands-on test of their ability to set up the digitization and digitize for 20 minutes. After the workshop was over, we settled into the rhythms of the digitization workflow that are described by Jeremy R. Brown in his essay elsewhere in this volume.

Figure 21: Second digitization workshop at the IES, December, 28 2009—January 1, 2010

In March we held another training workshop with other workers: Abdullahi Ali Sharif (the owner and operator of the Sharif Municipal Museum in Harrar), Gizaw Wakjira (employee at the National Library), Mimi Yohannes, Gebre Meskel Alemu (employee in the Reading Room at the IES), Bayu Kebede, Meseret Demisu, Emabet Tsega, Fasika Gebeyehu, Haji Mehammed Yesuf, Tadiyos Sisay, Abeselom Nekatibib Gebre Tsadik.

Figure 22: Participants in the third digitization workshop at the IES (left); Jeremy R. Brown, facilitating workshops and overseeing the digitization workflow of the EAP project (right)

The role of Jeremy R. Brown in the digitization workshops and in the daily work of EAP digitization project can hardly be overestimated. Daily productivity was maintained with an expectation of eight hundred shots per day from each digitizer. This comes to four to six books a day. Within a week or two, this rate was achieved and maintained for the better part of six months—at least on the days when there was steady electricity. Frequent interruptions would stop the work for hours or even days at a time.

The administrators of the IES made daily decisions about which manuscripts were next to be digitized. Manuscripts were set out for us on a cart or a table. Brown would make assignments to the digitizers and day after day we worked our way through what would eventually be 488,885 shots for 5,749 manuscripts in the IES collection.

Figure 23: Carts of manuscripts set out each day for digitization

One of the participants in the third digitization workshop at the IES was Abdullahi Ali Sharif, the remarkable creator and curator of the Harar Municipal Museum in Harar. Abdullahi had spent years collecting and preserving items of cultural heritage from the region of Harar, particularly Arabic manuscripts of the Islamic tradition. Several of us in Addis wanted to see his work in Harar. A delegation, including two representatives from the British Library, made the drive from Addis to Harar with Abdullahi. There we looked over the museum and strategized with him about his work of preservation and collecting. We had heard he was doing his work of digitization with very primitive equipment, and we made it a point to present him with a complete digitization station and a supply of hard drives for storage. His collection of Arabic materials became foundational for the study of the Arabic manuscripts of Ethiopia and informed the work of assessing and describing the IES collection of Arabic manuscripts.

Figure 24: Harar Municipal Museum (left); Abdullahi Ali Sharif, owner and operator of the museum (right)

Back at the IES we settled into the work of placing fragile items into conservation boxes which we had committed to the EAP. We identified about 1,500 of the most fragile items in the collection. On a series of flights to Ethiopia, I had brought nearly 2,000 conservation boxes to the IES. Each book had to be matched up with the box blank of the correct size and then the box blank had to be folded and glued in place along with fasteners to secure the flaps of the boxes. We personally boxed up over eight hundred items, trained staff at the IES to do the same, and left them with all of the materials to complete the work.

Preface xxxv

Figure 25: Items in the IES storage lockers inside their new conservation boxes (left); images from digitization workshop at the Mahibire Kiddusan building—work and observers (top); participants (center); a visit from one of the EOTC bishops (right)

In May, yet another story was playing out. In one of my trips to work with Professor Getatchew at HMML, we came across the manuscript given the project number EMIP 161. It was a rather remarkable Psalter, with several superb features. The materials and workmanship were very fine. There was an array of works included in the book that were out of the ordinary. There was a strophe summary text (f. 109v) that enumerated all of the strophes in Psalms and the Biblical Canticles. These summaries were usual in fifteenth century manuscripts but had died out after the sixteenth century. Even more interesting were land ownership records in the end pages of the book, complete with stamps. And tucked in the space between the end of the Song of Songs and the beginning of Praises of Mary was a one-line text and a seal of the royal household. The one line of text is written in a rare form of "negative writing" whose translation is

"This book belongs to Emperor Menilek." Getatchew looked at me and said, "Steve, this is a national treasure."

Some months later Professor Getatchew was contacted by Engineer Terefe Ras Warq who was seeking support for the establishment of a center of restoration in Ankobarr. He thought of that Psalter and contacted me to see if I would ask the owner to donate it to the center.

Figure 26: The Menilek Psalter (EMIP 161, Weiner Codex 56), folio 110r, the inscription of Menilek and seal of the family

The owner was Mr. Gerald Weiner of Highland Park, Illinois, a financier, and philanthropist, who had been acquiring Ethiopian manuscripts in North America for several years and ended up donating them eventually to the libraries of University of California at Los Angeles and the Catholic University of America (Washington, DC). We explained the details around the manuscript and its importance as an artifact of Ethiopian history. Mr. Weiner immediately consented to send it to Ankobär.

The manuscript came first to the IES, where it was presented in a news conference to Engineer Terefe Ras Warq. Richard and Rita Pankhurst both made speeches as did Ato Demeke Berhane and others. Dr. Elizabeth hosted the event. The manuscript was held for a week at the IES so that people could come to view it. Then, it was taken by car caravan from

Addis to Ankobär on June 9, 2010. As the caravan approached the city with horns honking, the road was lined with hundreds of people singing, and shouting, and holding signs. One of these—obviously written in English for my benefit—stated "Our Heritage is Our Identity." At the city center, the bishop of the region was there to certify the Psalter and oversee a ceremony in honor of its return. The ceremonies and return of the Menilek Psalter served as something of a closing of the EAP project at the IES. Jeremy and I returned to Portland, Oregon and within a few weeks, *ato* Demeke was retired by the IES.

Figure 27: Ceremonial handover of the Psalter on June 2, 2010 at a press conference at the IES (top left); return of the Menilek Psalter to Ankobarr, June 9, 2010—the three IES digitizers conferring with the district bishop (top right); entering Ankobarr in the caravan (bottom)

The work of the EAP 286 was far from over, though. We now had several products that needed to be delivered to London to fulfill the terms of the grant. The first of these was a full set of images in TIFF format. The second was a spreadsheet listing the content and dating and other metadata for each of the 5,749 items that had been digitized.

The production of a set of TIFF images required more than two months of processing time running nearly twenty-four hours a day, seven days a week, on what was a powerful computer for the time. The images shot at the IES were taken on Nikon D200 and D300 cameras which generated simultaneous RAW files and fine JPG files. The IES wanted JPGs and RAW images as well as digitally foliated PDF files of the manuscripts. In order to meet all of these specifications, we had to set up a chain of steps to generate all of these image sets and then mail the drives off to London.

As demanding as the processes were to digitize the manuscripts, the processes for creating metadata were at least as challenging and even more time consuming. It took more than two years to complete the basic work of creating metadata. This was due in large part to the decision to retire *ato* Demeke at that moment in June of 2010. The task of creating the metadata was to have fallen to the team at the IES. When they were unable to follow through with that requirement, the task fell to me and Jeremy and to whomever we could recruit to help with the task. Provision came in the form of several key persons, first among whom was *qäsis* Melaku Terefe, the Ethiopian Orthodox priest working in Los Angeles with whom I had been cataloguing manuscripts for a few years by then. He and I took up a routine that had us working for two to three hours some three or four days a week. We did this month after month. As we mentioned above, Dr. Alessandro Gori, graciously stepped in to list the Arabic materials in the IES collection. It took a further two years to complete the work and submit the listing required by EAP. This was due primarily to the vast size of the collection of digitized materials.

The most recent provision arrived in the person of Jacopo Gnisci, a fine scholar of art history who moved back and forth between centers in England and Italy. I had worked with him for the first time in the preparation of a volume for an exhibition at the Bodleian Library in Oxford.[10] I

---

10. Jocopo Gnisci, Sebastian Brock, David Appleyard, Sean M. Winslow, Steve Delamarter, Siam Bhayro, Antonella Brita, Girma Getahun, and Dan Levene, *Treasures of Ethiopia and Eritrea in the Bodleian Library, Oxford*, Manar Al-Athar Monograph 5 (Oxford: Oxford University Press, 2019).

had been asked to contribute an article on Ethiopian Psalters. Jacopo was the editor and clearly knew the task. In 2021, I approached him about taking on the task of the final editing of this volume. His participation has brought us to the final publication.

It did, indeed, require a host of people to see this project through to completion. I extend my own heartfelt appreciation to each of the people mentioned in this account. The British Library Endangered Archives Programme is, of course, the proximate cause for both the digitization and the cataloguing of the IES collection. At that time, their representative to us in Addis was Claudia Rapp who went on to take important roles in Vienna and give leadership with Michael Phelps (director of the Early Manuscripts Electronic Library, EMEL) to the amazing Sinai Palimpsest Project. She had to bear the brunt of a few of our communications from Addis that reflected something of the pressure we felt in Addis. For her patience and leadership through the challenges, we remain grateful.

The History of the Collection at the IES

Demeke Berhane
Former Head of the Department of Manuscripts and Archives

Ethiopia is an African country that is home to one of the continent's oldest writing systems. It is also one of the earliest Christian and Muslim nations of the world that has a very rich tradition of literature and fine arts.

The country has long and highly developed systems of Christian, Quranic, and other traditions of education. The ancient schools of the Ethiopian Orthodox Church, in particular, embraced philosophical, historical, medical, linguistic, and, especially, theological studies.

Because of its strategic position, Ethiopia has often suffered the experience of military conflicts. These have led to the looting and theft of precious documents (especially towards Western institutions) as well as to their destruction.

Nonetheless, modern-day Ethiopia is the repository of an immense number of manuscripts. Printing was introduced into the country only at the end of the nineteenth century, so many Ethiopian churches and monasteries possess numerous volumes in parchment.

The value of this cultural material has been recognized by libraries internationally. Ethiopian manuscripts can thus be found in many institutions including several Italian and British libraries, the Vatican library, and the Bibliothèque nationale de France. In fact, well over 10,000 Ethiopian manuscripts are found in European and American public libraries and in private hands. These valuable historical manuscripts are important not only for Ethiopian studies, but also for the reconstruction of African history as a whole. Our past cannot be told without evidence, and Ethiopic manuscripts are important and unique witnesses to Ethiopia's history.

Studying these manuscripts (records, archives and documents) is rather like studying a country's long-lived political, economic, social, military and cultural history. They are valuable to scholarly research. That is why they can be called "information banks."

The challenges of preserving records for posterity were and still are very acute. Churches and monasteries have been the primary institutions that played a major role in preserving and documenting the materials of medieval Ethiopia. However, a significant amount of records of ancient Ethiopia were ruthlessly destroyed by foreign invaders, and sometimes even by its citizens as a result of rivalry. To preserve this important historical and cultural heritage is the duty of Ethiopians and peoples of the world through various institutions and organizations. One of the academic institutions which history has provided for carrying this burden is the Institute of Ethiopian Studies (IES).

The IES is a leading research institution that holds and displays historical and cultural artifacts from Ethiopia. The Institute came into being in 1963. But the genesis of the museum and of the library which the Institute houses can be traced back to the 1950s.

The IES is located in the main campus of Addis Ababa University, which was formerly known as Gännätä Lə'ul ("Princely Paradise") when it served as the residence of Emperor Haylä Səllasse. Originally, this property belonged to the Emperor's father, *ras* Mäkonnən Wäldä Mika'él, one of the best-known statesmen of Emperor Mənəlik II. After the coup of General Mängəstu Nəway and his brother Gärmame Nəway in December 1960, Emperor Haylä Səllasse gave the whole compound as well as the buildings inside the compound to the then Haylä Səllasse I University in 1961.

The IES is the oldest of the five research institutions within the Addis Ababa University system and was officially opened in January 1963. It was founded with the mission to encourage, promote and undertake research in all fields relating to Ethiopia with emphasis on the humanities and cultural studies and to preserve Ethiopia's cultural heritage.

The beginnings of the IES's library and of the ethnological collection of the museum can be traced back sixty years to the work of collecting books and other cultural artifacts which began in the early 1950s. The

University College of Addis Ababa (UCAA) started collecting books on Ethiopia (Ethiopiana) right from its beginning in 1950. The nucleus of the collection, containing books on Ethiopia, in foreign and Ethiopian languages, maps, and microfilms, etc. was moved from the former University College Library Arat Kilo campus to the Gännätä Lə'ul Palace of Emperor Haylä Səllasse I, at Səddəst Kilo, which later become the main campus of the University.

Since its founding in 1963, the IES had made substantial progress in carrying out its mission. Various developments and changing circumstances led to the need for the Institute to have a more fitting organizational system, with administrative autonomy and a more streamlined set of objectives, focused on the humanities and cultural studies. Accordingly, a statute defining the administrative autonomy of the Institute was issued by the Senate of the University in 1995. On the sixteenth of August, 1995, the Addis Ababa University Senate issued the "Statute of the Institute of Ethiopian Studies, 1995." According to this document, the Institute would pursue the following broad objectives:

1. To conduct, promote and coordinate research and publication on Ethiopian studies with special emphasis on humanities, and cultural studies; and

2. To aid in the conservation of Ethiopia's cultural heritage by collecting, classifying, cataloguing, preserving, and displaying in a museum objects reflecting the material and spiritual culture of the diverse nationalities of Ethiopia.

Currently the Institute manages a library, the Ethnological museum, a postgraduate cultural studies program and publishes the *Journal of Ethiopian Studies*, among many other academic publications. The library therefore, is one of the main pillars of the Institute and has as its objectives:

1. To form a center that should facilitate serious research on subjects related to Ethiopia and the Greater Horn of Africa;

2. To form and maintain within its premises a collection of Ethiopian manuscripts (in particular those of antiquity or of special historical, sociological, or linguistic interest), photographs, and archival documents of historical and research interest, including manuscripts of present-day authors;

3. To maintain within its premises a library of books in all languages concerning Ethiopia and Ethiopian studies of all kinds; also as complete a collection as possible of books (on any subject) printed in Ethiopian languages (including news papers and periodicals).

The library of the IES started initially with a core of 1,800 books (including manuscripts), which it inherited from the University College Library, and to which it steadily continued to add.

The IES functions as Addis Ababa University's main documentation and research library for the humanities and social sciences. It currently houses no less than 200,000 books, 2,000 MA and PhD theses, over 10,000 senior essays, 2,000 periodical titles and many archives of manuscripts, scrolls, photographs, and other archival documents and records. These are kept in the Department of Manuscript and Archives, and reflect materials in local, as well as foreign languages, on Ethiopia and the greater horn of Africa.

For the last several years, the Institute has functioned as an arm of the National Archives, as well as a repository of Addis Ababa University for rare manuscripts, records, and materials from various individuals, and from some government offices.

For administrative purposes, the library is divided into five departments:

1. The Manuscript and Archives Department;
2. The Ethiopian Languages and Periodical Department;
3. The Foreign Languages Department;
4. The Technical Processing Department (including the departments of Cataloguing and Acquisition);
5. Administration.

All of these library departments serve the same purpose, which is to deliver library and information services to researchers and scholars of local and foreign origin. The library also supports the research needs of university faculty members and staffs. Beginning, senior, and postgraduate students of Addis Ababa University and the sister Regional State Universities all use the resources of the library to produce their senior essays and theses. Since the IES library is the only national research and reference library, we should also note that government workers, journalists, writers, NGO members, and members of institutions like the Society of Friends of Ethiopian Studies (SOFIES) continually make use of the IES resources.

The Manuscript and Archive Department of the IES has a considerable amount of manuscripts written in Gə'əz and Amharic made of parchment (vellum), magic scrolls on skin (leather), Islamic manuscripts (on paper) written in Arabic and Old Harari (Adarie), archival materials, various research papers written in several Ethiopian and foreign languages, photographic collections, slides, films, documents in micro-formats, correspondences, private letters and papers, an archive of clandestine literature, and many more such materials.

This department, established in the early 1970s simply as the "manuscript section," was reorganized in a new form beginning Mäskäräm 1979 EC (AD September 1986). In 1973 EC, the manuscript section of the Institute had a modest 350 manuscripts and scrolls, with a few archival documents. Today, the collections of the department are wide in scope. The recent project supported by a grant from the British Library Endangered Archives Programme digitized 5,749 items, which is still not everything in the collection. The holdings of the IES Department of Manuscript and Archives include manuscripts on parchment, the earliest of which are from the fourteenth century, containing biblical works, apocryphal and pseudo-pseudepigraphical literature, chronologies, service books, prayer and hymn books, books of theology, lives of saints, homilies, commentaries, vocabularies and grammars, magical divinations, and medical writings. On paper there are religious and medical writings in Arabic, land records, histories, creative writings and poetry collections, magic scrolls, various archival documents, and personal papers. There are also historical and ethnographic collections of photographs, documenting various personalities, places and social life. There are films and slides, recordings, and a large collections of microfilms and microfiches of manuscripts and archival materials dealing with correspondences, fugitive materials, notices, calendars, agendas, visiting cards, and the like.

The Institute of Ethiopian Studies came in time to save the records of Ethiopia. Valuable documents were gathered after the Ethiopian revolution of AD 1974 from various places, especially from Harar and Dire-Dawa. These included books and documents written in Arabic, French, English, and Amharic dealing with court cases, the Djibouti-Addis Ababa Railway, missionary correspondences, various municipal records dealing especially with reserved areas, the cement factory, and official and personal letters of Emperor Haylä Səllasse I, the royal family and other officials of the time.

As a result of these efforts at preservation we can now identify, in broad terms, some 86,000 items beyond manuscripts that are now in the holdings of the Department; namely:

- 3,110 research and archival materials in Ethiopian and foreign languages;
- 3,380 pieces of clandestine literature from the country and abroad;
- ca. 35,000 photographs, of historic and diplomatic occasion as well as of individual Ethiopians and foreigners, mostly during the period of Emperor Haylä Səllasse. 12,000 of these are in 280 albums; 500 are in frames; 22,000 are loose photographs in boxes and envelopes, including copies and Italian period photos of 1936–41 AD;
- ca. 10,000 letters (official and personal) of Emperor Haylä Səllasse I and the royal family;
- ca. 10,000 reels of microfilms and microfiches. The microfilms and microfiches of the British archive is the largest, and contains about 25,000 pages of documents from the Foreign Office, Colonial Office, and War Office archives in the Public Record Office, as well as from the Indian Office which covered the period of 1808–1964;
- 1,000 slides of manuscripts;
- ca. 12,000 folders of various archival materials of government offices such as the Attorney General (3,420 folders), the Ministry of Interior (3,865 folders), the State Property (854 folders), the Election Board (153 folders), the Haylä Səllasse I Prize Trust and the HIS Welfare Association (97 folders), the Rent House Administration (2,257 folders) which include a few letters from the period of Mənəlik II as well as Enemy Properties, State Properties, Haylä Səllasse I Bétä Rəst, Empress Mänän Asfaw Bétä Rəst, Princess Tänañé Wärq Haylä Səllasse Bétä Rəst, Prince Sahlä Səllasse Haylä Səllasse Bétä Rəst, etc); Ministry of Agriculture (516 folders), etc. kept in the ṣäḥafe tə'əzaz Wäldä Mäsqäl Tariku Memorial Research Center;

- numerous letters, reports, telegrams, video recordings, maps, post-cards, identity-cards, calendars, speeches, agendas, invitation cards, posters, notices, charts, and the like are also collected in the department; and
- not less than 12,000 folders of documents on land, estates, other properties, litigation, etc., which were being discarded by many public agencies after the 1974 revolution.

How did these materials come to light and how were they gathered and collected?

Perhaps the single most significant factor that drew attention to the artifacts of Ethiopia's cultural heritage was the opening of the country to travelling and tourism in the 1960s and 1970s. This brought about positive and negative consequences. On opening the country to tourism, Ethiopia was in the unfortunate position of having very little to offer visitors in terms of current production. Instead, tourists and foreign residents discovered the beauty and exotic appeal of the art and artifacts of the ancient churches and mosques. They started buying paintings, crosses, manuscripts and other antiquities which appeared in large quantities on the curio and art markets in Addis Ababa. They were also buying in the provinces, directly from the people entrusted with the safe-keeping of church treasures, these people being often ignorant of the historical and artistic importance of the objects they were selling. As a result, much valuable evidence of Ethiopia's cultural heritage started to leave the country. This, of course, caused much concern.

What was the role of the Institute with respect to this emergency situation?

The main problem was funding. It is clear from the outset that the project had to be self-supporting, the small allocation from the University budget for the museum acquisitions being quite insufficient for the purchase. The Institute had therefore to find its own sources of income. These came from various donations, public and private, including membership fees of the Society of Friends, as well as organized social events such as lectures, bridge and tea parties, dinner-dances, and even theatrical performances. Two organizations were set up to run these programs. The first was the committee of Preservation and Restoration of Old Ethiopian Paintings, active from 1965 to 1967, and the second was the Society of Friends of the Institute of Ethiopian Studies (SOFIES), active from 1968 until today. SOFIES was founded in 1968 and has played a major role in collecting and introducing the Ethiopian and foreign community to many aspects of Ethiopia's diverse and unique culture.

When considering the successes signaled by today's enormous collection at the IES, we should not forget the efforts of highly-devoted individuals: the first Director of the IES and the Chairman of SOFIES, the late Prof. Richard Pankhurst; the founder of the IES Museum and Library, the late Prof. Stanislaw Chojnacki; the dedicated and tireless IES Librarian for more than ten years, the late *ato* Degifie Gebre Tsadik. These were at the vanguard of this challenging and demanding task. Officials of Addis Ababa University, Presidents and Officers, the Directors of the Institute of Ethiopian Studies (such as Prof. Taddese Tamrat, Prof. Taddese Beyene, Prof. Bahru Zewde, Prof. Baye Yimam, Dr. Elizabeth W. Giyorgis and others), friends of the institute like the late Prof. Merid Wolde Aregay, Dr. Alemie Eshetie, Prof. Husen Ahmed of history department, the late Dr. Amsalu Aklilu of the Institute of languge studies (Ethiopian languge dept.), Dr. Sergew Gelaw of langage studies research Institute, Prof. Shiferaw Bekele of history department, *ato* Ahmed Zekaria of the IES Museum etc., the Staff members of IES, the Addis Ababa University community, the members of the Society of Friends of the Institute of Ethiopian Studies (SOFIES), such as Mrs. Rita Pankhurst, Engineer Fikermariam Yifru, Ambasador David Shin and his wife Mrs. Shin, Mr. Ian Cambell and many others, the Friends of Ethiopia, and the Ethiopian people, who, as a whole, worked hand in hand to build this collection.

The Society and its founders have been instrumental in transforming the IES Library and Museum into the foremost "Ethiopian culture and history information bank" in the world and at the same time saved for posterity innumerable works of Ethiopian indigenous knowledge and traditional art which the country would almost certainly have lost.

Ethiopian manuscripts represent original sources for studying the country's economical, social, political, and cultural history and provide invaluable information for the study of languages, arts, and religion in Ethiopia and its neighboring countries. These manuscripts are full of illustrations, illuminations, colophons, marginal notes, musical notations, etc., which are valuable for the study of Ethiopian history, culture, traditions, daily life, and the like. Like all other religious communities, Ethiopia has also produced indigenous literature, art, and music that are the integral part of the history of the religions.

The collections of the IES Manuscript and Archive Department bears comparison in quality and quantity with the most significant collections of Ethiopian manuscripts abroad. Containing as it does much unpublished material, it has attracted the attention of scholars and constitutes an invaluable corpus of research materials. All these historical documents and artifacts of the Ethiopian people need restoration and preservation due to their material nature.

It has been said repeatedly the IES Library was not purposely built as a library. The expansion of the collections over the last fifty years or so has been so great that is poses a threat to the building, which was erected for state receptions, not to hold tons of books and bound volumes of newspapers and other heavy documents. The Library's huge and ever increasing collection has been a major problem for our time in that it is now far too large to be housed in its present premises in the former palace building. The collection is now so crowded that there is scarcely space for proper cataloguing.

Thanks to the fund raising efforts of SOFIES, and with the support of Mohammed International Development Research and Organization Companies (MIDROC) Ethiopia, the private Investment Group owned by Sheikh Mohammed Hussein Ali Al-Amoudi, the new library of the IES is under construction adjacent to the old palace and current location of the IES. This new facility promises to solve some of the chronic problems experienced by the current library.

The goal to preserve images of the manuscripts in digital format is an old plan. The problem was how to get funding to do so. At an international conference held in 2004 at Africa Hall, I met Dr. Vrej Nersessian, head of Oriental collections at the British Library, and explained to him the problems we have faced regarding the preservation of the manuscripts in the care of the IES. Nersessian advised me to write a proposal to the Endangered Archives Programme (EAP) of the British Library. I did as I was advised. In a second stage of the grant writing process, we invited Prof. Steve Delamarter to cooperate with us and were finally granted the funds and carried out the digitization project. And now we come to the stage of the work that we can offer a series of catalogues of the materials thus digitized.

It brings me great satisfaction to see the catalogue work finalized. This is a goal for which I have worked for more than a decade. The purpose is especially to provide the necessary information for users of our collection in the manuscript department at the IES Library. In closing,

1 *The History of the Collection at the IES*

I express my endebtedness to my colleagues who have worked so hard for the last twenty-five years to increase the stature of the IES and the Department of Manuscript and Archives.

Introduction to the Handlist

Steve Delamarter and Jacopo Gnisci

The 1,530 entries described in this handlist attest to the extensive amount of work that had to be carried out in order to digitize the collection of the IES. Given the complexity of the enterprise, it was perhaps inevitable that this volume has been several years in the making. In order to bring the project to a close, Steve Delamarter contacted Jacopo Gnisci in 2021 and the two of us agreed to work collaboratively to tie up any loose ends and make the data contained in this volume available to the public.

Steve, as the driving force behind the project together with Demeke Berhane, was tasked with liaising with the volume's other contributors to put together a set of introductory essays; whereas Jacopo was entrusted with the task of editing the entries for consistency. During the process, it became evident that the field had developed in new and interesting directions from where it was in 2009–10 when, as detailed in the introductory essays by Jeremy R. Brown and Steve, work on this volume begun in earnest. In a series of meetings between the contributors we decided that attempting to bring this volume up to date with current scholarly trends would risk delaying its publication even further. Thus, keeping in mind the fact that the primary purpose of this volume is to provide readers with an overview of the Ethiopic holdings of the IES, we agreed not to overhaul the entries.

Some observations are in order to provide the reader with an adequate background to understand the data that is presented in the handlist. First, it is important to note that, for technical reasons, the folio numbers given in this handlist correspond to those assigned to the digital copies of the manuscripts and that these do not always correspond to the pencil foliation on the manuscripts themselves.

There are also some discrepancies in the amount and type of information contained in the various entries. Generally, those entries that focus on manuscripts that had already been catalogued by the EMML catalogues contain more detailed data than those that had not been described by this project. Moreover, due to the nature of the holdings of the IES, not all the works described below are actually Christian Ethiopic manuscripts. For instance, some of the entries refer to photocopies of manuscripts kept at different locations across Ethiopia, while others describe handwritten notes or book drafts produced by Ethiopian scholars that were subsequently deposited at the IES. As for the titles of literary works, we strove to be internally consistent, and, as far as possible, to align them with the titles given in the *Encylopaedia Aethiopica*, as long as this did not require a major overhaul of the existing records. In some cases, the Ethiopic titles of the works are also provided, but this has not been systematically done.

The handlist singles out a group of manuscripts that can be dated with more confidence than the other through internal evidence, but we make no claim to comprehensiveness. Moreover, in line with the introductory character of this volume, references were kept to a minimum. Ultimately, the reader should bear in mind that the primary goal of this work is to foster research by providing readers with an entry point to the collection of the IES. No doubt, as additional work on the institute's collection is undertaken, the data contained here will need to be revised and updated.

The Digitization of the Materials in the Department of Manuscript and Archives of the IES

Jeremy R. Brown

The digitization of the Institute of Ethiopian Studies (IES) collection was a complicated task requiring six months to complete. Every day, four or more photographers worked together in order to produce several thousand images. These images then needed to be organized and backed up. Subsequently, we began to collect metadata so that we could track the progress of the project as well as the individual productivity of the photographers. In this article I explain the equipment and processes involved in this project and discuss the procedures for balancing quality and quantity as well as how we overcame several challenges faced by the project.

The Photography Stations

We designed the photography stations for this project to be compact, mobile, and low in power requirements. Nikon D200 and D300 cameras served as the workhorses of the stations. The Nikon D200's 10.2 megapixel resolution was more than sufficient for the vast majority of the collection. A Nikon D300, with its 12.3-megapixel resolution, was employed for larger format items such as IES 77.

We mounted the camera on a tripod with a center column rotated parallel to the tabletop. The camera was then tethered to a laptop and operated with Camera Control Pro software. Through this software we could control settings such as aperture and shutter speed. Every image was captured both in high-quality JPEG and in NEF (Nikon's RAW format). We saved these images directly to a 500 gigabyte (GB) external hard drive, which we called the "daily drive."

In order to light the items evenly, each station had four lamps with full-spectrum light bulbs purchased in Addis Ababa. The local availability of these light bulbs enabled us to purchase replacements as bulbs burnt out during the project.

We operated at least four of these photography stations throughout the project and they proved to be reliable and durable, fitting the needs of the project and enabling us to digitize thousands of items.

The Digitization Workshop

The digitization of the IES collection began with a three-day workshop on the skills required for such a project. Staff members from the IES as well as several community members attended. Each person received hands-on training in photography. Additionally, we taught seminars on image processing and metadata collection. By the conclusion of the workshop, each attendant understood the issues of carrying out a digitization project of this scale.

During the workshop, we identified three people who quickly learned the processes and demonstrated an ability to photograph quickly and accurately. Hailemariam Ayalew, Mekonnen Desta, Sileshi Kassaye Kebede, and I served as the primary photographers for the project. Steve Delamarter often ran one of the digitization stations. Additionally, several IES staff members partnered to operate a station. Thus, five or six photographers often could be found working on the IES collection. After identifying our team, we began the work of digitizing the collection.

The Daily Work of Digitization and Metadata Collection

Between late-December 2009 and mid-May 2010, the work of photography was carried out Monday through Friday. We started work when the doors of the IES opened and we stopped work when they began to close up the building for the evening. Other than a short tea break in the afternoon, the photographers could be found working at their stations.

Each day of digitization began with the IES librarians bringing out a cart of materials to be photographed. As the director of digitization, I would go through the cart and assess any items that might require special attention. Such items included those of a particularly large or small size as well as items that were fragile or with loose bindings.

After the materials had been assessed, the photographers would take an item from the cart, photograph it, and then place it on a second cart. The IES librarians would then return these materials to their locations. To photograph an item meant to take a succession of images of two-page spreads through the book (being careful not to skip any pages), followed by shots of the six external sides of the book.

At the end of each work day, the photographers would turn in their "daily drive" with the day's images saved in an individual folder for each item digitized. In addition, they would also turn in a written report that included a list of the items photographed, the number of images for each item, the external measurements of each item, and the language of each item. I would collect these lists and enter the information into the metadata spreadsheet that we had created for the collection. These lists served as the first stage of metadata creation for the project.

Backing up the Data

At the end of each workday, I would take the collected "daily drives" home with me. There I would begin the process of compiling these drives into a master set containing a copy of all of the images taken in the project. Each master set consisted of five 2-terabyte (TB) external hard drives and there were three master sets containing a complete set of images. These were updated daily. One master set remained off-site at my apartment at all times. The second master set traveled with me during the day. The third master set remained on-site at the IES. This served to protect the project from data loss in the case of theft or disaster. All of the eggs were never left in the same basket.[1] The consistent, daily compiling and backing up of data was essential, because things did go wrong and equipment did fail.

Productivity and Accuracy

We also built in ways of tracking productivity and accuracy for each of the photographers. The daily compilation of the master set and

---

1. This was taken to the extreme that the two master sets carried back to the United States were on separate flights, just in case.

accompanying metadata entry provided a regular opportunity to assess the production of each individual photographer as well as check for accuracy both in the images taken and in the metadata listed.

The number of images taken by each of the digitizers was totaled each day of the project so that they had regular feedback on their work. We desired for each photographer to average at least 800 images during an eight-hour work day. In fact, most of the photographers averaged well over a thousand images a day after a few weeks of training and work. The regular totaling of the number of images allowed us to offer the photographers feedback as well as assistance and tips if their productivity dipped below the desired amount.

In tension with productivity is accuracy. The number of images is meaningless if the quality is insufficient. As we compiled the master set, we would review several image sets from each photographer. This enabled us to offer training to further reduce the number of blurry shots and to improve image composition.

After the first few months of work, our colleague in Portland, OR, Sara Vulgan, reviewed many of the image sets and listed the location of any illegible images. She sent us lists of pages that needed to be reshot. We then proceeded to retake those images so that the new image could replace the blurred or missing shot in the final image set. The process of identifying these images and then going to the physical item, locating the folio, and finally retaking the image was painstaking. However, it greatly improved dozens of image sets by replacing illegible frames.

Overcoming Challenges

We faced a number of challenges over the course of the digitization of the IES collection. Power outages, limited work hours, and equipment failures were among them.

During 2010, entire sections of Addis Ababa would lose power for hours. These blackouts often cost us an entire work day over the span of two weeks. Although our photography stations required very little power to operate and could operate on batteries alone, the loss of our lights often caused us to shut down operations. In addition to these lost hours, we also lost a number of work days to civic and religious holidays. Nevertheless, our team worked whenever the doors were opened to us.

We also faced several equipment failures during the project. The shutter in the Nikon D200 is rated for 150,000 shots. For this project, several of the cameras were pushed far beyond this threshold and one shutter did completely fail after 250,000 shots. Fortunately, we were prepared for this and had a spare camera available. We used a number of external hard drives for this project: sixteen 500 GB drives and fifteen 2 TB drives. We only suffered one hard drive failure and, fortunately, the data had been backed up so nothing was lost.

The threat of computer viruses was also a concern. No drives were allowed to be attached to the laptops other than those supplied by the project. Additionally, we brought spare laptop hard drives preloaded with the required software so that if computer contracted a virus, then the hard drive could be swapped for a clean drive. This spare equipment kept us from losing any significant work time due to equipment failure or malfunction.

Conclusions

After six months of work, we had digitized 5,749 items consisting of 488,885 shots. At the end of the project, we gave all of the equipment purchased through the Endangered Archives Programme to the IES. This included four photography stations complete with camera, tripod, laptop loaded with software, hard drives, and lamps. Moreover, a number of IES employees were trained through the digitization workshops hosted at the IES during the course of the project and also worked as photographers during the project and gained valuable experience in the skills of digitization.

As for the data, one complete set of images was copied onto the server at Addis Ababa University. Additionally, one complete master set of five two-TB hard drives was left at the IES. This served as the back-up to the image set uploaded to the server.

This project was an immense undertaking and I am grateful to the full-time photographers that worked with us. Hailemaryam, Mekonnen, and Sileshi were diligent and faithful workers who helped make the success of this project possible. I am also very grateful for the hard work and help of the IES librarians and staff, particularly Walatta Heywot and *ato* Gebre Masqal, who brought out materials in the morning and reshelved them after they had been photographed.

The Urgent Need for Digitizing and Cataloging Ethiopic Manuscripts

Qäsis Melaku Terefe

Throughout its extensive history, the Ethiopian Orthodox Tewahedo Church has cultivated a remarkable literary culture. This Church has translated and passed down numerous monastic, liturgical, and theological texts, along with the chronicles of saints, which were translated from Greek, Arabic, and possibly Syriac into Gəʿəz. Its literary heritage also contains various spiritual works penned by Ethiopian scholars, monastic leaders, and even kings.

In the absence of modern printing tools, these books were painstakingly handwritten and passed down to subsequent generations. Scholars studying scribal practices attest that the early copyists possessed a high degree of specialized knowledge, from the preparation of the skins of sheep and goats to the creation of inks and instruments for tooling bindings and trimming folios.

In tandem with the literary tradition, the Ethiopian Church also developed an iconographic tradition, which formed an integral part of its manuscript culture. Ethiopic manuscripts are adorned with images that relate to the content of the books and uphold the traditions and rules of the church.

The Ethiopian Church's corpus of texts also comprises books that outline the liturgical calendar, investigate the ancient course of celestial bodies, enumerate diseases based on their symptoms, and prescribe lesser-known medicinal herbs for treatment. Thus, Christian Ethiopian writers did not limit themselves solely to religious matters. Indeed, they also chronicled national events and the history of famines and wars from various eras. Moreover, they often wrote about personal records and transactions between individuals in the margins and flyleaves of their manuscripts. As such, the manuscripts of the Ethiopian Orthodox Tewahedo Church can be considered an archive of Ethiopian history, both public and private.

When Steve Delamarter, founder of the Ethiopian Manuscript Imaging Project, invited me to assist in cataloging the Gəʿəz and Amharic codices in Addis Ababa University's Institute of Ethiopian Studies, I enthusiastically joined, recognizing the project's importance in preserving the Ethiopian Church's legacy and the country's history. Unfortunately, historical records have been among the primary casualties of Ethiopia's changing governments and wars. In this respect, the impact of recent conflicts on the nation's most treasured historical manuscripts, particularly in the northern region, has yet to be assessed.

But recent events show that digitizing and cataloging these records using modern technology is an urgent need. Thanks to the British Library's Endangered Archives program, large steps have been taken to preserve many of the records of the Institute of Ethiopian Studies for future generations. With digitized manuscripts available to scholars and institutions, researchers worldwide can easily access these resources and significantly contribute to Ethiopian research.

While researching these records, I was struck by what the late Professor Getachew Haile, a renowned Ethiopian studies scholar, once told me about the manuscripts of Ethiopia: "These books are like an ocean; every time you come back, you will find something new." Indeed, these records constantly provide new insights. Some of them encapsulate truths, condensed into a few pages that could be expanded into thousands.

The benefits of studying these records extends beyond the interests of specialized researchers. These documents offer a rich account of the interactions among the various groups that make up Ethiopia's ethnicities. A knowledge of these can help to counteract the ethnic tensions prevalent in our time and promote a national vision that fosters unity and respect between peoples. Conversely, the destruction of these records by fire, water damage, or theft—or simply their sequestration when left in the hands of private individuals—equates to demolishing the country itself. After all, a country without a history has no identity.

Illuminated Ethiopic Manuscripts at the IES

Jacopo Gnisci

The collection of illuminated Ethiopic manuscripts at the IES is among the most significant in the world. From a chronological standpoint, the collection offers examples dating from the fourteenth century to our times, but it does not hold manuscripts dating back to late antiquity. While some of its illuminated treasures have been the object of scholarly attention, as a whole the collection remains understudied. Carla Zanotti-Eman's article on the headpieces (*ḥaräg*) in IES manuscripts from the fourteenth to the twentieth centuries is the only art historical piece that sets out to look at the collection in a diachronic and systematic way.[1] I am thus grateful that the other contributors to this volume invited me to edit their data and allowed me to write a piece on the illuminated manuscripts in the collection. My aim here is to explain my role in this volume, as well as draw attention to some of the outstanding visual features of the manuscripts in the IES and to the comprehensive data contained in this handlist in order to encourage further research on the collection.

To start, I must acknowledge that by the time I was asked to look at the data in the handlist the bulk of the descriptive work had already been carried out by the other contributors and my principal task was to identify discrepancies or typos across the existing entries. Nevertheless,

---

1. Carla Zanotti Eman, "Gli Areg nei Manoscritti dell'Institute of Ethiopian Studies," in *Orbis Aethiopicus: Studia in honorem Stanislaus Chojnacki natali septuagesimo quinto dicata, septuagesimo septimo oblata*, edited by Piotr O. Scholz, Bibliotheca Nubica 3 (Albstadt: Schuler, 1992), 2:475–99.

because my own research focuses on Ethiopian illumination, I inevitably paid particular attention to those sections of the handlist that are devoted to this feature of the manuscripts and so I feel that I should clarify the small part I played in revising the valuable information offered by this volume. My approach was to retain as much of the existing data as possible as long as I believed it to be factually correct, but for several entries I proposed revisions to the dating of the miniatures or reviewed, in agreement with the other contributors, the identification of certain art themes.

I should also spend a few words on the approach adopted in the handlist to describe the miniatures. All the figurative images in the manuscripts of the IES are identified as separate entities with increasing numbers associated to the folio on which they are found. It is important to note that the folio numbers listed in the handlist are based on the photographs and not on the foliation of the manuscripts when this is present. When two separate scenes appear on a page, the handlist contains two separate entries for each miniature and the folio number is accompanied by an indication of whether that image is found in the upper or lower part of the page by means of the terms "above" and "below" (e.g., IES 315).

A slightly different approach was adopted by the original catalogers to describe the images found on protective scrolls. These have been also categorized as "miniatures," but they are listed consecutively from top to bottom and distinguished by letters in alphabetical order. The terminology used to describe these images is generic for sake of clarity. Some of the figures on the scrolls have been identified as "demons," but it is worth noting that not all art historians agree with this identification so the matter remains open to debate. Here, I opted to retain the terminology employed by the other catalogers to expedite the publication of the volume. It is also worthwhile pointing out that large drawings found in the manuscripts are also described under the "miniature" category and that the handlist does not offer a systematic description of all the doodles or headpieces found in the collection.

Among the oldest illuminated manuscripts in the collection are IES 377, which contains portraits of standing holy figures executed by two different hands, and IES 74, which is richly decorated with headpieces and full-page prefatory portraits of Old Testament figures (Plates 11–12). The IES also owns a richly decorated late fifteenth-century Ethiopic Gospel that contains Evangelist portraits and a prefatory cycle showing three miniatures in which twelve apostles stand before an image of the Virgin and Child (Plates 20–22). Also worth mentioning is a an early sixteenth-century copy of the Miracles of Mary, decorated with headpieces as well as a portrait of the Virgin and Child. The features of this latter image bear witness to some of the artistic and cultural exchanges between Europe and Ethiopia in this period. Additionally, there are several manuscripts from the late fifteenth and early sixteenth centuries decorated with colourful and elaborate headpieces such as IES 721 and IES 722 (Plates 24–27). Among these latter manuscripts, is also IES 496, which has a drawing of an equestrian saint at its beginning that, based on its style, would appear to date to the late fifteenth or early sixteenth century.

While the IES holds only few illustrated manuscripts dating to the seventeenth century—including one (IES 103) with headpieces that brings to mind the style of examples associated to the region around Lalibäla[2]—it has a considerable collection of works dating to the eighteenth century that feature images executed in the Second Gondarine style of painting. Among the noteworthy manuscripts from this period are: IES 73, one of several manuscript in the collection which features multiple representations of donors in proskynesis (Plate 9); IES 315, which features a scene where the Ethiopian Emperor Yoḥannəs I and Iyasu I are visually paralleled to Constantine the Great; IES 422, a multiple-text manuscript which contains over thirty miniatures showing episodes from the life of Jesus, Mary and various saints, including one that shows *abunä* Ewosṭatewos travelling to Armenia; and IES 4175, a loose folio with a representation of the Council of Nicaea in which Arius is trapped within a net. Finally, within this group, IES 75 stands out especially for the sheer number of images. This manuscript, which must have been a personal object of a prominent person, is decorated with seventy scenes, including an extensive cycle showing episodes from the life and death of Jesus, as well as numerous representations showing episodes of apostolic martyrdom.

Turning our attention to the manuscripts dating to the late eighteenth and nineteenth centuries, I would like to mention: a copy of the Miracles of the Saint Michael (IES 2958), which has a prefatory image showing the donor in proskynesis before the archangel and a copy of the

---

2. See the discussion in Claire Bosc-Tiessé, "Géopolitique, Art et Production Manuscrite Au Lāstā Aux XVIIe et XVIIIe Siècles," in *Lalibela: Site Rupestre Chrétien d'Éthiopie*, edited by Claire Bosc-Tiessé and Marie-Laure Derat, Sites et Cités d'Afrique (Toulouse: Presses Universitaires du Midi, 2019), 112–66.

Miracles of Mary (IES 1051) with images executed in the Shewan style first described by Stanisław Chojnacki.[3]

As we move towards the turn of the twentieth century, we find a number of manuscripts painted in a style that can be associated to the imperial scriptorium of Emperor Mənilək and Emperor Ḥaylä Śəllase (IES 4; IES 31; IES 77: IES 108; IES 193; IES 240; Plate 1). The latter ruler appears in proskynesis before an unusual Crucifixion in a Psalter and Psalter of the Virgin manuscript dating to 1931/32 CE in which the blood of Jesus pours over two maps of the world (IES 1085). There are also a number of manuscripts from the first decades of the twentieth century executed in other styles which were employed in Addis Ababa in this period. Among them, IES 7 deserves special mention for the exceptional presence of popular scenes that are not directly connected with the Christian Ethiopian Orthodox repertoire of imagery (Plates 2–5).

Lastly, among the more recent manuscripts in the collection, one finds images executed by artists who also painted other objects, such as icons, for the tourist market (IES 1) as well as later additions to old manuscripts (IES 84). In some cases, it is clear that we are looking at the work of a forger who hoped to enhance the value of a manuscript through the addition of miniatures. The best example is offered by a group of manuscripts (IES 2411–14 and IES 2416) that all feature recent miniatures painted by the same illustrator.

---

3. Chojnacki, Stanisław, *Major Themes in Ethiopian Painting: Indigenous Developments, the Influence of Foreign Models, and Their Adaptation from the 13th to the 19th Century*. ÄF 10. Wiesbaden: Franz Steiner, 1983, 469–524.

Abbreviations

AF	Äthiopistische Forschungen (Stuttgart/Wiesbaden, 1977–)
CSCO	Corpus Scriptorum Christianorum Orientalium (Louvain, 1930–)
EA	*Encyclopaedia Aethiopica* (Hamburg, 2003–14)
EC	Ethiopian Calendar, seven to eight years behind AD
EMML	Getatchew Haile and William F. Macomber. *A Catalogue of Ethiopian Manuscripts Microfilmed for the Ethiopian Manuscript Microfilm Library, Addis Ababa, and for the Hill Monastic Manuscript Library, Collegeville* (Collegeville, MN: Hill Museum and Manuscript Library, 1973–)
EMIP	Ethiopic Manuscript Imaging Project (Portland, OR, 2009–)
EMTS	Ethiopic Manuscripts, Texts, and Studies (Eugene, OR, 2009–)
SA	Scriptores Aethiopici (within CSCO)

Catalogue of the Manuscripts

IES 00001, Mar Yeshaq or Isaac of Nineveh, ማር ይስሐቅ (= Book III of the spiritual writings of Isaac of Nineveh), in Gəʿəz with Amharic translation and commentary. Parchment and paper, 320 x 210 x 60 mm, iv + 246 folios, two columns, 30 lines, Gəʿəz, Amharic, late nineteenth/early twentieth century. EMML 6.

Miniatures:

1. F. iii r(ecto), Ləbnä Dəngəl, the king of Ethiopia, sitting in judgment in court, before an accuser and an accused.
2. F. 30r, a depiction of the translator of this book, *Mämhər* Akalä Wäld, in the process of translation and in teaching.
3. F. 244r, the celebration of the ark of the covenant (*tabot*).
4. F. 245r, Saint George and the Dragon.

IES 00002, Synaxarium, መጽሐፈ ስንክሳር, Part I. Parchment, 348 x 290 x 90 mm, iii + 201 folios, three columns, 35–36 lines, Gəʿəz, 1964. EMML 8.

IES 00003, Synaxarium, መጽሐፈ ስንክሳር, Part II. Parchment, 320 x 260 x 100 mm, ii + 202 folios, three columns, 30–32 lines, Gəʿəz, 1964. EMML 7.

IES 00004, Psalter, ዳዊት; Angels Praise Her, ይዜድስዋ መላእክት ለማርያም; produced in the Government Scriptorium. Parchment, 310 x 235 x 80 mm, iv + 190 folios, one column and two columns, 20 lines, Gəʿəz, twentieth century. EMML 1283.

Miniatures:

1. F. iv v(erso): King David playing the harp.

IES 00005, Commentary on Pauline Epistles; Commentary on the Catholic Epistles; Commentary on Revelation. Parchment, 360 x 260 x 50 mm, xiv + 154 folios, two columns, 40 lines, Amharic, twentieth century. EMML 9.

IES 00006, Harp of Praise, አርጋኖን ውዳሴ; Image of the Covenant of Mercy, መልክአ ኪዳነ ምሕረት; Image of the Assumption, መልክአ ፍልሰታ ለማርያም; Image of Saint George, መልክአ ጊዮርጊስ; Image of Jesus (incomplete), መልክአ ኢየሱስ; Image of Michael, መልክአ ሚካኤል; Image of Gabriel, መልክአ ገብርኤል; Angels Praise Her, ይዌድስዎ መላእክት ለማርያም. Parchment, 300 x 270 x 70 mm, i + 132 folios, two columns, 19 lines, Gəʿəz, early eighteenth century. EMML 1284.

Miniatures:

1. F. i r(ecto): Crude drawings of three figures.

IES 00007, Book of Icons. Parchment, 320 x 240 x 75 mm, ii + 141 folios, two columns, 25–26 lines, Amharic, 1909. EMML 10.

Miniatures:

1. F. 2r: The Holy Trinity surrounded by the four Living Creatures.
2. F. 4r: The devil capturing five men in a cage of thorns.
3. F. 5r: The five men freed from the cage of thorns by two angels. The devil holds the shattered remnants of the cage.
4. F. 7r: Two saints with halos and hands upraised inside of a church.
5. F. 8r: Man and woman seated in a church. Woman nurses a baby.
6. F. 9v: Flight into Egypt.
7. F. 11r: Anne in the temple.
8. F. 13r: Annunciation.
9. F. 15r: Madonna and Child.
10. F. 17r: The Crucifixion, the piercing of Jesus' side, and a man offering gall to drink.
11. F. 18r: An elder holding an olive branch before a younger person.

12. F. 19r: Vision of a sacred being surrounded by creatures.
13. F. 20r: The fall of the horse of a wealthy man chasing a rabbit.
14. F. 21r: A dog with meat in his mouth, being followed by another dog who wants the meat; the dog enters water, sees his reflection and tries to fight the dog he sees, and the dog who is following gets the meat.
15. F. 22r: A serpent, on orders from the devil, tries to extinguish the light from a lampstand.
16. F. 24r: Three philosophers encounter a person who lost his camel.
17. F. 25v: A scene from the book narrated by በረላንም, in which he caught a bird with his snare.
18. F. 26r: The bird spoke in human language and begged for his life by promising three pieces of advice: (1) don't believe anyone; (2) don't regret the past; (3) don't desire what you don't have.
19. F. 28r: Scene from the story of the good Samaritan with his donkey tending to the man who fell among thieves.
20. F. 30r: A man climbs a tree whose base has been eaten by a white and a black mouse; a serpent awaits to attack the man and another man with a gun lies in wait for the man, but he eats the fruit of the tree, oblivious to the dangers.
21. F. 31r: A crow in a tree has bread in its mouth, while a fox tries to get the bread by flattering the bird and getting it to open its mouth to speak.
22. F. 31v: A shrewd fox lies down as though dead; when four crows arrive (surrounding) to feast on the body, the fox leaps up and captures one of them. A note in the text cites the source as ፊልጶስ ክፍል ፲፮.
23. F. 32r: A hyena attacks a foolish and rebellious ram, while a good shepherd tends the rest of his flock of rams.
24. F. 32v: A fruitful tree with poisonous leaves and thorns.
25. F. 33r: A blind man with a walking staff and a paralyzed man on his shoulders.

26. F. 35r: A father, under a canopy, advising his seven children at his feet (four lower right; three lower left) with an object lesson about the strength of a bundle of seven sticks together.

27. F. 36v: A large and beautiful tree with colourful fruit neglected by the people of the land, but used by strangers.

28. F. 37r: A lion napping in front of his cave is disturbed by a small stinging creature called *Ǝnz*.

29. F. 39r: Two of the four horsemen in Revelation 6:2. The white horse with rider wearing crown (top); the red horse with rider carrying sword (bottom).

30. F. 41r: Two of the four horsemen in Revelation 6:5 and 6. The black horse with rider holding balance (top); the green horse with rider called Death (bottom).

31. F. 42r: How a small boy found a precious stone, and how a man deceived the boy and took the precious stone.

32. F. 42v: How a cat purred to get a piece of meat from a boy, but growled when it had the meat, thus revealing her nature.

33. F. 44r: A scene from a vision in which the devil tries to burn down a church and how a Great Eagle and an angel came out from the church and saved the church from burning.

34. F. 45r: Children playing near a river filled with frogs, throw stones in the river and are chastised by one of the frogs.

35. F. 46r: A scene from a vision in which four people stand together. One (upper left) stretches his hands to heaven. Another (upper right) holds a sword. Another (lower left) holds a cup filled with blood in one hand and a turtle in the other. A final person (lower right) a cup filled with blood in one hand and a hyssop branch in the other.

36. F. 47r: A person runs to catch the fog and falls off a cliff.

37. F. 47v: In a dream, a man sees an egg which sprouts wings.

38. F. 48r: A wise man, bitten by a snake on the finger, takes a knife and cuts off his finger to save his life.

39. F. 48v: A man (second from left) is married to an old lady. The philosopher (second from right) tells him to leave the old lady to marry a beautiful, young woman.

Catalogue of the Manuscripts 5

40. F. 50r: A scene from a vision of an island on which there is a great snake attacking a woman. A fish and a whale deliver the woman. The whale proposes to the woman, but the other animals counsel against it.

41. F. 50v: The great whale, a lion and a hyena.

42. F. 51r: A fly and a turtle laugh together; an ox stands nearby (above); and a fox kills the sheep and then wears the skin of the sheep in order to attack the other sheep (below).

43. F. 51v: One sheep surrounded by a lion, an elephant, a leopard, a goat, a pig, and a turtle. An angel of God protects the sheep.

44. F. 52r: Creatures called *Akädäma* who look like men in their upper parts and like crocodiles in their lower part.

45. F. 53r: A beautiful tree gives bark and wood for medicine. A philosopher sees the tree dry up and die. He observes that groundhogs have eaten the roots of the tree.

46. F. 55r: For 30 years a man searches all things but comes again to the same place.

47. F. 55v: Children (upper left and f. 56r) play with an angel (lower right).

48. F. 56r: Continuation of scene on f. 55v.

49. F. 57r: The devil mates with a hyena which tries to attack a sheep; but the sheep triumphs with a cross.

50. F. 58r: The devil (above) is slain by the sheep with the cross.

51. F. 58v: A man climbs through a window (no text accompanies this scene).

52. F. 59r: A philosophers carries a medicine chest on his head (f. 59r). People ask him what the medicine does, but except for one wise man, they do not believe him.

53. F. 60r: A man draws water from the river and fills a broken container (left and center), while the author looks on in his dream.

54. F. 61v: A foolish man carries wheat in a basket on his head (above) while a bird eats the wheat. Another foolish man uses water as ink. A wise man carves on stone (lower left). Another foolish man digs for water but stops short before finding water (lower right), while a wise man digs deeper (lower center) and finds water.

55. F. 62r: The Stingy Man, scene one: A poor neighbor kneels and feigns blindness with a hand covering his eyes; the stingy man looks on. Below are two animals.

56. F. 64r: The Stingy Man, scene two: A poor neighbor feigns blindness to trick the stingy man into showing him where he has buried his money.

57. F. 64v (described on f. 63v, column 2): A great snake devours a man who enters a cave to take gold.

58. F. 66r (described on ff. 65rv): The devil, disguised as a medicine man, gives a man medicine which changes his sheep into a fox.

59. F. 66v (continuation of 66r): Hyenas, killed by snakes and scorpions.

60. F. 67r (continuation of 66r): The angel of God saves the lion from the fox and hyenas.

61. F. 67v: A man with a small telescope watches a man with a scorpion nearby, a man writing, and a man measuring.

62. F. 68r: The angel of God, riding a horse, comes to the aid of a faithful man and triumphs over the devil (bottom).

63. F. 68v: The devil sits on the head of a man with a cap. The angel of God cuts off his hand. A friend of the first man trembles in fear.

64. F. 69r: The lions, servants of God, attack and kill the hyena, servant of the devil.

65. F. 70r: A monkey serves the devil.

66. F. 70v: A man-beast serves the devil.

67. F. 71r: The sheep with a cross on his head serves the angel of the Lord (upper right) and kills the monkey and man-beast (lower left) who serve the devil (upper left).

68. F. 71v: The flesh of the monkey and man-beast (below) is stripped off by crows (above).

69. F. 75r: How a father built a great building for the King of Egypt, but left a hidden door for his children to be able to take treasures from the king. The king set a trap for the thieves and ensnared one of the children. They cut off his head to avoid identification of the body.

70. F. 77r: Women of a city demand to know why they are not included in the deliberations of the town council (above). The council agrees to include them but on the condition they receive a box and leave it closed. When the men leave, the women open the box and a bird which was in it flew out (below). From this point forward they withdrew from the council.

71. F. 79r: A king went to war with another and promised to kill all the men in the city. The women of the city asked to be allowed to carry out their children and property before the king attacked. The king agreed. The women carried out their husbands and when challenged they explained that they owned no more important property than their husbands.

72. F. 82r: A farmer with a beautiful wife serves a landlord. The landlord has an affair with the wife. When the farmer appeals to God, God gives him two sticks: one will turn a human into a monkey; the other will turn a monkey into a human. The wife is tricked and turns the landlord into a monkey which is then chased by the dog (below) and eventually killed.

73. F. 82v: The farmer and his wife.

IES 00008, Image of Saint George, መልክአ ጊዮርጊስ; Psalter, ዳዊት. Parchment, 245 x 160 x 65 mm, iv + 154 folios, one column and two columns, 23 lines, Gəʿəz, nineteenth century. EMML 1285.

IES 00009, Psalter, ዳዊት. Paper, 130 x 90 x 25 mm, ii + 126 folios, one column and two columns, 23 lines, Gəʿəz, 1883 EC = 1890–91 (f. 1r has colophon). EMML 1296.

Miniatures:

1. F. ii v(erso): Ornate cross.

IES 00010, Psalter, ዳዊት. Parchment, 130 x 120 x 63 mm, ii + 166 folios, one column and two columns, 18 lines, Gəʿəz, eighteenth century. EMML 10 & 1293.

IES 00011, Gəʿəz Vocabulary and Grammar, ሰዋሰው፡ ግዕዝ. Paper, 200 x 155 x 50 mm, iv + 339 folios, two columns, 20 lines, Gəʿəz, twentieth century. EMML 1286.

IES 00012, Psalter, ዳዊት; Angels Praise Her, ይዌድስዋ መላእክት ለማርያም. Parchment, 165 x 120 x 50 mm, ii + 140 folios, one column and two columns, 25 lines, Gəʿəz, nineteenth century. EMML 1291.

IES 00013, Gospel of John, ወንጌል ዘዮሐንስ. Parchment, 140 x 100 x 40 mm, ii + 116 folios, two columns, 16 lines, Gəʿəz, mid-twentieth century. EMML 1295.

IES 00014, Prayer; Petition; Supplication; Anaphora of Our Lady Mary, ቅዳሴ ማርያም. Parchment, 155 x 110 x 40 mm, ii + 56 folios, two columns, 16 lines, Gəʿəz, nineteenth/twentieth century. EMML 1289.

IES 00015, Praises of Mary, ውዳሴ ማርያም; Gate of Light, አንቀጸ ብርሃን; Angels Praise Her, ይድስዋ መላእክት ለማርያም; Hymn to Mary, "For She is Glorious"; Hymn to Mary, "I Worship Thee"; Image of the Praises of Mary, መልከአ ውዳሴ ማርያም. Parchment, 140 x 100 x 45 mm, 82 folios, two columns, 12–13 lines, Gəʿəz, nineteenth century. EMML 1290.

IES 00016, Praises of God, ውዳሴ አምላክ; Hymn to God, "God of the Ancient Time"; Hymn to Mary; Prayer to God; Prayer to Jesus Christ, "Prayer of the Elderly"; Prayer of the Laity, "O Lord Save Me, Thou Who Saved." Parchment, 125 x 110 x 58 mm, ii + 153 folios, three columns, 17 lines, Gəʿəz, seventeenth and eighteenth centuries (composite). EMML 1294.

IES 00017, Psalter, ዳዊት. Parchment, 200 x 150 x 60 mm, ii + 142 folios, one column and three columns, 23–24 lines, Gəʿəz, early nineteenth century. EMML 1287.

Miniatures:

1. F. i v(erso): Equestrian saint.
2. F. ii r(ecto): Madonna and Child.

IES 00018, Five Pillars of Mystery, አምስቱ አዕማደ ምሥጢር; Beauty of Creation, ሥነ ፍጥረት; Prayer to God, in Amharic. Parchment, 175 x 130 x 30 mm, ii + 32 folios, one column, 13 lines, Gəʿəz, Amharic, twentieth century. EMML 1288.

IES 00019, Gəʿəz Grammar, ሰዋስው፡ ግዕዝ. Parchment, 150 x 110 x 40 mm, i + 86 folios, one column, 30–31 lines, Gəʿəz, nineteenth century. EMML 1292.

IES 00020, History of Ethiopia. Parchment, 200 x 135 x 45 mm, ii + 78 folios, two columns, 23–24 lines, Gəʿəz, Ḫədar 1905 = Nov./Dec. 1912 (dated colophon on ff. 76v–77a). EMML 1313.

Miniatures:

1. Inside front cover: Drawing of a cross.
2. Inside back cover: Drawing of a cross.

IES 00021, Harp of Praise, አርጋኖ ውዳሴ; Book of Christening, መጽሐፈ ክርስትና; Hymn to Mary with the saints; Catechism called here "Gate of Faith"; Image of Apostles, መልክአ ሐዋርያት; One Miracle of Mary, ተአምረ ማርያም. Parchment, 190 x 180 x 64 mm, ii + 145 folios, two columns, 17–18 lines, Gəʿəz, eighteenth/nineteenth/sixteenth centuries (composite). EMML 1307.

IES 00022, Harp of Praise, አርጋኖ ውዳሴ; Miscellanea. Parchment, 175 x 190 x 70 mm, ii + 144 folios, two columns, 16 lines, Gəʿəz, eighteenth century. EMML 1309.

IES 00023, Collection of Homilies in Amharic, "Religious Education and Guidance." Paper, 175 x 170 x 28 mm, i + 105 folios, one column, 15 lines, Amharic, twentieth century. EMML 1310.

Miniatures:

1. F. i r(ecto): Crude drawing of a figure.
2. Inside back cover: Crude drawing of a face.

IES 00024, Prayer Book; Canticle of the Flower, ማኅሌተ ጽጌ. Paper, 205 x 160 x 15 mm, i + 88 folios, one column, 18 lines, Amharic, 1941–50 (ff. 2rv). EMML 1312.

IES 00025, Psalter, ዳዊት. Parchment, 155 x 135 x 43 mm, iv + 158 folios, one column and two columns, 22 lines, Gəʿəz, 1887 EC = 1894–95 (dated on f. 158v). EMML 1316.

IES 00026, Harp of Praise, አርጋኖ ውዳሴ. Parchment, 187 x 180 x 70 mm, 117 folios, two columns, 19 lines, Gəʿəz, eighteenth/nineteenth century. EMML 1306.

Miniatures:

1. F. 99r: Crude drawing of three faces.

IES 00027, Collection of Homilies (in Amharic) "Religious Education and Guidance"; Collection of Treatises (in Amharic) called *Mäṣḥafä estegubu*'; Beauty of Creation, ሥነ ፍጥረት; Horologium for the Night, ስዓታት ዘሌሊት. Parchment, 174 x 113 x 41 mm, 355 folios, one column, 15–18 lines, Gəʿəz, Amharic, 1865–1913 (f. 353v mentions Emperor Mənilək II). EMML 1315. Inner half of double-slip maḥdär.

IES 00028, Forty-Six Miracles of Mary, ተአምረ ማርያም. Parchment, 238 x 185 x 53 mm, ii + 52 folios, two columns, 22–23 lines, Gəʿəz, nineteenth/twentieth century. EMML 1304.

Miniatures:

1. F. ii r(ecto): Madonna and Child.

IES 00029, Homiliary in Honor of Elijah; Homily on Saint George by Theodotus of Ancyra; Nine Miracles of Saint George. Paper, 276 x 190 x 27 mm, i + 165 folios, two columns, 25 lines, Gəʿəz, 1932 EC = 1939–40 (dated on f. 5r). EMML 1302.

IES 00030, Funeral Ritual, መጽሐፈ ግንዘት. Parchment, 303 x 228 x 63 mm, i + 103 folios, three columns, 24–27 lines, Gəʿəz, 1913–26 (dating based on a prayer for the Metropolitan Matewos [r. 1889–1926] and the fact that the place for the mention of the king has been left blank which might suggest the period between Emperor Mənilək II and Empress Zäwditu). EMML 1298.

IES 00031, On the importance of celebrating the feasts of Saint Michael; Image of Michael, መልክአ ሚካኤል; Homiliary in Honor of the Archangel Michael, ድርሳን ሚካኤል; Prayer with the secret names that God gave to Saint Michael. Parchment, 280 x 225 x 70 mm, iii + 139 folios, two columns, 18 lines, Gəʿəz, twentieth century. EMML 1299.

Miniatures:

1. Inside front cover: Angel with processional cross.
2. F. ii v(erso): God surrounded by the four Living Creatures.
3. F. iii r(ecto): Angel with processional cross.
4. F. iii v(erso): Ornate cross.
5. F. 6v: Angel with sword and scabbard standing over a bound devil.

IES 00032, Praises of God, ውዳሴ አምላክ. Parchment, 268 x 250 x 75 mm, i + 146 folios, two columns, 18 lines, Gəʿəz, seventeenth/eighteenth century. EMML 1300.

Miniatures:

1. F. 145v: Crude drawing of an ornate cross.

2. F. 146r: Crude drawing of a figure.

3. F. 146v: Crude drawing of a figure and an ornate cross.

IES 00033, Funeral Ritual, መጽሐፈ ግንዘት. Parchment, 280 x 220 x 85 mm, ii + 90 folios, two columns, 27–28 lines, Gəʿəz, 1841–67 (f. 43b, prayer for Metropolitan Sälama [1841–67] but also mentions the year 1871 EC = 1878–79). EMML 1301.

IES 00034, Images Collection, መልክአ ጉባኤ. Parchment, 290 x 250 x 95 mm, 226 folios, two columns, 16 lines, Gəʿəz, eighteenth century. EMML 1297.

IES 00035, Forty-Six Miracles of Mary, ተአምረ ማርያም; Four Miracles of Saint George, ተአምረ ጊዮርጊስ; Three Miracles of Jesus, ተአምረ ኢየሱስ. Parchment, 210 x 170 x 45 mm, 65 folios, two columns, 20 lines, Gəʿəz, 1865–1913 (f. 11r, prayer for Emperor Mənilək II). EMML 1305.

IES 00036, Praises of God, ውዳሴ አምላክ; Miscellanea. Parchment, 185 x 200 x 90 mm, 198 folios, two columns, 16 lines, Gəʿəz, seventeenth/eighteenth century. EMML 1308.

IES 00037, Homiliary in Honor of the Archangel Michael, ድርሳነ ሚካኤል; Homiliary in Honor of the Archangel Gabriel, ድርሳነ ገብርኤል. Parchment, 240 x 160 x 60 mm, iii + 144 folios, two columns, 25 lines, Gəʿəz, 1847–55 (copied for Ḥaylä Mäläkot, father of Emperor Mənilək II). EMML 1311.

Miniatures:

1. F. i r(ecto): portrait of Ḥaylä Maryam.

2. F. i v(erso): Wäldä Mädḫan before Michael, the Archangel.

3. F. ii r(ecto): Michael, the Archangel.

4. F. iii r(ecto): Ornate cross.

5. F. 144r: Portrait of a nobleman or woman (possibly Ḥaylä Mäläkot).

IES 00038, The Life of John of the East; The Acts of John of the East; Twenty-One Miracles of John of the East. Paper, 235 x 180 x 40 mm, iii + 169 folios, two columns, 23 lines, Gəʿəz, 1938 EC = 1945–46 (f. 120r, dated colophon). EMML 1303.

IES 00039, Gospel of John, ወንጌል ዘዮሐንስ; Miscellanea. Parchment, 160 x 130 x 45 mm, ii + 97 folios, two columns, 17 lines, Gəʿəz, nineteenth century. EMML 1314.

Miniatures:

1. F. ii v(erso): Saint.

IES 00040, Acts of John the Baptist, ገድለ ዮሐንስ መጥምቅ; Image of John the Baptist, መልክአ ዮሐንስ መጥምቅ; Life of *Abba* Bula/Abib (also called the *Gädl* for 25th of *Ṭəqəmt*); Image of Abib (i.e., Bula), መልክአ አቢብ. Parchment, 160 x 145 x 40 mm, 78 folios, two columns, 15 lines, Gəʿəz, eighteenth century. EMML 1344.

IES 00041, Book of Christening, መጽሐፈ ክርስትና. Parchment, 175 x 155 x 53 mm, i + 88 folios, two columns, 15 lines, Gəʿəz, eighteenth century. EMML 1334.

IES 00042, Praises of Mary, ውዳሴ ማርያም; School Chants, የቃል ትምህርት. Parchment, 105 x 80 x 37 mm, ii + 69 folios, two columns, 13 lines, Gəʿəz, eighteenth century. EMML 1347. Single-slip maḥdär.

IES 00043, *Məʾraf* Chants, ምዕራፍ. Parchment, 145 x 125 x 60 mm, iv + 129 folios, two columns, 17 lines, Gəʿəz, early twentieth century. EMML 1343.

IES 00044, Vision of Mary, ራዕየ ማርያም, in Amharic; Journey to Heaven, መንገደ ሰማይ; Computus, *Baḥərä Ḥasab*, ባሕረ ሐሳብ. Parchment, 125 x 80 x 35 mm, ii + 69 folios, one column, 15 lines, Gəʿəz, Amharic, 1899–1900. EMML 1346.

IES 00045, Image of Mary, መልክአ ማርያም; Image of Jesus, መልክአ ኢየሱስ; Image of Saint George, መልክአ ጊዮርጊስ. Parchment, 125 x 80 x 30 mm, ii + 38 folios, one column, 16 lines, Gəʿəz, nineteenth century. EMML 1342.

IES 00046, Study of *Qəne*, called *Fənotä qəne*. Parchment, 180 x 125 x 30 mm, i + 45 folios, two columns, 22–27 lines, Gəʿəz, nineteenth century. EMML 1340.

Miniatures:

1. F. i r(ecto): Crude drawing of Madonna and Child.

2. F. 45v: Crude drawing of Madonna and Child.

IES 00047, Homiliary in Honor of the Archangel Michael, ድርሳነ ሚካኤል. Parchment, 205 x 140 x 53 mm, ii + 126 folios, two columns, 21 lines, Gəʻəz, 1907 EC = 1914–15 (f. 124v, dated colophon). EMML 1335.

IES 00048, Collection of Chants called *Mäzmur*, መዝሙር. Parchment, 175 x 120 x 50 mm, ii + 78 folios, two columns, 20–21 lines, Gəʻəz, twentieth century. EMML 1336.

IES 00049, Homiliary in Honor of the Archangel Michael, ድርሳነ ሚካኤል; Two Miracles of Gabriel, ተአምረ ገብርኤል; Image of Gabriel, መልክአ ገብርኤል; Five Miracles of Michael, ተአምረ ሚካኤል. Parchment, 180 x 140 x 80 mm, iii + 205 folios, two columns, 16 lines, Gəʻəz, 1912 EC = 1919–20. EMML 1333.

Miniatures:

1. F. 35v: Drawings of three figures in pencil.

IES 00050, Psalter, ዳዊት. Parchment, 150 x 145 x 85 mm, ii + 183 folios, one column and two columns, 16 lines, Gəʻəz, eighteenth century. EMML 1345.

Miniatures:

1. F. 8v: Three crosses.

2. F. 24v: Drawing of a cross in pencil.

3. F. 25v: Drawing of a cross in pencil.

4. F. 26r: Drawing of a cross in pencil.

5. F. 38v: Crosses.

6. F. 47v: Crosses.

7. F. 54r: Crosses.

8. F. 71r: An angel marking the mid-point of the Psalms.

9. F. 132r: Crosses.

10. F. 140r: Angels.

IES 00051, *Asmat* Prayers, arranged for the days of the week. Parchment, 120 x 95 x 25 mm, iv + 50 folios, one column, 15 lines, Gəʽəz, nineteenth century. EMML 1341.

IES 00052, Antiphonary for the Fast of Lent, ጾመ ድጓ. Parchment, 160 x 120 x 55 mm, iv + 104 folios, two columns, 23–26 lines, Gəʽəz, nineteenth/twentieth century. EMML 1339.

IES 00053, Abbreviated antiphonary for the Fast of Lent, ጾመ ድጓ; notes of commentary on the New Testament; brief discourses (in Amharic) on baptism, reading with attention, the creation of nature, and on faith and commandments. Parchment, 180 x 140 x 50 mm, vi + 76 folios, two columns, 21 lines, Gəʽəz, Amharic, twentieth century. EMML 1337.

IES 00054, Prayers; Image of the Trinity, መልክአ ሥላሴ; Wisest of the Wise, ጠቢበ ጠቢባን; Image of Saint George, መልክአ ጊዮርጊስ; Image of Michael, መልክአ ሚካኤል; Five Miracles of Mary, ተአምረ ማርያም; Image of Täklä Haymanot, መልክአ ተክለ ሃይማኖት; Miscellanea; Two Miracles of Mary, ተአምረ ማርያም; Prayer to Mary, "O my Lady, Mary, Sanctify Me with Your Sanctity." Parchment, 200 x 130 x 40 mm, ii + 57 folios, one column, 20–21 lines, Gəʽəz, early eighteenth century. EMML 1338.

IES 00055, Acts of Näʾakkwəto Läʾab (including his Life, Miracles, Memorial Day). Parchment, 165 x 160 x 30 mm, 80 folios, two columns, 15 lines, Gəʽəz, eighteenth century. EMML 1356.

IES 00056, School Chants, የቃል ትምህርት. Parchment, 130 x 100 x 40 mm, i + 33 folios, two columns, 16 lines, Gəʽəz, nineteenth century. EMML 1360.

IES 00057, Vision of Sinoda, ራዕየ ሲኖደ. Parchment, 195 x 145 x 15 mm, i + 19 folios, two columns, 18 lines, Gəʽəz, November 24, 1950 (f. 14r, colophon). EMML 1351.

IES 00058, Gəʽəz Grammar, ሰዋስወ ግዕዝ. Parchment, 103 x 80 x 13 mm, 38 folios, one column, 17 lines, Gəʽəz, nineteenth century.

IES 00059, Acts of *Abunä* Tärbu, ገድለ አቡነ ተርቡ; Praises of Mary, ውዳሴ ማርያም; Covenant of the Morning, ኪዳን ዘነግሀ; Mystagogical Catechesis, ትምህርተ ኅቡዓት; A Chapter from the Book of the Dead.

Parchment, 160 x 100 x 40 mm, iv + 80 folios, one column, 16 lines, Gəʿəz, eighteenth century. EMML 1363. Double-slip maḥdär.

IES 00060, Prayer of Incense, ጸሎተ ዕጣን. Parchment, 215 x 155 x 20 mm, ii + 30 folios, two columns, 17 lines, Gəʿəz, 1916–26 (f. 8r Empress Zäwditu is mentioned). EMML 1349.

IES 00061, Covenant of the Morning, ኪዳን ዘነግህ, etc. Parchment, 150 x 140 x 60 mm, iv + 34 folios, two columns, 13 lines, Gəʿəz, 1930–74 (f. 19v, prayer for Emperor Ḫaylä Śəllase). EMML 1354.

Miniatures:

1. F. iii r(ecto): John praying.

2. F. 33v: Yared with sistrum and prayer staff.

IES 00062, Missal, መጽሐፈ ቅዳሴ. Parchment, 155 x 135 x 50 mm, ii + 78 folios, two columns, 12–20 lines, Gəʿəz, 1755–69 (f. 5v, prayer for Emperor Iyoʾas I). EMML 1357.

IES 00063, Praises of Mary, ውዳሴ ማርያም. Parchment, 235 x 190 x 11 mm, 25 folios, two columns, 18–21 lines, Gəʿəz, 1916–30 (f. 8r mentions Empress Zäwditu [r. 1916–30]).

Miniatures:

1. Inside front cover: Ornate cross, in pencil.

IES 00064, Anaphora of Our Lady Mary, ቅዳሴ ማርያም. Parchment, 147 x 110 x 25 mm, ii + 40 folios, two columns, 11 lines, Gəʿəz, 1881–1926 (ff. 4v and passim, prayer for Metropolitan Matewos). EMML 1353.

IES 00065, Praises of Mary, ውዳሴ ማርያም; Gate of Light, አንቀጸ ብርሃን; Angels Praise Her, ይዌድስዎ መላእክት ለማርያም. Parchment, 125 x 90 x 30 mm, ii + 44 folios, one column, 14–18 lines, Gəʿəz, nineteenth century. EMML 1364.

Miniatures:

1. F. ii v(erso): Crude drawing of a face.

IES 00066, Revelation, ራእየ ዮሐንስ. Parchment, 190 x 170 x 20 mm, i + 35 folios, two columns, 17 lines, Gəʿəz, eighteenth century. EMML 1352.

IES 00067, Psalter, ዳዊት. Parchment, 190 x 140 x 80 mm, iii + 119 folios, one column and two columns, 26-28 lines, Gəʿəz, nineteenth century. EMML 1361.

IES 00068, Covenant of the Morning, ኪዳን ዘነግህ. Parchment, 135 x 95 x 43 mm, ii + 48 folios, one column, 9-11 lines, Gəʿəz, twentieth century. EMML 1359.

Miniatures:

1. F. i v(erso): Jesus blessing a man.
2. F. 47r: Yared with a sistrum.
3. F. 48r: Elijah being fed by the raven.

IES 00069, *Asmat* Prayers, አስማት; Image of Michael, መልክአ ሚካኤል. Parchment, 135 x 100 x 48 mm, iv + 79 folios, two columns, 14-15 lines, Gəʿəz, twentieth century. EMML 1358.

Miniatures:

1. F. iv v(erso): Madonna and Child.

IES 00070, *Zəmmare* Chants for the Whole Year, ዝማሬ. Parchment, 220 x 170 x 60 mm, vi + 81 folios, three columns, 27 lines, Gəʿəz, 1909 (f. 57v, 20th year of the reign of Emperor Mənilək II). EMML 1350.

IES 00071, Horologium for the Night, ሰዓታት ዘሌሊት; Horologium for the Day, ሰዓታት ዘመዓልት; Hymn to Mary, "Rejoice, Mary, Virgin in mind and body," ተፈሥሒ ማርያም ድንግልት ሥጋ ወሕልና; Image of the Praises of Mary, መልክአ ውዳሴ ማርያም. Parchment and paper, 135 x 125 x 55 mm, i + 92 folios, two columns, 20-23 lines, Gəʿəz, seventeenth and twentieth centuries (composite). EMML 1362.

IES 00072, Antiphonary for the Fast of Lent, ጾመ ድጓ. Parchment, 183 x 140 x 45 mm, iii + 68 folios, two columns, 22-25 lines, Gəʿəz, twentieth century. EMML 1355.

IES 00073, Praises of Mary, ውዳሴ ማርያም; Gate of Light, አንቀጸ ብርሃን; Angels Praise Her, ይዌድስዋ መላእክት ለማርያም; Hymn to the Covenant of Mercy, ሰላም ለኪ ኪዳነ ምሕረት; Hymn to Gälawdewos (Claudius), ሰላም ለከ ሰግዔት መዋዒ; Praise and Thanksgiving, ውዳሴ ወግናይ; Image of the Icon, መልክአ ሥዕል; Image of the Assumption, መልክአ ፍልሰታ ለማርያም; Image of Anne Mother of Mary, መልክአ ሐና እመ ማርያም.

Parchment, 200 x 120 x 50 mm, ii + 111 folios, one column, 15 lines, Gəʿəz, late eighteenth/early nineteenth century.

Miniatures:

1. F. ii v(erso): The owner of the manuscript, *Abba* Näṣärä Ab, bowing before the two saints, *abunä* Täklä Haymanot and *abunä* Ewosṭatewos.
2. F. 47v: Saint George and the Dragon.
3. F. 95v: Madonna and Child with *Abba* Näṣärä Ab praying to the Virgin.
4. F. 96r: The Crucifixion.
5. F. 110r: The Assumption of Mary.

IES 00074, Psalter, ዳዊት (missing Praises of Mary and Gate of Light); *Asmat* Prayer; Excerpts from Horologium for the Night, ስኣታት ዘሌሊት. Parchment, 235 x 170 x 60 mm, i + 128 folios, one column and two columns, 28 lines, Gəʿəz, late fifteenth century.

Miniatures:

1. Inside front cover: Crude drawing of two figures.
2. F. 4v: Crude drawing of a figure.
3. F. 8v: Crude drawing of an equestrian saint.
4. F. 116v: King Solomon holding a sword.
5. F. 124v: Saint Anthony.
6. Inside back cover: Crude drawing of an angel.

IES 00075, Prayer to Jesus Christ, "For the sake of Your Trinity," በእንተ ሥላሴከ; Prayer to Jesus Christ, "O, Who Descended," ኦ ዘወረድከ; Hymn to the Apostles. Parchment, 170 x 100 x 60 mm, i + 78 folios, one column, 7–9 lines, Gəʿəz, late eighteenth century.

Miniatures:

1. F. 1v: *Abunä* Gäbrä Mänfäs Qəddus.
2. F. 2r: Martyrdom of *abunä* Abib, also known as *abba* Bula or Paul of Egypt.
3. F. 3r: Martyrdom of Saint George.

4. F. 3v: An Equestrian Saint on a white horse.
5. F. 4r: *Abba* Samu'el of Waldəbba riding a lion.
6. F. 5v: God surrounded by the Four Living Creatures.
7. F. 13v: The flight into Egypt.
8. F. 14v: Covenant of Mercy (*Kidanä Məhrät*).
9. F. 15v: Mary and Jesus at Däbrä Qwəsqwam (lamentation of our Lady Mary).
10. F. 16v: The Prophets.
11. F. 17v: The Apostles.
12. F. 18v: The Saints.
13. F. 19v: Saint George and the Dragon.
14. F. 20v: Madonna and Child.
15. F. 21r: Saint adores Mary and Her beloved son.
16. F. 21v: Annunciation.
17. F. 23r: Annunciation with God the Father.
18. F. 24r: The Nativity.
19. F. 25r: Baptism of Jesus.
20. F. 26v: Last Supper.
21. F. 27r: Foot Washing.
22. F. 28r: The Temptation of Jesus.
23. F. 29r: Betrayal of Christ by Judas.
24. F. 30r: The arrest of Jesus.
25. F. 31r: Jesus led off with a rope tied around his neck.
26. F. 32r: The seated Jesus is spat upon and mocked.
27. F. 33r: Jesus before Annas.
28. F. 34r: The Flagellation of Jesus.
29. F. 35r: The blindfolding of Jesus.
30. F. 36r: The Crown of Thorns.
31. F. 37r: Jesus disrobed and being crowned with a crown of thorns.
32. F. 38r: Jesus carrying the Cross.

33. F. 39r: Jesus stripped of his clothes.
34. F. 40r: Jesus with his hands and feet tied to the column.
35. F. 41r: Jesus before the High Priest.
36. F. 42r: Jesus before Pilate.
37. F. 43r: Pontius Pilate washes his hands.
38. F. 44r: Jesus before King Herod.
39. F. 45r: Jesus nailed to the Cross.
40. F. 46r: Raising the Cross.
41. F. 47r: Casting lots for Jesus' robes.
42. F. 48r: Jesus within a doorway.
43. F. 49r: The Crucifixion.
44. F. 50r: Longinus Piercing Jesus' side.
45. F. 51r: Jesus offered gall to drink while on cross.
46. F. 52r: The deposition.
47. F. 53r: The shrouding of Jesus' body.
48. F. 54r: Entombment of Jesus.
49. F. 55r: The Resurrection of Jesus, raising Adam and Eve (Anastasis).
50. F. 56r: The Ascension.
51. F. 57r: Second Coming of Christ and the day of judgment.
52. F. 60v: Angel reaching down to two kings (by a different artist).
53. F. 61r: *Abunä* Täklä Haymanot (by a different artist).
54. F. 62r: *Abunä* Ewosṭatewos at sea on the way to Armenia.
55. F. 62v: Nero and Peter.
56. F. 63r: The Beheading of Paul.
57. F. 64r: Peter hanged upside down.
58. F. 65r: Andrew dragged over rocky ground.
59. F. 66r: Stoning of James.
60. F. 67r: John with an evil man.
61. F. 68r: An angel rescues the dead body of Philip from fire.

62. F. 69r: Martyrdom of Saint Bartholomew. Placed within a weighted sack, he is cast into the sea.

63. F. 70r: Thomas carries his flayed skin with which he will raise the dead wife of the governor.

64. F. 71r: The Beheading of Matthew.

65. F. 72r: The Hanging of Thaddeus.

66. F. 73r: The Beheading of Nathaniel.

67. F. 74r: Martyrdom of Matthias.

68. F. 75r: Martyrdom of Mark.

69. F. 76v: Martyrdom of an unidentified saint.

70. F. 77r: Martyrdom of an unidentified saint.

IES 00076, Psalter, ዳዊት, Praises of Mary, with musical notation, ውዳሴ ማርያም. Parchment, 185 x 80 x 75 mm, 133 folios, one column and two columns, 20–21 lines, Gəʻəz, late eighteenth and seventeenth centuries (composite).

IES 00077, Holy Bible ordered by Emperor Ḫaylä Śəllase. Parchment, 523 x 390 x 130 mm, iv + 671 folios, three columns, 66 lines, Gəʻəz, 1934/1935.

IES 00078, Commentary on Genesis. Parchment, 143 x 95 x 10 mm, 42 folios, two columns, 24–25 lines, Amharic, nineteenth century. EMML 1382.

Miniatures:

1. F. 42v: Crude drawing of crosses, in pencil.

IES 00079, Cycle of Kings, ዐውደ ነገሥት. Parchment, 182 x 140 x 40 mm, 100 folios, two columns, 18–20 lines, Gəʻəz, 7383 AM = 1890/1891 (f. 3v, colophon). EMML 1379.

Miniatures:

1. F. 1v: Crude drawing of a horse and an angel.

2. F. 12v: Crude drawing of an ornate cross.

3. F. 88r: Crude drawing of a figure before an angel.

4. F. 89v: Drawing of marginal cross.

5. F. 100v: Crude drawing of two figures.

IES 00080, Glossary of Gəʿəz Words. Paper, 165 x 105 x 20 mm, i + 139 folios, one column, 19 lines, Gəʿəz, early twentieth century. EMML 1373.

Miniatures:

1. F. 138v: A lion, in pencil.

IES 00081, Anaphora of Our Lady Mary, ቅዳሴ ማርያም; Anaphora of Our Lord, ቅዳሴ እግዚእ; Sword of the Trinity, ሠይፈ ሥላሴ; Image of Gäbrä Krəstos, መልክአ ገብረ ክርስቶስ. Parchment, 137 x 110 x 30 mm, 79 folios, two columns, 14–15 lines, Gəʿəz, late nineteenth century. EMML 1381.

IES 00082, *Asmat* Prayers, አስማት. Parchment, 130 x 90 x 10 mm, i + 7 folios, one column, 15–16 lines, Gəʿəz, twentieth century. EMML 1383.

IES 00083, Image of Saint Peter, መልክአ ጴጥሮስ; Image of Saint Paul, መልክአ ጳውሎስ. Parchment, 129 x 90 x 3 mm, 14 folios, one column, 14 lines, Gəʿəz, early twentieth century. EMML 1384.

IES 00084, Psalter, ዳዊት. Parchment, 182 x 165 x 73 mm, ii + 181 folios, one column and two columns, 17 lines, Gəʿəz, seventeenth century. EMML 1376.

Miniatures:

1. F. ii v(erso): King David playing the harp.

2. F. 25v: Jesus giving the key (of the kingdom) to Peter.

IES 00085, Personal Prayer to the Trinity composed for Emperor Haylä Śəllase; Prayer to the Trinity (*Tamaḥezanku bekemu*); A Story of the Trinity. Parchment, 198 x 153 x 15 mm, ii + 166 folios, two columns, 13 lines, Gəʿəz, twentieth century. EMML 1369.

IES 00088, Acts of Saint George, ገድለ ጊዮርጊስ; Five Miracles of Saint George, ተአምረ ጊዮርጊስ; Martyrdom of Saint George. Paper, 278 x 110 x 10 mm, i + 27 folios, one column, 42 lines, Gəʿəz, twentieth century. EMML 1366.

IES 00089, Computus of Demetrius, patriarch of Alexandria (189–232), ሐሳብ ድሜጥሮስ (called here *Marḥa 'ewwer*). Paper, 255 x 197 x 30 mm, 18 folios, one column, 31–37 lines, Amharic, 7378 AM = 1885–86. EMML 1374.

IES 00090, Acts of Saint George, ገድለ ጊዮርጊስ. Parchment, 137 x 95 x 3 mm, ii + 10 folios, two columns, 18 lines, Gəʻəz, nineteenth century. EMML 1371.

IES 00091, Photograph of Microfilm of Chronicle of Emperor Tewodros II of Ethiopia, in Amharic (perhaps a copy of Cambridge OR. 883) by *aläqa* Wäldä Maryam. Parchment, 210 x 170 x 10 mm, i + 101 folios, one column, 16 lines, Amharic, 1904 (f. 100). EMML 1348 & 1349.

IES 00092, Image of Michael, መልክአ ሚካኤል; Covenant of the Morning, ኪዳን ዘነግህ; Anaphora of Our Lady Mary, ቅዳሴ ማርያም; Commentary on the Introductory Rite from *Muʻälläqa* of the Miracles of Mary, in Amharic; Commentary on Our Father (in Amharic), የአቡነ ዘበሰማያት ትርጓሜ, Horologium for the Night, ሰዓታት ዘሌሊት. Parchment, 150 x 110 x 45 mm, ii + 111 folios, two columns, 17–21 lines, Gəʻəz, Amharic, nineteenth century. EMML 1380.

Miniatures:

1. F. i v(erso): Portrait of a friend of Emperor Mənilək II before Raguel.

2. F. ii r(ecto): Raguel, the Archangel, with sword and processional cross.

IES 00093, Minor Prophets; Notes on Various Symbols. Parchment, 195 x 140 x 40 mm, ii + 49 folios, two columns, 26–29 lines, Gəʻəz, early twentieth century. EMML 1370.

IES 00094, Fragment of the Computus work known as *Märḥä 'əwwur*. Parchment, 145 x 105 x 10 mm, 24 folios, one column, 21–23 lines, Gəʻəz, second half of the nineteenth/first half of the twentieth century.

Miniatures:

1. F. 5v: Crude drawing of Madonna and Child.

IES 00095, Image of the Archangel Phanuel, መልክአ ፋኑኤል. Parchment, 90 x 60 x 20 mm, ii + 27 folios, one column, 13 lines, Gəʿəz, early twentieth century.

Miniatures:

1. F. i v(erso): Saint George and the Dragon.
2. F. i r(ecto): Madonna and Child.
3. F. ii v(erso): Angel with sword and scabbard.
4. F. 5v: Gäbrä Mänfäs Qəddus.
5. F. 6r: Angel with sword and scabbard.
6. F. 6v: Täklä Haymanot.
7. F. 7r: Gäbrä Mänfäs Qəddus.
8. F. 7v: Angel with sword and scabbard.
9. F. 8r: Madonna and Child.
10. F. 8v: Angel with sword and scabbard.

IES 00096, Missal, መጽሐፈ ቅዳሴ. Parchment, 243 x 170 x 68 mm, ii + 50 folios, two columns, 27 lines, Gəʿəz, twentieth century. EMML 1367.

IES 00097, Gospel of John arranged for the days of the week, ወንጌል ዘዮሐንስ. Parchment, 163 x 120 x 50 mm, ii + 90 folios, two columns, 14–18 lines, Gəʿəz, twentieth century. EMML 1378.

Miniatures:

1. F. 88v: Madonna and Child.
2. F. 89r: Saint George and the Dragon.
3. F. 90v: Crude drawing of an angel.

IES 00098, Covenant of Gäbrä Mänfäs Qəddus, ኪዳነ ገብረ መንፈስ ቅዱስ; Twelve Miracles of Gäbrä Mänfäs Qəddus, ተአምረ ገብረ መንፈስ ቅዱስ; Image of Michael, መልክአ ሚካኤል. Parchment, 92 x 90 x 40 mm, ii + 82 folios, one column, 11 lines, Gəʿəz, 1682–92 (f. 82r mentions Emperor Iyasu I [1682–1706] and Metropolitan Sinoda [1670/71–92]). EMML 1385.

Miniatures:

1. F. 63r: Gäbrä Mänfäs Qəddus.

IES 00099, Book of Disciples, መጽሐፈ ኦርድእት. Parchment, 130 x 100 x 37 mm, 50 folios, two columns, 13 lines, Gəʿəz, late eighteenth century.

IES 00100, Antiphonary for the Fast of Lent, ጾመ ድጓ. Parchment, 170 x 145 x 48 mm, i + 68 folios, two columns, 22 lines, Gəʿəz, early nineteenth century. EMML 1375.

IES 00101, Psalter, ዳዊት. Parchment, 190 x 140 x 60 mm, ii + 145 folios, one column and two columns, 21–23 lines, Gəʿəz, nineteenth century. EMML 1372.

Miniatures:

1. F. ii v(erso): Crude drawings of figures and a small painting of Madonna and Child has been stitched into the folio.

2. F. 128r: Crude drawing of an angel with sword and scabbard.

IES 00102, Harp of Praise, ኦርጋነ ውዳሴ, arranged for the days of the week. Parchment, 162 x 150 x 59 mm, ii + 203 folios, two columns, 14–15 lines, Gəʿəz, seventeenth century. EMML 1377.

Miniatures:

1. F. ii r(ecto): Crude drawing of Madonna and Child.

2. F. ii v(erso): Crude drawing of a man.

3. F. 202v: Crude drawing of a church.

IES 00103, Eight Miracles of Raphael, ተኣምረ ሩፋኤል; Image of Raphael, መልክአ ሩፋኤል; Image of Täklä Haymanot, መልክአ ተክለ ሃይማኖት; One Miracle of Mary, ተኣምረ ማርያም; Image of the Four Creatures, መልክአ ኦርባዕቱ እንስሳ. Parchment, 195 x 190 x 6 mm, iv + 69 folios, two columns, 13–14 lines, Gəʿəz, early eighteenth century.

Miniatures:

1. F. ii v(erso): The Second Coming of Jesus.

2. F. iii v(erso): A king (David?) seated before two attendants.

3. F. iv v(erso): Angel with sword and scabbard with the faces of people on his wings.

4. F. 26v: Madonna and Child.

5. F. 39v: *Abunä* Täklä Haymanot and *abunä* Ewosṭatewos.

6. Ff. 66v–67r: Equestrian King Nääkweto Lääb with his servants.

7. Ff. 67v–68r: Saint George and the Dragon and the servants of Saint George.

IES 00104, Philoxenus of Mabbug (245 numbered questions raised by Egyptian monks with their answers); Eight Sayings and a Homily of Evagrius of Pontes; Monastic Orders of Pachomius, ሥርዓተ ጳኩሚስ, the Spiritual Elder, አረጋዊ መንፈሳዊ. Parchment, 225 x 200 x 85 mm, i + 205 folios, two columns, 24–25 lines, Gəʿəz, eighteenth century. EMML 1387.

IES 00105, Apocryphal Acts of the Apostles, ገድለ ሐዋርያት. Parchment, 370 x 320 x 70 mm, 82 folios, three columns, 28 lines, Gəʿəz, 1682–1788 (f. 1r mentions an Emperor Iyasu, could be I, II, or III).

Miniatures:

1. F. 1v: Stoning of an Apostle (Matthias?) by two men.

2. F. 5v: The patron Täklä Ǝstifanos lays prostrate before a scene on the opposite page.

3. F. 6r: The martyrdom of Matthias by burning.

4. F. 10r: How James, son of Zebedee, was beheaded.

5. F. 13r: How they stretched Saint Mark with ropes.

6. F. 23v: How they inflated the skin of Saint Thomas and forced him to carry it.

7. F. 59r: The beheading of Matthew.

8. F. 62r: The beheading of Luke.

9. F. 67r: How the angel of God rescued Philip from fire.

10. F. 80v: How the fire of the Holy Spirit fell at Pentecost.

IES 00106, Psalter, ዳዊት. Parchment, 205 x 145 x 55 mm, iv + 138 folios, one column and two columns, 25 lines, Gəʿəz, eighteenth/nineteenth century. EMML 1390.

Miniatures:

1. F. ii v(erso): The Crucifixion.
2. F. iii r(ecto): Madonna and Child.

IES 00107, Images, Anaphora of Our Lady Mary, ቅዳሴ ማርያም, Miscellanea. Parchment, 250 x 140 x 47 mm, 103 folios, two columns, 13–17 lines, Gəʿəz, eighteenth century. EMML 1391.

IES 00108, Psalter, ዳዊት. Parchment, 263 x 205 x 85 mm, iv + 182 folios, one column and two columns, 22 lines, Gəʿəz, early twentieth century. EMML 1386.

Miniatures:

1. F. iii v(erso): The Archangel Michael Enthroned.
2. F. iv v(erso): The Crucifixion.
3. F. 167v: Madonna and Child flanked by two donors.
4. F. 181r: A dignitary is seated by a Psalter. His wife stands beside him.

IES 00109, Psalter, ዳዊት; Angels Praise Her, ይዌድስዋ መላእክት ለማርያም. Parchment, 230 x 180 x 80 mm, iv + 164 folios, one column and two columns, 21 lines, Gəʿəz, late nineteenth century. EMML 1388.

Miniatures:

1. F. ii r(ecto): The Crucifixion.
2. F. iii r(ecto): Angel with sword and scabbard.
3. F. iv r(ecto): King David playing the harp.
4. F. 162v: Saint George and the Dragon.
5. F. 163r: Madonna and Child with donor in proskynesis.

IES 00115, Directory for the Divine Office and the Rules of Chanting the Antiphonary (in Amharic); Miscellanea. Parchment, 130 x 100 x 3 mm, 8 folios, one column, 23–30 lines, Gəʿəz, Amharic, nineteenth century. EMML 1397.

IES 00116, Book of the Sun, መጽሐፈ ፀሐይ; Pillars of Wisdom of the Old and New Testaments, አዕማደ ምሥጢረ ብሊት ወሐዲስ. Parchment, 220 x 160 x 25 mm, ii + 51 folios, two columns, 25 lines, Gəʿəz, twentieth century. EMML 1389.

IES 00117, Beauty of the Creation, ሥነ ፍጥረት. Parchment and paper, 165 x 130 x 25 mm, iv + 84 folios, ff. 1r–30v two columns, ff. 31r–83r one column, 25 lines in two column section, 16 lines in one column section, Gəʿəz, nineteenth/twentieth century. EMML 1392.

IES 00118, Introduction to the Faith of Fathers (ሃይማኖተ አበው). Parchment, 235 x 160 x 5 mm, i + 10 folios, two columns, 38 lines, Gəʿəz, nineteenth century. EMML 1393.

IES 00119, Image of Ḫaylä Śəllase, መልክአ ኃይለ ሥላሴ; Image of Walatta Giyorgis, መልክአ ወለተ ጊዮርጊስ. Paper, 215 x 160 x 3 mm, ii + 31 folios, two columns, 19 lines, Gəʿəz, twentieth century. EMML 1396.

IES 00122, Gurage—English Dictionary, draft, Volume 1 by Wolf Leslau. Paper, 290 x 230 x 80 mm, ii + 937 folios, two columns, 26 lines, Gurage, English, 1979.

IES 00123, Sidamo—English Dictionary, draft, Volume 1 by Wolf Leslau. Paper, 290 x 235 x 80 mm, ii + 331 folios, two columns, 30 lines, Sidamo, English, 1979.

IES 00124, Gäbrä Mäsqäl, The Slave [A Story], draft, by ʿAlämayyähu Mogäs; Paper, 340 x 215 x 10 mm, i + 33 folios, one column, 38 lines, Amharic, 1961–62.

IES 00125, Etymological Dictionary of Harari, draft, by Wolf Leslau. Paper, 290 x 222 x 70 mm, iii + 583 folios, one column, 27 lines, Harari, English, 1963.

IES 00126, The Methods of Gəʿəz Poetry, ፍኖተ ቅኔ ዘአቢዳራ. Parchment, 192 x 128 x 21 mm, ii + 26 folios, two columns, 32–33 lines, Amharic, twentieth century.

IES 00127, *Asmat* Prayer for binding demons, ጸሎት በእንተ ማዕሠረ አጋንንት; *Asmat* Prayer against Evil Eye, ጸሎት በእንተ ሕማም ዓይነ ጥላ ወሌጌዎን; Prayer against demons, ተማኅፅንኩ በኢየሱስ ክርስቶስ ወልዱ ለአብ ከሣቴ ብርሃን. Parchment, 151 x 113 x 28 mm, ii + 17 folios, one column, 15 lines, Gəʿəz and Amharic, twentieth century.

IES 00128, *Asmat* Prayer to protect the shinbone ጸሎት በእንተ አቋያጻት; Image of Phanuel as *Asmat* Prayer against Epilepsy and Legewon; *Asmat* Prayer against Epilepsy and Legewon and the Evil Eye; *Asmat* Prayer of the Archangel Michael which is written on his left and right wings; *Asmat* Prayer against demons, አውግዞሙ ለአጋንንት; *Asmat* Prayer for drowning demons, ጸሎት በእንተ መስጦመ አጋንንት. Parchment, 68 x 60 x 9 mm, ii + 20 folios, one column, 7–10 lines, Gəʿəz, twentieth century.

IES 00129, Image of Saint George, መልክአ ጊዮርጊስ. Parchment, 82 x 65 x 22 mm, iv + 40 folios, one column, 10 lines, Gəʿəz, late nineteenth century.

IES 00130, Image of the Trinity, መልክአ ሥላሴ. Parchment, 75 x 50 x 15 mm, 26 folios, one column, 12–13 lines, Gəʿəz, nineteenth century.

IES 00131, Amharic Poems and Poetry, draft, by ʿAlämayyähu Mogäs. Paper, 350 x 256 x 13 mm, i + 75 folios, one column, 37 lines, Amharic, 1962.

IES 00132, A Novel, draft, by ʿAlämayyähu Mogäs. Paper, 350 x 256 x 7 mm, i + 50 folios, one column, 36 lines, Amharic, 1953 EC = 1960–61.

IES 00133, Book of Drawings. Paper, 350 x 256 x 5 mm, i + 37 folios, Amharic, twentieth century.

IES 00134, Wax and Gold (Collection of Amharic stories and sayings), draft, by ʿAlämayyähu Mogäs. Paper, 321 x 248 x 28 mm, i + 268 folios, one column, 31 lines, Amharic, 1954 EC = 1961–62.

IES 00135, Wax and Gold: Collection of Amharic stories and sayings, draft, by ʿAlämayyähu Mogäs. Paper, 330 x 215 x 35 mm, i + 404 folios, one column, 31 lines, Amharic, 1954 EC = 1961–62.

IES 00136, Record of Persons Cured by *mämhər* Wäldä Tənsaʾe Gəzaw. Paper, 346 x 204 x 26 mm, iii + 145 folios, one column, 32 lines, Amharic, 1955–57.

IES 00136A, Log of the people healed by exorcisms by the hand of *mämhər* Wäldä Tənsaʾe Gəzaw, በመምህር ወልደ ትንሣኤ ግዛው እጅ በጥምቀት የተፈወሱትን ሰዎች የሚገልጽ ሡሌዳ by *mämhər* Wäldä Tənsaʾe Gəzaw. Paper, 320 x 210 x 20 mm, i + 176 folios, one column, 35 lines, Amharic, early twentieth century.

IES 00136B, Log of the people healed by exorcisms by the hand of *mämhər* Wäldä Tənsa'e Gəzaw, part two, በመምህር ወልደ ትንሣኤ ግዛው እጅ በጥምቀት የተፈወሱትን ሰዎች የሚገልጽ ሡሌዳ by *mämhər* Wäldä Tənsa'e Gəzaw. Paper, 308 x 211 x 34 mm, ii + 199 folios, one column, 28 lines, Amharic, early twentieth century.

IES 00137, Excerpts of the Antiphonary for the Fast of Lent, ጾመ ድጓ. Parchment, 170 x 125 x 3 mm, i + 13 folios, two columns, 18–19 lines, Gəʿəz, twentieth century.

IES 00138, History of the Oromo. Paper, 174 x 115 x 5 mm, i + 19 folios, one column, 33–34 lines, Gəʿəz, twentieth century.

IES 00139, Image of the Patriarch Peter, መልክአ ጴጥሮስ. Parchment, 165 x 110 x 2 mm, 6 folios, one column, 26 lines, Gəʿəz, early twentieth century.

IES 00140, History of Monasticism, የምንኩስና ታሪክ. Parchment, 173 x 110 x 4 mm, 11 folios, one column, 23–25 lines, Amharic, twentieth century.

IES 00141, Bandlet of Righteousness, ልፋፈ ጽድቅ. Parchment, 70 x 55 x 25 mm, 28 folios, one column, 8–9 lines, Gəʿəz, late nineteenth century.

IES 00142, Excerpts of the Horologium for the Night, ሰዓታት ዘሌሊት. Parchment, 145 x 120 x 25 mm, 26 folios, one column, 18–24 lines, Gəʿəz, twentieth century.

IES 00144, *Asmat* Prayers, ክታብ. Parchment, 196 x 19.0 cm, three strips, two columns, Gəʿəz, twentieth century. Copied for ገድለ ተክለ ሃይማኖት.

Miniatures:
- Three miniatures: (a) talismanic symbol with face in center; (b) angel with sword and scabbard, and (c) ornate cross.

IES 00145, *Asmat* Prayers, ክታብ. Parchment, 242 x 19.0 cm, three strips, three columns, Gəʿəz, nineteenth century. Copied for ወለተ ተክለ ሃይማኖት, erased and substituted with ተስፋ ማርያም.

Miniatures:

- Three miniatures: (a) three figures with swords and processional crosses; (b) figure with sword and scabbard and a person on each side (Anastasis?), and (c) ornate cross with a figure on either side.

IES 00146, Prayer against the Tongue of People, ልሳነ ሰብእ (በእንተ ልሳነ ዘመድ ወባእድ). Parchment, 53 x 40 x 21 mm, ii + 32 folios, one column, 9–10 lines, Gəʿəz, twentieth century.

IES 00147, *Asmat* Prayers, ከታብ. Parchment, 66 x 4.2 cm, one strip, one column, Gəʿəz, twentieth century. Copied for ደብሪቱ and ወለተ ሕይወት.

Miniatures:

- One miniature: (a) three ornate crosses.

IES 00148, *Asmat* Prayers, ከታብ. Parchment, 61 x 9.0 cm, one strip, one column, Gəʿəz, twentieth century. Copied for ገብሪ ማርያም.

IES 00149, *Asmat* Prayers, ከታብ. Parchment, 128 x 5.0 cm, two strips, one column, Gəʿəz, twentieth century. Copied for ጽጌ ማርያም.

Miniatures:

- One miniature: (a) ornate cross.

IES 00150, *Asmat* Prayers, ከታብ. Parchment, 174 x 4.7 cm, three strips, one column, Gəʿəz, twentieth century. Copied for ወልደ እግዚአብሔር ኦርኃያ.

Miniatures:

- Two miniatures: (a) talismanic symbol; and (b) an angel.

IES 00151, *Asmat* Prayers, ከታብ. Parchment, 40 x 32 x 18 mm, accordion-fold codex, Gəʿəz, twentieth century. Copied for ኃይለ ማርያም.

IES 00152, Prayer Book (*Mäṣḥafä Ṣälot*). Paper, 162 x 100 x 8 mm, 33 folios, one column, 16 lines, Gəʿəz, twentieth century.

Miniatures:

1. F. 1r: Crude drawing of a figure.

IES 00153, Images Collection, መልክአ ጉባዔ. Paper, 187 x 177 x 5 mm, 28 folios, two columns, 31 lines, Gəʿəz, twentieth century.

IES 00154, Prayer during Service Granting Diaconate Orders. Paper, 163 x 110 x 10 mm, i + 37 folios, one column, 12 lines, Gəʿəz, late twentieth century.

IES 00155, *Asmat* Prayers, ክታብ. Parchment, 190 x 14.0 cm, three strips, one column, Gəʿəz, nineteenth century. Copied for ሥራሐ ድንግል by the scribe አባ ማኅፀን እዳየሱስ.

Miniatures:

- Three miniatures: (a) ornate cross with a figure on either side; (b) talismanic symbol; and (c) three figures.

IES 00156, *Asmat* Prayers, ክታብ. Parchment, 200 x 13.2 cm, three strips, one column, Gəʿəz, early nineteenth century. Copied for ፍሥሐ ጊዮርጊስ, erased and replaced by ወለተ ኢየሱስ.

Miniatures:

- Three miniatures: (a) angel with sword and scabbard; (b) equestrian saint spearing a lion; and (c) two angels with swords and scabbards.

IES 00158, *Asmat* Prayers, ክታብ. Parchment, 208 x 9.7 cm, three strips, one column, Gəʿəz, nineteenth century. Copied for ወለተ ዋህድ.

Miniatures:

- Three miniatures: (a) multi-box panel with face in center; (b) talismanic symbol; and (c) talismanic symbol.

IES 00159, *Asmat* Prayers, ክታብ. Parchment, 158 x 13.2 cm, three strips, one column, Gəʿəz, nineteenth century. Original name erased and replaced with ገብረ ሕይወት.

Miniatures:

- Three miniatures: (a) talismanic symbol; (b) ornate cross; and (c) multi-box panel.

IES 00160, The Shepherd of Hermas, ሔርማ ኖላዊ. Paper, 176 x 115 x 14 mm, i + 101 folios, one column, 18 lines, Gəʿəz, twentieth century.

IES 00161, Mystery of the Trinity, ምሥጢረ ሥላሴ; Mystery of the Incarnation, ምሥጢረ ሥጋዌ. Paper, 147 x 85 x 10 mm, i + 49 folios, one column, 21 lines, Amharic, twentieth century.

IES 00162, Remedies against Sorcery and Names of Various Herb Treatments for Different Diseases. Paper, 185 x 160 x 10 mm, 30 folios, one column, 19 lines, Gəʿəz, 1949.

IES 00163, *Asmat* Prayers, ከታብ. Parchment, 163 x 9.5 cm, two strips, one column, Gəʿəz, eighteenth/nineteenth century. Copied for ወለተ ሐና and the name ደርቤ አራጋሙ appears at the top of the scroll in different ink.

Miniatures:

- Three miniatures: (a) multi-box panel; (b) angel with sword and scabbard; and (c) talismanic symbol.

IES 00164, *Asmat* Prayers, ከታብ. Parchment, 142.5 x 11.5 cm, three strips, two columns, Gəʿəz, early nineteenth century. Copied for ወለተ ሕይወት.

Miniatures:

- Three miniatures: (a) fragment of an angel; (b) talismanic symbol, and (c) *Abba* Samuʾel riding a lion.

IES 00165, *Asmat* Prayers, ከታብ. Parchment, 192 x 10.0 cm, three strips, one column, Gəʿəz, eighteenth century. Copied for ወልደ ኪዳን.

Miniatures:

- Three miniatures: (a) ornate cross with a figure on either side; (b) angel; and (c) talismanic symbol.

IES 00166, *Asmat* Prayers, ከታብ. Parchment, 164 x 11.0 cm, three strips, one column, Gəʿəz, twentieth century. Copied for ወለተ ማርያም.

Miniatures:

- Four miniatures: (a) talismanic symbol with angel below; (b) angel with sword and scabbard; (c) lion of Judah; and (d) ornate cross.

IES 00167, *Asmat* Prayers, ከታብ. Parchment, 170.5 x 9.7 cm, three strips, one column, Gəʿəz, nineteenth/twentieth century. Copied for ወለተ እግዚእ, erased and replaced with ወለተ ሕይወት.

Miniatures:
- Three miniatures: (a) angel with sword and scabbard; (b) figure surrounded by eyes, and (c) ornate cross.

IES 00168, *Asmat* Prayers, ከታብ. Parchment, 58 x 5.0 cm, one strip, one column, Gəʿəz, 1950–75. Copied for ጆን ወልዳ ዮሐንስ ሐናይስኪ.

Miniatures:
- Three miniatures: (a) talismanic symbol; (b) talismanic symbol; and (c) angel with a sword.

IES 00169, *Asmat* Prayers, ከታብ. Parchment, 131 x 6.5 cm, three strips, one column, Gəʿəz, twentieth century. Copied for ገብረ መድኅን, added later in a different hand and ink.

Miniatures:
- Three miniatures: (a) multi-box panel; (b) angel with sword and scabbard; and (c) ornate cross.

IES 00170, *Asmat* Prayers, ከታብ. Parchment, 224 x 8.5 cm, four strips, one column, Gəʿəz, early twentieth century. Copied for ወለተ ሚካኤል ይኂላየ.

Miniatures:
- Four miniatures: (a) King Solomon; (b) talismanic symbol; (c) x-shaped pattern with people in each of the four corners; and (d) Archangel Phanuel stabbing Legewon with a sword.

IES 00171, *Asmat* Prayers, ከታብ. Parchment, 189 x 8 cm, three strips, one column, Gəʿəz, early nineteenth century. Copied for አሰን, erased and replaced with ደብረ ማርያም.

Miniatures:
- Three miniatures: (a) multi-box panel; (b) talismanic symbol; and (c) angel with sword and scabbard.

IES 00172, *Asmat* Prayers, ክታብ. Parchment, 178 x 9.3 cm, three strips, one column, Gəʿəz, twentieth century. Copied for ብሥራተ ማርያም and ተስፋ ሥላሴ.

Miniatures:

- Four miniatures: (a) angel with sword and scabbard; (b) ornate cross with a figure on either side; (c) ornate cross; and (d) talismanic symbol.

IES 00173, Photocopy of History of the Oromo, by *aläqa* Aṭme. Paper, 223 x 350 x 14 mm, i + 64 folios, one column, 39–40 lines, Amharic, early twentieth century.

IES 00174, Faith of The Fathers, ሃይማኖት አበው. Parchment, 350 x 300 x 80 mm, i + 221 folios, three columns, 29–30 lines, Gəʿəz, eighteenth century. EMML 1399.

IES 00175, Code of Kings, ፍትሐ ነገሥት. Parchment, 290 x 230 x 80 mm, iii + 163 folios, three columns, 30 lines, Gəʿəz, 1881/1882 (f. 163r, dated colophon). EMML 1401.

IES 00176, Epistles of Paul, መልእክታተ ጳውሎስ; Acts of the Apostles, ግብረ ሐዋርያት; Catholic Epistles, ሰብዓቱ መልእክታት; Revelation, ራዕየ ዮሐንስ. Parchment, 210 x 205 x 70 mm, iv + 172 folios, two columns, 20 lines, Gəʿəz, eighteenth century. EMML 1403.

Miniatures:

1. F. i r(ecto): Crude drawing of an angel.
2. F. ii v(erso): Crude drawing of figures and a horse.

IES 00177, Kings (1 Samuel, 2 Samuel, 1 Kings, 2 Kings), መጽሐፈ ነገሥት ቀዳማዊ, መጽሐፈ ነገሥት ካልዕ; a list of the kings of Judah and Israel. Parchment, 231 x 205 x 70 mm, ii + 140 folios, two columns, 21 lines, Gəʿəz, eighteenth century. EMML 1402.

Miniatures:

1. F. 68v: Figures and designs in red and black ink.

IES 00178, *Asmat* Prayers, ክታብ. Parchment, 176 x 11 cm, three strips, one column, Gəʿəz, nineteenth century. Copied for ወለተ ጊዮርጊስ ወልደ ተክለ ሃይማኖት.

Miniatures:

- Three miniatures: (a) angel with sword and scabbard; (b) multi-box panel; and (c) talismanic symbol.

IES 00179, *Asmat* Prayers, ክታብ. Parchment, 178 x 11 cm, three strips, one column, Gəʿəz, nineteenth century. Name of original owner was erased and replaced with ኪዳነ ማርያም.

Miniatures:

- Three miniatures: (a) talismanic symbol; (b) ornate cross; and (c) talismanic symbol.

IES 00180, *Asmat* Prayers, ክታብ. Parchment, 247 x 17 cm, four strips, two columns, Gəʿəz, late nineteenth/early twentieth century. Copied for ኃይለ ሚካኤል, ግብረ መስቀል, and ወለተ ተክለ ሃይማኖት, and one illegible name.

Miniatures:

- Six miniatures: (a) three figures (Trinity?); (b) two snakes around a lamb surrounded by the Tetramorph; (c) two talismanic symbols; (d) ornate cross; (e) angel with sword and processional cross; and (f) two talismanic symbols.

IES 00181, *Asmat* Prayers, ክታብ. Parchment, 163 x 14.4 cm, three strips, two columns, Gəʿəz, early twentieth century. Copied for ወለተ ሴት.

Miniatures:

- Two miniatures: (a) two angels with swords and scabbards, and (b) multi-box panel.

IES 00182, Psalter, ዳዊት. Parchment, 190 x 118 x 100 mm, i + 161 folios, one column and two columns, 21 lines, Gəʿəz, eighteenth century. EMML 1404.

Miniatures:

1. F. 110r: Crude drawing of a face.
2. F. 161r: Crude drawing of a figure.
3. Inside back cover: Crude drawing of figures.

IES 00184, Discourse on Christian life; Learn Religion, Do Good Deeds (an Amharic treatise on the judgment of the soul); Discourse on the Trinity. Parchment, 132 x 93 x 28 mm, ii + 42 folios, one column, 16 lines, Amharic, early nineteenth century. EMML 1406.

IES 00185, The History, Geography and Culture of the Region of Asosa-Beni Sangul. Paper, 341 x 222 x 13 mm, i + 42 folios, one column, 37–38 lines, Gəʿəz, 1967.

IES 00186, *Asmat* Prayers, ከታብ. Parchment, 150 x 7.8 cm, three strips, one column, Gəʿəz, nineteenth century. Copied for መልክአ ማርያም and ወለተ ሥላሴ.

Miniatures:

- Three miniatures: (a) five ornate crosses; (b) angel with sword and scabbard; and (c) multi-box panel with face in center.

IES 00190, *Asmat* Prayers, ከታብ. Parchment, 171 x 10 cm, three strips, one column, Gəʿəz, late nineteenth century. Copied for ኃይለ እግዚአብሔር and ወለተ ተክለ ሃይማኖት is written in a different hand and ink.

Miniatures:

- Three miniatures: (a) angel with sword; (b) person and child holding an umbrella; and (c) talismanic symbol.

IES 00191, *Asmat* Prayers, ከታብ. Parchment, 219.5 x 11 cm, three strips, one column, Gəʿəz, nineteenth century. Copied for ወለተ ገብርኤል ቦሰና.

Miniatures:

- Three miniatures: (a) angel with sword and processional cross; (b) Saint Susənyos; and (c) ornate cross.

IES 00192, *Asmat* Prayers, ከታብ. Parchment, 123 x 13 cm, three strips, two columns, Gəʿəz, late eighteenth/early nineteenth century. Copied for ርግበ ዳዊት and ወለተ ማርያም was added in a later hand.

Miniatures:

- Three miniatures: (a) two angels with swords and scabbards; (b) king with two attendants; and (c) talismanic symbol.

IES 00193, Psalter, ዳዊት; Angels Praise Her, ይቤድስዋ መላእክት ለማርያም. Parchment, 340 x 250 x 90 mm, iv + 179 folios, one column and two columns, 23 lines, Gəʿəz, 1924 EC = 1931–32 (f. 179r, dated). EMML 1400.

Miniatures:

1. F. i r(ecto): Flowers.
2. F. iv v(erso): King David playing the harp.
3. F. 15v: The Crucifixion.
4. F. 42v: The Devil, bound in chains underneath a drawing of Jesus in glory.
5. F. 49v: Portrait of a seated man with a beard, surrounded by an oval border of yellow and pink (the patron?).
6. F. 55v: Ethiopia, pictured as a woman with flowers, stretches out her hand to God, who was pictured in a roundel.
7. F. 57r: Jesus carrying the cross.
8. F. 66v: Celebration of the children of Israel with music and dancing, left. Destruction of the Egyptian Army (shown in profile) in the waters of the Red Sea, right.
9. F. 72v: The Israelites eating Mana.
10. F. 82v: Symbolic representation of the communion cup, here called the Cup of Life.
11. F. 89v: A hermit in prayer.
12. F. 104v: The Crucifixion of Jesus with Emperor Ḫaylä Śəllase below.
13. F. 120v: Temple of Jerusalem.
14. F. 125v: When David prayed to build the temple the birth of Christ was revealed to him.
15. F. 139r: David and Goliath.
16. F. 162v: Madonna and Child, surrounded by the four Living Creatures and a standing patron in the lower right.

IES 00194, Antiphonary for the Fast of Lent, ጾመ ድጓ. Parchment, 175 x 125 x 30 mm, ii + 57 folios, two columns, 21 lines, Gəʿəz, nineteenth century. EMML 1405.

IES 00195, *Asmat* Prayers, ክታብ. Parchment, 176 x 14 cm, three strips, three columns, Gəʿəz, eighteenth/nineteenth century. Copied for አመተ ኢየሱስ.

Miniatures:

- Two miniatures: (a) two angels with swords and scabbards; and (b) multi-box panel.

IES 00196, Inventory of Books and Manuscripts at Däbrä Dima, Book 1. Paper, 227 x 177 x 12 mm, 54 folios, one column, 23 lines, Amharic, 1967/1968.

IES 00197, Inventory of Books and Manuscripts at Däbrä Dima, Book 2. Paper, 227 x 177 x 12 mm, 55 folios, one column, 23 lines, Amharic, 1967/1968.

IES 00198, Inventory of Books and Manuscripts at Däbrä Dima, Book 3. Paper, 227 x 177 x 12 mm, i + 53 folios, one column, 22 lines, Amharic, 1968.

IES 00199, Inventory of Holy Objects of Dima Giyorgis. Paper, 227 x 177 x 12 mm, i + 53 folios, one column, 22 lines, Amharic, 1968.

IES 00200, Inventory of Manuscripts and Holy Objects of Däbrä Ṣəmmuna Monastery. Paper, 227 x 177 x 12 mm, i + 53 folios, one column, 23 lines, Amharic, 1968.

IES 00201, Inventory of Manuscripts and Holy Objects of Däbrä Wärq. Paper, 227 x 177 x 12 mm, i + 53 folios, one column, 23 lines, Amharic, 1969.

IES 00202, Inventory of Manuscripts and Holy Objects of Däbrä Marqos, Goǧǧam. Paper, 227 x 177 x 12 mm, 54 folios, one column, 23 lines, Amharic, 1968.

IES 00203, Inventory of Books, Manuscripts and Holy Objects at Däbrä Marqos, Bəčäna Giyorgis, Yäräz Mikaʾel, and Yätäb Gäbrä Mänfäs Qəddus. Paper, 227 x 177 x 12 mm, i + 54 folios, one column, 23 lines, Amharic, 1968.

IES 00209, A collection of Amharic folk songs. Paper, 287 x 220 x 25 mm, vii + 260 folios, one column, 30 lines, Amharic, 1961 EC = 1968–69. EMML 1409.

IES 00210, *Asmat* Prayers, አስማት. Parchment, 132 x 84 x 32 mm, i + 55 folios, one column, 15–16 lines, Gəʿəz, 1889 EC = 1996–97. EMML 1438.

Miniatures:

1. F. 41v: Talismanic symbol with face in center.

IES 00212, Missal, መጽሐፈ ቅዳሴ. Parchment, 223 x 190 x 75 mm, i + 122 folios, two columns, 20 lines, Gəʿəz, 1779–96 (ff. 13v, 25v, and passim, refer to Emperor Täklä Giyorgis [r. 1779–1800]; ff. 24r and passim refer to Metropolitan Yosab II [r. 1770–1803]; and ff. 83v, 113v, and passim refer to Patriarch Yoḥannəs [1769–96]). EMML 1421.

IES 00213, *Asmat* Prayers, ከታብ. Parchment, 103 x 80 x 40 mm, ii + 104 folios, one column, 14–15 lines, Gəʿəz, early twentieth century. EMML 1439.

Miniatures:

1. F. ii v(erso): Ornate cross.

2. F. 76v: Geometric design.

3. F. 87v: A church, in pencil.

IES 00214, Gəʿəz Vocabulary and Grammar, ሰዋስው፡ ግዕዝ. Parchment, 197 x 183 x 30 mm, 58 folios, two columns, 26–31 lines, Gəʿəz, seventeenth and nineteenth centuries (composite). EMML 1423.

Miniatures:

1. F. 33r: Crude drawing of Madonna and Child.

IES 00216, History of *däǧǧazmač* Näsibu Zäʾamanuʾel. Paper, 340 x 239 x 15 mm, i + 49 folios, one column, 38 lines, Amharic, ca. 1935. EMML 1410.

IES 00217, *Asmat* Prayers, ከታብ. Parchment, 186 x 10 cm, three strips, one column, Gəʿəz, late nineteenth century. Copied for ገብረ እግዚአብሐር and the name ገብረ ሥላሴ was added in a different hand and ink.

Miniatures:

- Three miniatures: (a) multi-box panel; (b) angel with sword and scabbard; and (c) ornate cross.

IES 00218, *Asmat* Prayers, ከታብ. Parchment, 185 x 12 cm, three strips, two columns, Gəʿəz, twentieth century. Copied for ወለተ ሥላሴ and ወለተ ማርያም.

Miniatures:

- Four miniatures: (a) angel with sword and scabbard; (b) four talismanic symbols; (c) talismanic symbol; and (d) ornate cross.

IES 00219, *Asmat* Prayers, ከታብ. Parchment, 240 x 10.5 cm, three strips, two columns, Gəʿəz, twentieth century. The name of the owner is insufficiently legible.

Miniatures:

- Three miniatures: (a) multi-box panel; (b) angel with sword and scabbard; and (c) ornate cross.

IES 00220, *Asmat* Prayers, ከታብ. Parchment, 220 x 13 cm, three strips, one column, Gəʿəz, twentieth century. Copied for ንግሥተ አዜብ.

Miniatures:

- Four miniatures: (a) talismanic symbol; (b) talismanic symbol; (c) four wings with eyes; and (d) talismanic symbol.

IES 00221, *Asmat* Prayers, ከታብ. Parchment, 142 x 9.4 cm, three strips, one column, Gəʿəz, late nineteenth century. Name of original owner was erased and replaced with ወልደ ገብርኤል in a poor hand.

Miniatures:

- Four miniatures: (a) talismanic symbol; (b) figure; (c) talismanic symbol; and (d) three ornate crosses.

IES 00222, *Ziq* Chants, መጽሐፈ ዚቅ. Parchment, 125 x 100 x 17 mm, ii + 22 folios, two columns, 17 lines, Gəʿəz, early twentieth century. EMML 1478.

IES 00223, Gəʿəz Grammar, **ሰዋስው፡ ግዕዝ**. Parchment, 186 x 116 x 20 mm, 128 folios, one column, 17 lines, Gəʿəz, twentieth century. EMML 1437.

Miniatures:

1. F. 128v: Crude drawing of an angel.

IES 00224, *Asmat* Prayers, **ከታብ**. Parchment, 187 x 14 cm, three strips, two columns, Gəʿəz, early twentieth century. Copied for **ወለተ ተክለ ሃይማኖት**.

Miniatures:

- Three miniatures: (a) angel with sword and scabbard; (b) multi-box panel; and (c) lion.

IES 00225, *Asmat* Prayers, **ከታብ**. Parchment, 242 x 11.5 cm, three strips, one column, Gəʿəz, early twentieth century. Copied for **ወለተ ሩፋኤል**.

Miniatures:

- Three miniatures: (a) multi-box panel; (b) talismanic symbol; and (c) angel with sword and scabbard.

IES 00226, *Asmat* Prayers, **ከታብ**. Parchment, 179 x 12 cm, three strips, two columns, Gəʿəz, twentieth century. Copied for **ወለተ ዓቢየ እግዚእ**.

Miniatures:

- Three miniatures: (a) angel with sword and scabbard; (b) multi-box panel; and (c) talismanic symbol.

IES 00227, *Asmat* Prayers, **ከታብ**. Parchment, 166 x 14 cm, three strips, two columns, Gəʿəz, twentieth century. Copied for **ወለተ ሃይማኖት**.

Miniatures:

- Three miniatures: (a) angel with sword and scabbard; (b) ornate cross with a figure on either side; and (c) multi-box panel.

IES 00228, *Asmat* Prayers, **ከታብ**. Parchment, 166 x 12 cm, three strips, one column, Gəʿəz, twentieth century. Copied for **ወለተ ሥላሴ**, erased and replaced by **ወለተ ሕይወት** and **ወለተ ዓቢየ እግዚእ**.

Miniatures:

- Four miniatures: (a) talismanic symbol; (b) talismanic symbol; (c) three ornate crosses; and (d) talismanic symbol.

IES 00229, *Asmat* Prayers, ከታብ. Parchment, 141 x 12 cm, three strips, one column, Gəʿəz, late nineteenth century. Copied for ወለተ ጊዮርጊስ, erased and replaced by ወለተ ሚካኤል.

Miniatures:

- Three miniatures: (a) Saint Susənyos in prayer; (b) Saint Susənyos spearing Wərzəlya; and (c) ornate cross with human faces.

IES 00230, *Asmat* Prayers, ከታብ. Parchment, 181 x 11 cm, three strips, one column, Gəʿəz, twentieth century. Original name erased and replaced with ወለተ ጸድቃን.

Miniatures:

- Four miniatures: (a) talismanic symbol; (b) angel with sword and scabbard; (c) four crosses inside of circles; and (d) ornate cross.

IES 00231, *Asmat* Prayers, ከታብ. Parchment, 187 x 11 cm, three strips, one column, Gəʿəz, twentieth century. Copied for ጸዳለ ማርያም ጨዳል.

Miniatures:

- Three miniatures: (a) angel with sword and scabbard; (b) talismanic symbol; and (c) talismanic symbol.

IES 00232, *Asmat* Prayers, ከታብ. Parchment, 176 x 10.5 cm, three strips, two columns, Gəʿəz, twentieth century. Copied for ወለተ ማርያም.

Miniatures:

- Three miniatures: (a) angel with sword and scabbard; (b) ornate cross with figure on either side; and (c) talismanic symbol.

IES 00233, *Asmat* Prayers, ከታብ. Parchment, 184 x 10.5 cm, three strips, one column, Gəʿəz, twentieth century. Original name was erased and replaced by ወለተ ኢየሱስ.

Miniatures:

- Three miniatures: (a) angel with sword and scabbard; (b) multi-box panel; and (c) talismanic symbol.

IES 00234, *Asmat* Prayers, ክታብ. Parchment, 202 x 18 cm, three strips, two columns, Gəʿəz, late nineteenth century. Copied for ገብረ ማርያም and ወልደ ማርያም, erased and replaced with ወለተ ተክለ ሃይማኖት and ወለተ ሕይወት ገብረ ሕይወት.

Miniatures:

- Three miniatures: (a) figure with arms uplifted; (b) angels with swords and scabbards; and (c) Gäbrä Mänfäs Qəddus and the Devil.

IES 00235, *Asmat* Prayers, ክታብ. Parchment, 170 x 17 cm, three strips, one column, Gəʿəz, late nineteenth century. Copied for ወለተ ሥላሴ.

Miniatures:

- Three miniatures: (a) figure with arms uplifted; (b) talismanic symbol, and (c) two ornate crosses.

IES 00236, *Asmat* Prayers, ክታብ. Parchment, 187 x 16.5 cm, three strips, two columns, Gəʿəz, nineteenth century. Copied for ወልደ ሚካኤል and his wife, erased and replaced with ወልደ ሥላሴ and ወለተ ማርያም.

Miniatures:

- Four miniatures: (a) angel with sword and scabbard; (b) talismanic symbol; (c) talismanic symbol; and (d) a lion.

IES 00237, *Asmat* Prayers, ክታብ. Parchment, 155 x 20.5 cm, two strips, two columns, Gəʿəz, late nineteenth century. Copied for ወልደ ዮሐንስ.

Miniatures:

- Two miniatures: (a) figure with arms uplifted; and (b) angel with sword and scabbard.

IES 00238, *Asmat* Prayers, ክታብ. Parchment, 230 x 21 cm, four strips, two columns, Gəʿəz, nineteenth century. Copied for ገብረ ሕይወት and ወልደ ሥላሴ, erased and replaced with ወልደ አረጋይ and his wife ወለተ ሙሴ.

Miniatures:

- Three miniatures: (a) three figures; (b) multi-box panel; and (c) ornate cross with a figure on either side.

IES 00239, *Asmat* Prayers, ከታብ. Parchment, 191 x 13.5 cm, four strips, one column, Gəʿəz, early twentieth century. Original name has been erased and replaced with ወለተ ሥላሴ.

Miniatures:

- Four miniatures: (a) angel with sword and scabbard; (b) talismanic symbol; (c) talismanic symbol; and (d) ornate cross.

IES 00240, Psalter, made in Emperor Mənilək's Government Scriptorium, ዳዊት; Image of Mary, መልክአ ማርያም; Image of Jesus, መልክአ ኢየሱስ; Image of Saint George, መልክአ ጊዮርጊስ; Image of Täklä Haymanot, መልክአ ተክለ ሃይማኖት; Image of Gäbrä Mänfäs Qəddus, መልክአ ገብረ መንፈስ ቅዱስ; Image of Michael, መልክአ ሚካኤል; Image of Gabriel, መልክአ ገብርኤል; Image of Raphael, መልክአ ሩፋኤል; Three Miracles of Mary, ተአምረ ማርያም; One Miracle of Saint George, ተአምረ ጊዮርጊስ; One Miracle of Täklä Haymanot, ተአምረ ተክለ ሃይማኖት; One Miracle of Gäbrä Mänfäs Qəddus, ተአምረ ገብረ መንፈስ ቅዱስ; One Miracle of Michael, ተአምረ ሚካኤል; One Miracle of Gabriel, ተአምረ ገብርኤል; One Miracle of Phanuel, ተአምረ ፋኑኤል; Image of Phanuel, መልክአ ፋኑኤል; Anaphora of Our Lady Mary, ቅዳሴ ማርያም. Parchment, 235 x 180 x 80 mm, iv + 275 folios, one column and two columns, 20 lines, Gəʿəz, Reign of Mənilək II (mentioned throughout). EMML 1414.

IES 00241, English-Afar Lexicon, draft, by Enid Parker. Paper, 320 x 240 x 40 mm, iii + 229 folios, two columns, 71 lines, Afar, English, 1969.

IES 00242, Four Gospels, አርባዕቱ ወንጌል. Parchment, 315 x 245 x 115 mm, ii + 163 folios, two columns, 27 lines, Gəʿəz, late fifteenth century.

Miniatures:

1. Ff. 2rv: The Twelve Apostles.
2. F. 3r: Madonna and Child.
3. F. 3v: Matthew the Evangelist.

4. F. 75v: Luke the Evangelist.

5. F. 122v: John the Evangelist.

IES 00243, Medical formulae or prescriptions, magico-religious prayers. Paper, 163 x 80 x 10 mm, i + 60 folios, one column, 16–17 lines, Amharic, 1968.

IES 00244A, Photocopy of a Collection of *Asmat* Prayers. Paper, 225 x 285 x 10 mm, i + 64 folios, one column, 17–19 lines, Gəʿəz, 1930–62 (f. 37 mentions Ḫaylä Śəllase, and Empress Manan who died in 1962). EMML 1407 & 1408.

Miniatures:

1. F. 5, left: Faces.

2. F. 6, left: Talismanic symbol.

3. F. 6, right: Talismanic symbol.

4. F. 7r: Talismanic symbol.

IES 00245, Amharic Commentary on the Psalter. Paper, 150 x 105 x 60 mm, iv + 371 folios, one column, 26–27 lines, Amharic, twentieth century. EMML 1426.

IES 00246, Sword of the Trinity, ሠይፈ ሥላሴ. Parchment, 145 x 103 x 33 mm, iv + 74 folios, two columns, 12–13 lines, Gəʿəz, twentieth century. EMML 1436.

IES 00247, Missal, መጽሐፈ ቅዳሴ. Parchment, 290 x 228 x 80 mm, iv + 112 folios, two columns, 19–22 lines, Gəʿəz, 1930–74 (f. 111v, mentions Emperor Ḫaylä Śəllase). EMML 1422. Single-slip maḥdär.

Miniatures:

1. F. iii r(ecto): Chart depicting the division of the Host.

IES 00248, Five Pillars of Mystery, አምስቱ አዕማደ ምሥጢር. Parchment, 160 x 105 x 50 mm, ii + 95 folios, two columns, 20 lines, Gəʿəz, nineteenth century. EMML 1425.

Miniatures:

1. F. i r(ecto): Crude drawing of Madonna and Child.

2. F. 93r: Crude drawing of a figure.

IES 00249, Prayer book; Praises of Mary, ሙዳሰ ማርያም; Anaphora of Our Lady Mary, ቅዳሴ ማርያም; Misc. Parchment, 152 x 110 x 37 mm, iv + 68 folios, two columns, 18 lines, Gəʿəz, 1889–1917 (ff. 49v–50r mention Metropolitan P̣eṭros IV [r. 1881–1917] and Metropolitan Matewos [r. 1889–1926]). EMML 1428.

IES 00250, *Asmat* Prayers. Parchment, 155 x 98 x 40 mm, ii + 98 folios, two columns, 20–22 lines, Gəʿəz, nineteenth century. EMML 1427.

IES 00251, Amharic-English Dictionary, Volume I, draft, by Thomas Kane. Paper, 345 x 211 x 67 mm, iv + 568 folios, one column, Amharic, English, 1961.

IES 00252, Amharic-English Dictionary, Volume II, draft, by Thomas Kane. Paper, 340 x 210 x 55 mm, i + 479 folios, one column, Amharic, English, 1961.

IES 00253, Amharic-English Dictionary, Volume III, draft, by Thomas Kane. Paper, 340 x 210 x 98 mm, i + 570 folios, one column, Amharic, English, 1961.

IES 00254, Photocopy of History of Ethiopia with special emphasis on the house of Goǧǧam. Paper, 227 x 335 x 25 mm, i + 161 folios, two columns, 36 lines, Amharic, twentieth century. EMML 1411.

IES 00278, Prayer of Mary at Bartos, ባርቶስ. Parchment, 130 x 96 x 32 mm, ii + 80 folios, one column, 15–17 lines, Gəʿəz, twentieth century.

IES 00292, Code of Kings, ፍትሐ ነገሥት. Parchment, 293 x 250 x 90 mm, ii + 186 folios, two columns, 25–29 lines, Gəʿəz, twentieth century. EMML 1412.

IES 00293, *Asmat* Prayers, ክታብ. Parchment, 224 x 18 cm, three strips, two columns, Gəʿəz, early twentieth century. Copied for ተክለ ሚካኤል and ወለተ ሃይማኖት, occasionally substituted with ተክለ ሃይማኖት.

Miniatures:

- Three miniatures: (a) equestrian saint; (b) *Abba* Samu'el riding a lion; and (c) Gäbrä Mänfäs Qəddus beside an ornate cross.

IES 00294, Octateuch, አሪት, with commentaries. Parchment, 288 x 190 x 180 mm, 291 folios, two columns, 33 lines, Gəʿəz, fifteenth century.

IES 00295, *Asmat* Prayers, ክታብ. Parchment, 213 x 22 cm, three strips, three columns, Gəʿəz, late nineteenth century. Copied for ዘሥላሴ.

Miniatures:
- Three miniatures: (a) angel with sword and scabbard; (b) Saint George and the Dragon; and (c) talismanic symbol.

IES 00296, Cycle of Kings, ዑዉደ ነገሥት. Parchment, 220 x 147 x 34 mm, ii + 57 folios, two columns, 26 lines, Gəʿəz, nineteenth century. EMML 1424.

IES 00297, Harp of Praise, አርጋኖነ ውዳሴ, arranged for the days of the week. Parchment, 255 x 210 x 50 mm, iv + 129 folios, two columns, 18–19 lines, Gəʿəz, nineteenth century. EMML 1413.

IES 00298, History of Lasta Kings, *Yälasta Nägäśtat Tarik*, by Krəstos Haräyo, translated into Amharic by *mämhər* Gäbrä Mäsqäl Täsfaye of Gännätä Maryam. Paper, 330 x 210 x 25 mm, iii + 79 folios, one column, 33 lines, Amharic, Gəʿəz, 1969.

IES 00312, Photocopy of Grammar Notes and Vocabulary of Ethiopian Languages, draft, by Marvin Lionel Bender. Paper, 330 x 225 x 30 mm, i + 228 folios, one column, English, 1965.

IES 00313, Photocopy of Word Lists of Different Languages of Ethiopia, draft, by Harold Fleming. Paper, 336 x 223 x 19 mm, i + 171 folios, one column, English, 1969.

IES 00314A, Language survey of Ethiopia, word-lists collected from various sources, Volume 1, draft. Paper, 290 x 220 x 35 mm, i + 287 folios, one column, English, 1969.

IES 00314B, Language survey of Ethiopia, word-lists collected from various sources, Volume 2, draft. Paper, 290 x 220 x 30 mm, i + 244 folios, one column, English, 1969.

IES 00314C, Language survey of Ethiopia, word-lists collected from various sources, Volume 3, draft. Paper, 290 x 220 x 38 mm, i + 222 folios, one column, English, 1969.

IES 00315, Book of Prayers, Miracles of Mary, ተአምረ ማርያም. Parchment, 385 x 330 x 20 mm, i + 23 folios, one column, 22 lines, Gəʿəz, eighteenth century.

Miniatures:

1. F. 8v, above: Apostles.
2. F. 8v, below: Saint George and the Dragon with a patron prostrate before him; an emperor, probably Iyasu I, is shown praying in a church.
3. F. 9r: Mary at Däbrä Mäṭmaq (above); priests receive her with singing and the martyrs bow down to her (below).
4. F. 9v: Salome and Joseph and Madonna and Child at Däbrä Qwəsqwam (above); a figure with an attendant in proskynesis (below).
5. F. 10r: Presentation of Mary.
6. F. 10v: The Nativity (above); and figures playing *gänna* (below).
7. F. 11r: Madonna and Child.
8. F. 11v: The Crucifixion.
9. F. 12r: The Holy Trinity with a patron in proskynesis.
10. F. 12v: A group of saints including Ewosṭatewos, Täklä Haymanot, Gäbrä Mänfäs Qəddus, *abba* Samu'el, *abba* Abib, and *abba* Kiros (above); and the Nine Saints (below).
11. F. 13r: Saint George.
12. F. 13v, above: Saint Yosṭos on horseback.
13. F. 13v, below: Saint Abali on horseback.
14. F. 14r, above: Saint Filatäwos on horseback.
15. F. 14r, below: Saint Awsabyos on horseback.
16. F. 14v, above: Saint Fiqṭor on horseback.
17. F. 14v, below: Saint Sebastian on horseback.
18. F. 15r, above: Saint Tewodros on horseback.
19. F. 15r, below: Saint Behnam on horseback.
20. F. 15v, above: Saint Mercurius on horseback.
21. F. 15v, below: Saint Gälawdewos on horseback.
22. F. 16r, above: Saint Fasiladas on horseback.
23. F. 16r, below: Saint Tewodros Masəriqawi on horseback.

24. F. 16v, above: Covenant of Mercy, *Kidanä Məhrät*.
25. F. 16v, below: Martyrdom of Sebastian.
26. F. 17r, above: *Abunä* Täklä Haymanot addresses three people.
27. F. 17r, below: Two rows of saints and apostles.
28. F. 17v, above: The Beheading of John the Baptist.
29. F. 17v, below: Salome dances before Herod.
30. F. 18r: Michael and a patron in proskynesis.
31. F. 18v, above: Cyricus and his mother, Julitta are shown among flames next to the three Israelite children Hananiah, Mishael, and Azariah.
32. F. 18v, below: The Stoning of Stephen.
33. F. 19r: Emperor Iyasu I departs for war.
34. F. 19v: Emperor Iyasu I returns from war as victor.
35. F. 20r: Priests celebrate the emperor's return.
36. F. 20v: Four biblical kings, seated on their thrones; David (upper left); Solomon (upper right); Hezekiah (lower left); Josiah (lower right).
37. F. 21r, above: Emperor Yoḥannəs I (upper left), and Emperor Iyasu I seated on their thrones.
38. F. 21r, below: Emperor Constantine, presides over the Council of Nicaea attended by Arius, the Archbishop Alexander and the 300 Orthodox Fathers.
39. F. 21v: A group of 20 holy men, including Arsenius, Kiros, Shenute, Ammonius, Paul of Thebes, and Pachomius.
40. F. 22r: A group of 20 holy men, including Pishoy, John, *abba* Aron, Mark, Saint Alexis, and Simeon Stylites.
41. F. 22v, above: Abraham, Isaac, and Jacob (represented like the Trinity), Moses receiving the Ten Commandments, Aaron with his blooming rod.
42. F. 22v, below: A group of holy men including Daniel, Jonah, Habakkuk.

IES 00316, Image of the Covenant of Mercy, መልክአ ኪዳነ ምሕረት; Image of Michael, መልክአ ሚካኤል; Hymn to the Trinity, "I Worship"; Image of the Covenant of Mercy, መልክአ ኪዳነ ምሕረት; *Asmat* Prayer of Saint Thomas the Apostle. Parchment, 115 x 90 x 35 mm, 75 folios, one column, 12–14 lines, Gəʽəz, early twentieth century. EMML 1477.

Miniatures:

1. F. 1r: Equestrian saint spearing an enemy.
2. F. 33r: Angel with sword and scabbard.
3. F. 33v: Angel.
4. F. 75v: Saint Thomas holding his flayed skin.

IES 00317, Book of Christening, መጽሐፈ ክርስትና. Parchment, 127 x 105 x 25 mm, ii + 26 folios, one column, 15–16 lines, Gəʽəz, 1945 EC = 1952–53. EMML 1475.

IES 00318, Harp of Praise, አርጋኖነ ውዳሴ, arranged for the days of the week. Parchment, 175 x 180 x 65 mm, ii + 140 folios, two columns, 15–17 lines, Gəʽəz, seventeenth century. EMML 1469.

Miniatures:

1. F. 138v: Crude drawing of an angel.

IES 00321, Photocopy of manuscript of History of Kings, ታሪክ ነገሥት. Paper, 220 x 335 x 20 mm, 111 folios, one column, 18 lines, Gəʽəz, twentieth century. EMML 1466.

IES 00322, Antiphonary for the Whole Year, ድጓ. Parchment, 325 x 270 x 85 mm, iv + 176 folios, three columns, 32–42 lines, Gəʽəz, 1930–74 (f. 1r mentions Emperor Ḫaylä Śəllase). EMML 1462.

IES 00323, A Message (*Mälaʼəkt*) to Ethiopian Christians to revive their faith by embarrassing Catholicism, addressed to Emperor Täklä Giyorgis II (r. 1869–71) and the Ethiopian faithful by "monks who live on the border of the land." Paper, 152 x 115 x 20 mm, v + 100 folios, one column, 14 lines, Amharic, 1874. EMML 1472.

IES 00324, Book of History (a collection of notes on history with special emphasis on Ethiopia, compiled by Gäbrä Mika'el Gərmu). Paper, 220 x 170 x 35 mm, iv + 207 folios, one column, 19–20 lines, Gə'əz, 1911–13 (ff. 1r and 3r, dated). EMML 1470.

IES 00325, History of Emperor Yoḥannəs IV (a collection of notes, compiled by Gäbrä Mika'el Gərmu). Paper, 212 x 153 x 10 mm, ii + 24 folios, one column, 21 lines, Gə'əz, 1909 EC = 1916–17.

IES 00326, The Amharic Chronicle of King Tewodros II by *däbtära* Zännäb (copied from the printed edition by Enno Littmann [Princeton, 1902]); Additional Notes on Emperor Tewodros II; History of Ethiopia in Tigrinya as narrated by the professors and elders; short notes in Tigrinya on the history of Ethiopia with special emphasis on the meaning of places and nations or tribe names; notes in Tigrinya on nineteenth-century history of Ethiopia. Paper, 244 x 182 x 15 mm, i + 70 folios, one column, 25–27 lines, Amharic, Gə'əz, Tigrinya, 1952–54. EMML 1473.

IES 00327, *Mäṣḥafä məkr*, Book of Advice, መጽሐፈ ምክር, an apologetic treatise in Amharic in defence of Catholicism in Ethiopia. Paper, 320 x 212 x 20 mm, iii + 123 folios, one column, 33 lines, Amharic, twentieth century. EMML 1467.

IES 00329, Gə'əz Grammar, ሰዋሰው፡ ግዕዝ. Paper, 177 x 120 x 8 mm, 68 folios, one column, 17–18 lines, Gə'əz, 1930.

IES 00330, Amharic Commentary on the Covenant of the Morning, ኪዳን ዘነግህ. Parchment, 170 x 110 x 7 mm, i + 15 folios, one column, 20–21 lines, Amharic, late nineteenth century. EMML 1474.

IES 00333, Image of Gäbrä Mänfäs Qəddus, መልክአ ገብረ መንፈስ ቅዱስ. Parchment, 120 x 95 x 8 mm, ii + 12 folios, one column, 9 lines, Gə'əz, early twentieth century.

IES 00345, *Asmat* Prayers, አስማት, for the days of the week. Paper, 160 x 100 x 13 mm, ii + 61 folios, one column, 16 lines, Gə'əz, twentieth century. EMML 1476.

Miniatures:

1. F. i v(erso): Six-pointed star, in blue ink.

2. F. ii r(ecto): A woman and a six-pointed star, in pencil.

IES 00348, The Dialect of Gondär, draft, by R. Cowley. Paper, 338 x 218 x 5 mm, i + 13 folios, one column, English, 1970.

IES 00350, Psalter, ዳዊት. Parchment, 200 x 190 x 65 mm, ii + 122 folios, one column and two columns, 20 lines, Gəʿəz, eighteenth century. EMML 1465.

Miniatures:

1. F. 121v: King David playing the harp.
2. F. 122r: An enthroned figure (Solomon?) with an attendant.

IES 00351, Short List of Church Properties in Moret District. Paper, 326 x 220 x 4 mm, i + 6 folios, one column, 20 lines, Amharic, 1971.

IES 00355, Beauty of the Creation, ሥነ ፍጥረት; The Mystery of Incarnation, ምሥጢረ ሥጋዌ; Amharic Commentary on the Introduction to the Miracles of Mary; An Amharic Treatise on Computus, ባሕረ ሐሳብ. Paper, 200 x 145 x 50 mm, 158 folios, two columns, 23 lines, Amharic, 1912 EC = 1919–20 (f. 143v). EMML 1468.

IES 00357, An Amharic catechetical treatise in defence of *Täwahədo* or the teaching of Ethiopian Orthodox church on the oneness of the nature of Christ. Parchment, 257 x 187 x 67 mm, ii + 48 folios, one column, 17 lines, Amharic, early twentieth century. EMML 1471.

IES 00358, Homiliary in Honor of the Archangel Michael, ድርሳነ ሚካኤል. Parchment, 210 x 135 x 37 mm, iv + 166 folios, two columns, 20 lines, Gəʿəz, 1909. EMML 1464.

Miniatures:

1. F. ii v(erso): Saint George and the Dragon.
2. F. iii r(ecto): Madonna and Child.
3. F. iv v(erso): Michael, the Archangel.
4. F. 63v: Samson, holding the jawbone, standing above slain Philistines.
5. F. 165r: The devil holding pitchfork flees from Euphemia who holds an icon.
6. F. 166r: Saint Michael, the archangel, riding a horse meets Saint Bahəran.

IES 00361, Photocopy of the History of Kings, ታሪክ ነገሥት. Translated by *ato* Gärima Täfärra from a Gəʿəz manuscript found in Däbrä Bərhan Śəllase church at Gondär and copied by ʾAnduʿaläm Mulaw. Paper, 330 x 220 x 8 mm, ii + 62 folios, one column, 36–42 lines, Amharic, 1971.

IES 00371, Image of the Archangel Raguel, መልአክ ራጉኤል. Parchment, 90 x 70 x 20 mm, vi + 40 folios, one column, 13 lines, Gəʿəz, twentieth century.

Miniatures:

1. F. 1v: Raguel, the Archangel. Text says "paint Raguel here."
2. F. 2v: Two snakes devouring each other. Text says "paint Behemoth."
3. F. 6r: Two snakes devouring each other. Text says "paint Behemoth around the text."
4. F. 9v: Three snakes devouring each other. Text says "paint Behemoth around the text."
5. F. 10v: Two snakes devouring each other. Text says "paint Behemoth around the text."
6. F. 13r: A cross inside a box of red and blue ink.
7. F. 14r: Two snakes devouring each other. Text says "paint Behemoth inside."
8. F. 14v: Four-headed bird. Text says "paint four-headed bird."
9. F. 17r: Two snakes devouring each other around the text.
10. F. 18v: Two snakes devouring each other around the text.
11. F. 20v: Lamb of God holding cross. Text says "paint lamb."
12. F. 22r: Raguel, the Archangel, with sword and scabbard.
13. F. 22v: Raguel, the Archangel, with sword.
14. F. 25v: Madonna and Child.
15. F. 27v: Raguel, the Archangel.
16. F. 28r: Two snakes devouring each other.
17. F. 29r: Madonna and Child.
18. F. 30r: Gäbrä Mänfäs Qəddus.
19. F. 31v: A frog.

20. F. 33r: An angel and a lion. Text says, "paint the angel and, under him, the lion."

21. F. 33v, upper: The Holy Trinity surrounded by the four Living Creatures.

22. F. 33v, lower: An angel riding a horse.

IES 00372, List of people healed and assisted by Saint Gabriel and Saint Michael. Paper, 217 x 160 x 2 mm, 2 folios, one column, 23 lines, Amharic, 1972.

IES 00373, Four Gospels, አርባዕቱ ወንጌል. Parchment, 373 x 295 x 80 mm, i + 166 folios, two columns, 21 lines, Gəʻəz, 1682–92 (f. 166r, mentions the reign of Iyasu I [r. 1682–1706] while Sinoda [1671/72–92] was Metropolitan). EMML 1463.

IES 00374, Praises to the Lord, ምስጋና ለአምላክ by Mekibib Zeleke. Paper, 357 x 255 x 37 mm, i + 68 folios, one column, 16 lines, Amharic, 1958.

IES 00375, List of Ethiopian cultural objects in the Museum of the University of Zurich collection by Raunib. Paper, 304 x 216 x 5 mm, i + 14 folios, one column, German, 1972.

IES 00377, Testaments of Abraham, Isaac and Jacob; Homily of Saint Ephrem on Abraham and Sarah; Acts of *abba* Nob; The Report of Paphnutius on his Visit to the Ascetics in the desert in Egypt; Homily of Saint Basil for the dedication of the church of Saint Mary; Book of Christening, መጽሐፈ ክርስትና. Parchment, 200 x 145 x 70 mm, iii + 142 folios, ff. 1r–56r and 96r–142v two columns, ff. 58r–95r one column, 20 lines, Gəʻəz, late fourteenth/early fifteenth century. EMML 5 & 1496.

Miniatures:

1. F. iii v(erso): Abraham.

2. F. 57v: *Abba* Nob; "Image of Saint *abba* Nob, how he prayed standing. May his prayer be with us. Amen."

3. F. 95v: "Image of Abunafer, how he prayed standing. May his prayer be with us. Amen"

4. F. 115v: "Image of Mary, How she prayed for all creation to her beloved Son that he might forgive us. May the prayer and blessing of her beloved son be with us. Amen."

IES 00378A, Photocopy of the History of *ras* Alula. Edited by Haggai Erlich, "A Contemporary Biography of *ras* Alula," BSOAS 39 (1976). Paper, 280 x 220 x 7 mm, i + 31 folios, one column, 18 lines, Amharic, late twentieth century. EMML 1491.

IES 00378B, History of *ras* Alula, introduction and translation in English. Paper, 328 x 219 x 7 mm, i + 57 folios, one column, 36 lines, Amharic, English, late twentieth century. EMML 1491 & 1500.

IES 00378C, Photocopy of History of *ras* Alula. Paper, 180 x 145 x 10 mm, i + 39 folios, one column, 18 lines, Amharic, late twentieth century. EMML 1500.

IES 00379, Catalogue of Wolaita Sodo Museum by Bruce and Barbie Van Meter. Paper, 340 x 250 x 17 mm, i + 33 folios, English, 1972.

IES 00380A, The History of the Oromo by *aläqa* Aṭme. Paper, 276 x 216 x 22 mm, ii + 190 folios, one column, 29 lines, Amharic, 1913.

IES 00380B, The History of the Oromo by *aläqa* Aṭme. Paper, 276 x 216 x 20 mm, ii + 191 folios, one column, 28–29 lines, Amharic, 1913.

IES 00381, Gəʿəz vocabulary and Grammar, ሰዋስው፡ ግዕዝ. Parchment, 145 x 130 x 42 mm, i + 75 folios, two columns, 13 lines, Gəʿəz, eighteenth century. EMML 1499.

Miniatures:

1. F. 3v: Saint George and the Dragon.
2. F. 8r: Madonna and Child.

IES 00382, *Asmat* Prayers, ኪታብ. Parchment, 180 x 18 cm, two strips, two columns, Gəʿəz, nineteenth century. Copied for ሥላሴ, erased and replaced with አቡየ ገብረ እግዚአብሐር.

Miniatures:

- Four miniatures: (a) King Solomon; (b) Archangels Michael and Gabriel with swords; (c) Archangels Phanuel and Raguel with swords, and (d) talismanic symbols.

IES 00383, Book of the Disciples, መጽሐፈ አርድእት. Parchment, 172 x 100 x 35 mm, ii + 40 folios, one column, 18 lines, Gəʿəz, early nineteenth century. EMML 1501.

IES 00385, Photocopy of the Book of Medicine, መጽሐፈ መድኃኒት; *Asmat* Prayers, አስማት. Paper, 335 x 220 x 15 mm, i + 85 folios, one column, 31 lines, Gəʿəz, twentieth century. EMML 1486.

Miniatures:

1. F. 27r: Talismanic figures.
2. F. 42r: Three six-pointed stars.
3. F. 67r: A three-box panel (1 x 3) with a face in center.
4. F. 68r: A four box panel (2 x 2) of geometric patterns.
5. F. 69r: Talismanic symbols.
6. F. 70r: Talismanic symbol.
7. F. 71r: Talismanic symbols.
8. F. 72r: Talismanic symbols.
9. F. 73r: Talismanic symbol.

IES 00386, *Asmat* Prayers, ከታብ; Image of Saṭnaʾel. Parchment, 140 x 100 x 21 mm, ii + 26 folios, one column, 14 lines, Gəʿəz, twentieth century. EMML 1502.

Miniatures:

1. F. ii v(erso): An angel.
2. F. 13r: An angel with sword and scabbard.

IES 00387, Photocopy of the Commentary on the Code of Kings, part II. Paper, 330 x 220 x 25 mm, i + 200 folios, two columns, 29 lines, Gəʿəz, twentieth century. EMML 1483.

IES 00388, Photocopy of The King and the Crown [Poems], draft, by Nəguśənna Zäwdu. Paper, 320 x 220 x 4 mm, v + 26 folios, one column, 27 lines, Amharic, 1939 EC = 1956–57. EMML 1489.

IES 00392, Book of Enoch, መጽሐፈ ሄኖክ; Book of Jubilees, መጽሐፈ ኩፋሌ. Parchment, 320 x 250 x 60 mm, 94 folios, two columns, 27–29 lines, Gəʿəz, fifteenth century.

IES 00393, Image of Gäbrä Mänfäs Qəddus, መልክአ ገብረ መንፈስ ቅዱስ. Paper, 164 x 117 x 5 mm, i + 10 folios, one column, 8 lines, Gəʿəz, twentieth century. EMML 1493.

IES 00394, Greeting to the Church, ሰላም ለኪ ቤተ ክርስቲያን ሎዛ; Greeting to the Christian Sabbath, ሰላም ለኪ ዕለተ ሰንበት; Greeting to the Guardian Angel, መልክአ ዐቃቤ መልአክ. Paper, 160 x 107 x 5 mm, i + 9 folios, one column, 14 lines, Gəʿəz, twentieth century. EMML 1494.

IES 00395, Abbreviated Funeral Ritual prepared by *qes* Badəmma Yaläw. Paper, 175 x 120 x 8 mm, ii + 9 folios, one column, 14 lines, Amharic, 1928 EC = 1935–36. EMML 1492.

IES 00396, Photocopy of *Alfabeticum Æthiopicum pro linguâ Ghéz et Amhara: Dizionario Etiopico-Latino* (Ethiopic-Latin Dictionary), draft, by F. Giusto da Urbino (= Jacopo Curtopassi). Paper, 300 x 230 x 25 mm, i + 214 folios, two columns, 31 lines, Latin, Gəʿəz, 1868.

IES 00397, The Five Pillars of Mystery, አምስቱ አዕማደ ምሥጢር; Beauty of Creation, ሥነ ፍጥረት; Passion of the Cross, በእንተ ሕማማተ መስቀል; Computus, ባሕረ ሐሳብ. Parchment, 237 x 183 x 70 mm, ii + 195 folios, two columns, 21 lines, Gəʿəz, 1878 EC = 1885–86. EMML 1495.

IES 00398, Psalter, ዳዊት. Parchment, 130 x 130 x 70 mm, 176 folios, one column and two columns, 18 lines, Gəʿəz, eighteenth century. EMML 1498.

IES 00400, Photocopy of History of *däǧǧazmač abba* Wəqaw by Sirak Fekade Sellasie. Paper, 330 x 215 x 10 mm, i + 52 folios, two columns, 30 lines, Amharic, 1931 EC = 1938–39. EMML 1484.

IES 00401, Photocopy of Chronicle of Emperor Yoḥannəs I. Paper, 337 x 225 x 20 mm, 140 folios, two columns, 32 lines, Gəʿəz, Amharic, nineteenth/twentieth century. EMML 1485.

IES 00402, Acts of Gäbrä Mänfäs Qəddus, ገድለ ገብረ መንፈስ ቅዱስ; Miracles of Gäbrä Mänfäs Qəddus, ተአምረ ገብረ መንፈስ ቅዱስ; Image of Gäbrä Mänfäs Qəddus, መልክአ ገብረ መንፈስ ቅዱስ, Miscellanea. Parchment, 168 x 161 x 51 mm, i + 113 folios, two columns, 16 lines, Gəʿəz, nineteenth century. EMML 1497.

IES 00403, *Asmat* Prayers, ከታብ. Parchment, 208 x 10 cm, three strips, one column, Gəʿəz, nineteenth century. Copied for ወለተ ኢየሱስ, erased and replaced in some places with ንግሥተ ማርያም.

Miniatures:

- Three miniatures: (a) talismanic symbol; (b) angel with sword and scabbard, and (c) multi-box panel.

IES 00404, *Asmat* Prayers, ከታብ. Parchment, 166 x 10 cm, three strips, one column, Gəʿəz, twentieth century. Copied for ወለተ ሐርገዪን.

Miniatures:

- Three miniatures: (a) four circles containing four smaller circles; (b) two circles containing smaller circles; and (c) talismanic symbol.

IES 00405, *Asmat* Prayers, ከታብ. Parchment, 178 x 10.5 cm, three strips, one column, Gəʿəz, twentieth century. Copied for ወለተ መድኅን.

Miniatures:

- Three miniatures: (a) talismanic symbol; (b) angel with sword and scabbard; and (c) talismanic symbol.

IES 00406, *Asmat* Prayers, ከታብ. Parchment, 166 x 13 cm, three strips, one column, Gəʿəz, late nineteenth/early twentieth century. Copied for ገብረ እግዚአብሔር, erased and replaced by ዓቢየ እግዚእ and then by ወልደ አምላክ.

Miniatures:

- Three miniatures: (a) talismanic symbol; (b) ornate cross; and (c) talismanic symbol.

IES 00407, *Asmat* Prayers, ከታብ. Parchment, 186 x 11 cm, three strips, one column, Gəʿəz, late eighteenth century. Copied for ወለተ ሩፋኤል.

Miniatures:

- Three miniatures: (a) angel with sword and scabbard; (b) talismanic symbol; and (c) talismanic symbol.

IES 00408, *Asmat* Prayers, ከታብ. Parchment, 182 x 10 cm, three strips, one column, Gəʽəz, early twentieth century. Copied for ገብረ አናንያ.

Miniatures:

- Four miniatures: (a) angel with sword and scabbard; (b) multi-box panel; (c) angel with sword and scabbard; and (d) talismanic symbol.

IES 00409, *Asmat* Prayers, ከታብ. Parchment, 162 x 8.5 cm, three strips, one column, Gəʽəz, twentieth century. Copied for ወለተ ተክለ ሃይማኖት.

Miniatures:

- Four miniatures: (a) angel with sword and scabbard; (b) talismanic symbol; (c) table of letters, eyes, and x-shaped patterns; and (d) talismanic symbol.

IES 00410, *Asmat* Prayers, ከታብ. Parchment, 152 x 12 cm, two strips, one column, Gəʽəz, late eighteenth century/early nineteenth century. Copied for ወለተ ማርያም, ገብረ እግዚአብሔር, ወለተ ዮሐንስ, and ወለተ ኢየሱስ.

Miniatures:

- Three miniatures: (a) angel with sword and scabbard; (b) talismanic symbol; and (c) talismanic symbol.

IES 00411, *Asmat* Prayers, ከታብ. Parchment, 181 x 9 cm, three strips, one column, Gəʽəz, twentieth century. Copied for አመተ ጸድቃን.

Miniatures:

- Three miniatures: (a) angel with sword and scabbard; (b) a king and a demon; and (c) talismanic symbol.

IES 00412, *Asmat* Prayers, ከታብ. Parchment, 163.5 x 8 cm, two strips, one column, Gəʽəz, twentieth century. The name አመተ ኢየሱስ appears in a different hand and ink.

Miniatures:

- Two miniatures: (a) angel with sword; and (b) ornate cross.

IES 00413, *Asmat* Prayers, ክታብ. Parchment, 178 x 9 cm, three strips, two columns, Gəʿəz, twentieth century. Copied for ወለተ አመተ ኢየሱስ.

Miniatures:

- Three miniatures: (a) angel with sword and scabbard; (b) talismanic symbol; and (c) talismanic symbol.

IES 00414, *Asmat* Prayers, ክታብ. Parchment, 159 x 10 cm, three strips, one column, Gəʿəz, twentieth century. Copied for ወለተ ማርያም.

Miniatures:

- Three miniatures: (a) angel with sword and scabbard; (b) angel; and (c) angel.

IES 00415, *Asmat* Prayers, ክታብ. Parchment, 214 x 14 cm, three strips, two columns, Gəʿəz, twentieth century. Original name erased and replaced with ኃመተ ማርያም.

Miniatures:

- Three miniatures: (a) angel with sword and scabbard; (b) figure with arms uplifted and angel above; and (c) talismanic symbol.

IES 00416, *Asmat* Prayers, ክታብ. Parchment, 187 x 16.6 cm, three strips, two columns, Gəʿəz, twentieth century. Copied for ወለተ ገብርኤል.

Miniatures:

- Four miniatures: (a) figure with arms uplifted; (b) two people with swords and scabbards; (c) Gäbrä Mänfäs Qəddus holding a handcross; and (d) an angel with sword.

IES 00417, Psalter, ዳዊት; Angels Praise Her, ይዌድስዋ መላእክት ለማርያም. Parchment, 213 x 155 x 60 mm, v + 192 folios, one column and two columns, 18–20 lines, Gəʿəz, 1924 EC = 1931–32. EMML 1511.

Miniatures:

1. F. v v(erso): King David playing the harp.

IES 00419, Published edition of Amharic commentary on the Praises of Mary; Amharic commentary on the Anaphora of Our Lady Mary by Cyriacus; Amharic theological treaties. Paper, 200 x 165 x 33 mm, i

+ 282 folios, one column, 18–28 lines, Amharic, Gəʿəz, 1925 EC = 1932–33. EMML 1514.

IES 00420, Photocopy of a manuscript of the Combat and Miracles of Qäwəsṭos. Paper, 245 x 178 x 30 mm, ii + 227 folios, two columns, 22 lines, Gəʿəz, twentieth century. EMML 1513.

IES 00421A, List of manuscripts in Addis Ababa Churches, Volume I. Paper, 365 x 260 x 29 mm, ii + 150 folios, one column, English, Gəʿəz, Amharic, 1972.

IES 00421B, List of manuscripts in Addis Ababa Churches, Volume II. Paper, 360 x 260 x 10 mm, ii + 112 folios, one column, English, Gəʿəz, Amharic, 1972.

IES 00421C, List of manuscripts in Addis Ababa Churches, Volume III. Paper, 370 x 260 x 28 mm, iii + 123 folios, one column, English, Gəʿəz, Amharic, 1972.

IES 00422, Prayer to Jesus Christ, "For the sake of Your Trinity," በእንተ ሥላሴክ; Praise of the Beloved, ስብሐተ ፍቁር; Two Miracles of Mary, ተአምረ ማርያም; Three Miracles of Gäbrä Mänfäs Qəddus, ተአምረ ገብረ መንፈስ ቅዱስ; One Miracle of Saint George, ተአምረ ጊዮርጊስ; One Miracle of Täklä Haymanot, ተአምረ ተክለ ሃይማኖት; One Miracle of Ewosṭatewos, ተአምረ ኤዎስጣቴዎስ; Image of John the Baptist, መልክአ ዮሐንስ መጥምቅ; Hymn to Jesus Christ, "O, for the sake of us," አ በእንቲአነ; Image of the Icon, መልክአ ሥዕል; One Miracle of Michael, ተአምረ ሚካኤል. Parchment, 186 x 129 x 54 mm, vi + 92 folios, one column, 8 lines, Gəʿəz, eighteenth century. EMML 1487.

Miniatures:

1. F. vi r(ecto): The Holy Trinity surrounded by the Four Living Creatures.
2. F. 6v: God the Father, sending forth Gabriel (lower) for the Annunciation.
3. F. 7v: The Annunciation.
4. F. 8v: The Nativity.
5. F. 9v: The Baptism of Jesus.
6. F. 10v: The Temptation of Jesus.

7. F. 11v: The Arrest of Jesus.
8. F. 12v: Jesus with arms bound.
9. F. 13v: Jesus with rope around his neck.
10. F. 14v: The striking of Jesus by the guards.
11. F. 15v: The Flagellation of Jesus.
12. F. 16v: Removing the robe of Jesus.
13. F. 17v: The soldiers place a robe on Jesus.
14. F. 18v: The Blindfolding of Jesus.
15. F. 19v: The Striking of the Head.
16. F. 20r: Two patrons in proskynesis before Jesus.
17. F. 20v: Jesus carrying the Cross.
18. F. 21v, above: Nailing Jesus to the cross.
19. F. 21v, below: Pilate washes his hands.
20. F. 22v: The Crucifixion.
21. F. 23r: A patron in proskynesis before Jesus.
22. F. 23v: Jesus is offered gall when he is on the cross.
23. F. 24r: A patron prostrate before the Crucifixion.
24. F. 24v: Piercing Jesus' side.
25. F. 25v: The Deposition.
26. F. 26v: Wrapping the body of Jesus in the burial shroud.
27. F. 27v: The Entombment of Jesus.
28. F. 28v: The Resurrection of Jesus, raising Adam and Eve (Anastasis).
29. F. 29v: The Ascension.
30. F. 31v: The Last Judgment.
31. F. 55v: Our Lady Mary, beside a building.
32. F. 58r: Our Lady Mary saves a soul being taken by demons.
33. F. 60r: Our Lady Mary, appears as a white bird to George the Younger.
34. F. 64r: Gäbrä Mänfäs Qəddus.

35. F. 65v: Saint George and the Dragon.

36. F. 68r: Täklä Haymanot.

37. F. 71v: *Abunä* Ewosṭatewos at sea on the way to Armenia.

38. F. 79r: The beheading of John the Baptist.

IES 00424, Collection of Gəʿəz *Qəne*, with their Translations, Volume VI, pp. 361–78, and I, pp. 1–30, by *blatten geta* Ḫəruy Wäldä Śəllase. Paper, 345 x 220 x 5 mm, iii + 49 folios, one column, Gəʿəz, Amharic, 1956 EC = 1963–64. EMML 1506.

IES 00425, Collection of Gəʿəz *Qəne*, with their Translations, Volume II, pp. 31–110 by *blatten geta* Ḫəruy Wäldä Śəllase. Paper, 345 x 215 x 15 mm, iii + 82 folios, one column, Gəʿəz, Amharic, 1956 EC = 1963–64. EMML 1505.

IES 00426, Collection of Gəʿəz *Qəne*, with their Translations, Volume III, pp. 111–200 by *blatten geta* Ḫəruy Wäldä Śəllase. Paper, 320 x 210 x 12 mm, ii + 95 folios, one column, Gəʿəz, Amharic, 1956 EC = 1963–64. EMML 1503.

IES 00427, Collection of Gəʿəz *Qəne*, with their Translations, Volume IV, pp. 201–80 by *blatten geta* Ḫəruy Wäldä Śəllase. Paper, 315 x 200 x 12 mm, ii + 83 folios, one column, Gəʿəz, Amharic, 1956 EC = 1963–64. EMML 1508.

IES 00428, Collection of Gəʿəz *Qəne*, with their Translations, Volume V, pp. 281–361 by *blatten geta* Ḫəruy Wäldä Śəllase. Paper, 320 x 200 x 7 mm, ii + 83 folios, one column, Gəʿəz, Amharic, 1956 EC = 1963–64. EMML 1507.

IES 00429A, Photocopy of the Inventory of Church Antiquities in the Ethiopian Church, Saint Stephen dei Mori, inside Saint Peter compound of Vatican City, Rome, *Inventario delle robbe che si ritrovano nella Chiesa, et Casa di S. Stefano delli Frati Mori dietro S. Pietro fatto dal Sr. D. Eran: de Sanctis, Capp. nodid a Chiesa*. Paper, 298 x 212 x 12 mm, i + 46 folios, one column, Italian, Latin, 1630–1705.

IES 00430, Aksum Museum Catalogue Book, Volume I (Numbers 001–1850). Paper, 323 x 200 x 10 mm, 62 folios, English, 1965.

IES 00431, Permanent Register Book of Aksum Museum Artefacts by S. Dempster Boyd, S.D., Peace Corps volunteer. Paper, 323 x 200 x 10 mm, 37 folios, English, 1965.

IES 00434, What Should Christians Do During the Mass?. Paper, 330 x 205 x 2 mm, i + 3 folios, one column, 34 lines, Amharic, twentieth century.

IES 00435, Songs by Beggars about Riches. Parchment, 255 x 187 x 1 mm, 2 folios, one column, 23 lines, Amharic, twentieth century.

IES 00436, Combined fragments of two biblical manuscripts. First Manuscript: Book of Jubilees (1–3v, incomplete at the beginning and end); Susanna (4rv); Daniel (5r); Additions to Daniel (8v); Amos (10r); Micah (14r); Joel (18r); Obadiah (21r); Jonah (22r); Nahum (23v); Habakkuk (25v); Zephaniah (26v); Haggai (28v); Zechariah (32r); Malachi (37v–39v incomplete at the end). Second Manuscript: Matthew (40r); and the end of John (68r). Parchment, 355 x 269 x 47 mm, 69 folios, two columns, 28–29 lines, Gəʿəz, late fifteenth century/early sixteenth century.

IES 00439, Book of Jubilees, መጽሐፈ ኩፋሌ. Parchment, 225 x 168 x 58 mm, iv + 85 folios, two columns, 30–31 lines, Gəʿəz, 1505–6. EMML 3 & 1510.

IES 00440, Acts of Gäbrä Mänfäs Qəddus, ገድለ ገብረ መንፈስ ቅዱስ; Miracles of Gäbrä Mänfäs Qəddus, ተአምረ ገብረ መንፈስ ቅዱስ; Image of Gäbrä Mänfäs Qəddus, መልክአ ገብረ መንፈስ ቅዱስ; Homily of Jacob of Serugh. Parchment, 193 x 163 x 58 mm, iv + 104 folios, two columns, 17–18 lines, Gəʿəz, eighteenth century. EMML 1512.

IES 00441, Acts of Gäbrä Mänfäs Qəddus, ገድለ ገብረ መንፈስ ቅዱስ; Fourteen Miracles of Gäbrä Mänfäs Qəddus, ተአምረ ገብረ መንፈስ ቅዱስ; Image of Gäbrä Mänfäs Qəddus, መልክአ ገብረ መንፈስ ቅዱስ; and Anthems for the commemoration of Gäbrä Mänfäs Qəddus. Parchment, 172 x 158 x 59 mm, ii + 97 folios, two columns, 16 lines, Gəʿəz, eighteenth century. EMML 1526.

IES 00442, Image of Phanuel, መልክአ ፋኑኤል; Prayer to bind demons; Prayer to Gabriel; Greeting to Gabriel; Prayer to Raphael; Greeting to Raphael; Prayer to Sachiel; Greeting to Sachiel; Prayer to Phanuel; Greeting to Phanuel; Prayer to Raguel; Prayer to Afnin; Greeting to

Afnin. Parchment, 116 x 91 x 9 mm, ii + 16 folios, one column, 18 lines, Gəʿəz, twentieth century. EMML 1541.

IES 00443, Acts of Saint George, ገድለ ጊዮርጊስ; Two Miracles of Saint George, ተአምረ ጊዮርጊስ. Parchment, 182 x 174 x 48 mm, 80 folios, two columns, 17–18 lines, Gəʿəz, nineteenth century. EMML 1528.

IES 00444, Image of Mary, መልከአ ዘማርያም; Greeting to a Saint whose name is not filled in; Greeting to Saint Ḫətä Krəstos; Greeting to Ḫbäyä Dəngəl; Horologium for the Night, ስኣታት ዘሌሊት; Praise of the Beloved ascribed to Emperor Zärʾa Yaʿəqob, ስብሓተ ፍቁር. Parchment, 173 x 162 x 42 mm, vi + 93 folios, two columns, 18 lines, Gəʿəz, early seventeenth century and eighteenth centuries (composite). EMML 1529.

Miniatures:

1. F. i r(ecto): A man with a hand cross.

IES 00445, *Asmat* Prayers, ክታብ. Parchment, 157 x 11.5 cm, three strips, one column, Gəʿəz, nineteenth century. Copied for ወልደ ገብርኤል, erased and replaced with ገብረ ሥላሴ.

Miniatures:

- Three miniatures: (a) multi-box panel; (b) talismanic symbol; and (c) talismanic symbol.

IES 00446, *Asmat* Prayers, ክታብ. Parchment, 177 x 11 cm, three strips, two columns, Gəʿəz, nineteenth century. Copied for ወልደ ኢየሱስ.

Miniatures:

- Four miniatures: (a) angel with sword and scabbard; (b) multi-box panel; (c) ornate cross; and (d) talismanic symbol.

IES 00447, *Asmat* Prayers, ክታብ. Parchment, 171 x 11.5 cm, two strips, one column, Gəʿəz, nineteenth century. Copied by ወለተ ሙሴ.

Miniatures:

- Four miniatures: (a) angel with sword and scabbard; (b) talismanic symbol; (c) talismanic symbol; and (d) talismanic symbol.

IES 00448, *Asmat* Prayers, ክታብ. Parchment, 174 x 9 cm, three strips, one column, Gəʽəz, twentieth century. Copied for ጊፉት ሥላሴ ደስታ.

Miniatures:

- Two miniatures: (a) angel with sword and scabbard; and (b) King Solomon and a demon.

IES 00450, *Asmat* Prayers, ክታብ. Parchment, 167 x 11.5 cm, three strips, one column, Gəʽəz, twentieth century. Copied for ተጠምቀ መድኀን.

Miniatures:

- Three miniatures: (a) angel; (b) talismanic symbol; and (c) talismanic symbol.

IES 00451, *Asmat* Prayers, ክታብ. Parchment, 143 x 7 cm, three strips, one column, Gəʽəz, nineteenth century. Copied for ዓመተ ዮሐንስ.

Miniatures:

- Three miniatures: (a) ornate cross; (b) figure with arms uplifted; and (c) geometric design.

IES 00452, *Asmat* Prayers, ክታብ. Parchment, 172 x 8 cm, three strips, one column, Gəʽəz, nineteenth century. Copied for ወለተ መድኀን.

Miniatures:

- Three miniatures: (a) angel; (b) talismanic symbol; and (c) talismanic symbol.

IES 00453, *Asmat* Prayers, ክታብ. Parchment, 190 x 10.5 cm, four strips, two columns, Gəʽəz, twentieth century. Copied for ወለተ ማርያም, later replaced in some places with ወለተ ሚካኤል.

Miniatures:

- Four miniatures: (a) angel with sword and scabbard; (b) angel in frame surrounded by four angels; (c) talismanic symbol surrounded by four angels; and (d) talismanic symbol.

IES 00454, *Asmat* Prayers, ክታብ. Parchment, 202.5 x 13 cm, three strips, one column, Gəʽəz, nineteenth century. Copied for ወለተ ሚካኤል.

Miniatures:

- Four miniatures: (a) angel; (b) four eyes; (c) talismanic symbol; and (d) talismanic symbol.

IES 00455, *Asmat* Prayers, ክታብ. Parchment, 195 x 13 cm, two strips, one column, Gəʿəz, nineteenth century. Copied for ላህያ ድንግል, erased and replaced with ዓመተ ማርያም.

Miniatures:

- Three miniatures: (a) angel with sword and scabbard; (b) talismanic symbol; and (c) multi-box panel with face in center.

IES 00456, *Asmat* Prayers, ክታብ. Parchment, 170 x 9 cm, three strips, one column, Gəʿəz, nineteenth century. Copied for ወለተ ኪዳን, replaced with ወለተ ሚካኤል.

Miniatures:

- Four miniatures: (a) multi-box panel; (b) angel; (c) talismanic symbol; and (d) ornate cross.

IES 00457, *Asmat* Prayers, ክታብ. Parchment, 184 x 9 cm, three strips, one column, Gəʿəz, early twentieth century. Copied for አመተ ዮሐንስ በሃብታ.

Miniatures:

- Three miniatures: (a) angel with sword and scabbard; (b) ornate cross with figure on either side; and (c) Saint Susənyos killing Wərzəlya.

IES 00458, *Asmat* Prayers, ክታብ. Parchment, 111 x 12.5 cm, two strips, two columns, Gəʿəz, nineteenth century. Original name erased and replaced with ወለተ ብርሃን.

Miniatures:

- Two miniatures: (a) angel with sword and scabbard; and (b) two ornate crosses.

IES 00459, *Asmat* Prayers, ክታብ. Parchment, 156 x 5 cm, two strips, one column, Gəʿəz, late twentieth century. Copied for ንግሥቴ ንግሥት.

Miniatures:

- Three miniatures: (a) multi-box panel; (b) talismanic symbol; and (c) talismanic symbols.

IES 00460, Letters of *däǧǧazmač* Ḫaylä Maryam Lämma. Paper, 158 x 107 x 9 mm, i + 58 folios, one column, 17–31 lines, Amharic, 1915 EC = 1922–23. EMML 1539.

Miniatures:

1. F. 55v: Crude drawing of a figure and a face.

IES 00461, Fragments of the Four Gospels, አርባዕቱ ወንጌል. Parchment, 363 x 280 x 43 mm, 56 folios, two columns, 26–28 lines, Gəʿəz, fifteenth century.

IES 00462, Monastic Rules and Conduct. Parchment, 125 x 84 x 42 mm, ii + 135 folios, one column, 14 lines, Gəʿəz, twentieth century. EMML 1536.

Miniatures:

1. F. i v(erso): Gäbrä Mänfäs Qəddus.
2. F. ii r(ecto): Täklä Haymanot.
3. F. ii v(erso): Madonna and Child.
4. F. 135r: Saint George and the Dragon.

IES 00463, *Asmat* Prayers, ክታብ. Parchment, 61 x 39 x 10 cm, ii + 18 folios, one column, 13–15 lines, Gəʿəz, twentieth century.

IES 00464, Antiphonary for the Fast of Lent, ጾመ ድጓ. Paper, 188 x 129 x 34 mm, ii + 98 folios, two columns, 19 lines, Gəʿəz, nineteenth/twentieth century. EMML 1530.

IES 00466, Series of Gurage Poems, collected by P. Gabriele Sartori, Missionario Cappuccino di Trento. Paper, 330 x 220 x 7 mm, i + 44 folios, Italian, 1975.

IES 00467, Photocopy of manuscript of Senodos and the Law of the Kings, ፍትሐ ነገሥት. Paper, 333 x 221 x 51 mm, 449 folios, one column, 37 lines, Gəʿəz, twentieth century. EMML 1516.

IES 00468, Photocopy of Paris, Bibliothèque nationale de France, Eth. MS 302 containing the History of Galla, in Amharic. Paper, 333 x 221 x 57 mm, iii + 467 folios, one column, 22–23 lines, Amharic, nineteenth/twentieth century. EMML 1517.

IES 00469, Typed transcription of the Chronicle of Emperor ʿAmdä Ṣəyon, translated into Amharic by Yəkunno Amlak. Paper, 330 x 215 x 8 mm, i + 47 folios, one column, 40 lines, Amharic, twentieth century. EMML 1519.

IES 00470, Handwritten Transcription of the Chronicles of Emperors Zärʾä Yaʾəqob and Bäʿədä Maryam, translated into Amharic by Enbaqom Qalä Wäld. Paper, 330 x 215 x 8 mm, 51 folios, one column, 37–38 lines, Amharic, twentieth century. EMML 1519.

IES 00471, Homiliary of the Lifegiver, ድርሳነ ማኅየዊ; Litany, ሊጦን; Litany for Tuesday; Litany; One Miracle of Mary, ተአምረ ማርያም, The Five Dolors; Hymn to Jesus Christ. Parchment, 197 x 140 x 59 mm, vi + 130 folios, two columns, 17 lines, Gəʿəz, nineteenth/twentieth century. EMML 1525.

Miniatures:

1. F. ii v(erso): Equestrian saint, in pencil.
2. F. v r(ecto): A woman, in pencil.

IES 00472, Image of Saint George, መልክአ ጊዮርጊስ. Parchment, 85 x 74 x 9 mm, i + 27 folios, one column, 7 lines, Gəʿəz, late eighteenth century.

Miniatures:

1. F. 1r: Saint George is tortured with an ax (left).
2. F. 1v: Saint George, is impaled and tortured by a man with an ax.
3. F. 2r: A burning object (boiling lead?) is placed on Saint George.
4. F. 2v: Saint George is placed in boiling tar.
5. F. 3r: A stake is driven through the head of Saint George.
6. F. 3v: Saint George is strangled with ropes.
7. F. 4r: An individual worships an idol.
8. F. 4v: Saint George prays.

9. F. 5r: Saint George is forced to drink molten metal.
10. F. 5v: Saint George and the Dragon.
11. F. 6r: Two men torture Saint George with a wheel of knives.
12. F. 6v: Saint George stands before King Dadyanos.
13. F. 7r: Saint George raises the dead.
14. F. 7v: Saint George is fed poison.
15. F. 8r: Milk flows out from the cuts of Saint George.
16. F. 8v: Saint George is covered with stones.
17. F. 9r: Saint George is flogged.
18. F. 9v: Stakes are driven through the body of Saint George.
19. F. 10r: Saint George hears a warning from a messenger to recant.
20. F. 10v: Saint George is bound in prison.
21. F. 11r: Saint George and the Dragon.
22. F. 11v: Saint George binds the dragon.
23. F. 12r: Saint George is imprisoned and bound to stakes.
24. F. 12v: Saint George prays to God.
25. F. 13r: Saint George is burnt on a gridiron.
26. F. 13v: Saint George's skin is pierced with knives.
27. F. 14r: Saint George is crushed by a pillar.
28. F. 14v: Saint George prays in prison.
29. F. 15r: The Lord appears to Saint George in prison.
30. F. 15v: The Dragon and Birutawit.
31. F. 16r: Saint George is impaled.
32. F. 16v: Saint George is scorched.
33. F. 17r: Birutawit prays to the Lord.
34. F. 17v: Saint George is pierced by a pillar.
35. F. 18r: Saint George argues with two elders.
36. F. 18v: Saint George is bound to a stake.
37. F. 19r: Saint George is bound in a furnace.

38. F. 19v: Saint George is weighed down with tar on hands and feet and flogged.
39. F. 20r: Saint George is in prison.
40. F. 20v: Saint George is seated and robed in a cloak.
41. F. 21r: Three figures, wearing crowns, in a fire.
42. F. 21v: The beheading of Saint George.
43. F. 22r: The body of Saint George.
44. F. 22v: The Lamentation for Saint George.
45. F. 23r: The entombment of Saint George.
46. F. 23v: The Striking of the Head.
47. F. 24r: A weeping Mary.
48. F. 24v: Saint George is pierced with a stake.
49. F. 25r: Saint George is cut with a saw.
50. F. 25v: Mary grieves over the crucifixion.
51. F. 26r: A saint or patron stands to receive a blessing (unfinished drawing).

IES 00473, *Asmat* Prayers, ከታብ. Parchment, 150 x 5 cm, two strips, one column, Gəʿəz, late twentieth century. Space for a name was left blank.

Miniatures:
- One miniature: (a) angel.

IES 00474, *Asmat* Prayers, ከታብ. Parchment, 67 x 3.5 cm, one strip, one column, Gəʿəz, late twentieth century. Copied for ዋጋዬ.

IES 00475, *Asmat* Prayers, ከታብ. Parchment, 169 x 3 cm, six strips, one column, Gəʿəz, twentieth century. Copied for ውልቅቱ ጨሬ.

IES 00476, *Asmat* Prayers, ከታብ. Parchment, 93 x 4.7 cm, two strips, one column, Gəʿəz, early twentieth century. Copied for ገብረ ኢየሱስ ዳርጌ.

IES 00477, *Asmat* Prayers, ከታብ. Paper, 110 x 5 cm, five strips, one column, Gəʿəz, early twentieth century. Copied for ወልደ ማርያም.

IES 00478, *Asmat* Prayers, ከታብ. Parchment, 99 x 4.7 cm, two strips, one column, Gəʻəz, twentieth century. Copied for ገብረ ኢየሱስ ዳርጌ.

Miniatures:

- Two miniatures: (a) angel with sword and scabbard; and (b) talismanic symbol.

IES 00479, *Asmat* Prayers, ከታብ. Parchment, 54 x 2 cm, one strip, one column, Gəʻəz, twentieth century. Copied for ሮማን.

IES 00480, *Asmat* Prayers, ከታብ, includes Mystagogia, ትምህርተ ኅቡዓት, and other *Asmat* Prayers. Paper, 5.7 x 4.5 x.5 cm, ii + 27 folios, one column, 12 lines, Gəʻəz, twentieth century. No owner was mentioned.

IES 00481, *Asmat* Prayers, ከታብ. Parchment, 31 x 5.5 cm, one strip, one column, Gəʻəz, late twentieth century. Copied for ወልደ ጊዮርጊስ መላኩ.

Miniatures:

- One miniature: (a) talismanic symbol.

IES 00482, *Asmat* Prayers, ከታብ. Paper, 68 x 9.2 cm, one strip, one column, Gəʻəz, late twentieth century. Copied for መንገሻ.

Miniatures:

- One miniature: (a) angel.

IES 00483, *Asmat* Prayers, ከታብ. Parchment, 37.5 x 4 cm, one strip, one column, Gəʻəz, twentieth century. Copied for እልፉ.

Miniatures:

- One miniature: (a) talismanic symbol.

IES 00484, *Asmat* Prayers, ከታብ. Paper, 127.5 x 7.5 cm, three strips, one column, Gəʻəz, late twentieth century. Copied for ተክለ ጊዮርጊስ.

IES 00485, *Asmat* Prayers, ከታብ. Parchment, 77.5 x 5 cm, one strip, one column, Gəʻəz, late nineteenth century. Copied for ገብረ ኢየሱስ ዳርጌ.

Miniatures:

- One miniature: (a) multi-box panel.

IES 00486, *Asmat* Prayers, ከታብ. Parchment, 19 x 4.2 cm, one strip, one column, Gəʿəz, twentieth century. Copied for ገብረ ጊዮርጊስ የሿነው.

Miniatures:

- One miniature: (a) talismanic symbol.

IES 00487, *Asmat* Prayers, ከታብ. Paper, 32.5 x 11 cm, one strip, one column, Gəʿəz, late twentieth century. Copied for ጌትነት.

IES 00488, *Asmat* Prayers, ከታብ. Parchment, 63 x 3.3 cm, one strip, one column, Gəʿəz, late twentieth century. Copied for ጥሩነሽ አስካለ ማርያም.

Miniatures:

- One miniature: (a) table of letters.

IES 00489, *Asmat* Prayers, ከታብ. Parchment, 24.5 x 7.4 cm, one strip, one column, Gəʿəz, late twentieth century. Copied for ኃይለ ሥላሴ ኃይሉ.

IES 00490, *Asmat* Prayers, ከታብ. Parchment, 66 x 2 cm, one strip, one column, Gəʿəz, twentieth century. Copied for ወለተ ሚካኤል.

IES 00491, *Asmat* Prayers, ከታብ. Parchment, 140 x 5.5 cm, two strips, one column, Gəʿəz, twentieth century. Copied for ዓፀ ማርያም ወርቅነሽ.

Miniatures:

- Three miniatures: (a) Holy Trinity surrounded by the four Living Creatures; (b) angel with sword and scabbard; and (c) angel with sword and scabbard.

IES 00492, Collection of Prayers against Charms; Image of the Trinity, መልክአ ሥላሴ. Parchment, 135 x 91 x 24 mm, ii + 54 folios, one column, 14 lines, Gəʿəz, twentieth century. EMML 1537.

IES 00493, Amharic-Oromiffa Vocabulary. Paper, 166 x 110 x 12 mm, 76 folios, two columns, 18 lines, Amharic, Oromiffa, nineteenth/twentieth century. EMML 1538.

Miniatures:

1. F. 20r: Four birds.
2. F. 44r: Crude drawing of a figure.

3. F. 65r: Crude drawing of a figure.

4. F. 73v: Crude drawing of a figure.

5. F. 74r: Crude drawing of a figure.

6. Inside back cover: Crude drawing of a figure.

IES 00494, Manual for Telling the Future and *Asmat* Prayer. Paper, 161 x 107 x 10 mm, ii + 75 folios, one column, 18–19 lines, Gəʿəz, twentieth century. EMML1524.

IES 00495, Image of the Guardian Angel, መልአከ ዐቃቢ መልአክ; Greeting to the Guardian Angel. Paper, 124 x 77 x 8 mm, i + 21 folios, one column, 18 lines, Gəʿəz, early twentieth century. EMML 1540.

IES 00496, The Acts of the Holy Fathers and Brothers who dwelt at Däbrä Dammo; The History of Our Father Saint Stephen and all his Disciples. Parchment, 228 x 169 x 74 mm, ii + 154 folios, two columns, 24–25 lines, Gəʿəz, early sixteenth century. EMML 4.

Miniatures:

1. F. ii v(erso): Equestrian saint (drawing).

2. F. 153r: Crude drawing of an equestrian saint.

IES 00497, Abbreviated Antiphonary for the Whole Year, ድጓ; Collection of Chants called *Mästägabəʾ*, መስተጋብዕ; Collection of Chants called *Arbaʿət*, አርባዕት; Collection of Chants called *Śäläst*, ሠለስት; Collection of Chants called *Aryam*, አርያም. Parchment, 158 x 139 x 44 mm, ii + 83 folios, two columns, 17–18 lines, Gəʿəz, early nineteenth century. EMML 1534.

IES 00498, *Asmat* Prayers, አስታብ. Parchment, 158.5 x 6 cm, two strips, one column, Gəʿəz, twentieth century. Copied for ዘውዲቱ.

Miniatures:

- Three miniatures: (a) ornate cross; (b) angel; and (c) multi-box panel.

IES 00499, Image of Yəmrəḥannä Krəstos, and Praises of God, ውዳሴ አምላክ. Parchment, 68 x 67 x 16 mm, five strips, 297 cm long, 48 folios, one column, 7–10 lines, Gəʿəz, early twentieth century.

Miniatures:

1. F. 23v: Ornate cross.

IES 00500, *Asmat* Prayers, ክታብ. Parchment, 80.5 x 5.4 cm, one strip, one column, Gəʿəz, early twentieth century. Copied for ቪፈራው ገብረ ተክለሃይማኖት.

IES 00501, *Asmat* Prayers, ክታብ. Parchment, 120 x 3.8 cm, two strips, one column, Gəʿəz, twentieth century. Copied for ስለሺ.

Miniatures:

- Three miniatures: (a) angel with sword and scabbard; (b) angel with sword and scabbard; and (c) ornate cross.

IES 00502, *Asmat* Prayers, ክታብ. Parchment, 90 x 4.4 cm, two strips, one column, Gəʿəz, twentieth century. Copied for ወለተ ጻድቅ (ቦጋለች).

IES 00503, *Asmat* Prayers, ክታብ. Parchment, 146 x 3.8 cm, two strips, one column, Gəʿəz, twentieth century. Copied for ወርቃፈራሁ እንተማርያም.

Miniatures:

- One miniature: (a) multi-box panel.

IES 00504, *Asmat* Prayers, ክታብ. Paper, 203 x 6.5 cm, four strips, one column, Gəʿəz, twentieth century. Copied for ወለተ ጻድቅ ወርቂ (ወርቅነሽ).

Miniatures:

- Three miniatures: (a) angel with sword and scabbard; (b) talismanic symbol; and (c) ornate cross.

IES 00505, *Asmat* Prayers, ክታብ. Parchment, 123 x 3.5 cm, two strips, one column, Gəʿəz, twentieth century. Copied for አሥራተ ማርያም ከበበ.

IES 00506, *Asmat* Prayers, ክታብ. Parchment, 61.5 x 4.1 cm, one strip, one column, Gəʿəz, twentieth century. Copied for ተሲላ.

IES 00507, *Asmat* Prayers, ክታብ. Parchment, 55.5 x 5.4 cm, one strip, one column, Gəʿəz, twentieth century. Copied for ጸጌ ሐና.

Miniatures:

- One miniature: (a) three ornate crosses.

IES 00508, *Asmat* Prayers, ክታብ. Parchment, 70 x 4 cm, one strip, one column, Gəʿəz, twentieth century. Copied for የሽአራግ ወለተ ዮሐንስ.

Miniatures:

- One miniature: (a) three figures.

IES 00509, *Asmat* Prayers, ክታብ. Parchment, 90 x 3.9 cm, one strip, one column, Gəʿəz, twentieth century. Copied for ሰሎሞን ክፍለ ማርያም.

IES 00510, *Asmat* Prayers, ክታብ. Parchment, 118 x 3.4 cm, two strips, one column, Gəʿəz, twentieth century. Copied for ክበበ ፀሐይ.

IES 00511, *Asmat* Prayers, ክታብ. Parchment, 140.5 x 3.6 cm, two strips, one column, Gəʿəz, twentieth century. Copied for ገብረ ስንበት ኬራ.

Miniatures:

- One miniature: (a) x-shaped pattern.

IES 00512, *Asmat* Prayers, ክታብ. Parchment, 70 x 3.5 cm, one strip, one column, Gəʿəz, twentieth century. Copied for ገርጋሩ and ወልደ ዮሐንስ.

Miniatures:

- One miniature: (a) two figures.

IES 00513, *Asmat* Prayers, ክታብ. Parchment, 80 x 4.5 cm, one strip, one column, Gəʿəz, twentieth century. Copied for ዓስካለ ማርያም (ፋናየ).

Miniatures:

- Two miniatures: (a) ornate cross with a lamb surrounded by two snakes; and (b) talismanic symbol.

IES 00514, *Asmat* Prayers, ክታብ. Parchment, 134.5 x 5 cm, two strips, one column, Gəʿəz, twentieth century. Copied for ወለተ ጻድቅ (አሰለፈች).

Miniatures:

- One miniature: (a) ornate cross.

IES 00515, *Asmat* Prayers, ኪታብ. Parchment, 81 x 4 cm, one strip, one column, Gəʿəz, twentieth century. Copied for ወለተ ወልድ (ስመኝ).

Miniatures:

- Four miniatures: (a) figure; (b) talismanic symbol; (c) ornate cross; and (d) six figures.

IES 00516, *Asmat* Prayers, ኪታብ. Parchment, 62.3 x 52 cm, one strip, one column, Gəʿəz, early twentieth century. Copied for ወለተ ኪዳን አበበች.

Miniatures:

- One miniature: (a) talismanic symbol.

IES 00517, *Asmat* Prayers, ኪታብ. Parchment, 146 x 5 cm, three strips, one column, Gəʿəz, twentieth century. Copied for እትአለማሁ.

Miniatures:

- One miniature: (a) angel with sword and scabbard.

IES 00518, *Asmat* Prayers, ኪታብ. Parchment, 67.5 x 4.5 cm, one strip, one column, Gəʿəz, twentieth century. Copied by ጥላሁን ኃይለ ሥላሴ.

Miniatures:

- One miniature: (a) ornate cross.

IES 00519, *Asmat* Prayers, ኪታብ. Parchment, 138 x 5 cm, three strips, one column, Gəʿəz, twentieth century. The name ወለተ ወልድ (ወርቅነሽ) is added in a different ink.

Miniatures:

- One miniature: (a) ornate cross.

IES 00520, *Asmat* Prayers, ኪታብ. Parchment, 139 x 4 cm, two strips, one column, Gəʿəz, twentieth century. Copied for ወለተ ማርያም (ብዙዓለም).

Miniatures:

- Eight miniatures: (a) angel with sword and scabbard; (b) talismanic symbol; (c) talismanic symbol; (d) two-headed figure; (e) two snakes and a figure; (f) talismanic symbol; (g) cross; and (h) ornate cross.

IES 00521, *Asmat* Prayers, ካታብ. Parchment, 58.6 x 4.7 cm, one strip, one column, Gəʽəz, twentieth century. Copied for ኃፀ ማርያም.

IES 00522, *Asmat* Prayers, ካታብ. Parchment, 52 x 4.5 cm, two strips, one column, Gəʽəz, early twentieth century. Copied for ተክለ ሃይማኖት (ሸፈራው).

IES 00523, *Asmat* Prayers, ካታብ. Parchment, 190 x 4.7 cm, three strips, one column, Gəʽəz, twentieth century. Copied for ገብረ ኪዳን ንጉሤ.

IES 00524, *Asmat* Prayers, ካታብ. Parchment, 94 x 5 cm, two strips, one column, Gəʽəz, twentieth century. Copied for ወለተ ሥላሴ (ዝማነሽ).

Miniatures:

- One miniature: (a) talismanic symbol.

IES 00525, *Asmat* Prayers, ካታብ. Parchment, 173 x 8 cm, three strips, one column, Gəʽəz, twentieth century. Copied for ወለተ ማርያም (ማይተጌጢቱ).

Miniatures:

- Three miniatures: (a) three figures; (b) angel with sword and hand cross; and (c) talismanic symbol.

IES 00526, *Asmat* Prayers, ካታብ. Parchment, 73 x 4 cm, one strip, one column, Gəʽəz, twentieth century. Copied for ወልደ አግኑኤል.

IES 00527, *Asmat* Prayers, ካታብ. Parchment, 82 x 5 cm, one strip, one column, Gəʽəz, twentieth century. Copied for ኃፀ ማርያም.

IES 00528, *Asmat* Prayers, ካታብ. Parchment, 106 x 5 cm, two strips, one column, Gəʽəz, twentieth century. Copied for ዘውዲቱ (ዘውዬ).

IES 00529, *Asmat* Prayers, ካታብ. Parchment, 106 x 4.4 cm, two strips, one column, Gəʽəz, twentieth century. Copied for ወለተ ማርያም ቡላቂት.

IES 00530, *Asmat* Prayers, ካታብ. Parchment, 87 x 4.4 cm, one strip, one column, Gəʽəz, twentieth century. Copied for ኃይለ ማርያም (ኃይሉ).

Miniatures:

- Three miniatures: (a) ornate cross; (b) angel; and (c) ornate cross.

IES 00531, *Asmat* Prayers, ክታብ. Parchment, 70.5 x 4.6 cm, one strip, one column, Gəʿəz, twentieth century. Copied for አጸደ ማርያም (ሎሚ).

IES 00532, *Asmat* Prayers, ክታብ. Parchment, 60.5 x 5 cm, one strip, one column, Gəʿəz, twentieth century. Copied for ለማ ገብረ ጻድቅ.

Miniatures:

- One miniature: (a) ornate cross.

IES 00533, *Asmat* Prayers, ክታብ. Parchment, 180 x 5 cm, three strips, one column, Gəʿəz, twentieth century. Copied for ብዙነሽ ወለተ ማርያም.

Miniatures:

- Four miniatures: (a) geometric design; (b) angel; (c) ornate cross; and (d) person with a branch and a book.

IES 00534, *Asmat* Prayers, ክታብ. Parchment, 89.5 x 4.5 cm, one strip, one column, Gəʿəz, twentieth century. Copied for ወልደ ሰማዕት ከበደ.

Miniatures:

- Two miniatures: (a) multi-box panel; and (b) x-shaped pattern.

IES 00535, *Asmat* Prayers, ክታብ. Parchment, 64 x 4.4 cm, one strip, one column, Gəʿəz, twentieth century. Copied for ወለተ ዮሐንስ ባች አምላክ.

Miniatures:

- Four miniatures: (a) multi-box panel; (b) talismanic symbol; (c) talismanic symbol; and (d) multi-box panel.

IES 00536, *Asmat* Prayers, ክታብ. Parchment, 41 x 4.5 cm, one strip, one column, Gəʿəz, twentieth century. Copied for ቀነኒ ኃይለ ማርያም.

IES 00537, *Asmat* Prayers, ክታብ. Parchment, 166 x 6.5 cm, three strips, one column, Gəʿəz, twentieth century. Copied for አክሊሉ ገብረ ሚካኤል.

Miniatures:

- Four miniatures: (a) angel; (b) ornate cross; (c) ornate crosses; and (d) ornate cross.

IES 00538, *Asmat* Prayers, ካታብ. Parchment, 100 x 3.5 cm, two strips, one column, Gəʿəz, twentieth century. Copied for አስገዶች ጽጌ ማርያም.

Miniatures:

- Two miniatures: (a) angel; and (b) talismanic symbol.

IES 00539, *Asmat* Prayers, ካታብ. Parchment, 154 x 6 cm, two strips, one column, Gəʿəz, twentieth century. Copied for ተሾመ ተፈራ (አክሊለ ማርያም).

Miniatures:

- Three miniatures: (a) angel; (b) multi-box panel; and (c) ornate cross.

IES 00540, *Asmat* Prayers, ካታብ. Parchment, 94 x 3.4 cm, two strips, one column, Gəʿəz, twentieth century. Copied for ገብረ ወልድ ሞላ.

Miniatures:

- One miniature: (a) ornate cross.

IES 00541, *Asmat* Prayers, ካታብ. Parchment, 62 x 4 cm, two strips, one column, Gəʿəz, twentieth century. Copied for አስካለ ማርያም.

IES 00542, *Asmat* Prayers, ካታብ. Parchment, 121 x 4.5 cm, two strips, one column, Gəʿəz, twentieth century. Copied for በየነ ወልደ ሐዋርያት.

IES 00543, *Asmat* Prayers, ካታብ. Parchment, 105 x 5 cm, two strips, one column, Gəʿəz, twentieth century. Copied for ወለተ ሚካኤል.

IES 00544, *Asmat* Prayers, ካታብ. Parchment, 79 x 5 cm, two strips, one column, Gəʿəz, twentieth century. Copied for ክንፈ ገብርኤል.

Miniatures:

- One miniature: (a) three talismanic symbols.

IES 00545, *Asmat* Prayers, ካታብ. Parchment, 179 x 4.5 cm, three strips, one column, Gəʿəz, twentieth century. Copied for ከበደ (ገብረ ኢየሱስ).

Miniatures:

- One miniature: (a) ornate cross.

IES 00546, *Asmat* Prayers, ክታብ. Parchment, 194 x 5 cm, three strips, one column, Gəʽəz, twentieth century. Copied for ይግለጡ ተክለ ሥላሴ.

Miniatures:

- One miniature: (a) angel.

IES 00547, *Asmat* Prayers, ክታብ. Parchment, 84 x 5 cm, one strip, one column, Gəʽəz, twentieth century. Copied for ጠጋየ ገብረ ማርያም.

IES 00548, *Asmat* Prayers, ክታብ. Parchment, 120 x 6.5 cm, two strips, one column, Gəʽəz, twentieth century. Copied for ገብቶ ወለተ መድኅን.

Miniatures:

- Three miniatures: (a) talismanic symbol; (b) talismanic symbol; and (c) figure with arms uplifted.

IES 00549, *Asmat* Prayers, ክታብ. Parchment, 134.5 x 4.4 cm, two strips, one column, Gəʽəz, twentieth century. Copied for ብዙነሽ (ወለተ ሐና).

Miniatures:

- Two miniatures: (a) angel; and (b) multi-box panel.

IES 00550, *Asmat* Prayers, ክታብ. Parchment, 140 x 7 cm, two strips, one column, Gəʽəz, twentieth century. Copied for ታክለ (ኃይለ ሚካኤል).

Miniatures:

- One miniature: (a) multi-box panel.

IES 00551, *Asmat* Prayers, ክታብ. Parchment, 61 x 5 cm, one strip, one column, Gəʽəz, twentieth century. Copied for ወለተ ወልደ.

IES 00552, *Asmat* Prayers, ክታብ. Parchment, 139 x 5.5 cm, two strips, one column, Gəʽəz, twentieth century. Copied for አጽሞ ጊዮርጊስ, replaced with ጊታንህ ገብረ መድህን.

Miniatures:

- One miniature: (a) ornate cross.

IES 00553, *Asmat* Prayers, ክታብ. Parchment, 160 x 7.5 cm, three strips, one column, Gəʽəz, twentieth century. Copied for ድብሪቱ, replaced with ስመኝ.

Miniatures:

- Two miniatures: (a) angel with sword and scabbard; and (b) talismanic symbol.

IES 00554, *Asmat* Prayers, ክታብ. Parchment, 99 x 4.2 cm, two strips, one column, Gəʿəz, twentieth century. Copied for ጽጌ ማርያም አባት.

Miniatures:

- Two miniatures: (a) multi-box panel, and (b) talismanic symbol.

IES 00555, *Asmat* Prayers, ክታብ. Parchment, 209 x 5 cm, three strips, one column, Gəʿəz, twentieth century. Copied for ወልደ ተክለ ሃይማኖት ይንገሥ.

Miniatures:

- Seven miniatures: (a) angel with sword and scabbard; (b) ornate cross; (c) talismanic symbol; (d) talismanic symbol; (e) figure; (f) three birds; and (g) ornate cross.

IES 00556, *Asmat* Prayers, ክታብ. Parchment, 207.5 x 3.5 cm, three strips, one column, Gəʿəz, twentieth century. Copied for ወልደ ሚካኤል አያሌው.

IES 00557, *Asmat* Prayers, ክታብ. Parchment, 83 x 5 cm, one strip, one column, Gəʿəz, twentieth century. Copied for ወለተ ገብርኤል ኪዳኔ.

IES 00558, *Asmat* Prayers, ክታብ. Parchment, 105.5 x 4 cm, two strips, one column, Gəʿəz, twentieth century. Copied for ብርሃነ ሚካኤል, later replaced with ከንፈ ሚካኤል.

IES 00559, *Asmat* Prayers, ክታብ. Parchment, 136 x 4.8 cm, three strips, one column, Gəʿəz, twentieth century. Copied for አስካለ ማርያም, later replaced with ዓመተ ማርያም ወርቂቱ.

Miniatures:

- Two miniatures: (a) ornate cross of four faces; and (b) angel.

IES 00560, *Asmat* Prayers, ክታብ. Parchment, 173.5 x 5 cm, three strips, one column, Gəʿəz, twentieth century. Copied for እኅተ ማርያም.

Miniatures:

- Two miniatures: (a) talismanic symbol; and (b) talismanic symbol.

IES 00561, *Asmat* Prayers, ከታብ. Parchment, 213 x 9 cm, three strips, one column, Gəʿəz, twentieth century. Copied for ማርያም እናኑ.

Miniatures:

- Three miniatures: (a) ornate cross; (b) angel with sword and scabbard; and (c) talismanic symbol.

IES 00562, *Asmat* Prayers, ከታብ. Parchment, 59.5 x 5 cm, one strip, one column, Gəʿəz, twentieth century. Copied ጥላሁን ገብረ ሥላሴ.

Miniatures:

- One miniature: (a) cross.

IES 00563, *Asmat* Prayers, ከታብ. Parchment, 142 x 3.5 cm, two strips, one column, Gəʿəz, twentieth century. Copied for ወለተ ገብርኤል (ይሻረግ), in some places እንተ ገብርኤል (ይሻረግ).

Miniatures:

- One miniature: (a) ornate cross.

IES 00564, *Asmat* Prayers, ከታብ. Parchment, 139 x 4.5 cm, two strips, one column, Gəʿəz, twentieth century. Copied for አበበች ወለተ ሚካኤል.

IES 00565, *Asmat* Prayers, ከታብ. Parchment, 169 x 4.5 cm, three strips, one column, Gəʿəz, twentieth century. Copied for ወልደ ሚካኤል አያሌው.

Miniatures:

- Two miniatures: (a) geometric design; and (b) ornate cross.

IES 00566, *Asmat* Prayers, ከታብ. Parchment, 116 x 5 cm, two strips, one column, Gəʿəz, twentieth century. Copied for ጥላሁን ገብረ ሥላሴ.

Miniatures:

- Three miniatures: (a) ornate cross; (b) geometric design; and (c) talismanic symbol.

IES 00567, *Asmat* Prayers, ክታብ. Parchment, 48 x 4.5 cm, one strip, one column, Gəʿəz, twentieth century. Copied for ወለተ ማርያም (በቀለች).

IES 00568, *Asmat* Prayers, ክታብ. Parchment, 60 x 7 cm, one strip, one column, Gəʿəz, twentieth century. Copied for ዘነበች.

Miniatures:

- Two miniatures: (a) three talismanic symbols; and (b) ornate cross.

IES 00569, *Asmat* Prayers, ክታብ. Parchment, 147.5 x 4.7 cm, four strips, one column, Gəʿəz, twentieth century. Copied for ወለተ ሩፋኤል (አስናቀች).

Miniatures:

- Two miniatures: (a) cross; and (b) angel.

IES 00570, *Asmat* Prayers, ክታብ. Parchment, 188 x 5.3 cm, two strips, one column, Gəʿəz, twentieth century. Copied for አውላቸው ወልደ መድህን.

Miniatures:

- Twelve miniatures: (a) cross; (b) angel; (c) multi-box panel; (d) talismanic symbol; (e) multi-box panel; (f) geometric design; (g) geometric design; (h) angel; (i) ornate cross; (j) multi-box panel; (k) talismanic symbol; and (l) talismanic symbol.

IES 00571, *Asmat* Prayers, ክታብ. Parchment, 153 x 4.5 cm, two strips, one column, Gəʿəz, twentieth century. Copied for ቦጋለች (ወለተ ጸድቅ).

IES 00572, *Asmat* Prayers, ክታብ. Parchment, 143 x 4.3 cm, two strips, one column, Gəʿəz, twentieth century. Copied for ወለተ ማርያም (ሌንሴ).

Miniatures:

- Two miniatures: (a) geometric design; and (b) geometric design.

IES 00573, *Asmat* Prayers, ክታብ. Parchment, 73 x 4.5 cm, one strip, one column, Gəʿəz, twentieth century. Copied for ገብረ ማርያም ገብሬ, erased and replaced with ስይፈ ሥላሴ.

Miniatures:

- Two miniatures: (a) multi-box panel; and (b) talismanic symbol.

IES 00574, *Asmat* Prayers, ክታብ. Parchment, 50.3 x 5 cm, one strip, one column, Gəʽəz, twentieth century. Copied for ቀነኒ ኃይለ ማርያም.

IES 00575, *Asmat* Prayers, ክታብ. Parchment, 118 x 4.5 cm, two strips, one column, Gəʽəz, twentieth century. Copied for እሸቴ ገብረ ማርያም.

Miniatures:

- Two miniatures: (a) angel; and (b) geometric design.

IES 00576, *Asmat* Prayers, ክታብ. Parchment, 147.2 x 5.6 cm, three strips, one column, Gəʽəz, twentieth century. Copied for ጽጌ ማርያም.

IES 00577, *Asmat* Prayers, ክታብ. Parchment, 155.2 x 3.9 cm, three strips, one column, Gəʽəz, twentieth century. Copied for ወለተ ስንበት ደለደዋ.

Miniatures:

- Three miniatures: (a) angel; (b) angel; and (c) talismanic design.

IES 00578, *Asmat* Prayers, ክታብ. Parchment, 110 x 4 cm, three strips, one column, Gəʽəz, twentieth century. Copied for አጥናፉ ገብረ ሥላሴ.

IES 00579, *Asmat* Prayers, ክታብ. Paper, 191 x 5.7 cm, two strips, one column, Gəʽəz, twentieth century. Copied for ወለተ ሥላሴ.

Miniatures:

- Twelve miniatures: (a) multi-box panel; (b) multi-box panel; (c) multi-box panel; (d) multi-box panel; (e) ornate cross; (f) multi-box panel; (g) multi-box panel; (h) multi-box panel; (i) geometric design; (j) angel; (k) talismanic symbol; and (l) talismanic symbol.

IES 00580, *Asmat* Prayers, ክታብ. Parchment, 171 x 5.4 cm, three strips, one column, Gəʽəz, twentieth century. Copied for ገብረ ወልድ.

Miniatures:

- One miniature: (a) talismanic symbol.

IES 00581, *Asmat* Prayers, ክታብ. Parchment, 133 x 6 cm, two strips, one column, Gəʽəz, early twentieth century. Copied for ወለተ ጻድቅ አበበች.

Miniatures:

- Three miniatures: (a) talismanic symbol; (b) winged creature; and (c) talismanic symbol.

IES 00582, *Asmat* Prayers, ከታብ. Parchment, 43 x 3.8 cm, one strip, one column, Gəʿəz, twentieth century. Copied for ወልደ ማርያም በቲ.

Miniatures:

- One miniature: (a) talismanic symbol.

IES 00583, *Asmat* Prayers, ከታብ. Parchment, 61 x 7 cm, one strip, one column, Gəʿəz, twentieth century. Copied for ወለተ መድህን መንን.

IES 00584, *Asmat* Prayers, ከታብ. Parchment, 32.5 x 5.5 cm, one strip, one column, Gəʿəz, twentieth century. Copied for ወልደ ማርያም.

IES 00585, *Asmat* Prayers, ከታብ. Paper, 160 x 7.5 cm, five strips, one column, Gəʿəz, twentieth century. Copied for ኃብተ ማርያም ዬቃ.

Miniatures:

- Three miniatures: (a) talismanic symbol; (b) ornate cross of four faces; and (c) talismanic symbol.

IES 00586, *Asmat* Prayers, ከታብ. Parchment, 69.7 x 4.3 cm, one strip, one column, Gəʿəz, twentieth century. Copied for መስፍን አየለ.

IES 00587, *Asmat* Prayers, ከታብ. Parchment, 72.5 x 3.8 cm, one strip, one column, Gəʿəz, twentieth century. Copied for አሌሉዓፆየ ማርያም.

Miniatures:

- Two miniatures: (a) angel with sword; and (b) talismanic symbol.

IES 00588, *Asmat* Prayers, ከታብ. Parchment, 92 x 4.5 cm, one strip, one column, Gəʿəz, twentieth century. Copied for ደስታ ዓመተ ማርያም.

Miniatures:

- Two miniatures: (a) three figures; and (b) angel.

IES 00589, *Asmat* Prayers, ከታብ. Parchment, 197 x 5.3 cm, two strips, one column, Gəʿəz, twentieth century. Copied for በየኑ.

Miniatures:

- Two miniatures: (a) crosses and figures; and (b) three faces.

IES 00590, *Asmat* Prayers, ካታብ. Paper, 85 x 6.5 cm, one strip, one column, Gəʿəz, twentieth century. Copied for ከበደ.

IES 00591, *Asmat* Prayers, ካታብ. Parchment, 142 x 3.5 cm, two strips, one column, Gəʿəz, twentieth century. Copied for ወለተ ስንበት የብልጫ.

Miniatures:

- Two miniatures: (a) x-shaped pattern; and (b) x-shaped pattern.

IES 00592, *Asmat* Prayers, ካታብ. Parchment, 80 x 3.5 cm, one strip, one column, Gəʿəz, twentieth century. Copied for ጉቱ ገብረ ስንበት.

Miniatures:

- One miniature: (a) x-shaped pattern.

IES 00593, *Asmat* Prayers, ካታብ. Parchment, 84 x 4.8 cm, three strips, one column, Gəʿəz, twentieth century. Copied for ወለተ ተክለ ሃይማኖት አየለች.

Miniatures:

- Two miniatures: (a) talismanic symbol; and (b) multi-box panel.

IES 00594, *Asmat* Prayers, ካታብ. Parchment, 115 x 5.3 cm, two strips, one column, Gəʿəz, twentieth century. Copied for ወርቅአፈራሁ እገተ ማርያም.

Miniatures:

- Six miniatures: (a) three faces; (b) cross surrounded by two snakes; (c) three faces above a geometric design; (d) two faces; (e) talismanic symbol; and (f) geometric design.

IES 00595, *Asmat* Prayers, ካታብ. Parchment, 159.5 x 4.8 cm, three strips, one column, Gəʿəz, twentieth century. Copied for ከበበ ፀሐይ.

Miniatures:

- One miniature: (a) geometric design.

IES 00596, *Asmat* Prayers, ካታብ. Parchment, 131.3 x 4.3 cm, two strips, one column, Gəʿəz, twentieth century. Copied for እንተ ጊዮርጊስ ምንትዋብ.

IES 00597, *Asmat* Prayers, ካታብ. Parchment, 196.5 x 8 cm, three strips, one column, Gəʿəz, twentieth century. Copied for ዘውዲ.

IES 00598, *Asmat* Prayers, ካታብ. Parchment, 152 x 4 cm, two strips, one column, Gəʿəz, twentieth century. Copied for ወለተ ማርያም አበበች.

Miniatures:

- Two miniatures: (a) angel with sword; and (b) ornate cross.

IES 00599, *Asmat* Prayers, ካታብ. Parchment, 67 x 4.5 cm, one strip, one column, Gəʿəz, twentieth century. Copied for ተከልኝ.

Miniatures:

- One miniature: (a) three faces.

IES 00600, *Asmat* Prayers, ካታብ. Parchment, 152 x 5.3 cm, three strips, one column, Gəʿəz, twentieth century. Copied for ወለተ ሥላሴ ጥሩነሽ.

Miniatures:

- Two miniatures: (a) angel; and (b) multi-box panel.

IES 00601, *Asmat* Prayers, ካታብ. Parchment, 112 x 3.5 cm, two strips, one column, Gəʿəz, twentieth century. Copied for ታፈስ ኃይለ ኢየሱስ.

IES 00602, *Asmat* Prayers, ካታብ. Parchment, 137 x 4.2 cm, two strips, one column, Gəʿəz, twentieth century. Copied for በቀለች.

Miniatures:

- Five miniatures: (a) ornate crosses; (b) ornate crosses; (c) snakes; (d) talismanic symbol; and (e) snakes.

IES 00603, *Asmat* Prayers, ካታብ. Parchment, 158 x 5 cm, three strips, one column, Gəʿəz, twentieth century. Copied for ወለተ ማርያም ሻሼ.

Miniatures:

- Four miniatures: (a) talismanic symbol; (b) two angels; (c) three figures and three crosses; and (d) talismanic symbols.

IES 00604, *Asmat* Prayers, ክታብ. Parchment, 54 x 6.6 cm, one strip, one column, Gəʿəz, twentieth century. Copied for ጽጌ ማርያም.

IES 00605, *Asmat* Prayers, ክታብ. Parchment, 72 x 4.8 cm, two strips, one column, Gəʿəz, twentieth century. Original name erased and replaced with ገብረ ጻድቅ.

Miniatures:

- Two miniatures: (a) angel with sword and scabbard; and (b) talismanic symbol.

IES 00606, *Asmat* Prayers, ክታብ. Parchment, 103 x 7.5 cm, one strip, one column, Gəʿəz, twentieth century. Copied for ኃይለ ሚካኤል ተክለ.

Miniatures:

- One miniature: (a) talismanic symbol of four faces.

IES 00607, *Asmat* Prayers, ክታብ. Parchment, 57 x 7.3 cm, one strip, one column, Gəʿəz, twentieth century. Copied for አበበች.

IES 00608, *Asmat* Prayers, ክታብ. Parchment, 85 x 5 cm, three strips, one column, Gəʿəz, twentieth century. Copied for ቦጋለች አስካላ ሥላሴ.

Miniatures:

- Two miniatures: (a) three talismanic symbols; and (b) multi-box panel.

IES 00609, *Asmat* Prayers, ክታብ. Parchment, 68.7 x 4 cm, one strip, one column, Gəʿəz, twentieth century. Copied for ወልደ ትንግኤ and በግጹ አበቱ.

Miniatures:

- Two miniatures: (a) talismanic symbol; and (b) cross.

IES 00610, *Asmat* Prayers, ክታብ. Parchment, 84.5 x 5.8 cm, one strip, one column, Gəʿəz, twentieth century. Copied for አጸደ ማርያም ወርቅነሽ.

Miniatures:

- One miniature: (a) three crosses.

IES 00611, *Asmat* Prayers, ክታብ. Parchment, 19.5 x 5.8 cm, four strips, one column, Gəʽəz, twentieth century. Copied for ዓመተ ማርያም, erased and replaced with ወለተ ገብርኤል ዓለምነሽ.

Miniatures:

- Five miniatures: (a) talismanic symbols; (b) geometric design; (c) geometric design; (d) geometric design; and (e) multi-box panel.

IES 00612, *Asmat* Prayers, ክታብ. Parchment, 212 x 4.5 cm, three strips, one column, Gəʽəz, twentieth century. Copied for ወለተ ጸድቃ (ጸድቃን) እታለማሁ.

IES 00613, *Asmat* Prayers, ክታብ. Parchment, 89.5 x 4 cm, two strips, one column, Gəʽəz, twentieth century. Copied for አሥራተ ማርያም ክበበ.

Miniatures:

- One miniature: (a) multi-box panel.

IES 00614, *Asmat* Prayers, ክታብ. Parchment, 63.5 x 4 cm, one strip, one column, Gəʽəz, twentieth century. Copied for ገብረ ስንበት ገብሬ.

IES 00615, *Asmat* Prayers, ክታብ. Parchment, 64 x 4 cm, one strip, one column, Gəʽəz, twentieth century. Copied for ኃይለ ጊዮርጊስ.

Miniatures:

- One miniature: (a) talismanic symbol.

IES 00616, *Asmat* Prayers, ክታብ. Parchment, 154 x 4.3 cm, two strips, one column, Gəʽəz, twentieth century. Copied for ወለተ ጸድቅ አቻሽማነው.

Miniatures:

- One miniature: (a) angel above a multi-box panel.

IES 00617, *Asmat* Prayers, ክታብ. Parchment, 126.5 x 3.7 cm, two strips, one column, Gəʽəz, twentieth century. Copied for ወለተ መድገን እተነስ.

IES 00618, *Asmat* Prayers, ክታብ. Parchment, 41 x 6 cm, two strips, one column, Gəʽəz, twentieth century. Copied for እሴተ ማርያም.

Miniatures:

- Three miniatures: (a) geometric design; (b) geometric design; and (c) talismanic symbol.

IES 00618B, *Asmat* Prayers, ክታብ. Parchment, 36 x 4 cm, one strip, one column, Gəʿəz, twentieth century. Copied for ወለተ ማርያም በቀለች.

Miniatures:

- One miniature: (a) talismanic symbol.

IES 00619, *Asmat* Prayers, ክታብ. Parchment, 206.5 x 5.8 cm, three strips, one column, Gəʿəz, twentieth century. Copied for ኅፀ ማርያም ወርቅነሽ.

Miniatures:

- Six miniatures: (a) angel with sword and scabbard; (b) angel with sword and scabbard; (c) angel with sword and scabbard; (d) angel with sword and scabbard; (e) lamb with a cross surrounded by two snakes; and (f) angel with sword and scabbard.

IES 00620, *Asmat* Prayers, ክታብ. Parchment, 168 x 3.5 cm, three strips, one column, Gəʿəz, twentieth century. Copied for ተክለ ጊዮርጊስ ተክሉ.

Miniatures:

- Three miniatures: (a) multi-box panel; (b) ornate cross of four faces; and (c) talismanic symbol.

IES 00621, *Asmat* Prayers, ክታብ. Parchment, 213 x 8.3 cm, four strips, one column, Gəʿəz, early twentieth century. Copied for ወለተ ኪዳን.

Miniatures:

- Six miniatures: (a) multi-box panel; (b) angel with sword and scabbard; (c) angel with sword and scabbard; (d) talismanic symbol; (e) ornate cross of five faces; and (f) four crosses.

IES 00622, *Asmat* Prayers, ክታብ. Parchment, 116 x 6 cm, two strips, one column, Gəʿəz, twentieth century. Copied for ገብረ ጻድቅ.

Miniatures:

- One miniature: (a) cross.

IES 00623, *Asmat* Prayers, ክታብ. Parchment, 234 x 5.3 cm, four strips, one column, Gəʿəz, twentieth century. Copied for ገብረ ሐና ይማም.

IES 00624, *Asmat* Prayers, ክታብ. Parchment, 46.5 x 4.7 cm, one strip, one column, Gəʻəz, twentieth century. Copied for ወለተ ስንበት በሻዱ.

Miniatures:

- One miniature: (a) talismanic symbol.

IES 00625, *Asmat* Prayers, ክታብ. Parchment, 54 x 4.5 cm, one strip, one column, Gəʻəz, twentieth century. Copied for እሸቱ ገብረ ማርያም.

IES 00626, *Asmat* Prayers, ክታብ. Parchment, 46.7 x 5 cm, one strip, one column, Gəʻəz, twentieth century. Copied for አበበች ወለተ ማርያም.

IES 00627, *Asmat* Prayers, ክታብ. Parchment, 112.5 x 4.8 cm, two strips, one column, Gəʻəz, twentieth century. Copied for የሺ and ወለተ ማርያም is added in a later hand in blue ink.

IES 00628, *Asmat* Prayers, ክታብ. Parchment, 216.5 x 5.5 cm, three strips, one column, Gəʻəz, twentieth century. Original owner's name (ወልደ ሚካኤል?) is erased and replaced with ወለተ ማርያም.

Miniatures:

- Six miniatures: (a) multi-box panel; (b) multi-box panel; (c) multi-box panel; (d) ornate crosses; (e) ornate cross of four faces; and (f) crosses.

IES 00629, *Asmat* Prayers, ክታብ. Parchment, 134 x 5.3 cm, two strips, one column, Gəʻəz, twentieth century. Copied for ወለተ ሰማዕት አለማየሁ.

IES 00630, *Asmat* Prayers, ክታብ. Parchment, 83 x 5.8 cm, one strip, one column, Gəʻəz, twentieth century. Copied for ገብረ እግዚአብሔር.

Miniatures:

- Four miniatures: (a) ornate cross; (b) geometric design; (c) angel; and (d) talismanic symbol.

IES 00631, *Asmat* Prayers, ክታብ. Parchment, 144 x 4.3 cm, two strips, one column, Gəʻəz, twentieth century. Copied for አስበ.

IES 00632, *Asmat* Prayers, ክታብ. Parchment, 176 x 3.6 cm, two strips, one column, Gəʻəz, twentieth century. Copied for ወርቃፈራሁ እናተ ማርያም.

IES 00633, *Asmat* Prayers, ከታብ. Parchment and paper, 164 x 5.5 cm, four strips (three strips are parchment and one strip is paper), one column, Gəʿəz, twentieth century. Copied for ወለተ አረጋዊ.

IES 00634, *Asmat* Prayers, ከታብ. Parchment, 145 x 5.2 cm, two strips, one column, Gəʿəz, twentieth century. Copied for ታዮ ቀጸላ ጊዮርጊስ.

Miniatures:

- Two miniatures: (a) geometric design; and (b) talismanic symbol.

IES 00635, *Asmat* Prayers, ከታብ. Parchment, 175 x 4.6 cm, three strips, one column, Gəʿəz, twentieth century. Copied for ቱራ ገብረ ሚካኤል.

IES 00636, *Asmat* Prayers, ከታብ. Parchment, 98 x 4.6 cm, two strips, one column, Gəʿəz, twentieth century. Copied for አሰፋ ገብረ ሚካኤል.

IES 00637, *Asmat* Prayers, ከታብ. Paper, 167.5 x 5.5 cm, five strips, one column, Gəʿəz, twentieth century. Copied for ሙሉነህ ኃይለ መርያም.

Miniatures:

- Five miniatures: (a) three crosses; (b) three crosses; (c) geometric design; (d) geometric design; and (e) geometric design.

IES 00638, *Asmat* Prayers, ከታብ. Paper, 98 x 4.5 cm, two strips, one column, Gəʿəz, twentieth century. Copied for ወለተ ጊዮርጊስ ማሚተ.

Miniatures:

- Three miniatures: (a) talismanic symbol; (b) multi-box panel; and (c) geometric design.

IES 00639, *Asmat* Prayers, ከታብ. Parchment, 348.5 x 6.5 cm, six strips, one column, Gəʿəz, twentieth century. Copied for ወለተ መድህን መነን.

IES 00640, *Asmat* Prayers, ከታብ. Parchment, 98.2 x 8 cm, two strips, one column, Gəʿəz, nineteenth century. Copied for ፈለቀ ወልደ ሚካኤል.

Miniatures:

- Two miniatures: (a) cross; and (b) angel.

IES 00641, *Asmat* Prayers, ከታብ. Parchment, 11.8 x 11.8 cm, one strip, one column, Gəʿəz, twentieth century. Copied for ለማ.

IES 00642, *Asmat* Prayers, ኪታብ. Parchment, 137 x 5.2 cm, two strips, one column, Gəʿəz, early twentieth century. Copied for ኃጸ ማርያም ከቡሽ.

Miniatures:

- One miniature: (a) talismanic symbol surrounded by four faces.

IES 00643, *Asmat* Prayers, ኪታብ. Parchment, 53.5 x 5 cm, one strip, one column, Gəʿəz, twentieth century. Copied for ወለተ ሥላሴ ዝግነሺ.

Miniatures:

- Two miniatures: (a) multi-box panel; and (b) talismanic symbol.

IES 00644, *Asmat* Prayers, ኪታብ. Parchment, 58 x 2.7 cm, one strip, one column, Gəʿəz, twentieth century. Copied for ኃፀ ማርያም.

Miniatures:

- One miniature: (a) angel.

IES 00645, *Asmat* Prayers, ኪታብ. Parchment, 127 x 4.4 cm, two strips, one column, Gəʿəz, twentieth century. Copied for ተክለ ማርያም.

IES 00646, *Asmat* Prayers, ኪታብ. Parchment, 43.8 x 4.6 cm, one strip, one column, Gəʿəz, twentieth century. Name of patron is illegible.

Miniatures:

- Two miniatures: (a) three talismanic symbols; and (b) an angel with a sword.

IES 00649, *Asmat* Prayers, ኪታብ. Parchment, 65.5 x 4.1 cm, one strip, one column, Gəʿəz, twentieth century. Copied for ጽጌ ማርያም.

Miniatures:

- One miniature: (a) cross.

IES 00650, *Asmat* Prayers, ኪታብ. Parchment, 74 x 4.8 cm, one strip, one column, Gəʿəz, twentieth century. Copied for ጽጌ ማርያም.

Miniatures:

- Two miniatures: (a) cross; and (b) angel.

IES 00651, *Asmat* Prayers, ክታብ. Parchment, 159.7 x 5.7 cm, three strips, one column, Gəʿəz, late nineteenth century. Original name erased and replaced with ወለተ ማርያም ዘርጊ.

Miniatures:

- Two miniatures: (a) angel; and (b) talismanic symbols.

IES 00652, *Asmat* Prayers, ክታብ. Paper, 143 x 3.8 cm, one strip, one column, Gəʿəz, twentieth century. Copied for ወለተ ኤሊያስ ዛነበች.

Miniatures:

- Three miniatures: (a) talismanic symbol; (b) multi-box panel; and (c) talismanic symbol surrounded by four faces.

IES 00653, *Asmat* Prayers, ክታብ. Parchment, 130 x 5.5 cm, two strips, one column, Gəʿəz, twentieth century. Copied for አክሊሉ ሰማዕት.

IES 00654, *Asmat* Prayers, ክታብ. Parchment, 81.5 x 4.8 cm, one strip, one column, Gəʿəz, twentieth century. Copied for አየለች አስካላ ማርያም.

IES 00655, *Asmat* Prayers, ክታብ. Parchment, 142 x 4.8 cm, one strip, one column, Gəʿəz, twentieth century. Copied for የግሌ እንተ ገብርኤል.

Miniatures:

- Three miniatures: (a) angel with sword; (b) talismanic symbol; and (c) ornate cross.

IES 00656, *Asmat* Prayers, ክታብ. Parchment, 37 x 5.2 cm, one strip, one column, Gəʿəz, twentieth century. Copied for ልጅ ተክለ መድኃን and later replaced by ቄስ የሻነው አፈወርቅ.

Miniatures:

- Two miniatures: (a) cross; and (b) talismanic symbol.

IES 00657, *Asmat* Prayers, ክታብ. Parchment, 102.5 x 3 cm, one strip, one column, Gəʿəz, twentieth century. Copied for አርአያ ሥላሴ.

Miniatures:

- One miniature: (a) cross.

IES 00658, *Asmat* Prayers, ክታብ. Parchment, 49.2 x 6.3 cm, one strip, one column, Gəʿəz, twentieth century. Copied for ተክለ ወልድ ማሞ.

Miniatures:

- Three miniatures: (a) angel with sword and book; (b) ornate cross; and (c) geometric design.

IES 00659, *Asmat* Prayers, ክታብ. Paper, 95 x 4 cm, three strips, one column, Gəʿəz, twentieth century. Copied for ተረጨ አካለ ወልድ.

IES 00660, *Asmat* Prayers, ክታብ. Parchment, 34 x 4.7 cm, one strip, one column, Gəʿəz, twentieth century. Copied for ወለተ ሚካኤል.

IES 00661, *Asmat* Prayers, ክታብ. Parchment, 73 x 4.3 cm, one strip, one column, Gəʿəz, twentieth century. Copied for ዓመተ ማርያም.

Miniatures:

- One miniature: (a) talismanic symbol.

IES 00662, *Asmat* Prayers, ክታብ. Parchment, 161 x 11.5 cm, two strips, one column, Gəʿəz, twentieth century. Copied for ወለተ ሕይወት, ወለተ ሚካኤል, and ገብረ ሚካኤል.

Miniatures:

- Five miniatures: (a) three ornate crosses; (b) angel; (c) talismanic symbol; (d) ornate cross; and (e) five ornate crosses.

IES 00663, *Asmat* Prayers, ክታብ. Parchment, 195 x 11 cm, four strips, one column, Gəʿəz, twentieth century. Copied for ወለተ ቂርቆስ.

Miniatures:

- Three miniatures: (a) angel with sword; (b) talismanic symbol surrounded by four eyes; and (c) ornate cross.

IES 00664, *Asmat* Prayers, ክታብ. Parchment, 176.5 x 10 cm, three strips, one column, Gəʿəz, early twentieth century. Original name (ጸፈተ ሥላሴ?) is written over with the name ወለተ ተክለ ሃይማኖት.

Miniatures:

- Two miniatures: (a) ornate cross surrounded by four angels; and (b) cross with a figure on either side.

IES 00665, *Asmat* Prayers, ከታብ. Parchment, 168.5 x 9 cm, two strips, one column, Gəʿəz, late nineteenth century. Copied for ወልደ ኢየሱስ.

Miniatures:

- Three miniatures: (a) talismanic symbol; (b) talismanic symbol; and (c) talismanic symbol.

IES 00666, *Asmat* Prayers, ከታብ. Parchment, 135 x 9.5 cm, two strips, one column, Gəʿəz, early twentieth century. Copied for ጸምረ ቃል, ሣህለ ሥላሴ, and ገብረ ኤያቄም.

Miniatures:

- Three miniatures: (a) angel with sword and scabbard; (b) talismanic symbol; and (c) x-shaped pattern.

IES 00667, *Asmat* Prayers, ከታብ. Parchment, 186 x 11 cm, four strips, two columns, Gəʿəz, twentieth century. Copied for ገብረ መስቀል, ወለተ ማርያም, and ገብረ ሥላሴ.

Miniatures:

- Six miniatures: (a) angel with sword and scabbard; (b) talismanic symbol; (c) multi-box panel; (d) ornate cross; (e) two crosses; and (f) ornate cross.

IES 00668, *Asmat* Prayers, ከታብ. Parchment, 195 x 7 cm, three strips, one column, Gəʿəz, twentieth century. Copied for ገብረ ቂርቆስ and ገብረ ኢየሱስ.

Miniatures:

- Three miniatures: (a) talismanic symbol with a multi-box panel; (b) angel with sword and scabbard; and (c) geometric design.

IES 00669, *Asmat* Prayers, ከታብ. Parchment, 190 x 12 cm, two strips, one column, Gəʿəz, early twentieth century. Copied for ሰበን ጊዮርጊስ.

Miniatures:

- Three miniatures: (a) angel with sword and scabbard; (b) equestrian saint; and (c) talismanic symbol.

IES 00670, *Asmat* Prayers, ከታብ. Parchment, 188 x 11.5 cm, three strips, two columns, Gəʿəz, twentieth century. Copied for ወለተ ሕይወት and ወለተ ኪዳን.

Miniatures:

- Three miniatures: (a) angel with sword and scabbard; (b) angel with sword and scabbard; and (c) angel with sword and scabbard.

IES 00671, *Asmat* Prayers, ከታብ. Parchment, 158 x 9 cm, three strips, one column, Gəʿəz, twentieth century. Copied for ወለተ ስንበት.

Miniatures:

- Three miniatures: (a) angel with sword and scabbard; (b) talismanic symbol; and (c) ornate cross with a figure on either side.

IES 00672, *Asmat* Prayers, ከታብ. Parchment, 188 x 9.5 cm, three strips, one column, Gəʿəz, nineteenth century. Copied for ወለተ ጊዮርጊስ.

Miniatures:

- Three miniatures: (a) angel with sword; (b) talismanic symbol surrounded by four faces; and (c) ornate cross.

IES 00673, *Asmat* Prayers, ከታብ. Parchment, 175 x 10 cm, four strips, one column, Gəʿəz, twentieth century. Copied for ወለተ ኪዳን and ወልደ ማርያም.

Miniatures:

- Four miniatures: (a) multi-box panel; (b) talismanic symbol; (c) talismanic symbol; and (d) talismanic symbol.

IES 00674, *Asmat* Prayers, ከታብ. Parchment, 122 x 6.5 cm, two strips, one column, Gəʿəz, twentieth century. Copied for ገብረ ኢየሱስ.

Miniatures:

- Three miniatures: (a) angel with sword and scabbard; (b) talismanic symbol; and (c) ornate cross.

IES 00675, Book of Enoch, መጽሐፈ ሄኖክ, with marginal notes in Amharic. Paper, 211 x 143 x 13 mm, v + 85 folios, two columns, 21 lines, Gəʿəz, Amharic, nineteenth/twentieth century. EMML 1531.

IES 00677, History and hymns of Ezekiel, ዜና ሕዝቅኤል. Parchment, 288 x 234 x 10 mm, i + 12 folios, two columns, 25 lines, Gəʿəz, 1918.

IES 00679, Abbreviated Antiphonary for the Whole Year, ድጓ. Parchment, 212 x 164 x 43 mm, 78 folios, two columns, 26–37 lines, Gəʿəz, late fourteenth/early fifteenth century.

IES 00680, *Asmat* Prayers, ክታብ. Parchment, 195.5 x 8.5 cm, three strips, one column, Gəʿəz, twentieth century. Copied for ወለተ ኪዳን ድርጋ.

Miniatures:

- Three miniatures: (a) cross; (b) angel with sword and scabbard; and (c) talismanic symbol.

IES 00681, History of Ethiopia in Gəʿəz and Amharic, called here "The glory of kings," *Kəbrä Nägäśt*. The information for the first 50 pages comes from the *Kəbrä Nägäśt* and the *Mäṣḥafä 'Aksum*. Parchment, 265 x 211 x 44 mm, ii + 92 folios, two columns, 25 lines, Gəʿəz, Amharic, twentieth century. EMML 1515.

IES 00682, History of the Galla, the Invasion of Graññ and the Vision of Emperor Ləbnä Dəngəl, in Amharic; Chronicle of Emperor Tewodros by *däbtära* Zännäb. Paper, 300 x 220 x 12 mm, i + 69 folios, two columns, 31–32 lines, Amharic, twentieth century. EMML 1521.

IES 00683, History of Religious Controversies in Ethiopia, መጽሐፈ ነገረ ሃይማኖት; Commentary on the introductory rite to the Miracles of Mary, መጽሐፈ ሥርዓት. Parchment, 165 x 120 x 49 mm, vi + 62 folios, one column, 18–19 lines, Gəʿəz, early twentieth century. EMML 1533.

IES 00684, Photocopy of typed transcription of Brief history of Täklä Haymanot, king of Goǧǧam and Kaffa. Paper, 340 x 220 x 9 mm, ii + 22 folios, Amharic, twentieth century.

IES 00685, Amharic Poems by *aläqa* Ǝnbaqom Qalä Wäld. Paper, 345 x 228 x 10 mm, i + 87 folios, Amharic, 1965 EC = 1972. EMML 1520.

IES 00686, Gəʿəz Grammar, ሰዋስው፡ ግዕዝ; Mystery of the Sky, ምሥጢረ ሰማይ; The Gate of Belief, አንቀጸ አሚን; Miscellanea. Parchment, 180 x 115 x 39 mm, ii + 72 folios, ff. 1r–49v one column, ff. 50r–70v two columns, 21–28 lines, Gəʿəz, nineteenth/twentieth century. EMML 1535.

IES 00687, God Reigns, እግዚአብሔር ነግሠ (ነግሦ); Hymns from the Horologium, ኪሎሙ; Introductory Exhortations to the Miracles of Mary. Parchment, 112 x 109 x 52 mm, vi + 95 folios, two columns, 16 lines, Gəʿəz, seventeenth century. EMML 1542.

IES 00688, Photocopy of an unidentified twentieth century manuscript containing A History of the City of Dessie. Paper, 335 x 220 x 50 mm, i + 58 folios, one column, 31 lines, Amharic, twentieth century. EMML 1518.

IES 00690, Image of Mary, መልክአ ማርያም; Image of the Christian Sabbath, መልክአ ሰንበተ ክርስቲያን; Image of Phanuel, መልክአ ፋኑኤል. Parchment, 93 x 73 x 11 mm, 17 folios, one column, 15 lines, Gəʿəz, late nineteenth century.

IES 00691, History of Ethiopia gathered from different sources. Parchment, 255 x 185 x 65 mm, ii + 137 folios, two columns, 25 lines, Gəʿəz, nineteenth century. EMML 1527.

IES 00692, Hymn to Mary, "In heaven and on earth," በሰማይ ወበምድር; Canticle of Our Lady Mary (Luke 1:46–55); Praises of Mary, ውዳሴ ማርያም; Gate of Light, አንቀጸ ብርሃን. Parchment, 180 x 120 x 55 mm, 132 folios, one column, 11 lines, Gəʿəz, seventeenth/eighteenth century. EMML 1532.

IES 00693, History of Iyasu I (1682–1706). Parchment, 180 x 120 x 63 mm, ii + 66 folios, two columns, 15 lines, Gəʿəz, late nineteenth century. EMML 1584.

IES 00694, Treasure of Faith, መዝገበ ሃይማኖት. Parchment and paper, 200 x 170 x 32 mm, i + 48 folios, two columns, 14 lines, Gəʿəz, nineteenth/twentieth century. EMML 1568.

Miniatures:

1. F. i r(ecto): Crude drawing of figures.

2. F. 24v: Crude drawing of two faces.

3. F. 47r: Crude drawing of a figure.

IES 00695, Lectionary, ግጻዌ. Parchment, 150 x 120 x 42 mm, 78 folios, one column, 25 lines, Gəʿəz, early fifteenth. EMML 1571.

IES 00696, Chronicle of Emperor Mənilək II by *ṣäḥafe tə'əzaz* Gäbrä Śəllase Wäldä Arägay. Parchment, 255 x 200 x 85 mm, xviii + 341 folios, two columns, 19 lines, Amharic, twentieth century. EMML 1562.

IES 00697, Photocopy of a twentieth-century manuscript containing the Book of the Commemoration of the Savior of the World, መጽሐፈ ተዝካሩ ለመድኃኔ ዓለም. Paper, 214 x 334 x 12 mm, i + 91 folios, two columns, 17 lines, Gəʻəz, twentieth century. EMML 1553.

Miniatures:

1. F. i v(erso): The Crucifixion.

IES 00698, *Asmat* Prayers, አስማት. Parchment, 171.5 x 12 cm, three strips, two columns, Gəʻəz, twentieth century. Copied for አመተ ማርያም.

Miniatures:

- Three miniatures: (a) angel with sword and scabbard; (b) ornate cross with a figure on either side; and (c) ornate cross of figures.

IES 00699, Study notes of *aläqa* Kidanä Wäld Kəfle on Ethiopian Alphabet. Paper, 225 x 175 x 18 mm, 105 folios, one column, 17 lines, Amharic, 1934. EMML 1523.

IES 00700, Continuation of *aläqa* Kidanä Wäld Kəfle's study notes. Paper, 220 x 170 x 19 mm, 117 folios, one column, 24–25 lines, Amharic, 1942. EMML 1560.

IES 00701, Correspondence between a certain missionary of the Catholic church called *abba* Ǝndrəyas and Metropolitan Matewos on religious questions with the title "Debates of Mayofi (?) on faith." Paper, 210 x 165 x 10 mm, 47 folios, one column, 18–19 lines, Amharic, 1903. EMML 1561.

IES 00702, Treaties by *aläqa* Kidanä Wäld Kəfle on what he calls Orthodox Theology entitled "The Faith of the Earlier Fathers." Paper, 230 x 180 x 22 mm, i + 181 folios, one column, 23–24 lines, Amharic, 1935. EMML 1558.

IES 00703, Catechism of the Catholic Church, composed presumably by a foreigner. Paper, 235 x 175 x 20 mm, i + 161 folios, one column, 24 lines, Amharic, twentieth century. EMML 1559.

IES 00704, First draft of *aläqa* Kidanä Wäld Kəfle's Gəʿəz Grammar (Addis Ababa: Artistic Printing, 1948 EC = 1955–56). Paper, 230 x 175 x 40 mm, i + 356 folios, one column, 24 lines, Gəʿəz, Amharic, 1948 EC = 1955–56. EMML 1555.

IES 00705, First draft of *aläqa* Kidanä Wäld Kəfle's Gəʿəz Dictionary. Paper, 330 x 215 x 11 mm, 89 folios, one column, 33 lines, Gəʿəz, Amharic, 1927 EC = 1935. EMML 1557.

IES 00706A, Photocopy of twentieth-century manuscript containing the first part of an Amharic commentary on the Law of Kings, ፍትሐ ነገሥት. Paper, 305 x 218 x 13 mm, i + 102 folios, two columns, 31 lines, Amharic, twentieth century. EMML 1551.

IES 00706B, Photocopy of twentieth-century manuscript containing the second part of an Amharic commentary on the Law of Kings, ፍትሐ ነገሥት. Paper, 305 x 218 x 15 mm, i + 132 folios, two columns, 31 lines, Amharic, twentieth century. EMML 1550.

IES 00707, Autograph of The Traditional Church Education: The nature of the traditional church education in Ethiopia and the role played by the church in it, a study performed as part of the Bachelor of Theology degree earned at the Theological College, Addis Ababa University by ʿAlämayyähu Mogäs. Paper, 330 x 210 x 13 mm, iiv + 95 folios, one column, English, 1971.

IES 00708, Autograph of a work on Poetry by ʿAlämayyähu Mogäs. Paper, 340 x 223 x 20 mm, iii + 141 folios, one column, Amharic, 1968. EMML 1549.

IES 00709, Autograph of a work *Ḥaräg tərgwame* by ʿAlämayyähu Mogäs. Paper, 330 x 215 x 6 mm, ii + 52 folios, one column, Amharic, 1972. EMML 1554.

IES 00710, The writings of ʿAlämayyähu Mogäs (ten works). Paper, 334 x 220 x 12 mm, i + 6 folios, one column, Amharic, 1968. EMML 1556.

IES 00711, Language Teaching and Curricula in Traditional Education of the Ethiopian Orthodox Church. Departments of Ethiopian Languages and Literature, Faculty of Arts, Haile Selassie I University. A paper prepared for the Interdisciplinary Seminar of the Faculties of Arts and Education by ʿAlämayyähu Mogäs. Paper, 334 x 220 x 12 mm, ii + 16 folios, one column, English, 1972.

IES 00712, Three Chants of the Greek Orthodox Church for the feast days of Emperor Ḥaylä Śəllase. Translated into Gəʿəz under the title [Zəmmare] by ʿAlämayyähu Mogäs. Paper, 334 x 220 x 12 mm, 9 folios, one column, Gəʿəz, 1955. EMML 1556.

IES 00714, Amharic jokes of the famous [qəne] teacher Täkle of Wašära by ʿAlämayyähu Mogäs. Paper, 334 x 220 x 12 mm, 6 folios, one column, Amharic, 1941. EMML 1556.

IES 00715, The responsibility of the Church towards youth: A speech given at the conference of the *Haymanotä abäw* Association, [Miyazya 16, 1963 A.M.] by ʿAlämayyähu Mogäs. Paper, 334 x 220 x 12 mm, i + 8 folios, one column, Amharic, 1971.

IES 00716, A speech prepared for a youth organization in a rhyming composition by ʿAlämayyähu Mogäs. Paper, 334 x 220 x 12 mm, i + 12 folios, one column, Amharic, 1972.

IES 00717, Biography of *märigeta qes* Mogäs Däräso by ʿAlämayyähu Mogäs. Paper, 334 x 220 x 12 mm, i + 11 folios, one column, English, 1959 EC = 1967. EMML 1556.

IES 00718, Testimony to the fact that plants are medicine by ʿAlämayyähu Mogäs. Paper, 334 x 220 x 12 mm, i + 4 folios, one column, Amharic, 1963 EC = 1971. EMML 1556.

IES 00719, A critical review of M. Chaîne, *Grammaire éthiopienne* by ʿAlämayyähu Mogäs. Paper, 334 x 220 x 12 mm, ii + 24 folios, one column, English, 1961 EC = 1969. EMML 1556.

IES 00720, A collection of Gəʿəz and Amharic poems by ʿAlämayyähu Mogäs. Paper, 334 x 220 x 12 mm, 41 folios, one column, Gəʿəz, Amharic, ca. 1968–72. EMML 1556.

IES 00721, Excerpt from the Book of Isaiah; Book of Ezekiel, ዘሕዝቅኤል; Life of Ezekiel; 1 Maccabees, መጽሐፈ መቃብያን ቀዳማዊ (88r); 2 Maccabees, መጽሐፈ መቃብያን ካልዕ (143r); 3 Maccabees, መጽሐፈ መቃብያን ሣልስ (175r). Parchment, 200 x 155 x 80 mm, ii + 195 folios, two columns, 22 lines, Gəʿəz, late fifteenth/early sixteenth century.

IES 00722, Book of Jeremiah, ዘኤርምያስ (1r); Lamentations, ሰቆቃወ ኤርምያስ ነቢይ (61r and loose pages at the end of the codex); Baruch, መጽሐፈ ባሮክ (64v); Book of Ezekiel, ዘሕዝቅኤል (75r), incomplete at the end. Parchment, 230 x 190 x 17 mm, ii + 108 folios, two columns, 28 lines, Gəʽəz, late fifteenth century.

IES 00723, Thirty-Seven Miracles of Mary, ተአምረ ማርያም. Parchment, 210 x 154 x 54 mm, ii + 66 folios, two columns, 22–24 lines, Gəʽəz, sixteenth century. EMML 1573.

Miniatures:

1. F. ii v(erso): Madonna and Child.

IES 00724, Acts of *abunä* Tärbu, ገድለ አቡነ ተርቡ; Prayer of Ephrem the Syrian; Explanations of Jesus, ፍካሬ ኢየሱስ; Covenant of the Morning, ኪዳን ዘነግህ; Mystagogia, ትምህርተ ኅቡዓት. Parchment, 190 x 140 x 35 mm, iv + 38 folios, one column, 15 lines, Gəʽəz, eighteenth century. EMML 1569.

IES 00725, The Order of the Church, in Amharic; Prayer containing an interpretation of the letters of Hebrew alphabet; Chants concerning the resurrection of the dead; Image of the Guardian Angel, መልክአ ዐቃቤ መልአክ; Absolution of the Son, ፍትሐት ዘወልድ; Mystagogia, ትምህርተ ኅቡዓት; Covenant of the Morning, ኪዳን ዘነግህ; Prayer; Litany, ሊጦን; Anaphora of Our Lord, ቅዳሴ እግዚእ; Commentary on the opening Prayer, in Amharic; The Number of the Sufferings of Christ. Parchment, 150 x 95 x 48 mm, iv + 100 folios, ff. 1r–90v one column, ff. 91r–100v two columns, 16–18 lines, Gəʽəz, Amharic, eighteenth century. EMML 1570.

Miniatures:

1. F. 48r: Image of the Host.
2. F. 49v: Ornate cross with a figure standing on each side.
3. F. 50r: Cross with patterns extending from each corner.
4. F. 87v: Box filled with patterns of lines and circles.
5. F. 88v: Ornate cross with a figure standing on each side.
6. F. 89r: Box filled with geometric patterns.

IES 00726, Konso Dictionary, based largely on the dialects of Shako Otto of ólanta and Dinote Kusiya of Pátinkatto, and thus being representative of the speech of turayti in Eastern Konso in the area around Bakawlé, the capital of the then Konso wäräda by Paul Black and

Shako Otto. Paper, 340 x 220 x 31 mm, ii + 223 folios, one column, Konso, English, 1970.

IES 00727, Gidole Dictionary, based largely on the idiolects of Taye and Kusia Tolonge of šile in "Upper Gidole," to the immediate west of Gidole town by Paul Black. Paper, 330 x 220 x 19 mm, ii + 136 folios, one column, Gidole, English, 1970.

IES 00728, God Reigns, እግዚአብሔር ነግሠ (ነግሡ). Parchment, 140 x 100 x 80 mm, viii + 283 folios, two columns, 16 lines, Gəʿəz, twentieth century. EMML 1585.

IES 00729, Fragments from two manuscripts, bound as one. First work: Lessons on the Christian Religion; Second work: Beauty of Creation, ሥነ ፍጥረት; Five Pillars of Mystery, አምስቱ አዕማደ ምሥጢር. Parchment, 180 x 135 x 58 mm, 73 folios, two columns, 19 lines in first manuscript, 29 lines in second manuscript, Gəʿəz, nineteenth century.

IES 00730, Miracles of Mary, ተአምረ ማርያም; Rhyming homily of Emperor Zärʾa Yaʿəqob (1434–68) on the role of the Virgin Mary in our salvation, መጽሐፈ ጦማር. Parchment, 260 x 238 x 61 mm, iv + 117 folios, two columns, 19–20 lines, Gəʿəz, eighteenth century. EMML 1581.

Miniatures:

1. F. ii v(erso): The Striking of the Head.
2. F. iii v(erso): Madonna and Child.

IES 00731, Homiliary of the Lifegiver, ድርሳነ ማኅየዊ; Image of the Savior of the World, መልክአ መድኃኔ ዓለም; Image of Saint George, መልክአ ጊዮርጊስ; Hymn to Saint George, ነገረ ፊደላት ሳምን; Greeting to Saint George, ሰላም ለከ ጊዮርጊስ; Image of the Cross, መልክአ መስቀል. Parchment, 275 x 195 x 55 mm, iv + 100 folios, two columns, 21 lines, Gəʿəz, 1928 EC = 1936. EMML 1582.

Miniatures:

1. F. 70v: Italian card with print of Madonna and Child has been glued onto the folio.
2. F. 70v: Italian card with print of Jesus has been glued onto the folio.

IES 00732, *Asmat* Prayers, አስማት; Book of the Disciples, ነገረ አርድእት; One Miracle of the Trinity, ተአምረ ሥላሴ; Image of Täklä Haymanot, መልክአ ተክለ ሃይማኖት. Parchment, 240 x 175 x 51 mm, ii + 103 folios, two columns, 22 lines, Gəʿəz, twentieth century. EMML 1583.

IES 00735, Twenty-One Miracles of Aragawi, ተአምረ አረጋዊ. Parchment, 160 x 120 x 40 mm, ii + 50 folios, two columns, 17 lines, Gəʿəz, nineteenth century. EMML 633.

IES 00736, Order of Monastic Life, ሥርዓተ አሥረ መነኮሳት. Parchment, 135 x 118 x 39 mm, iv + 60 folios, two columns, 14 lines, Gəʿəz, late nineteenth century. EMML 634.

IES 00737, Horologium for the Night, ሰዓታት ዘሌሊት; Four Miracles of Mary, ተአምረ ማርያም; One Miracle of Saint George, ተአምረ ጊዮርጊስ; One Miracle of Jesus, ተአምረ ኢየሱስ. Parchment, 245 x 170 x 40 mm, iv + 66 folios, two columns, 22 lines, Gəʿəz, twentieth century. EMML 1572.

IES 00738, Psalter, ዳዊት; Psalter of the Virgin, መዝሙረ ድንግል. Parchment, 235 x 170 x 79 mm, iv + 225 folios, one column and two columns, 20 lines, Gəʿəz, 1939. EMML 708.

IES 00739, *Ziq* Chants, መጽሐፈ ዚቅ. Parchment, 145 x 115 x 35 mm, ii + 105 folios, one column, 17–21 lines, Gəʿəz, twentieth century. EMML 1595.

IES 00740, Calendar of the Feast Days of the Church Year; Gospel of John, ወንጌል ዘዮሐንስ; Genealogy of Ethiopian Monasticism; Litanical Prayer for the Seven Days of the Week, ሊጦን. Parchment, 165 x 110 x 38 mm, ii + 78 folios, two columns, 22 lines, Gəʿəz, nineteenth century. EMML 703.

IES 00741, Horologium for the Day, ሰዓታት ዘመዓልት; Horologium for the Night, ሰዓታት ዘሌሊት; One Miracle of Mary, ተአምረ ማርያም; One Miracle of Saint George, ተአምረ ጊዮርጊስ; One miracle of Gäbrä Mänfäs Qəddus; One Miracle of Jesus, ተአምረ ኢየሱስ; Greeting to the Church and to Saint Michael; Hymns to Saint Gabriel and Saint George; Hymns to the Virgin Mary. Parchment, 168 x 130 x 39 mm, ii + 93 folios, two columns, 21–28 lines, Gəʿəz, twentieth century. EMML 1593.

Miniatures:

1. F. i v(erso): Two images of the host, in pencil.
2. F. ii r(ecto): Image of the Host.
3. F. ii v(erso): Crude drawing of an angel, a figure, and faces.
4. F. 37r: Crude drawing of a figure.
5. F. 93r: Crude drawing of an angel.
6. F. 93v: Crude drawing of an angel and a figure.

IES 00743, Scriptural readings for the Night Hours for each day of the week. Parchment, 245 x 190 x 20 mm, i + 27 folios, two columns, 18–19 lines, Gəʿəz, 1930–74. EMML 1591.

IES 00744, Psalter, ዳዊት. Made in the Government Scriptorium. Parchment, 335 x 240 x 78 mm, iii + 186 folios, one column and two columns, 25 lines, Gəʿəz, twentieth century.

Miniatures:

1. Inside front cover: Photograph of *abunä* Yoḥannəs, archbishop of Ethiopia.
2. F. i v(erso): Ornate cross.
3. F. iii v(erso): Print of a Western Crucifixion painting.
4. F. 18r: Photograph of the "Governor" of Addis Ababa, *bitwäddäd* Wäldä Mäsqäl Tariku.
5. F. 186r: Print of "the future church at Kolfe".
6. Inside back cover: Photograph of *abunä* Abrəham, the first archbishop of Ethiopia.

IES 00745, Commentary on the Daily Prayer; Commentary on the Ten Commandments; Commentary on the Six Words of the Gospel; On the Trinity; Intercessory Prayer of Basil Bishop of Caesarea; Hymn to Mary, "Your Lamentation;" *Asmat* Prayer, አስማት; Personal Prayer of the Owner, *blatten geta* Maḫtämä Śəllase Wäldä Mäsqäl. Paper, 160 x 100 x 33 mm, ii + 258 folios, one column, 11–12 lines, Gəʿəz, Amharic, ca. 1929.

IES 00746, Commentary on the Horologium, written by *ṣäḥafe tä'äzaz* Wäldä Mäsqäl (Minister of Pen) in 1929 and copied in 1961. Parchment, 180 x 130 x 40 mm, iv + 131 folios, one column, 22–25 lines, Gəʿəz, 1961.

IES 00747, Daily Prayers (in Amharic); Praises of Mary (in Amharic), ውዳሴ ማርያም; At the Cross of Jesus Christ (in Amharic); Prayer for Mornings, Evenings, and Communion (in Amharic); Prayer of Ephrem the Syrian (in Amharic); Supplications and Intercession of Basil; Biblical Readings from Book of Hours (in Amharic); Table Prayer, "We beseech you," ሰአልናከ; Introduction to the Miracles of Mary (in Amharic and Gəʿəz); One Miracles of Mary, ተአምረ ማርያም; Praises of Mary, draft copy; Angels Praise Her, ይዌድስዎ መላእክት ለማርያም, belonging to *ṣäḥafe tä'äzaz* Wäldä Mäsqäl (Minister of Pen). Paper, 200 x 145 x 10 mm, i + 84 folios, one column, 30 lines, Gəʿəz, Amharic, twentieth century.

IES 00748, Commentary on Horologium written by *ṣäḥafe tä'äzaz* Wäldä Mäsqäl (Minister of Pen) in 1929. Paper, 205 x 145 x 20 mm, i + 142 folios, one column, 22 lines, Gəʿəz, 1929.

IES 00749, Book of Human Anatomy, belonging to *ṣäḥafe tä'äzaz* Wäldä Mäsqäl (Minister of Pen). Paper, 212 x 157 x 15 mm, i + 69 folios, one column, 21 lines, Amharic, twentieth century.

IES 00750, Copy of IES 745: Commentary on Daily Prayer; Commentary on the Ten Commandments; Commentary on the Six Words of the Gospel; On the Trinity; Intercessory Prayer of Basil Bishop of Caesarea; Hymn to Mary, "Your Lamentation;" *Asmat* Prayer, አስማት; Personal Prayer of the Owner, *blatten geta* Maḫtämä Śəllase Wäldä Mäsqäl. Parchment, 260 x 200 x 38 mm, iii + 114 folios, two columns, 17 lines, Gəʿəz, 1961.

IES 00751, Gospel of John, ወንጌል ዘዮሐንስ; Covenant of the Morning, ኪዳን ዘነግህ; Anaphora of Our Lady Mary attributed to Cyriacus of Bəhənsa, ቅዳሴ ማርያም. Parchment, 180 x 130 x 40 mm, ii + 91 folios, two columns, 15–21 lines, Gəʿəz, early twentieth century. EMML 1592.

IES 00752, Funeral Ritual, መጽሐፈ ግንዘት. Parchment, 265 x 185 x 77 mm, iv + 139 folios, two columns, 22–24 lines, Gəʿəz, early twentieth century. EMML 1152.

IES 00753, Missal, መጽሐፈ ቅዳሴ. Parchment, 252 x 185 x 70 mm, iii + 134 folios, two columns, 23–24 lines, Gəʿəz, nineteenth century. EMML 1153.

Miniatures:

1. F. ii r(ecto): Crude drawing of ornate crosses and a face.

2. F. 133v, bottom margin: Image of the Host, in blue ink.

3. F. 134r, right margin: Image of the Host, in purple ink.

4. F. 134v: Image of the Host, in pencil.

IES 00754, Gospel of John, ወንጌል ዘዮሐንስ; Anaphora of Our Lady Mary attributed to Cyriacus of Bəhənsa, ቅዳሴ ማርያም. Parchment, 150 x 97 x 42 mm, v + 104 folios, two columns, 17–20 lines, Gəʿəz, 1770–96. EMML 401.

Miniatures:

1. F. v r(ecto): Crude drawing of three angels with drawn swords.

2. F. v v(erso): John the Evangelist (fifteenth century?).

3. F. 101v: Drawing of a standing saint. Below, two figures battle.

4. F. 103v: Saint George and the Dragon (nineteenth century?).

5. F. 104r: Madonna and Child (nineteenth century?).

IES 00755, Collection of *Asmat* Prayers (ኣታብ), with magical squares and drawings. Parchment, 130 x 90 x 10 mm, i + 25 folios, one column, 16 lines, Gəʿəz, nineteenth century. EMML 1598.

Miniatures:

1. F. 8r: A lion.

2. F. 24r: Three ornate crosses.

IES 00756, Bandlet of Righteousness, ልፋፈ ጽድቅ. Parchment, 75 x 54 x 28 mm, ii + 24 folios, one column, 7–8 lines, Gəʿəz, twentieth century.

IES 00757, Greetings, Hymns, and glorifications for the Virgin Mary and the Saints for the hours. Parchment, 144 x 115 x 14 mm, i + 29 folios, one column, 11 lines, Gəʿəz, nineteenth/twentieth century. EMML 1596.

IES 00758, *Ziq* Chants, መጽሐፈ ዚቅ. Paper, 184 x 115 x 29 mm, 213 folios, one column, 16–17 lines, Gəʿəz, twentieth century. EMML 1594.

IES 00759, Miracles of Mary, ተአምረ ማርያም; Miracles of Jesus, ተአምረ ኢየሱስ. Parchment, 236 x 180 x 46 mm, i + 96 folios, two columns, 19 lines, Gəʿəz, twentieth century. EMML 933.

IES 00760, Horologium for the Night, ስኣታት ዘሌሊት. Parchment, 173 x 115 x 32 mm, ii + 68 folios, two columns, 17 lines, Gəʿəz, late nineteenth/early twentieth century. EMML 454.

IES 00761, Psalter, ዳዊት. Parchment, 172 x 112 x 48 mm, ii + 138 folios, one column and two columns, 24 lines, Gəʿəz, twentieth century.

Miniatures:

1. Inside front cover: Crude drawing of three figures.

IES 00762, Missal, መጽሐፈ ቅዳሴ, incomplete at the end. Parchment, 215 x 162 x 43 mm, 46 folios, two columns, 21 lines, Gəʿəz, 1889–1913. F. 30v mentions Emperor Mənilək II (r. 1889–1913). F. 31r mentions the Metropolitan P̣eṭros IV (r. 1881–1917) and the Metropolitan Matewos (r. 1889–1926). EMML 394.

Miniatures:

1. F. 2r: Crude drawing of an angel.
2. Ff. 8v–9r: The Twelve Apostles.

IES 00763, Psalter, ዳዊት; Greeting to the Savior of the World, ሰላም መድኃኔ ዓለም, incomplete at the end. Parchment, 197 x 130 x 56 mm, 142 folios, one column and two columns, 24 lines, Gəʿəz, twentieth century.

IES 00764, Image of Mary, መልክአ ማርያም; Image of Jesus, መልክአ ኢየሱስ; Hymn to the Virgin Mary; Image of Saint George, መልክአ ጊዮርጊስ; Greeting to the Saints; Horologium for the Night, ስኣታት ዘሌሊት. Parchment, 107 x 105 x 5 mm, 90 folios, two columns, 14 lines, Gəʿəz, nineteenth century. EMML 1597.

Miniatures:

1. F. 42v: Crude drawing of a figure with a crown.

IES 00765, Psalter, ዳዊት. Parchment, 146 x 100 x 60 mm, ii + 160 folios, one column and two columns, 23 lines, Gəʿəz, twentieth century.

Miniatures:
1. F. i v(erso): Crude drawing of a figure.
2. F. ii r(ecto): Crude drawing of a figure and a face.
3. F. ii v(erso): Ornate crosses.

IES 00766, Missal, መጽሐፈ ቅዳሴ. Parchment, 158 x 113 x 38 mm, v + 63 folios, two columns, 20 lines, Gəʿəz, 1930–74 (reign of Emperor Ḥaylä Śəllase). EMML 795.

IES 00767, History of Arero and Borana People, draft by Bäkurä Ṣəyon Ṭəlahun. Paper, 315 x 214 x 14 mm, i + 80 folios, one column, Amharic, 1966 EC = 1973–74.

IES 00768, Photocopy of History of Shoan Dynasty, draft. Paper, 335 x 222 x 18 mm, v + 118 folios, one column, Amharic, copied in 1959 EC = 1966–67.

IES 00770, Poetry of *aläqa* Ǝnbaqom Qalä Wäld, autograph. Paper, 348 x 212 x 10 mm, i + 31 folios, one column, Amharic, Gəʿəz, twentieth century.

IES 00772, List of Ethnological Objects at the Wollamo Sodu Regional Museum by Barbie and Bruce Van Meter. Paper, 330 x 217 x 6 mm, ii + 22 folios, English, 1969.

IES 00776, Gospel of John, ወንጌል ዘዮሐንስ. Parchment, 141 x 98 x 39 mm, iv + 102 folios, two columns, 14–16 lines, Gəʿəz, early twentieth century. EMML 799.

IES 00777, Two manuscripts bound together as one. First Manuscript (ff. 1–128): Sixty Miracles of Mary, ተአምረ ማርያም, written in the sixteenth century. Second Manuscript (ff. 129–41) Five Miracles of Jesus, ተአምረ ኢየሱስ, written in the sixteenth/seventeenth century. Parchment, 215 x 182 x 83 mm, iii + 139 folios, two columns, 19–23 lines, Gəʿəz, sixteenth/seventeenth century (composite). EMML 1692.

Miniatures:

1. F. ii r(ecto): Madonna and Child, flanked by two angels, Gabriel and Michael (fourteenth century).
2. F. ii v(erso): Empty Canon Tables.
3. F. iii v(erso): Madonna and Child.

IES 00778, Psalter, ዳዊት. Parchment, 185 x 127 x 52 mm, ii + 133 folios, one column and two columns, 25 lines, Gəʿəz, twentieth century.

Miniatures:

1. F. ii r(ecto): Crude drawing of a cross.
2. F. 133v: Crude drawing of a cross.

IES 00779, Gospel of John, ወንጌል ዘዮሐንስ. Parchment, 158 x 118 x 34 mm, iii + 92 folios, two columns, 19 lines, Gəʿəz, twentieth century. EMML 837.

IES 00780, Homiliary on the Sabbath of the Church, ድርሳነ ሰንበት. Parchment, 162 x 144 x 36 mm, iv + 42 folios, two columns, 16–17 lines, Gəʿəz, nineteenth century. EMML 624.

IES 00781, Psalter, ዳዊት. Parchment, 156 x 110 x 45 mm, ii + 99 folios, one column and two columns, 28 lines, Gəʿəz, nineteenth century. EMML 592.

IES 00782, Horologium for the Night, ሰዓታት ዘሌሊት; Book of the Jar, መጽሐፈ ቄደር; Book of the Pearl of Great Price, መጽሐፈ ባሕረይ; Image of Jesus, መልክአ ኢየሱስ; Hymn to Mary, "I Worship Thee"; One Miracle of Mary, ተአምረ ማርያም; Hymn to Mary, "I Praise Thy Grace"; Image of Mary, መልክአ ማርያም; Lament of the Virgin, ሰቆቃወ ድንግል; Image of the Assumption, መልክአ ፍልሰታ ለማርያም; Image of Saint George, መልክአ ጊዮርጊስ; Image of My Lady Mary, መልክአ እግዝእትየ ማርያም; Image of Gälawdewos (Claudius), መልክአ ገላውዴዎስ; Image of the Praises of Mary, መልክአ ውዳሴ ማርያም; Image of the Gate of Light, መልክአ አንቀጸ ብርሃን; Image of Arägawi/Zä-Mika'el, መልክአ አረጋዊ /ዘሚካኤል. Parchment, 166 x 140 x 59 mm, iv + 95 folios, two columns, 18 lines, Gəʿəz, seventeenth/eighteenth century. EMML 625.

Catalogue of the Manuscripts 113

IES 00783, Gospel of Mark, ወንጌል ዘማርቆስ. Parchment, 196 x 179 x 45 mm, 46 folios, two columns, 18 lines, Gəʽəz, seventeenth/eighteenth century. EMML 622.

IES 00784, Psalter, ዳዊት. Parchment, 110 x 78 x 65 mm, vi + 192 folios, one column and two columns, 22–23 lines, Gəʽəz, early twentieth century.

Miniatures:

1. F. 190v: Crude drawing of a bird.

2. F. 191r: Crude drawing of a bird.

3. F. 192r: Crude drawing of a figure with a sword and scabbard.

4. F. 192v: Crude drawing of two faces.

IES 00785, Book of Spiritual Healing, መጽሐፈ ፈውስ መንፈሳዊ. Parchment, 172 x 118 x 26 mm, 39 folios, two columns, 22–23 lines, Gəʽəz, early twentieth century. The manuscript has been foliated with numbers stamped in blue ink in the lower right corner and in the upper right corner of the recto side of the folios, just as though it were an EMML manuscript.

IES 00786, Canticle of the Flower, ማኅሌተ ጽጌ; Anaphora of Our Lady Mary attributed to Cyriacus of Bəhənsa, ቅዳሴ ማርያም; Image of Elijah, መልክአ ኤልያስ. Parchment, 160 x 110 x 30 mm, iii + 60 folios, one column, 19–21 lines, Gəʽəz, 1889–1926 (f. 42r mentions the Alexandrian Patriarch Cyril V [1874–1927] and the Metropolitan Matewos [1889–1926]).

Miniatures:

1. F. i v(erso): Crude drawing of a figure.

2. F. ii r(ecto): Crude drawing of angels.

3. F. iii r(ecto): Crude drawing of a face.

IES 00787, Commentary on the Octateuch, in Amharic; Commentary on the Book of Jubilees, in Amharic; Commentary on the Book of Enoch, in Amharic; Commentary on Isaiah, in Amharic. Parchment, 210 x 168 x 62 mm, iii + 237 folios, two columns, 34–38 lines, Amharic, Gəʽəz, 1902 EC = 1910. EMML 1694.

IES 00788, Commentary on 1–4 Kings, in Amharic; Commentary on Ecclesiasticus, in Amharic; Commentary on 1–2 Chronicles, in Amharic; Treatise on the Trinity and the Incarnation, in Amharic; Commentary on 1–3 Maccabees, in Amharic; Commentary on 2 Ezra; Commentary on the Book of Jubilees; Commentary on 1–2 Chronicles; Commentary on Jeremiah; Commentary on 1–3 Kings; Computus, ባሀረ ኅሳብ; Commentary on the Anaphora, in Amharic. Parchment, 210 x 164 x 62 mm, ii + 208 folios, two columns, 36–48 lines, Amharic, Gəʿəz, 1865–1913 (f. 72b mentions Mənilək II). EMML 1693.

IES 00789, Book of Sirach, መጽሐፈ ሲራክ. Parchment, 182 x 145 x 34 mm, ii + 55 folios, two columns, 24–27 lines, Gəʿəz, nineteenth century. EMML 1696.

IES 00790, Harp of Praise, አርጋኖ ውዳሴ. Parchment, 163 x 159 x 52 mm, i + 117 folios, two columns, 16 lines, Gəʿəz, seventeenth/eighteenth century. EMML 1697.

IES 00791, Epistles of Paul, መልእክታተ ጳውሎስ; Catholic Epistles, ሰብዓቱ መልእክታት; Revelation, ራእየ ዮሐንስ; Covenant of the Morning, ኪዳን ዘነግህ; Mystagogia, ትምህርተ ኅቡዓት. Parchment, 184 x 160 x 70 mm, iii + 133 folios, two columns, 21 lines, Gəʿəz, seventeenth century. EMML 1695.

IES 00792, Mystagogia, ትምህርተ ኅቡዓት. Parchment, 515 x 364 x 1 mm, 1 folio, 3 columns, 80 lines, Gəʿəz, late nineteenth century.

IES 00793, Homiliary in Honor of the Archangel Michael, ድርሳነ ሚካኤል. Parchment, 256 x 196 x 40 mm, i + 66 folios, two columns, 23 lines, Gəʿəz, twentieth century.

Miniatures:

1. Inside front cover: Crude drawing of an angel.
2. F. i v(erso): Crude drawing of an angel.
3. 66v: Crude drawing of an angel, a cross, and a figure.
4. Inside back cover: Crude drawing of a figure.

IES 00795, Net of Solomon interspersed with biblical passages, መርበብተ ሰሎሞን. Parchment, 134 x 94 x 29 mm, ii + 68 folios, one column, 13 lines, Gəʻəz, twentieth century. EMML 461.

Miniatures:

1. F. 19r: Ornate cross.

IES 00796, Book of the Jar, መጽሐፈ ቀደር; Book of Confession, መጽሐፈ ኑዛዜ. Parchment, 132 x 128 x 35 mm, ii + 56 folios, two columns, 15 lines, Gəʻəz, seventeenth century. EMML 1699.

IES 00836, Photocopy of a late nineteenth-century manuscript containing letters between Metropolitan Matewos and *abba* Andreas, from the Catholic Church. Paper, 333 x 225 x 12 mm, ii + 40 folios, one column, 18–19 lines, Amharic, late nineteenth century.

IES 00837, Psalter, ዳዊት. Parchment, 219 x 160 x 93 mm, ii + 183 folios, one column and two columns, 20 lines, Gəʻəz, fifteenth century.

Miniatures:

1. F. 140v: "Image of Moses, the prophet."

2. F. 155r: King Solomon.

3. F. 164v: Madonna and Child.

IES 00838, Amharic Introduction to the antiphonaries, entitled, Order of the *Dəggwa* and Məʻraf; Antiphonary for the Whole Year, ዱን. Parchment, 318 x 247 x 66 mm, vi + 170 folios, three columns, 37 lines, Gəʻəz, early twentieth century. EMML 707.

Miniatures:

1. F. ii v(erso): King Gäbrä Mäsqäl and Yared.

2. F. v v(erso): Madonna and Child.

IES 00842A, Photocopy of negative images of excerpts of Bibliothèque nationale de France, Mondon-Vidailhet Collection, Eth. MS 300 containing Letters of Emperor Yoḥannəs IV (r. 1872–89); see IES 845B. Paper, 220 x 303 x 10 mm, iii + 19 folios, one column, 16 lines, Gəʻəz, 1868–89.

IES 00842B, Photocopy of negative images of Bibliothèque nationale de France, Mondon-Vidailhet Collection, Eth. MS 291 containing Chronicles of 1868–75. Paper, 220 x 303 x 10 mm, ii + 19 folios, one column, 16 lines, Gəʿəz, late nineteenth century.

IES 00844, Photocopy of negative images of Bibliothèque nationale de France, Eth. MS 302 containing "*Histores Des Galla, Part II*" by *aläqa* Teme. Paper, 220 x 303 x 12 mm, ii + 47 folios, one column, 32 lines, French, Gəʿəz, late nineteenth century.

IES 00845A, Photocopy of negative images of letters of *däǧǧazmač* Kaśa (eventually Emperor Yoḥannəs IV). Paper, 212 x 302 x 9 mm, i + 16 folios, one column, Gəʿəz, late nineteenth century.

IES 00845B, Photocopy of negative images of excerpts of Bibliothèque nationale de France, Mondon-Vidailhet Collection, Eth. MS 300 containing Letters of Emperor Yoḥannəs IV; see IES 842A. Paper, 220 x 305 x 9 mm, ii + 9 folios, one column, Amharic, late nineteenth century.

IES 00846, Photocopy of negative images of excerpts of Bibliothèque nationale de France, Mondon-Vidailhet Collection, Eth. MS 259 containing a "History of Kings Täklä Giyorgis and Yoḥannəs IV," የአጼ ተክለ ጊዮርጊስ እና የአጼ ዮሐንስ ታሪክ በአለቃ ለምለም by *aläqa* Lämläm. Paper, 220 x 303 x 13 mm, iii + 58 folios, one column, 19 lines, Gəʿəz, late nineteenth century.

IES 00849, The Biography of *ras* Gugsa Wäle by *grazmač* Asfaw Täsäma Wärqe. Paper, 215 x 170 x 10 mm, iv + 34 folios, one column, 22 lines, Amharic, 1967 EC = 1974–75.

IES 00852, Psalter, ዳዊት; Psalter of the Virgin, መዝሙረ ድንግል, written in two columns throughout. Parchment, 185 x 165 x 60 mm, iii + 141 folios, two columns, 21 lines, Gəʿəz, eighteenth century. EMML 2344.

Miniatures:

1. F. iii v(erso): Madonna and Child (drawing).

2. F. 33v: Equestrian Saints (drawing).

IES 00853, Homiliary on the Sabbath of the Church, ድርሳነ ሰንበት; Image of the Christian Sabbath, መልክአ ሰንበተ ክርስቲያን. Parchment, 213 x 150 x 30 mm, iv + 50 folios, two columns, 14–15 lines, Gəʿəz, late nineteenth century.

IES 00854, God Reigns, እግዚአብሔር ነግሠ (ነግሥ), ascribed to Zärʾa Yaʿəqob. Parchment, 95 x 89 x 40 mm, 80 folios, one column, 11 lines, Gəʿəz, late eighteenth century.

IES 00855, Funeral Ritual, መጽሐፈ ግንዘት. Parchment, 309 x 252 x 126 mm, ii + 226 folios, two columns, 20 lines, Gəʿəz, late nineteenth/ early twentieth century.

Miniatures:

1. F. ii r(ecto): Crude drawing of an angel.
2. F. ii v(erso): Crude drawing of a face.
3. F. 225v: Crude drawing of three angels.
4. F. 226r: Crude drawing of two talismanic symbols with faces in the center.

IES 00856, *Asmat* Prayers, አስማት; Excerpts from the Psalter, ዳዊት; Image of Mary, መልክአ ማርያም; Image of Jesus, መልክአ ኢየሱስ; Image of Michael, መልክአ ሚካኤል; Image of Gabriel, መልክአ ገብርኤል. Parchment, 120 x 84 x 38 mm, viii + 89 folios, ff. 1r–16r, 43r–87r one column, ff. 17r–42v two columns, 16–19 lines, Gəʿəz, early twentieth century.

Miniatures:

1. F. 31v: Talismanic symbols.
2. F. 32v: Talismanic symbol.

IES 00874, Collection of letters and notes related to Gəʿəz grammar; Ethiopian history by Kidanä Wäld Kəfle. Paper, 340 x 225 x 10 mm, 41 folios, Amharic, twentieth century.

IES 00876, Short Biography of *ras* Arʾaya, የትልቁ ራስ አርአያ አጭር የሕይወት ታሪክ. Paper, 320 x 205 x 2 mm, 5 folios, one column, 37 lines, Amharic, English, late twentieth century.

IES 00877, Inventory from Bägemdər and Səmen Provinces, በበጎምድርና ስሜን ጠ/ግዛት የቀረቡ. Paper, 290 x 210 x 3 mm, 7 folios, Amharic, late twentieth century.

IES 00879, A Historical Tragedy about Tewodros, **ቴፖድሮስ ታሪካዊ ትራጄዲትያትር**. Paper, 320 x 200 x 2 mm, 4 folios, Amharic, late twentieth century.

IES 00977, Prayer Book of the Catholic Church. Paper, 193 x 146 x 17 mm, i + 112 folios, one column, 20 lines, Amharic, Gəʿəz, twentieth century.

Miniatures:

1. F. 19v: Geometric patterns.
2. F. 21v: Flowers (drawing).
3. F. 24v: Ornate cross (drawing).
4. F. 33r: Geometric pattern made up of letters (drawing).
5. F. 36v: Flowers (drawing).
6. F. 38v: Flowers (drawing).
7. F. 42v: Flowers (drawing).

IES 00984, List of Gəʿəz Literature compiled by *aläqa* Gäbrä Mädḫǝn of Harar. Paper, 270 x 205 x 7 mm, ii + 41 folios, Amharic, 1947 EC = 1954–55.

IES 00985, Antiphonary for the Whole Year, **ድጓ**. Parchment, 187 x 120 x 60 mm, iv + 114 folios, two columns, 20–21 lines, Gəʿəz, twentieth century.

IES 00986, "Holy Gospel," Ethiopic New Testament given as gift from Prof. S. Chojnacki, printed edition with annotations in red ink. Paper, 209 x 163 x 45 mm, iv + 360 folios, one column, 24 lines, Gəʿəz, 1830 EC = 1837–38.

IES 00988, Fourteen Miracles of Mary, **ተአምረ ማርያም**; Nine Miracles of Jesus, **ተአምረ ኢየሱስ**. Parchment, 179 x 135 x 41 mm, ii + 56 folios, two columns, 15–16 lines, Gəʿəz, twentieth century.

Miniatures:

1. F. i r(ecto): Crude drawing of a figure.
2. F. ii r(ecto): Crude drawing of three faces.
3. Inside back cover: Crude drawing of a face and a cross.

IES 00989, Photocopy of EMML 630, an early eighteenth-century manuscript containing an Amharic Introduction to the Gospel of Matthew and a Commentary in Gəʻəz on the Gospel. A Harmony of the four gospels is apparently envisaged. Paper, 320 x 225 x 25 mm, ii + 126 folios, three columns, 22–29 lines, Amharic, Gəʻəz, early eighteenth century. EMML 630.

Miniatures:

1. F. 123r: An angel.

IES 00990, Cycle of Kings, ዐውደ ነገሥት, incomplete at the beginning and end. Parchment, 129 x 92 x 17 mm, 35 folios, one column, 35 lines, Gəʻəz, twentieth century. Single-slip maḥdär.

IES 00991, Book of Nablis, መጽሐፈ ናብሊስ; Book of Victory of Obedience, መጽሐፈ ጌራ መዊዕ; Image of the Victory of Obedience, መልክአ ጌራ መዊዕ; Image of Michael and Gabriel, መልክአ ሚካኤል ወገብርኤል; Image of Saint George, መልክአ ጊዮርጊስ; Hymn to Saint George, "O who is quick for help," አ ፍጡነ ረድኤት; Image of Mary of Zion, መልክአ ማርያም ጽዮን; *Asmat* Prayer of the Archangel Michael which is written on his left and right wings (often included in *Dersana Mikaʼel* in the month of Ḫədar); Image of Anne Mother of Mary, መልክአ ሐና እሙ ማርያም; Psalms 118–20; made in the Government Scriptorium. Parchment, 213 x 150 x 38 mm, iv + 80 folios, ff. 1r–66r two columns, ff. 67r–79r one column, 15 lines, Gəʻəz, twentieth century.

IES 00992, Book of Medicine, መጽሐፈ መድኃኒት. Parchment, 170 x 135 x 21 mm, iii + 48 folios, one column, 19–25 lines, Amharic, early twentieth century.

IES 00994, Five Pillars of Mystery (formerly belonging to a group of Jesuits), አምስቱ አዕማደ ምሥጢር. Parchment, 187 x 144 x 50 mm, iv + 116 folios, two columns, 17–18 lines, Gəʻəz, late nineteenth century. The manuscript has been foliated with numbers stamped in blue ink in the lower right corner and in the upper right corner of the recto side of the folios, just as though it were an EMML manuscript.

IES 00995, Gəʻəz Vocabulary and Grammar, ሰዋስው፡ ግዕዝ. Parchment, 130 x 110 x 39 mm, 76 folios, two columns, 14 lines, Gəʻəz, seventeenth/eighteenth century. EMML 1543.

IES 00996, Psalter, ዳዊት. Parchment, 171 x 122 x 68 mm, iv + 168 folios, one column and two columns, 21 lines, Gəʿəz, early twentieth century.

IES 00998, Biography of *ras* Gugsa Wäle, autograph by *grazmač* Asfaw Täsäma Wärqe. Paper, 290 x 210 x 15 mm, 129 folios, one column, Amharic, 1969 EC = 1976–77.

IES 00998A, Biography of *ras* Gugsa Wäle, typed by *grazmač* Asfaw Täsäma Wärqe. Paper, 330 x 215 x 5 mm, 23 folios, one column, Amharic, 1969 EC = 1976–77.

IES 00999, History of the Exile; with a preface by *blatten* Märsəʿe Ḥazän Wäldä Qirqos, autograph by Śahəle Täkaləñ. Paper, 350 x 250 x 16 mm, ii + 112 folios, one column, Amharic, 1945 EC = 1952–53. EMML 3766.

IES 00999A, History of the Exile, typed by Śahəle Täkaləñ. Paper, 300 x 215 x 15 mm, i + 201 folios, one column, Amharic, 1967 EC = 1974–75.

IES 00999B, History of the Exile, typed, second copy by Śahəle Täkaləñ. Paper, 303 x 215 x 25 mm, i + 201 folios, one column, Amharic, 1967 EC = 1974–75.

IES 01000, Biography of *däǧǧazmač* Tašomä Šänquṭ, የደጃዝማች ተሾመ ሸንቁጥ የሕይወት ታሪክ. Paper, 315 x 210 x 12 mm, ii + 55 folios, one column, Amharic, late twentieth century.

IES 01001, Book of Prayer of Peter, መጽሐፈ ጸሎት ኤጥሮስ. Parchment, 131 x 100 x 37 mm, iv + 60 folios, two columns, 16–19 lines, Gəʿəz, twentieth century.

Miniatures:
1. F. ii r(ecto): Crude drawing of a face.
2. F. iii r(ecto): Crude drawing of a figure.
3. F. iii v(erso): Crude drawing of the Crucifixion.

IES 01002, Book of Greetings to the Saints, ጸሎት በእንተ ተአምኖ ቅዱሳን. Parchment, 120 x 99 x 52 mm, i + 130 folios, one column, 9 lines, Gəʿəz, eighteenth century.

IES 01003, The Story of Mr. Insatiable and Mr. Vanity: It teaches what is Sufficient for Dignity and Life, ያቶ ምንም ላይበቃንና የአቶ በከንቱ ታሪክ ለሰው ማእርግና ኑሮ የሚበቃውን by *fitawrari* Deresa, ፊታውራሪ ዴሬሳ. Paper, 255 x 205 x 2 mm, i + 8 folios, one column, 25 lines, Amharic, late twentieth century.

IES 01004, Creation and Its Way: Natural Law, third book, ፍጡርና መንገዱ የተፈጥሮ ሕግ 3ኛ መጽሐፈ. by Kirubel Bäšah. Paper, 225 x 170 x 10 mm, 87 folios, one column, 17–18 lines, Amharic, late twentieth century.

IES 01011, Antiphonary for the Fast of Lent, ጾም ድጓ. Parchment, 227 x 205 x 48 mm, iii + 99 folios, three columns, 25 lines, Gəʽəz, nineteenth century.

Miniatures:

1. F. 98v: Crude drawing of two faces.

IES 01012, Harp of Praise, አርጋኖነ ውዳሴ. Parchment, 145 x 130 x 75 mm, ii + 164 folios, two columns, 17 lines, Gəʽəz, early nineteenth century.

Miniatures:

1. F. 160r: Crude drawings of crosses and figures.
2. F. 164v: Crude drawing of crosses.

IES 01013, Book of Praises (of the Trinity), መጽሐፈ ነገረ ውዳሴ; The Prayer of Mary at Golgotha, ጸሎተ እግዝእትነ ማርያም ዘሰኔ ጎልጎታ; excerpt from Computus, ባህረ ኅሳብ. Parchment, 140 x 106 x 54 mm, i + 109 folios, two columns, 13–15 lines, Gəʽəz, twentieth century.

IES 01014, *Zəmmare* Chants, ዝማሬ. Parchment, 170 x 120 x 40 mm, iii + 89 folios, two columns, 25–26 lines, Gəʽəz, twentieth century.

IES 01015, Miracles of Mary, ተአምረ ማርያም. Parchment, 172 x 125 x 34 mm, i + 48 folios, two columns, 19 lines, Gəʽəz, ninteenth century. EMML 839.

Miniatures:

1. F. 25v: Saint George and the Dragon.
2. F. 26r: Madonna and Child.
3. F. 26v: The Crucifixion.

IES 01016, Image of Lalibäla, መልክአ ላሊበላ; Image of Yəmrəḥannä Krəstos, መልክአ ይምርሃነ ክርስቶስ; Image of Näʾakkwəto Läʾab, መልክአ ነአኩቶ ለአብ. Parchment, 86 x 70 x 25 mm, ii + 40 folios, one column, 11 lines, Gəʿəz, nineteenth century. EMML 1548.

IES 01017, Book of Qerəllos, መጽሐፈ ቄርሎስ. Parchment, 280 x 236 x 48 mm, 114 folios, two columns, 28–29 lines, Gəʿəz, twentieth century.

IES 01018, Gəʿəz Grammar, ሰዋሰው፡ ግዕዝ. Parchment, 120 x 97 x 23 mm, 70 folios, one column, 30–36 lines, Gəʿəz, twentieth century. EMML 1544.

IES 01019, Book of Unction, መጽሐፈ ባህርይ; Book of Confession, መጽሐፈ ኑዛዜ. Parchment, 72 x 65 x 30 mm, i + 52 folios, one column, 10–11 lines, Gəʿəz, twentieth century. Amulet case.

IES 01020, *Asmat* Prayers of Angels, አስማት መላእክት; Image of the Guardian Angel, መልክአ ዑቃቤ መልአክ. Parchment, 76 x 62 x 16 mm, i + 25 folios, one column, 11–12 lines, Gəʿəz, twentieth century.

IES 01021, Excerpt from Book of Hours for the Night. Parchment, 110 x 98 x 49 mm, 73 folios, two columns, 12 lines, Gəʿəz, nineteenth century.

IES 01022, Theological treatise on the Trinity, ምሥጢረ፡ ሥላሴ. Parchment, 110 x 110 x 32 mm, 48 folios, two columns, 10 lines, Amharic, nineteenth century. EMML 635.

Miniatures:
1. F. 48v: Crude drawing of figures.

IES 01023, Five Pillars of Mystery, አምስቱ አዕማደ ምሥጢር. Parchment, 140 x 125 x 24 mm, 65 folios, two columns, 15 lines, Gəʿəz, nineteenth century.

IES 01024, Homiliary of the Savior of the World, ድርሳነ መድኃኔ ዓለም. Parchment, 200 x 157 x 50 mm, iv + 126 folios, two columns, 16 lines, Gəʿəz, twentieth century.

IES 01025, Homiliary in Honor of the Archangel Michael, ድርሳነ ሚካኤል. Parchment, 245 x 165 x 63 mm, i + 140 folios, two columns, 18 lines, Gəʿəz, twentieth century.

Miniatures:

1. F. i r(ecto): Crude drawing of a horse.

2. F. i v(erso): Crude drawing of a figure.

3. F. 70r: Crude drawing of an angel.

IES 01026, Psalter, ዳዊት. Parchment, 164 x 111 x 62 mm, iv + 142 folios, one column and two columns, 22–24 lines, Gəʿəz, twentieth century.

IES 01027, Psalter, ዳዊት. Parchment, 165 x 112 x 57 mm, iv + 127 folios, one column and two columns, 26–27 lines, Gəʿəz, nineteenth century.

Miniatures:

1. F. iii v(erso): King David playing the harp.

2. F. 126v: Saint George and the Dragon.

3. F. 127r: Madonna and Child.

IES 01028, Psalter, ዳዊት. Parchment, 238 x 175 x 79 mm, 137 folios, one column and two columns, 25 lines, Gəʿəz, late nineteenth century.

IES 01029, Image of Mary, መልክአ ማርያም; Image of Jesus, መልክአ ኢየሱስ; Image of Michael, መልክአ ሚካኤል. Parchment, 122 x 92 x 34 mm, iv + 54 folios, two columns, 13 lines, Gəʿəz, twentieth century.

IES 01030, Angels Praise Her, ይዌድሰዋ መላእክት ለማርያም; Psalter, ዳዊት. Parchment, 194 x 130 x 70 mm, iii + 178 folios, one column and two columns, 20 lines, Gəʿəz, twentieth century.

IES 01031, Prayer of the Covenant, ጸሎተ ኪዳን; Absolution of the Son, ፍትሐት ዘወልድ; Prayer, "For the sake of the peaceful holy things," በእንተ ቅድሳት ሰላማዊት; Mystagogia, ትምህርተ ኅቡዓት; Anaphora of Our Lord, ቅዳሴ እግዚእ; God of the Luminaries, እግዚአብሔር ዘብርሃናት. Parchment, 160 x 116 x 32 mm, ii + 51 folios, two columns, 11 lines, Gəʿəz, twentieth century.

IES 01032, Psalter, ዳዊት. Parchment, 207 x 142 x 54 mm, ii + 153 folios, one column and two columns, 23 lines, Gəʿəz, twentieth century.

IES 01033, *Mäwaśəʾət* Chants, መዋሥዕት, with musical notation. Parchment, 157 x 115 x 22 mm, 100 folios, two columns, 13–14 lines, Gəʿəz, twentieth century.

IES 01034, Missal, መጽሐፈ ቅዳሴ, with musical notation. Parchment, 154 x 45 x 63 mm, ii + 153 folios, two columns, 20 lines, Gəʿəz, regency of ləǧ Iyasu, 1913–16 (f. 36r).

IES 01035, Psalter, ዳዊት. Parchment, 184 x 128 x 70 mm, ii + 160 folios, one column and two columns, 21 lines, Gəʿəz, twentieth century.

Miniatures:

1. F. 159r: Crude drawing of crosses and figures.

2. F. 159v: Crude drawing of a face.

IES 01036, The Orthodox Faith, ርቱዕ ሃይማኖት. Parchment, 310 x 220 x 66 mm, ii + 177 folios, two columns, 28 lines, Gəʿəz, twentieth century.

IES 01037, *Ziq* Chants, መጽሐፈ ዚቅ, with musical notation, arranged for the days of the week. Parchment, 162 x 107 x 36 mm, iii + 103 folios, two columns, 18–21 lines, Gəʿəz, twentieth century.

IES 01038, Homiliary in Honor of the Archangel Michael, ድርሳነ ሚካኤል. Parchment, 198 x 145 x 46 mm, viii + 116 folios, two columns, 20 lines, Gəʿəz, late eighteenth century.

Miniatures:

1. F. 89r: Crude drawing of an angel.

2. F. 95r: Crude drawing of a figure.

3. F. 98v: Crude drawing of a figure.

IES 01039, Harp of Praise, አርጋኖነ ውዳሴ. Parchment, 166 x 151 x 97 mm, 182 folios, two columns, 14 lines, Gəʿəz, early eighteenth century.

Miniatures:

1. F. 179v: Crude drawing of an angel.

IES 01040, The Code of Kings, Part two: on secular matters, ፍትሐ ነገሥት ሥጋዊ. Paper, 352 x 241 x 86 mm, iii + 406 folios, two columns, 29–30 lines, Gəʿəz, early twentieth century.

IES 01041, Canticle of the Flower, ማኅሌተ ጽጌ; Harp of Praise, አርጋኖነ ውዳሴ. Parchment, 226 x 188 x 73 mm, iv + 179 folios, two columns, 15 lines, Gəʿəz, early nineteenth century.

Miniatures:

1. F. i r(ecto): Crude drawing of an angel.

IES 01042, Psalter, ዳዊት. Parchment, 210 x 150 x 56 mm, iv + 147 folios, one column and two columns, 22–23 lines, Gəʿəz, twentieth century.

IES 01043, Book of Hours, መጽሐፈ ሰዓታት. Parchment, 150 x 105 x 29 mm, ii + 44 folios, one column, 17–19 lines, Gəʿəz, early twentieth century.

IES 01044, Acts of Gäbrä Mänfäs Qəddus, ገድለ ገብረ መንፈስ ቅዱስ; Miracles of Gäbrä Mänfäs Qəddus, ተአምረ ገብረ መንፈስ ቅዱስ. Parchment, 238 x 175 x 50 mm, 80 folios, two columns, 20–21 lines, Gəʿəz, late nineteenth century.

IES 01045, Gospel of John, ወንጌል ዘዮሐንስ. Parchment, 155 x 110 x 36 mm, iv + 82 folios, two columns, 18 lines, Gəʿəz, late nineteenth century.

IES 01046, Psalter, ዳዊት. Parchment, 165 x 167 x 79 mm, 164 folios, one column and two columns, 18–19 lines, Gəʿəz, nineteenth century.

IES 01047, Psalter, ዳዊት. Parchment, 159 x 111 x 64 mm, iv + 159 folios, one column and two columns, 21 lines, Gəʿəz, twentieth century.

IES 01048, *Mäwaśəʾət* Chants, መዋሥዕት; Sections from School Chants called ክሥተት ዓርያም with musical notation. Parchment, 171 x 122 x 25 mm, i + 72 folios, ff. 1r–44v, 61r–62r, and 69r–71v two columns, ff. 46r–60r one column, ff. 64r–66v four columns, 14–18 lines, Gəʿəz, 1951–1970, mentions Patriarch Basəlyos (f. 41r) and Emperor Ḫaylä Śəllase (f. 41v).

IES 01049, Four Gospels, አርባዕቱ ወንጌል. Parchment, 324 x 260 x 97 mm, i + 142 folios, two columns, 24–27 lines, Gəʿəz, late sixteenth century.

Miniatures:

1. F. i v(erso): Matthew the Evangelist.
2. F. 43r: Madonna and Child.
3. F. 43v: Mark the Evangelist.
4. F. 72v: Luke the Evangelist.
5. F. 121v: John the Evangelist.

IES 01051, Image of Paraclete, መልክአ ጳራቅሊጦስ; Prayer of Mary at Golgotha, ጸሎተ እግዝእትነ ማርያም ዘሰነ ጎልጎታ; Image of Saint George "I Beseech You," መልክአ ጊዮርጊስ ተማኅፀንኩ; Image of Saint George "Greeting to Your Acts," መልክአ ጊዮርጊስ ሰላም ለጥንተ ገድልከ; Image of the Savior of the World, መልክአ መድኃኔ ዓለም. Parchment, 132 x 98 x 48 mm, iv + 102 folios, one column, 12 lines, Gəʿəz, twentieth century.

IES 01052, Image of the Passion of the Cross, መልክአ ሕማማተ መስቀል; *Asmat* Prayer against Charm, ጸሎት በእንተ መፍትሔ ሥራይ; Prayer of Peter, ጸሎተ ጴጥሮስ. Parchment, 127 x 80 x 35 mm, iv + 69 folios, one column, 15–16 lines, Gəʿəz, twentieth century.

Miniatures:

1. F. i v(erso): Crude drawing of a figure.

IES 01053, Book of Spiritual Healing, መጽሐፈ ፈውስ መንፈሳዊ. Parchment, 135 x 95 x 21 mm, ii + 22 folios, one column, 17–22 lines, Gəʿəz, twentieth century.

IES 01054, History of the Kings of Gamo, የጋሞ ታሪክ ነገሥት. Parchment, 125 x 92 x 2 mm, i + 8 folios, one column, 11 lines, Gəʿəz, twentieth century.

IES 01055, Gospel of John, ወንጌል ዘዮሐንስ; Anaphora of Our Lady Mary, ቅዳሴ ማርያም. Parchment, 235 x 165 x 56 mm, iv + 116 folios, two columns, 18 lines, Gəʿəz, 1889–1926 (mentions the Metropolitan Matewos [r. 1889–1926] and the Alexandrian Patriarch Cyril V [1874–1927] on f. 95r and 96r).

Miniatures:

1. F. i v(erso): A saint.

2. F. ii r(ecto): A saint.

3. F. ii v(erso): A saint holding a hand cross.

4. F. iii r(ecto): A saint holding a hand cross.

5. F. iii v(erso): A saint holding a hand cross.

6. F. iv r(ecto): A saint holding a hand cross.

7. F. iv v(erso): Madonna and Child.

8. F. 113r: The Crucifixion.

9. F. 113v: The Last Supper.

10. F. 114r: A saint holding a book.

11. F. 114v: A saint with legs crouched underneath him.

12. F. 115r: A saint holding a hand cross.

13. F. 115v: A saint holding a hand cross.

14. F. 116r: A saint holding a hand cross.

IES 01056, Book of the Disciples, መጽሐፈ አርድእት; Sword of Divinity, ሠይፈ መለኮት; God of the Luminaries, እግዚአብሔር ዘብርሃናት; Three Miracles of Mary, ተአምረ ማርያም; Image of Raphael, መልክአ ሩፋኤል. Parchment, 223 x 114 x 37 mm, 53 folios, one column, 19–20 lines, Gəʿəz, nineteenth century.

Miniatures:

1. F. 36r: God surrounded by the four Living Creatures.

2. F. 42v: Saint George and the Dragon.

3. F. 43r: Madonna and Child.

4. F. 53r: Raphael performs a miracle with two donors in proskynesis.

IES 01057, Gəʿəz Grammar, ሰዋሰው፡ ግዕዝ. Parchment, 122 x 92 x 27 mm, iii + 63 folios, one column, 15 lines, Gəʿəz, late nineteenth and twentieth century.

IES 01058, Gəʿəz Grammar, ሰዋሰው፡ ግዕዝ, Five Pillars, አምስቱ አዕማደ ምሥጢር. Parchment, 162 x 135 x 38 mm, ii + 48 folios, two columns, 19 lines, Gəʿəz, twentieth century.

IES 01064, Psalter, ዳዊት, incomplete. Parchment, 195 x 180 x 50 mm, ii + 115 folios, one column and two columns, 20 lines, Gəʿəz, eighteenth century.

Miniatures:

1. F. 87v: Crude drawing of a figure.

IES 01065, Collection of pictures from a manuscript of the Net of Solomon, መርበብተ ሰሎሞን. Parchment, 305 x 250 x 2 mm, 10 folios, two columns, 26 lines, Gəʿəz, nineteenth century.

Miniatures:

1. Talismanic symbols are on every folio.

IES 01066, Catechism, ትምህርተ ክርስትና. Paper, 170 x 105 x 2 mm, i + 27 folios, two columns, 25–26 lines, Gəʿəz, twentieth century.

IES 01067, *Asmat* Prayer against Charm, ጸሎት በእንተ ፍትሐተ ሥራይ. Parchment, 115 x 84 x 19 mm, ii + 40 folios, one column, 14 lines, Gəʿəz, twentieth century.

IES 01068, *Asmat* Prayer against an Enemy, ጸሎት በእንተ መግረሬ ፀር. Parchment, 111 x 78 x 13 mm, i + 25 folios, one column, 14 lines, Gəʿəz, early twentieth century. The manuscript has been foliated with numbers stamped in blue ink in the lower right corner of the recto side of the folios, just as though it were an EMML manuscript.

IES 01080, The Philosophy of Zärʾa Yaʿəqob by B.A. Turaev, ሐተታ ዘርዓ ያዕቆብ. Paper, 244 x 192 x 18 mm, i + 64 folios, one column, 25 lines, Gəʿəz, Russian, 1904.

IES 01081, Lectionary for Passion Week, ግብረ ሕማማት. Parchment, 410 x 328 x 121 mm, iii + 267 folios, three columns, 31 lines, Gəʿəz, twentieth century.

IES 01082, Net of Solomon, መርበብተ ሰሎሞን, *Asmat* Prayer Against Charm, ጸሎት በእንተ ፍትሐተ ሥራይ. Parchment, 150 x 108 x 35 mm, vi + 105 folios, one column, 15 lines, Gəʿəz, twentieth century.

Miniatures:

1. Talismanic symbols are found throughout the codex (ff. 11r, 14v–15v, 17rv, 18v–19r, 20rv, 22r–23v, 24v, 45v, 48r–49r, 51r, 52v–53v, 54v, and 56v–62v).

IES 01083, Mystagogia, ትምህርተ ኅቡዓት; Image of Saint George, መልክአ ጊዮርጊስ; Image of Michael, መልክአ ሚካኤል. Parchment, 115 x 95 x 9 mm, ii + 29 folios, one column, 14–15 lines, Gəʿəz, late twentieth century.

Miniatures:

1. F. 14v: An angel.

IES 01084, Anaphora of Our Lady Mary, **ቅዳሴ ማርያም**; Image of Mary, **መልክአ ማርያም**; Image of Jesus, **መልክአ ኢየሱስ**; Image of the Assumption, **መልክአ ፍልሰታ ለማርያም**. Parchment, 165 x 120 x 50 mm, ii + 92 folios, one column, 12 lines, Gəʿəz, early twentieth century.

IES 01085, Homiliary in Honor of the Archangel Michael, **ድርሳን ሚካኤል**. Parchment, 231 x 180 x 70 mm, iv + 109 folios, two columns, 22 lines, Gəʿəz, Seal of King Mikaʾel of Wollo (f. 108v) suggests a *terminus ad quem* of 1918.

Miniatures:

1. F. ii v(erso): Saint George and the Dragon.
2. F. iii r(ecto): Madonna and Child.
3. F. iv v(erso): Saint Michael defeats the devil (lower). A saint holds a Psalter (left).
4. F. 6r: The angel Michael delivers souls from the clutches of the devil in Gehena.
5. F. 7v: The Archangel Michael, enthroned.
6. F. 23r: The Archangel Michael above a scene where a saint, holding a rod with a fish and standing beside a ram, stands before a woman in a church.
7. F. 34v: Bahəran (rights) shows a letter to the archangel Michael on horseback.
8. F. 49r: The archangel Michael stands before the governor (seated left) in order to release captives.
9. F. 52v: How the archangel Michael raised the dead before the governor.
10. F. 77r: How the archangel Michael rescued Saint Euphemia.
11. F. 88v: Bahəran (rights) shows a letter to the archangel Michael on horseback.
12. F. 99r: God surrounded by the four Living Creatures.

IES 01087, Life and Miracles of Saint George, **ገድለ ጊዮርጊስ**. Parchment, 358 x 252 x 73 mm, iv + 180 folios, three columns, 24 lines, Gəʿəz, twentieth century.

IES 01089, Brief Study on Philosophy, መጠነኛ የፍልስፍና ጥናት ከእ. ተስፋ ሥላሴ ሞጎስ by A. Täsfa Śǝllase Mogäs. Paper, 290 x 210 x 5 mm, ii + 16 folios, one column, Amharic, late twentieth century.

IES 01125, Photographs of folios in a manuscript recording a gift of Four Gospels and of land on Säne 11, 1926 EC (= 1935) from Emperor Ḫaylä Śǝllase to Bar Kidanä Mǝḥrät Monastery, ለባር ኪዳነ ምሕረት ገዳም የተሰጠ ወንጌላና ርስት ጉልት መረጃ ሰነድ. Photo paper, 257 x 200 x 3 mm, 9 folios, two columns, Gǝʿǝz, late twentieth century.

IES 01126.1, History of the Oromo People, by *abbä* Baḥǝry, translated from Gǝʿǝz to Amharic by *blatten* Märsǝʿe Ḫazän Wäldä Qirqos in 1959 EC, ዜናሁ ለእባ ባሕርይ። ዘጸሐፈ በልሳነ ግዕዝ ከግዕዝ ወደ አማርኛ በብላታ መርስዔ ኀዘን ወልደ ቂርቆስ ተተረጐመ። by Abbä Baḥǝry. Paper, 335 x 225 x 10 mm, i + 49 folios, one column, 23 lines, Gǝʿǝz, 1959 EC (=1967).

IES 01126.2, History of the Oromo People, [lit. Galla], by *abbä* Baḥǝry, translated from Gǝʿǝz to Amharic by *blatten* Märsǝʿe Ḫazän Wäldä Qirqos in 1959 EC, copy 2, ዜናሁ ለእባ ባሕርይ። ዘጸሐፈ በልሳነ ግዕዝ ከግዕዝ ወደ አማርኛ በብላታ መርስዔ ኀዘን ወልደ ቂርቆስ ተተረጐመ። by Abbä Baḥǝry. Paper, 335 x 225 x 10 mm, i + 50 folios, one column, 23 lines, Gǝʿǝz, 1959 EC.

IES 01130, Catalogue of the Manuscripts of the Institute of Ethiopian Studies. Paper, 350 x 225 x 7 mm, 105 folios, one column, Gǝʿǝz, Amharic, English, twentieth century.

IES 01133, List of Gǝʿǝz Books, እስትግቡዕ ዘመጸሕፍተ ግእዝ by *blatten* Märsǝʿe Ḫazän Wäldä Qirqos. Paper, 280 x 220 x 5 mm, 32 folios, one column, 30 lines, Amharic, late twentieth century.

IES 01136, Book of History, መጽሐፈ ታሪክ. Paper, 335 x 210 x 18 mm, i + 107 folios, two columns, 27–28 lines, Gǝʿǝz, Amharic, mid-twentieth century.

IES 01137, Five Pillars, አምስቱ አእማደ ምሥጢር, called here Word of Faith, ቃለ ሃይማኖት. Parchment, 150 x 105 x 30 mm, 72 folios, one column, 20–21 lines, Gǝʿǝz, early twentieth century.

IES 01148, Sword of Divinity, ሠይፈ መለኮት; Image of Edom (incomplete), መልክአ ኤዶም. Paper, 112 x 79 x 2 mm, 22 folios, one column, 11 lines, Gǝʿǝz, twentieth century.

IES 01213, Proverbs, መጽሐፈ ምሳሌ; Ecclesiastes, መጽሐፈ መክብብ; Wisdom of Solomon, መጽሐፈ ጥበበ ሰሎሞን; Song of Songs, መኃልየ መኃልይ, a gift from Emperor Ḫaylä Śəllase to the Holy Trinity Theological College on Miyazya 3, 1953 EC (= 1960). Parchment, 250 x 170 x 42 mm, iv + 60 folios, two columns, 28 lines, Gəʿəz, 1920 EC = 1927–28.

IES 01214, Commentary on the Gospel of Matthew, from Gəʿəz to Gəʿəz, a gift of Bishop Marqos of Goǧǧam to Holy Trinity Theological College, ትርንጓሜ ማቴዎስ ግዕዝ በግዕዝ የተተረጎመ. Parchment, 290 x 225 x 93 mm, iv + 177 folios, two columns, 31 lines, Gəʿəz, Ḥamle 29, 1960 EC = 1967.

IES 01243, Log Book of Parchment (*Branna*) Income and Expense for the Government Scriptorium for the years 1934–57, የብራና ገቢና ወጪ. Paper, 315 x 220 x 15 mm, i + 151 folios, Amharic, 1934–57 EC = 1941–65.

IES 01255, Image of Gäbrä Mänfäs Qəddus, መልክአ ገብረ መንፈስ ቅዱስ; Image of Jesus, መልክአ ኢየሱስ; Image of the Christian Sabbath, መልክአ ሰንበተ ክርስቲያን; Image of Raphael, መልክአ ሩፋኤል. Parchment, 108 x 78 x 50 mm, ii + 94 folios, one column, 9 lines, Gəʿəz, early twentieth century.

Miniatures:

1. F. ii r(ecto): Printed card of Saint Sebastian is stitched to the folio.
2. F. 94r: Printed card of Madonna and Child is stitched to the folio.

IES 01256, Fragment of a Psalter (Pss 81–144), ዳዊት, made in the Government Scriptorium. Parchment, 70 x 56 x 15 mm, 69 folios, one column, 19 lines, Gəʿəz, early twentieth century.

IES 01268, Receipt Book for Parchment (*Branna*) for the Government Scriptorium from Gənbot 1957 EC through Gənbot 1958 EC; የብራና መቀበያ ደረሰኝ መዝገብ. Paper, 210 x 150 x 10 mm, ca. 108 folios, Amharic, 1957–58 EC = 1964–66.

IES 01276, Who is the Author of the Computus?, የባሕረ ሃሳብ ደራሲ ማነው? መምህር ኪዳነ ማርያም ገ/ሕይወት by *mämhər* Kidana Maryam Gäbrä Ḥəywot. Paper, 345 x 225 x 9 mm, i + 26 folios, one column, 40 lines, Amharic, twentieth century.

IES 01279, Visual Report of the Accomplishments of Emperor Ḫaylä Śəllase for the Ethiopian Orthodox Church, ግርማዊ ንኀ ቀዳማዊ ኃይለ ሥላሴ ለኢትዮጵያ ቤተ ክርስቲያን የፈጸሙዋቸውን ክፍተኞች ጉዳዮች የሚያሳይ ሥዕላዊ መግለጫ prepared by the Mission Department of the Ethiopian Orthodox Church. Paper, 344 x 243 x 10 mm, 38 folios, Amharic, twentieth century.

IES 01280, List of Ethiopian Kings from the Queen of Sheba up to Emperor Dəlnaʿod, ከንግሥተ ሳባ እስከ አጼ ድልነዓድ ድረስ ያሉ የኢትዮጵያ ነገሥታት ዝርዝር. Paper, 330 x 240 x 11 mm, i + 24 folios, one column, 34–35 lines, Amharic, twentieth century.

IES 01285, A Log of Needed Parchment and Materials in the Government Scriptorium, beginning 1935 EC through 1958 EC, የብራናና ሌሎችም የጽሕፈት መዛግያዎች መጠየቂያ ቅጽ. Paper, 300 x 220 x 10 mm, i + 86 folios, one column, 34–36 lines, Amharic, 1935–58 EC = 1942–66.

IES 01288, Log Book of Parchment (*Branna*) Projects in the Government Scriptorium beginning Miyazya 1945 through 1960 EC = 1952–68, የብራና እና የቀለም ማስረከቢያ መዝገብ. Paper, 308 x 210 x 8 mm, 36 folios, Amharic, 1945–60 EC = 1952–68.

IES 01291, Photographs of Negative Images of Cambridge University 1887, a manuscript of Faith of the Fathers, in Amharic, of the early twentieth century [here called Book of Wisdom of the Apostles], according to the Unctionist Movement, መጽሐፈ ጥበብ ዘአበዊነ ሐዋርያት ንጹሐን እንተ ይእቲ ሃይማኖተ አበው (የቅብዓት ባህል). Paper, 296 x 210 x 15 mm, ii + 73 folios, two columns, 20 lines, Gəʿəz, Amharic, late twentieth century.

IES 01305, Photocopy of a manuscript of the Life of Alexander from the State Library Preussischer Kulturbesitz, with the shelf mark "Petermann II Nachtrag 38," Folios 4a–82b, ዜና እስክንድር ከብራና ፎቶ ኮፒ የተደረገ. Paper, 340 x 220 x 24 mm, i + 162 folios, two columns, 14 lines, Gəʿəz, seventeenth century.

IES 01315, Amharic Translation of the Quran, መጽሐፈ ቁርዓን. Paper, 350 x 220 x 37 mm, 277 folios, two columns, 39–41 lines, Amharic, twentieth century.

IES 01316, Log of Transfer of Skins from the Palace Butcher to the Scriptorium and charged to the Treasury, beginning Ṭəqəmt 1956

EC, ለብራና አገልግሎት የሚውል የበግ ቆዳ ከዐለቱ ሥጋ ቤት የሚጠየቅበትና መፈረሚያ ደረሰኝ. Paper, 225 x 180 x 15 mm, ii + 101 folios, Amharic, 1956 EC = 1963–64.

IES 01322, List of books assigned from the Special Treasury [of Emperor Ḥaylä Śəllase] to scribes in the Government Scriptorium to copy, beginning 1934 EC up to 1965 EC, የልዩ ግምጃ ቤት የቁም ጸሐፊዎች ለእያንዳንዳቸው የተሰጣቸው የመጻሕፍት ዝርዝር. Paper, 333 x 213 x 5 mm, i + 27 folios, Amharic, 1934–65 EC = 1941–73.

IES 01326, File of letters sent from the Government Scriptorium regarding the business of the Scriptorium, beginning 1955 EC; በግርማዊ ንጉሠ ነገሥት ልዩ ግምጃ ቤት የቁም ጽሕፈት ቤት ልዩ ልዩ ሰነዶች. Paper, 348 x 228 x 4 mm, ca. 24 folios, Amharic, 1955 EC = 1962–63.

IES 01340, Photocopies of folios from an eighteenth-century copy of the Acts of Täklä Haymanot and other manuscripts, ከገድለ ተክለ ሃይማኖት እና ከሌሎችም የተወጣጣ የብራና ጽሁፍ. Paper, 340 x 240 x 3 mm, 9 folios, two columns, 18–21 lines, Gəʿəz, mid-twentieth century.

IES 01342, Genealogical Table of King Täklä Haymanot. Paper, 490 x 450 x 1 mm, 2 folios, English, twentieth century.

IES 01348, Excerpts from the Book of Genesis and other biblical passages (perhaps from the Ḥaylä Śəllase Bible Project), ኦሪት ዘልደትና ሌሎችም ምዕራፎች (ምሉዕ ያይደለ). Paper, 342 x 225 x 15 mm, 180 folios, two columns, 37 lines, Gəʿəz, Amharic, mid-twentieth century.

IES 01350, Letters to the Imperial special Treasury from the Government Scriptorium, ከቁም ጽሕፈት ቤት ለንጉሡ ነገሥቱ ልዩ ግምጃ ቤት የተጻፉ ደብዳቤዎች ካርቦን ኮፒ. Paper, 244 x 189 x 9 mm, 38 folios, Amharic, Beginning 1962 EC = 1969–70.

IES 01368, The Church Among Gentiles, ቤተ ክርስቲያን በአሕዛብ መካከል, by *abba* Marqos. Paper, 270 x 210 x 15 mm, ii + 112 folios, one column, 30–31 lines, Amharic, mid-twentieth century.

IES 01373, Pauline Epistles, Text (Gəʾəz) and Commentary (Amharic), a collection of negative images of a late nineteenth century manuscript. Paper, 240 x 300 x 25 mm, ca. 205 folios, Gəʿəz, Amharic, mid-twentieth century.

IES 01377, List of Church Vestments and Gifts to the Priests for the Newly-Built Church in Aksum, አዲስ ለተሠራው ለአክሱም ጽዮን ቤተ ክርስቲያን የተሰጡ ንዋየ ቅድሳት ዝርዝር እና ለካህናቱ ሊሰጡ የተዘጋጁ የሽልማት ልብሶች ዝርዝር. Paper, 350 x 250 x 3 mm, i + 3 folios, Amharic, Ṭərr 20, 1957 EC = 1964.

IES 01381A, Orit [Exodus and following]; Kings; Maccabees; Proverbs; Wisdom of Solomon; Ecclesiastes; Ezekiel (perhaps from the Ḫaylä Śəllase Bible Project), first draft with corrections, ግዕዝና አማርኛመጽሐፈ ቅዱስ በከፊል. Paper, 345 x 255 x 90 mm, 874 folios, two columns, 37 lines, Gəʿəz, Amharic, mid-twentieth century.

IES 01381B, Job; Chronicles; Ezekiel; Minor Prophets; Daniel, and other books from the Old Testament (perhaps from the Ḫaylä Śəllase Bible Project), first draft with corrections, ግዕዝና አማርኛ መጽሐፈ ቅዱስ በከፊል. Paper, 340 x 250 x 103 mm, 669 folios, two columns, 35 lines, Gəʿəz, Amharic, mid-twentieth century.

IES 01382, Lectionary Readings for the weeks after Pentecost. Paper, 418 x 292 x 14 mm, 49 folios, two columns, 36 lines, Gəʿəz, twentieth century.

IES 01383, Published Edition of New Testament books from the Ḫaylä Śəllase Bible Project, መጽሐፍተ ሐዲሳት በግዕዝን በአማርኛ፤ ቀዳማዊ አጼ ኃይለ ሥላሴ ያስፉት መጽሐፈ ቅዱስ. Paper, 403 x 287 x 30 mm, 87 folios, four 65 lines, Gəʿəz, Amharic in facing columns, 1927 EC = 1934–35.

IES 01384, Log for parchment and ink in the Government Scriptorium, የብራናና የቀለም ወጪ. Paper, 403 x 250 x 16 mm, i + 66 folios, Amharic, 1913–28 EC = 1920–35.

IES 01397, Photocopies of negative images from the Order of the Church of Däbrä Marqos, Goǧǧam, ሥርዓት ቤተ ክርስቲያን ዘደብረ ማርቆስ እንተ ይእቲ ደብረ ፀሐይ. Paper, 210 x 296 x 8 mm, 58 folios, two columns, 27 lines, Gəʿəz, 1898 EC = 1905–6.

IES 01398, Photocopies of negative images from the Order of the Church of Däbrä Marqos, Goǧǧam, ሥርዓት ቤተ ክርስቲያን ዘደብረ ማርቆስ እንተ ይእቲ ደብረ ፀሐይ. Paper, 210 x 296 x 7 mm, 55 folios, two columns, 26 lines, Gəʿəz, 1898 EC = 1905–6.

IES 01399, Photocopies of the negative images of notes and transactions and wills written in eighteenth- and nineteenth-century manuscripts from Däbrä Wärq of Goǧǧam, ከጎጃም ደብረ ወርቅ ከተለያዩ የብራና መጻሕፍት ፎቶ ኮፒ የተደረጉ የግጒ የውል የኑዛዜ ማስታወሻዎች. Paper, 296 x 210 x 6 mm, i + 32 folios, two columns, 20 lines, Gəʿəz, eighteenth-nineteenth century.

IES 01400, Photocopies of the negative images of notes and transactions and wills written in nineteenth-century manuscript(s) from Bəčäna Goǧǧam, ከጎጃም ብቸና ጊዮርጊስ ከተለያዩ የብራና መጻሕፍት ፎቶ ኮፒ የተደረጉ የግጒ የውል የኑዛዜ ማስታወሻዎች. Paper, 296 x 210 x 6 mm, 31 folios, two columns, 22 lines, Gəʿəz, nineteenth century.

IES 01401, Photocopies of the negative images of notes written in manuscripts from Woynna Kidanä Məḥrät Monastery, Goǧǧam, በወይና ኪዳነ ምሕረት ጎጃም ከተለያዩ የብራና መጻሕፍት ፎቶ ኮፒ የተደረጉ የግጒ የውል የኑዛዜ ማስታወሻዎች. Paper, 296 x 210 x 5 mm, i + 201 folios, two columns, 27 lines, Gəʿəz, nineteenth century.

IES 01402, History of the Roman Catholic Church in Ethiopia, ስለ ሮማ ካቶሊክ ቤተ ክርስቲያን በኢትዮጵያ ታሪክ. Paper, 296 x 210 x 4 mm, i + 18 folios, one column, 16 lines, Gəʿəz, late nineteenth century.

IES 01555, Amharic poetry, አማርኛ ቅኔ, by *aläqa* Ǝnbaqom. Paper, 351 x 245 x 10 mm, 93 folios, one column, Amharic, 1963–65 EC = 1970–73.

IES 01556, Articles, Gəʿəz and Amharic poetry, ልዩ ልዩ ጽሑፎች የአማርኛና የግዕዝ ቅኔዎች by *aläqa* Ǝnbaqom. Paper, 341 x 240 x 35 mm, 232 folios, one column, Amharic, Gəʿəz, 1960–72 EC = 1967–80.

IES 01557, Amharic Poetry, አማርኛ ቅኔ, by *aläqa* Ǝnbaqom. Paper, 345 x 235 x 23 mm, 200 folios, one column, Amharic, 1963–70 EC = 1970–78.

IES 01558, Gəʿəz Poetry, የአማርኛና የግዕዝ ቅኔዎች, by *aläqa* Ǝnbaqom. Paper, 340 x 230 x 30 mm, 142 folios, one column, Gəʿəz, 1958–65 EC = 1965–73.

IES 01559, Articles, Gəʿəz and Amharic poetry, ልዩ ልዩ ጽሑፎች የአማርኛና የግዕዝ ቅኔዎች, by *aläqa* Ǝnbaqom. Paper, 345 x 255 x 10 mm, 112 folios, one column, Gəʿəz, 1956–63 EC = 1963–71.

IES 01560, Amharic and Gəʿəz Poetry, **የአማርኛና የግዕዝ ቅኔዎች**, collected by *aläqa* Ǝnbaqom. Paper, 320 x 200 x 10 mm, 87 folios, one column, Gəʿəz, Amharic, mid-twentieth century.

IES 01561, Amharic and Gəʿəz Poetry, **የአማርኛና የግዕዝ ቅኔዎች**, collected by *aläqa* Ǝnbaqom. Paper, 320 x 200 x 10 mm, 84 folios, one column, Gəʿəz, Amharic, mid-twentieth century.

IES 01562, Amharic and Gəʿəz Poetry, **የአማርኛና የግዕዝ ቅኔዎች**, collected by *aläqa* Ǝnbaqom. Paper, 310 x 200 x 8 mm, 86 folios, one column, Gəʿəz, Amharic, mid-twentieth century.

IES 01563, Amharic and Gəʿəz Poetry, **የአማርኛና የግዕዝ ቅኔዎች**, collected by *aläqa* Ǝnbaqom. Paper, 310 x 200 x 8 mm, 83 folios, one column, Gəʿəz, Amharic, mid-twentieth century.

IES 01564, Amharic and Gəʿəz Poetry, **የአማርኛና የግዕዝ ቅኔዎች** collected by *aläqa* Ǝnbaqom. Paper, 310 x 200 x 8 mm, i + 88 folios, one column, Gəʿəz, Amharic, mid-twentieth century.

IES 01565, Drafts of biblical books and other books (e.g., Faith of the Fathers, Code of the Kings, Qerəllos) for the Ḥaylä Śəllase Bible Project, **የሃይማኖተ አበውና ልዩ ልዩ መጻሕፍት ረቂቅ ጥራዝ**. Paper, 340 x 225 x 13 mm, 198 folios, two columns, 28–42 lines, Amharic, early twentieth century.

IES 01566, Autobiography of *aläqa* Ǝnbaqom, and Amharic Poetry, **የአለቃ እንባቆም የሕይወት ታሪክና ሌሎችም የአማርኛ ቅኔዎች**, by *aläqa* Ǝnbaqom. Paper, 340 x 230 x 11 mm, 131 folios, one column, 39 lines, Amharic, 1958 EC = 1965–66.

IES 01572, Collection of photos of an eighteenth-century Gəʿəz Grammar, **ሰዋስው፡ ግዕዝ**. Paper, 400 x 299 x 9 mm, 26 folios, two columns, 25 lines, Amharic, mid-twentieth century.

IES 01573, Collection of photos of an early twentieth-century manuscript of History from Emperor Susənyos to Emperor Mənilək II, **ከአፄ ሱስንዮስ እስከ አፄ ምኔልክ በአማርኛ ፎቶ ግራፍ**. Paper, 240 x 181 x 15 mm, 74 folios, one column, 31 lines, Amharic, mid-twentieth century.

IES 01579, A loose quire containing the whole of Acts of Saint Fiqṭor, **ገድለ ፊቅጦር**. Paper, 335 x 240 x 3 mm, 13 folios, two columns, 31–32 lines, Gəʿəz, mid-twentieth century.

IES 01591, Loose quire from a manuscript containing the biography of *ras* Wäldä Mika'el, written on paper, in rhyme, **የራስ ወልደ ሚካኤል የሕይወት ታሪክ በግጥም የተዘጋጀ። በኃይለ መለኮት ወልደ ሚካኤል** by Ḫaylä Mäläkot. Paper, 340 x 235 x 2 mm, i + 5 folios, one column, 30 lines, Tigrinya, mid-twentieth century.

IES 01609, Amharic Religious Poem and a Collection of Testimonies from various people about the Patriotism of Mäse Qosǝṭin, handwritten documents and one photograph copy, **አማርኛ የሃይማኖት ግጥም እና ስለ ሙሴቆስጢን አርበኝነት የተሰጠምስክርነት**. Paper, 350 x 230 x 2 mm, 10 folios, two columns, 33 lines, Amharic, 1938 EC = 1945–46.

IES 01617, Reflections: Amharic Poetry, **ነጸብራቅ አማርኛ ግጥሞች**, by Wänago Mǝnčǝle. Paper, 197 x 159 x 2 mm, i + 17 folios, one column, 20 lines, Amharic, 1972 EC = 1979–80.

IES 01624, Amharic Poetry and Notes About Culture, **አማርኛ ቅኔዎችና ስለ ባህል አንዳንድ አሳቦች**, by *aläqa* Ǝnbaqom. Paper, 340 x 245 x 13 mm, 70 folios, one column, 35–37 lines, Amharic, 1970–72 EC = 1977–80.

IES 01625, Text copied from the end of a Psalter, **ዳዊት**, found in an Addis Ababa Market. Paper, 255 x 203 x 1 mm, 3 folios, one column, Amharic, twentieth century.

IES 01626, Photographs of a nineteenth-century manuscript of Nägärä Maryam, **ነገረ፡ ማርያም**. Paper, 340 x 245 x 40 mm, 97 folios, two columns, 25 lines, Gǝʿǝz, nineteenth century.

IES 01627, Photographs of a nineteenth-century manuscript of Nägärä Maryam, **ነገረ፡ ማርያም**. Paper, 194 x 299 x 10 mm, 59 folios, two columns, 25 lines, Gǝʿǝz, nineteenth century.

IES 01631, Autobiography of *aläqa* Täsäma, **የአለቃ ተሰማ የሕይወት ታሪክ**. Paper, 355 x 214 x 2 mm, 12 folios, one column, 28 lines, Amharic, ca. 1965 EC = ca. 1972–73.

IES 01633, Two loose quires, the first contains parallel Gǝʿǝz and Amharic translations of Psalm 8, the second contains fragments from the Song of Songs, chapter one, in Gǝʿǝz only, and the Book of Hebrews. Parchment, 300 x 254 x 1 mm, 18 folios, one column and two columns, 28 lines, Gǝʿǝz, Amharic, twentieth century.

IES 01642, Gəʽəz Poetry, የግዕዝ ቅኔዎች. Paper, 340 x 245 x 2 mm, 33 folios, one column, Gəʽəz, 1973 EC = 1980–81.

IES 01667, Gəʽəz Poetry, published in the series Collection of Sources for the Study of Ethiopian Culture, Vol. 40, የኢትዮጵያን ባሕል ለማጥናት የተሰበሰቡ ጽሑፎች የግዕዝ ቅኔዎች። በቀዳማዊ ኃይለ ሥላሴ ዩንቨርሲቲ የኢትዮጵያ ጥናትና ምርመራ ክፍል. Paper, 279 x 219 x 3 mm, ii + 20 folios, one column, Gəʽəz, 1967 EC = 1974–75.

IES 01668, Gəʽəz Poetry, published in the series, Collection of Sources for the Study of Ethiopian Culture, Vol. 39, የኢትዮጵያን ባሕል ለማጥናት የተሰበሰቡ ጽሑፎች የግዕዝ ቅኔዎች። በቀዳማዊ ኃይለ ሥላሴ ዩንቨርሲቲ የኢትዮጵያ ጥናትና ምርመራ ክፍል. Paper, 280 x 223 x 3 mm, ii + 26 folios, one column, lines, Gəʽəz, 1967 EC = 1974–75.

IES 01672, Psalter, ዳዊት, incomplete at the end. Parchment, 145 x 144 x 64 mm, 145 folios, one column and two columns, 20 lines, Gəʽəz, eighteenth century.

Miniatures:

1. F. 68v: Crude drawing of two figures.
2. F. 78r: Crude drawing of a face.
3. F. 100r: Crude drawing of a face.

IES 01732, Book of Ḥawi, draft version in pencil, in Gəʽəz and Amharic, in parallel columns, የመጽሐፈ ሐዊ ረቂቅ. Paper, 350 x 230 x 55 mm, 597 folios, two columns, 37–38 lines, Amharic, Gəʽəz, twentieth century.

IES 01733–34, Letters from the Ministry of Pen to the Ministry of Treasury, 1938, ከጽሕፈት ሚ/ር ለገንዘብ ሚ/ር ለተለያዩ ሰዎች የተጻፉ ደብዳቤዎች. Paper, 350 x 230 x 44 mm, ii + 704 folios, Amharic, 1938 EC = 1945–46.

IES 01735–36, Psalms and Song of Songs, draft version in pencil, in Gəʽəz and Amharic, in parallel columns. Paper, 343 x 250 x 25 mm, i + 183 folios, two columns, 36 lines, Amharic, Gəʽəz, twentieth century.

IES 01736, Genesis; Joshua; Enoch; Sirach; Isaiah; Jeremiah; Baruch, draft version in pencil, in Gəʽəz and Amharic, in parallel columns. Paper, 350 x 240 x 40 mm, 432 folios, two columns, 36–37 lines, Gəʽəz, Amharic, twentieth century.

IES 01737, Law of Kings, ፍትሐ ነገሥት, draft version in pencil. Paper, 350 x 226 x 36 mm, i + 274 folios, two columns, 26–31 lines, Gəʿəz, Amharic, twentieth century.

IES 01738, Drafts of various works, in pencil. Paper, 330 x 255 x 20 mm, ii + 151 folios, two columns, 27–38 lines, Gəʿəz, Amharic, twentieth century.

IES 01739, Constitution of the Ethiopian Imperial Government, written in the Government Scriptorium, የኢትዮጵያ ንጉሠ ነገሥት መንግሥት ሕገ መንግሥት. Parchment, 273 x 205 x 1 mm, i + 9 folios, one column, 31–33 lines, Amharic, 1948 EC = 1955–56.

IES 01740, Law of the Kings, ፍትሐ ነገሥት, text and commentary, draft version in pencil, and fragments of other works. Paper, 385 x 270 x 35 mm, i + 205 folios, two columns, 37–39 lines, Gəʿəz, Amharic, twentieth century.

IES 01741, Tobit; Judith, draft version in pencil, and other works, መጽሐፈ ጦቢት ዮዲት እና ሌሎችም፡፡ ረቂቅ፡፡. Paper, 340 x 247 x 10 mm, i + 102 folios, two columns, 33 lines, Gəʿəz, Amharic, twentieth century.

IES 01742, Prayer of the Covenant, ጸሎተ ኪዳን; Praise of God, ውዳሴ አምላክ; and other works, draft version in pencil, in Amharic, ውዳሴ አምላክ እና ሌሎችም፡፡ ረቂቅ፡፡. Paper, 346 x 255 x 10 mm, ii + 58 folios, two columns, 30–31 lines, Gəʿəz, Amharic, Italian, twentieth century.

IES 01743, Homily of Saint Ephrem, draft version in pencil, and other works, ድርሳን ዘቅዱስ ኤፍሬም. Paper, 323 x 244 x 5 mm, 61 folios, two columns, 31 lines, Gəʿəz, Amharic, twentieth century.

IES 01744, Law of the Kings, ፍትሐ ነገሥት, draft version in pencil, and other works. Paper, 343 x 263 x 20 mm, 169 folios, two columns, 31 lines, Gəʿəz, Amharic, twentieth century.

IES 01745, Book of Ezra, መጽሐፈ ዕዝራ, a loose quire. Parchment, 467 x 358 x 6 mm, 6 folios, four columns, 74 lines, Gəʿəz, twentieth century.

IES 01747, Homily of Jacob of Serugh, How Abraham Offered His Son Isaac; Gospel of Matthew (first five chapters), draft version in pencil, and other works, ድርሳን ያዕቆብ ዘሥሩግ፡፡ ወንጌል ዘማቴዎስ. Parchment, 350 x 250 x 7 mm, 32 folios, two columns, 39 lines, Gəʿəz, Amharic, twentieth century.

IES 01759, Photocopies of negative images of folios from an illuminated, nineteenth-century manuscript of the Miracles of Jesus, ተአምረ ኢየሱስ. Paper, 330 x 230 x 5 mm, 12 folios, two columns, 19 lines, Gəʿəz, late nineteenth century.

Miniatures:

1. F. 5r: Tewodros on horseback.

IES 01760, Photocopies of negative images of folios from a manuscript of *Zena abba Elyas,* ዜና አባ ኤልያስ. Paper, 345 x 240 x 10 mm, i + 41 folios, two columns, 17 lines, Gəʿəz, twentieth century.

IES 01763, Photocopies of negative images of folios from a twentieth-century manuscript of the Chronicles of Täklä Giyorgis and King Yoḥannəs IV, commissioned by Mondon-Vidailhet. Paper, 300 x 220 x 3 mm, 55 folios, one column, 19 lines, Gəʿəz, twentieth century.

IES 01765, Photocopies of negative images of folios with colophons from several manuscripts in the IES collection. Paper, 300 x 210 x 6 mm, 50 folios, two columns, and three columns, Gəʿəz, twentieth century.

Miniatures:

1. F. 44r: Täklä Haymanot.
2. F. 45v: Image of four saints, Gäbrä Ṣəyon, Iyasus Moʾa, Zä-Iyasus, and Zä-Kərstos Täsfanä.
3. F. 46r: How two archangels escorted Mary into the temple.

IES 01766, Autograph of the Book of Gəʿəz Grammar and Dictionary, Volume 1, መጽሐፈ ሰዋስው ወግሥ ወመዝገበ ቃላት ሐዲስ። መምህር ክፍለ ጊዮርጊስ ኪዳነ ወልድ ክፍሌ። ደስታ ተክለ ወልድ። by *mämhər* Kəfle Giyorgis, Kidanä Wäld Kəfle, and Dästa Täklä Wäld. Paper, 230 x 180 x 70 mm, ii + 504 folios, ff. 1r–148v one column, ff. 149r–503v two columns, 25 lines, Amharic, twentieth century.

IES 01767, Autograph of Book of Gəʿəz Grammar and Dictionary, Volume 2, መጽሐፈ ሰዋስው ወግሥ ወመዝገበ ቃላት ሐዲስ። መምህር ክፍለ ጊዮርጊስ ኪዳነ ወልድ ክፍሌ። ደስታ ተክለ ወልድ። by *mämhər* Kəfle Giyorgis, Kidanä Wäld Kəfle, and Dästa Täklä Wäld. Paper, 249 x 178 x 60 mm, i + 504 folios, two columns, 25 lines, Gəʿəz, Amharic, twentieth century.

IES 01768, Amharic Translation of the Quran, ቁርአን. Paper, 330 x 220 x 70 mm, ix + 633 folios, one column, 27 lines, Amharic, twentieth century.

IES 01774, Senodos, or, Book of Canon, draft version in pencil, in Gəʿəz and Amharic, መጽሐፈ ቀኖና ዓዲ ሲኖዶስ. Paper, 340 x 240 x 15 mm, 161 folios, two columns, 33–36 lines, Gəʿəz, Amharic, twentieth century.

IES 01777, Wisdom of Sirach, መጽሐፈ ሲራክ. Parchment, 112 x 101 x 37 mm, 74 folios, one column, 17 lines, Gəʿəz, twentieth century.

IES 01778, Gəʿəz Grammar, ሰዋሰው፡ ግዕዝ. Parchment, 152 x 96 x 21 mm, 26 folios, two columns, 19 lines, Gəʿəz, twentieth century.

Miniatures:

1. F. 26r: An equestrian saint below two angels.

2. F. 26v: Two equestrian saints.

IES 01779, Catechism of the Orthodox Faith, ነገረ ሃይማኖት; Beauty of Creation, ሥነ ፍጥረት; *Asmat* Prayer against the medicine man; ጸሎት በእንተ ዐቃቤ ሥራይ. Parchment, 88 x 77 x 23 mm, 84 folios, two columns, 13 lines, Gəʿəz, nineteenth century.

IES 01780, Book of *Aslət* (Lectionary readings from the Bible), arranged for the ecclesiastical feasts and festivals, መጽሐፈ አስልጥ. Parchment, 273 x 228 x 34 mm, iii + 50 folios, two columns, 23 lines, Gəʿəz, twentieth century.

IES 01781, Five Pillars of Mystery, አምስቱ አዕማደ ምሥጢር. Parchment, 130 x 110 x 40 mm, i + 125 folios, two columns, 20–21 lines, Gəʿəz, eighteenth century.

Miniatures:

1. F. i r(ecto): Crude drawing of a figure.

IES 01782, Bandlet of Righteousness, ልፋፈ ጽድቅ; Vision of Mary, in Amharic, ራዕየ ማርያም. Parchment, 142 x 98 x 29 mm, ii + 58 folios, ff. 1r–30v two columns, ff. 31r–56v one column, 14–15 lines, Gəʿəz, Amharic, twentieth century.

IES 01800, Photocopy of negative images of UNESCO Microfilm, series 10, number 37, the Book of Hikar, a manuscript from Qəddus Giyorgis Church, Dima Monastery, Goǧǧam. Paper, 210 x 297 x 14 mm, ca. 142 folios, Gəʾəz, eighteenth century.

IES 01801, Acts of *abunä* Zärʾa Buruk, ገድለ አቡነ ዘርዓ ቡሩክ, autograph of a critical edition. Paper, 219 x 171 x 32 mm, ca. 227 folios, Amharic, English, German, twentieth century.

IES 01807, Homiliary in Honor of the Savior of the World, recounting the Revelation to *abunä* Mäbaʾa Ṣəyon; ድርሳነ መድኃኔ ዓለም ዘከሠተ ለገብሩ አቡነ መብዓ ጽዮን. Paper, 276 x 218 x 5 mm, i + 49 folios, two columns, 22 lines, Gəʿəz, twentieth century.

IES 01816, Photocopy of an eighteenth-century manuscript containing the Book of Ḥawi, መጽሐፈ ሐዊ. Paper, 340 x 250 x 20 mm, i + 109 folios, three columns, 42 lines, Gəʿəz, eighteenth century.

Miniatures:

1. F. 108r: Photograph of an illumination of "the ascension of Our Lord into heaven."

IES 01818A, Photographs of excerpts of manuscripts from the Bibliothèque nationale de France, MSS Eth. 594 and 184. Paper, 340 x 240 x 5 mm, v + 28 folios, one column, 14 lines, Gəʿəz, nineteenth century.

IES 01818B, Photographs of excerpts of manuscripts from the Bibliothèque nationale de France, MSS Eth. 594 and 184. Paper, 345 x 230 x 5 mm, v + 26 folios, one column, 14 lines, Gəʿəz, nineteenth century.

IES 01820, Cycle of Kings, ዐውደ ነገሥት. Paper, 290 x 210 x 12 mm, ii + 141 folios, one column, 18–19 lines, Amharic, twentieth century.

IES 01821, Book of Tuladan, መጽሐፈ ቱላዳን; *Asmat* Prayers. Paper, 165 x 115 x 7 mm, i + 30 folios, one column, 21–23 lines, Gəʿəz, twentieth century.

Miniatures:

1. F. 25v: The scribe stands beside a woman: "Bless my pen" (drawing).

2. F. 28v: Crude drawing of a man beside a tree.

3. F. 29r: Madonna and Child.

4. F. 29v: A saint stands beside an angel with sword outstretched, in pencil and purple ink.

IES 01823, Horologium for the Night, ሰዓታት ዘሌሊት. Parchment, 135 x 127 x 48 mm, ii + 79 folios, two columns, 16 lines, Gəʽəz, eighteenth century.

IES 01824, Book of Philosophy, መጽሐፈ ፈላስፉ. Parchment, 200 x 190 x 33 mm, 48 folios, two columns, 20–21 lines, Gəʽəz, eighteenth century.

IES 01825, Introduction to the Four Gospel, መቅድመ ወንጌል; Four Gospels, አርባዕቱ ወንጌል. Parchment, 248 x 185 x 40 mm, iii + 132 folios, two columns, 30–31 lines, Gəʽəz, early twentieth century.

IES 01826, Excerpts of an *Asmat* Prayer, አስማት; Prayer to Jesus Christ, "For the sake of Your Trinity," በእንተ ሥላሴክ; Praise of the Beloved, ስብሐተ ፍቁር; Petition and Supplication, ስእለት ወአስተብቁዖት; Image of the Assumption of Mary, መልክአ ፍልሰታ ለማርያም; Concluding Hymns from the Miracles of Mary, መርገፍ ዘተአምረ ማርያም; Image of Michael, መልክአ ሚካኤል; Image of Gabriel, መልክአ ገብርኤል; Hymn to Saint George, "Finisher of the Acts," ፈጻሜ ገድል. Parchment, 188 x 98 x 45 mm, ii + 84 folios, one column, 16–17 lines, Gəʽəz, nineteenth century.

IES 01827, Introduction to Book of Light; Rampart of the Cross, ሐጹረ መስቀል; Prayer of Forgiveness of Sin, ጸሎተ ስርየት ኃጢአት; Prayer when entering the Church, ጸሎት ሶበ ትበውእ ውስተ ቤተ ክርስቲያን; Daily Prayers interwoven with Praises of Mary and Gate of Light; Prayer of Mary at Bartos, ባርቶስ; One Miracle of Mary, ተአምረ ማርያም; Sword of the Trinity, ሠይፈ ሥላሴ; Image of Zena Marqos, መልክአ አቡነ ዜና ማርቆስ; Hymn to the Trinity. Parchment, 218 x 192 x 67 mm, i + 152 folios, two columns, 17–18 lines, Gəʽəz, eighteenth century and nineteenth century and twentieth century (composite).

Miniatures:

1. F. i r(ecto): Madonna and Child.

IES 01830, Photocopies of seven folios of manuscripts from the Vatican collection, concerning colophons about Ethiopian monasteries,

ከባቲካን የተገኙ የተለያዩ ስለኢትዮጵያ ገዳማት ታሪክ የሚናገሩ ከተለያዩ መጽሐፍት ፎቶኮፒ የተነሱ ማስታወሻዎች. Paper, 270 x 190 x 5 mm, ii + 9 folios, one column and two columns, Gəʻəz, fifteenth to eighteenth centuries.

IES 01832, Picture and some negative images of the Treaty of 1843 between Mənilək II, King of Shewa, and Queen Victoria of Britain, በሸዋ ንጉሥና በብሪታኒያ ንግሥት መካከል እአየተደረገውል. Paper, 4 folios, two columns, English, Amharic, 1843.

IES 01841, Wisest of the Wise, ጠቢበ ጠቢባን. Parchment, 132 x 99 x 15 mm, v + 37 folios, one column, 14 lines, Gəʻəz, 1968 EC = 1975–76.

IES 01842, Gəʻəz Grammar, ሰዋሰወ፡ ግዕዝ. Parchment, 104 x 90 x 40 mm, vii + 70 folios, one column, 16 lines, Gəʻəz, nineteenth century.

IES 01890, Faith of the Ancient Fathers, ሃይማኖተ አበው ቀደምት, by Kidanä Wäld Kəfle. Paper, 340 x 285 x 70 mm, i + 226 folios, one column and two columns, 28 lines, Amharic, twentieth century.

IES 01908, Introduction to Commentary on Ezekiel, unpublished, by Kidanä Wäld Kifle. Paper, 300 x 218 x 15 mm, i + 54 folios, one column, 33 lines, Amharic, late twentieth century.

IES 01918, Book of Prayer of Saint Peter, ጸሎተ ዼጥሮስ; Prayer of Mary, ጸሎተ ማርያም እሰመ ክብርት አንቲ; Image of the Icon, መልክአ ሥዕል; Image of Jesus, መልክአ ኢየሱስ; Image of the Savior of the World, መልክአ መድኃኔ ዓለም; Image of Saint George, መልክአ ጊዮርጊስ; Image of Täklä Haymanot, መልክአ ተክለ ሃይማኖት. Parchment, 222 x 168 x 71 mm, iv + 182 folios, two columns, 15 lines, Gəʻəz, late nineteenth century.

Miniatures:

1. F. ii r(ecto): Ornate cross.
2. F. ii v(erso): Ornate cross.
3. F. 1r: The Lord lays his hand on Peter's head.
4. F. 4r: The Lord lifts Peter by the hands.
5. F. 4v: The Lord lifts Peter by the hands.
6. F. 8r: Jesus stands before a herd of sheep.

IES 01919, Image of Raguel, መልክአ ራጉኤል; Image of John Son of Thunder, መልክአ ዮሐንስ ወልደ ነጉድጓድ. Parchment, 96 x 70 x 24 mm, ii + 58 folios, one column, 10 lines, Gəʿəz, twentieth century.

Miniatures:

1. F. 1v: Raguel, the Archangel.
2. F. 3r: Two snakes intertwined with text written between their bodies.
3. F. 4v: Four snakes intertwined with text written between their bodies.
4. F. 5r: Two snakes intertwined with text written between their bodies.
5. F. 6r: Two snakes intertwined with text written between their bodies.
6. F. 8v: Two snakes intertwined with text written between their bodies and the lamb with the cross at the center.
7. F. 9v: Four snakes intertwined with text written between their bodies.
8. F. 10r: Raguel, the Archangel.
9. F. 11r: Leopard.
10. F. 11v: Raguel, the Archangel.
11. F. 13r: Two snakes intertwined with text written between their bodies.
12. F. 14r: The Striking of the Head.
13. F. 16r: The Crucifixion.
14. F. 18r: Four-headed bird.
15. F. 18v: A bat in a tree, a lion to the right.
16. F. 19v: Four snakes intertwined with text written between their bodies.
17. F. 20r: Raguel, the Archangel.
18. F. 22r: The Holy Trinity surrounded by the four Living Creatures.
19. F. 24r: Madonna and Child.
20. F. 24v: A lamb.

21. F. 28v: Madonna and Child.

22. F. 31r: John.

23. F. 31v: Elijah and Peter.

24. F. 32r: John and one other saint.

25. F. 37r: John the Evangelist.

26. F. 38v: Romna and John.

27. F. 42r: The Crucifixion.

28. F. 43r: John, seated on a throne.

29. F. 43v: King David.

30. F. 44r: King Solomon.

31. F. 47v: God the Father.

32. F. 48r: Jerusalem.

33. F. 48v: John.

34. F. 50r: Abraham and Sarah.

35. F. 50v: Ezra.

36. F. 51v: Tewogolos (the theologian).

37. F. 52r: Yared.

38. F. 55v: John.

IES 01920, Anaphora of Our Lady Mary attributed to Cyriacus of Bəhənsa; Praises of Mary, ውዳሴ ማርያም; *Asmat* Prayer of the Seven Archangels, ድርሳን ዘሰባቱ ሊቃነ መላእክት. Parchment, 137 x 104 x 24 mm, ii + 50 folios, one column, 12 lines, Gə'əz, 1951–56 (Mentions the Patriarch Basəlyos [1951–70] and the Alexandrian Patriarch Joseph II [1946–56]).

IES 01921, Image of the Praises of Mary, መልክአ ውዳሴ ማርያም; Mystagogia, ትምህርተ ኅቡዓት; God of the Luminaries, እግዚአብሔር ዘብርሃናት; *'Ǝzəl* Chants, ዕዝል; Absolution of the Son, ፍትሐት ዘወልድ. Parchment, 109 x 71 x 34 mm, 56 folios, one column, 11–17 lines, Gə'əz, twentieth century.

IES 01930, Revelation, ራዕየ ዮሐንስ. Parchment, 188 x 156 x 31 mm, iii + 33 folios, two columns, 19 lines, Gə'əz, nineteenth century.

Miniatures:

1. F. ii r(ecto): Crude drawing of a man on a horse.

IES 01939, Treatise on Prayer Beads, ስለ መቁጠሪያ ታሪክ; Brief Notes on the Synaxarium; Calendar for the Feast Days and Fasting Days; Prayer on the End Times; Window on Heaven; The Paths of the Zodiak; Admonition and Prayer, መቅድመ ጸሎት ለምእመናን ትምህርት; Collected *sälamat* from the Synaxarium, የስንክሳር መርገፍ ስብስብ. Paper and parchment, 205 x 140 x 32 mm, iv + 107 folios, two columns, 24 lines, Amharic, Gəʿəz, 1930–74 (mentions Emperor Ḥaylä Śəllase).

IES 01959, Psalter, ዳዊት. Parchment, 176 x 124 x 60 mm, iv + 170 folios, one column and two columns, 21 lines, Gəʿəz, early-twentieth century.

Miniatures:

1. F. ii v(erso): A man standing, holding a book.
2. F. iii r(ecto): Gäbrä Mänfäs Qəddus.
3. F. 169v: Saint George and the Dragon.
4. F. 170r: Madonna and Child.

IES 01983, Palace papers related to the establishment of the Government Scriptorium, etc. Paper, 345 x 230 x 8 mm, 71 folios, Amharic, 1911 EC = 1918–19.

IES 01992, Gəʿəz Poetry for the Heroism of *ras* Alula, ስለራስ አሉላ አርበኝነት የቀረበ የግእዝ ቅኔ። ከመሪጌታ ልሳነ ወርቅ ገብረ ጊዮርጊስ ገብረ ሥላሴ። by *märigeta* Ləsanä Wärq Gäbrä Giyorgis Gäbrä Śəlase, lecturer in the Yared Music School. Paper, 270 x 210 x 3 mm, 5 folios, one column, 28 lines, Gəʿəz, 1979 EC = 1986–87.

IES 01996, Chronicle of Ethiopian Kings up to Ḥaylä Śəllase, ዋልቄ ነገሥት. Paper, 276 x 219 x 35 mm, ii + 333 folios, one column, 24 lines, Amharic, twentieth century.

IES 01998, *Asmat* Prayers, ክታብ. Parchment, 180 x 10 cm, four strips, one column, Gəʿəz, twentieth century. Space for a name was left blank.

Miniatures:

1. Three miniatures: (a) face surrounded by four angels; (b) angel with sword and scabbard; and (c) a person.

IES 02000, Autobiography of *nägadras* ꓱšäte Täkätäläw. Paper, 290 x 220 x 10 mm, 44 folios, one column, 22 lines, Amharic, twentieth century.

IES 02032, Genealogy of Ethiopian Kings, through Emperor Iyasu II (1755), ፖልቄ ነገሥት; Petition and Supplication, ስእለት ወአስተብቍዖት. Parchment, 222 x 198 x 62 mm, vii + 127 folios, two columns, 17 lines, Gəʿəz, late seventeenth/early eighteenth century.

IES 02055, Photocopy of a twentieth-century manuscript of Book of Qerəllos, መጽሐፈ ቄርሎስ. Paper, 332 x 221 x 30 mm, i + 227 folios, two columns, 24 lines, Gəʿəz, twentieth century.

IES 02073, History of Baffana. Parchment, 140 x 81 x 30 mm, ii + 44 folios, one column, 18 lines, Gəʿəz, twentieth century.

Miniatures:

1. Inside front cover: Ornate cross.
2. F. I r(ecto): Ornate crosses.
3. F. i v(erso): Crude drawings of ornate crosses, prayer staffs, and faces.
4. F. 43r: Ornate cross.
5. F. 43v: Crude drawing of a man.
6. F. 44r: Ornate crosses.
7. F. 44v: Ornate crosses.
8. Inside back cover: Ornate cross.

IES 02081, Brief Homily on the Life of Zechariah; Image of Zechariah with *Asmat*; Acts of Märqorewos, ገድለ መርቆሬዎስ; Image of Raguel, መልአክ ሩጉኤል. Parchment, 124 x 88 x 11 mm, 80 folios, one column, 9 lines, Gəʿəz, twentieth century.

IES 02083, Psalter, ዳዊት. Parchment, 225 x 158 x 72 mm, iv + 142 folios, one column and two columns, 23 lines, Gəʿəz, twentieth century.

Catalogue of the Manuscripts 149

IES 02084, Harp of Praise, አርጋኖነ ውዳሴ. Parchment, 125 x 105 x 55 mm, ii + 182 folios, two columns, 14 lines, Gəʿəz, seventeenth century.

IES 02137, Psalter, ዳዊት. Parchment, 155 x 100 x 57 mm, 200 folios, one column, 17–18 lines, Gəʿəz, twentieth century.

IES 02138, Fountain of Blood, የደም ምንጭ ቤት ወደድ መኮንን, by *bitwäddäd* Mäkwännən. Parchment, 195 x 140 x 22 mm, iii + 66 folios, one column, 13 lines, Amharic, 1939 EC = 1946–47.

IES 02145, Antiphonary for the Whole Year, ድጓ. Parchment, 290 x 270 x 78 mm, ii + 181 folios, three columns, 37 lines, Gəʿəz, 1773 EC = 1780–81.

IES 02146, Image of Tewodros, መልክአ ቴዎድሮስ. Parchment, 600 x 550 x 1 mm, 1 folio, four columns, 56 lines, Gəʿəz, 1868–1905 (mentions Emperor Mənilək II).

IES 02147, Image of John, መልክአ ዮሐንስ. Parchment, 555 x 555 x 1 mm, 1 folio, four columns, 54 lines, Gəʿəz, 1917–30 (mentions Empress Zäwditu).

IES 02148, Abbreviated Antiphonary for the Whole Year, ድጓ. Parchment, 240 x 230 x 60 mm, v + 92 folios, three columns, 26 lines, Gəʿəz, eighteenth century.

IES 02149, Five Pillars of Mystery, አምስቱ አዕማደ ምሥጢር. Parchment, 130 x 100 x 50 mm, ii + 106 folios, one column, 13 lines, Amharic, Gəʿəz, nineteenth century.

Miniatures:

1. F. i v(erso): Crude drawing of a church, in pencil.
2. F. ii r(ecto): Crude drawing of churches, in pencil.
3. F. ii v(erso): Crude drawing of a church, in pencil.
4. F. 104r: Crude drawing of a church, in pencil.
5. F. 104v: Crude drawing of a church, in pencil.

IES 02150, Five Pillars of Mystery, አምስቱ አዕማደ ምሥጢር. Parchment, 150 x 110 x 22 mm, 45 folios, one column, 18–24 lines, Gəʿəz, Amharic, twentieth century.

IES 02151, Book of the Disciples, መጽሐፈ አርድእት. Parchment, 250 x 210 x 40 mm, iii + 66 folios, two columns, 19–20 lines, Gəʿəz, early twentieth century.

IES 02152, Abbreviated Antiphonary for the Whole Year, ድጓ; Hymns, መዝሙር. Paper, 160 x 125 x 20 mm, ii + 111 folios, two columns, 13 lines, Gəʿəz, twentieth century.

IES 02153A, Cycle of Kings, ዐውደ ነገሥት. Parchment, 159 x 160 x 50 mm, 133 folios, two columns, 20–28 lines, Gəʿəz, early nineteenth century.

IES 02153B, Various *Asmat* Prayers, አስማት. Paper, 170 x 100 x 7 mm, iii + 70 folios, one column, 16 lines, Gəʿəz, twentieth century.

Miniatures:

1. Talismanic symbols are found throughout (ff. 2v–3r, 8r, 13r, 14v, 15v, 24r–26r, 32r, 40rv, 47r–49r, 53v–54r, 55r, 57r, 58r, 59v–60r, 68v).

2. F. 10r: Ornate cross.

3. F. 17r: Ornate cross.

IES 02153C, Various *Asmat* Prayers, አስማት. Paper, 160 x 100 x 9 mm, ii + 25 folios, one column, 16 lines, Gəʿəz, twentieth century.

Miniatures:

1. F. ii v(erso): A cross with angels on all four sides, surrounded by two snakes.

2. F. 10v: Box with lines and circles inside of it.

IES 02153D, Various *Asmat* Prayers, አስማት; Prayer of Peter, ጸሎተ ኢጥሮስ. Paper, 140 x 95 x 15 mm, ii + 58 folios, one column, 14 lines, Gəʿəz, twentieth century.

Miniatures:

1. F. ii v(erso): Ornate cross.

IES 02154, Photocopy of the Book of Furqan, የፉርቃን መጽሐፈ, translated from Arabic into Amharic. Paper, 339 x 220 x 19 mm, iii + 138 folios, two columns, 26 lines, Amharic, twentieth century.

IES 02157, Psalter, ዳዊት. Parchment, 175 x 170 x 90 mm, i + 173 folios, one column and two columns, 18 lines, Gəʿəz, eighteenth/nineteenth century.

IES 02158, Psalter, ዳዊት; Angels Praise Her, ይዌድስዋ መላእክት ለማርያም. Parchment, 215 x 140 x 55 mm, iv + 142 folios, one column and two columns, 25 lines, Gəʿəz, late nineteenth/early twentieth century.

Miniatures:

1. F. 21v: An angel with a sword.
2. F. 141v: Madonna and Child.

IES 02159, Hymn to Our Lady Mary, ተአምኖታ ለእግዝእትነ ማርያም; bound with published edition of Mystagogia, ትምህርተ ኅቡዓት; Prayer of the Covenant, ጸሎተ ኪዳን (published in 1943). Parchment and paper, 120 x 90 x 40 mm, viii + 57 folios, one column, 10 lines, Gəʿəz, twentieth century.

Miniatures:

1. F. i v(erso): "The Priests praise her."
2. F. ii r(ecto): Our Lady Mary, flanked by the two archangels.
3. F. ii v(erso): An equestrian saint, with the caption, "The Martyrs praise and greet her."
4. F. iii r(ecto): Other equestrian saints and soldiers.
5. F. iii v(erso): A crowd of saints, with the caption, "The faithful praise and greet her."
6. F. iv v(erso): Saint George and the Dragon.
7. F. v r(ecto): Madonna and Child.
8. F. vi r(ecto): Seated scribe and painter.
9. F. vii v(erso): The Holy Trinity surrounded by the four Living Creatures.
10. F. viii r(ecto): Abraham stands with hands clasped together, with the caption, "tent of Abraham."
11. F. 34r: Two angels at the top of the folio.
12. F. 37v: Our Lady Mary, enthroned.
13. F. 38r: "How the (five) monks praised her in the monastery."

14. F. 38v: Crude drawing of a figure.

15. F. 39v: Madonna and Child.

16. F. 40r: Two women before Madonna and Child.

17. F. 40v: Ornate cross.

18. F. 41r: Madonna and Child.

IES 02160, Acts of Saint Mark the Evangelist, ገድለ ማርቆስ; Miracles of Saint Mark the Evangelist, ተአምረ ማርቆስ. Parchment, 150 x 120 x 40 mm, iv + 85 folios, two columns, 15–16 lines, Gəʿəz, nineteenth century.

Miniatures:

1. F. iv r(ecto): Talismanic symbol with face in center, surrounded by four angels.

2. F. 66v: Mark the Evangelist.

3. F. 67r: "How Däbrä Ṣəyon, baptismal name Wäldä Maryam, prayed."

IES 02161, Psalter, in Amharic, made in the Government Scriptorium, ዳዊት. Parchment, 260 x 195 x 68 mm, iv + 192 folios, one column and two columns, 24 lines, Amharic, twentieth century.

IES 02166, Petition and Supplication, arranged for the days of the week, ስእለት ወአስተብቍዖት; Harp of Praise, አርጋኖነ ውዳሴ. Parchment, 320 x 290 x 70 mm, iii + 182 folios, three columns, 21 lines, Gəʿəz, nineteenth/twentieth century.

IES 02167, Acts of Täklä Haymanot, ገድለ ተክለ ሃይማኖት. Parchment, 310 x 250 x 58 mm, ii + 99 folios, three columns, 29–30 lines, Gəʿəz, late nineteenth/early twentieth century.

IES 02168, Acts of Saint George, ገድለ ጊዮርጊስ; Miracles of Saint George, ተአምረ ጊዮርጊስ. Parchment, 280 x 230 x 58 mm, ii + 124 folios, two columns, 26–27 lines, Gəʿəz, twentieth century.

IES 02178, Image of Arsema, መልክአ አርሲማ; One Miracle of Mary (concerning Arsema), ተአምረ ማርያም; Acts of Arsema of Armenia, ገድለ አርሲማ ዘአርማንያ. Parchment, 220 x 165 x 45 mm, iv + 71 folios, two columns, 19–20 lines, Gəʿəz, twentieth century.

Catalogue of the Manuscripts 153

IES 02180, Computus, ባሕረ ሐሳብ. Paper, 160 x 110 x 14 mm, 61 folios, one column, 15 lines, Gəʿəz, twentieth century.

IES 02181, Acts of *abunä* Mäbʻa Ṣəyon, ገድለ አቡነ መብዓ ጽዮን. Paper, 160 x 105 x 5 mm, i + 27 folios, one column, 19 lines, Gəʿəz, twentieth century.

IES 02182, *Ziq* Chants, መጽሐፈ ዚቅ. Parchment, 120 x 90 x 45 mm, iii + 63 folios, two columns, 17 lines, Gəʿəz, nineteenth century.

IES 02183, Prayer for Undoing Charm, መፍትሐ ሥራይ. Parchment, 83 x 60 x 25 mm, ii + 45 folios, one column, 17–18 lines, Gəʿəz, twentieth century.

IES 02184, Bandlet of Righteousness, ልፋፈ ጽድቅ, leporello codex. Parchment, 85 x 60 x 25 mm, i + 52 folios, one column, 11 lines, Gəʿəz, twentieth century.

IES 02185, History of Ethiopia, here called *Kəbrä nägäśt*, in Amharic; History of Shewa; Japanese Religion and Culture; History of Kings; List of Caliphates; List of Alexandrian Bishops; List of Ethiopian Kings; History of Ethiopia from Mənilək I to Mənilək II. Parchment and paper, 205 x 170 x 110 mm, ii + 701 folios, ff. 1r–417v, 619r–696r one column, ff. 418r–617v two columns, 19 lines, Amharic, 1905 EC = 1912–13.

Miniatures:

1. F. ii v(erso): A hand, holding a balance with a cluster of grapes (?) on the left side and a sword on the right side.

IES 02187, Commentary on Code of Kings, መጽሐፈ ፍትሐ ነገሥት ከነትርጓሜው; Commentary on the Book of Sirach, መጽሐፈ ሲራክ አንድምታ ትርጓሜ, by Mälə'akä Bərhan. Parchment and paper, 280 x 220 x 38 mm, i + 302 folios, ff. 1r–192r one column, ff. 199r–290v two columns, 21–27 lines, Amharic, Gəʿəz, 1901 EC and 1907 EC = 1908–14.

Miniatures:

1. Inside back cover: Printed card of Madonna and Child.

IES 02188, Didascalia. Paper, 320 x 245 x 28 mm, i + 131 folios, two columns, 26–29 lines, Gəʻəz, 1930–50 (f. 1r mentions Emperor Ḫaylä Śəllase and the Metropolitan Qerəllos VI).

IES 02189, Homiliary of the Savior of the World, made in the Government Scriptorium, ድርሳነ መድኃኔ ዓለም. Parchment, 190 x 133 x 50 mm, iv + 143 folios, two columns, 15 lines, Gəʻəz, early twentieth century. EMML 7454.

IES 02190, Book of Ḥawi, መጽሐፈ ሐዊ. Paper, 345 x 217 x 29 mm, i + 363 folios, two columns, 31 lines, Gəʻəz, Amharic, twentieth century.

IES 02193, Prayer to Jesus, arranged for the days of the week. Parchment, 130 x 95 x 35 mm, iv + 60 folios, one column, 11–12 lines, Gəʻəz, twentieth century.

IES 02199, Image of the Guardian Angel, መልክአ ዐቃቤ መልአክ; Daily Prayers, ጸሎት ዘዘወትር; Prayer of the Covenant, ጸሎተ ኪዳን; Prayer, "I beseech you by God, the Father"; Prayer, "I Praise God"; Prayer, "O, Lord Jesus Christ, Son of the Living God"; Image of Gabriel, መልክአ ገብርኤል; Image of the Guardian Angel, መልክአ ዐቃቤ መልአክ. Parchment, 115 x 90 x 38 mm, iv + 65 folios, one column, 11 lines, Gəʻəz, twentieth century.

IES 02203, Book of Tuladan, መጽሐፈ ቱላዳን. Parchment, 180 x 130 x 39 mm, v + 83 folios, one column, 14 lines, Gəʻəz, 1960 EC = 1967–68.

Miniatures:

1. F. iii r(ecto): Ornate cross.
2. F. iv r(ecto): John the Evangelist.

IES 02204, Book of Confession, መጽሐፈ ኑዛዜ; Bandlet of Righteousness, ልፋፈ ጽድቅ; Image of John, መልክአ ዮሐንስ. Parchment, 130 x 90 x 39 mm, ii + 49 folios, one column, 13–14 lines, Gəʻəz, twentieth century.

Miniatures:

1. F. i r(ecto): Crude drawing of an equestrian saint.

IES 02205, Antiphonary for the Whole Year, ዱን. Parchment, 230 x 140 x 55 mm, iii + 125 folios, two columns, 20–23 lines, Gəʻəz, twentieth century.

Catalogue of the Manuscripts 155

IES 02209, Miracles of Saint Michael, ተአምረ ሚካኤል; Homiliary in Honor of the Monthly Feast of the Archangel Michael for the Month of Ḫədar, ድርሳን ዘጎዳር ቅዱስ ሚካኤል. Parchment, 210 x 170 x 50 mm, iii + 86 folios, two columns, 17–18 lines, Gəʿəz.

IES 02210, Computus, ባሕረ ሐሳብ; Image of the Passion Week, መልክአ ሕማማት; Lectionary of the Passion Week, ግብረ ሕማማት; Lamentation of the Virgin, ሰቆቃወ ድንግል; Mystery of the Trinity, in Amharic, ምሥጢረ ሥላሴ; Table Prayer, "We beseech you," ሰአልናከ; Image of the Eucharist, መልክአ ቁርባን; Excerpt of the Horologium for the Night called Prayer to Mary, "All the Hosts of Heaven Glorify You" ኮሎሙ ሠራዊተ ሰማያት; Hymn called *Məqnay*, ምቅናይ; Miracle of Mary, ተአምረ ማርያም; Miracle of *abba* Samuʾel, ተአምረ አባ ሳሙኤል; Miracles of Jesus, ተአምረ ኢየሱስ; Image of *abba* Samuʾel, መልክአ አባ ሳሙኤል. Parchment, 150 x 110 x 50 mm, iv + 120 folios, two columns, 18 lines, Gəʿəz, early twentieth century.

Miniatures:

1. F. 104v: Print card of Madonna and Child is stitched onto the folio.

IES 02211, Rampart of the Cross, ሐጹረ መስቀል. Parchment, 70 x 70 x 30 mm, ii + 54 folios, one column, 10 lines, Gəʿəz, nineteenth century.

IES 02212, Prayer of Moses, ጸሎተ ሙሴ. Parchment, 90 x 60 x 19 mm, ii + 24 folios, one column, 14 lines, Gəʿəz, twentieth century.

IES 02213, Bandlet of Righteousness, ልፋፈ ጽድቅ; Days on which the Heavens are Open to Receive Prayer, ርጉወ ሰማይ. Parchment, 95 x 70 x 12 mm, iv + 43 folios, one column, 12 lines, Gəʿəz, twentieth century.

IES 02228, In praise of the Patriarch Basəlyos and Emperor Ḫaylä Śəllase, in the style of the school chant called *aryam*, በአርያም መልክ ለብፁዕ ወቅዱስ አቡን ባስልዮስ እና ለቀዳማዊ ኃይለ ሥላሴ የቀረበ. Paper, 351 x 293 x 1 mm, i + 1 folios, three columns, 29 lines, Gəʿəz, twentieth century.

IES 02243, Bandlet of Righteousness, ልፋፈ ጽድቅ; the Prayer of Mary at Golgotha, ጸሎተ እግዝእትነ ማርያም ዘኔ ጎልጎታ; Sword of the Trinity, arranged for the days of the week, ሠይፈ ሥላሴ; Prayer to Mary; Prayer to Jesus; Computus, ባሕረ ሐሳብ; Anaphora of Our Lady Mary attributed to Cyriacus of Bəhənsa, ቅዳሴ ማርያም. Parchment, 130 x 90 x 60 mm, 174 folios, one column, 15–17 lines, Gəʿəz, twentieth century.

Miniatures:

1. F. 46r: Madonna and Child, in pencil.

IES 02244, *Asmat* Prayers, with talismanic symbols, አስማት. Parchment, 90 x 72 x 40 mm, i + 100 folios, one column, 12 lines, Gəʿəz, twentieth century.

Miniatures:

1. Talismanic symbols are found throughout the codex (ff. 2r, 3rv, 4v, 7v–9v, 11r, 12r–15v, 17r–19v, 94v, 99v).

2. F. 99r: Equestrian saint.

IES 02256, Book of Philosophers, መጽሐፈ ፈላስፋ. Parchment, 195 x 140 x 35 mm, ii + 35 folios, two columns, 22 lines, Gəʿəz, twentieth century.

IES 02257, *Mäwaśəʾat* Chants, መዋሥዕት. Parchment, 170 x 140 x 48 mm, iv + 92 folios, two columns, 13 lines, Gəʿəz, twentieth century.

IES 02260, *Ziq* Chants, መጽሐፈ ዚቅ. Parchment, 180 x 135 x 73 mm, vi + 198 folios, two columns, 22–23 lines, Gəʿəz, twentieth century.

IES 02261, Image of Täklä Haymanot, መልክአ ተክለ ሃይማኖት; Prayer of Dəmeṭros and *abunä* Sälama for Long Life and Repentance, ጸሎት ዘእድሜ ወንስሐ. Parchment, 126 x 80 x 21 mm, ii + 32 folios, one column, 13–14 lines, Gəʿəz, twentieth century.

IES 02263, Book of Advice and Admonition, written by seven saintly monks, ምዕዳን ዘአስተጋብእዎ ፯ ቅዱሳን መነኮሳት. Parchment, 110 x 75 x 30 mm, ii + 43 folios, one column, 14 lines, Amharic, twentieth century.

Miniatures:

1. F. 43v: Crude drawing of a saint holding a necklace.

IES 02268, Proverbs, ምሳሌያተ ሰሎሞን; Commentary on the Book of Daniel, ትርጓሜ ዳንኤል, incomplete; On the Rise of Mohamad Grañ, ነገረ ግራኝ. Paper, 160 x 160 x 20 mm, i + 70 folios, ff. 1r–58r one column, ff. 58v–68v two columns, 15–33 lines, Gəʿəz, 1928 EC = 1935–36.

IES 02269, Genealogy of the Fathers from Adam up to the last of the Ethiopian Emperors (Mənilək II), ሦልቄ ነገሥት; Amharic Poem in Praise of Mənilək II; History of the Kings of Ethiopia, ታሪከ ነገሥት; Acts of Gäbrä Krəstos, ገድለ ገብረ ክርስቶስ; Image of Gäbrä Krəstos, መልክአ ገብረ ክርስቶስ; Five Pillars of Mystery, አምስቱ አዕማደ ምሥጢር, combined with the Beauty of Creation, ሥነ ፍጥረት. Paper, 228 x 140 x 19 mm, iii + 170 folios, one column, 21–23 lines, Amharic, 1914 EC = 1921–22.

IES 02282, Zəmmare Chants, ዝማሬ Mäwaśə'ət Chants, መዋሥዕት. Parchment, 220 x 180 x 65 mm, iv + 134 folios, ff. 1r–98r two columns, ff. 99r–132v three columns, 21–24 lines, Gə'əz, nineteenth century.

Miniatures:

1. F. 98v: Madonna and Child.

IES 02283, Psalter, ዳዊት; Praises of Mary, ውዳሴ ማርያም, is combined with Image of the Praises of Mary, መልክአ ውዳሴ ማርያም; Gate of Light, አንቀፀ ብርሃን, is combined with Image of the Gate of Light, መልክአ አንቀፀ ብርሃን; Prayer of Supplication for the Departed, መስተብቁዕ ዘሙታን. Parchment, 270 x 230 x 90 mm, ii + 209 folios, one column and two columns, 18 lines, Gə'əz, nineteenth century.

IES 02291, Gospel of John, ወንጌል ዘዮሐንስ; Anaphora of Our Lady Mary attributed to Cyriacus of Bəhənsa, ቅዳሴ ማርያም; Absolution of the Son, ፍትሐት ዘወልድ. Parchment, 160 x 95 x 42 mm, ii + 116 folios, two columns, 15–19 lines, Gə'əz, early twentieth century.

IES 02292, Homiliary on the Sabbath of the Church, ድርሳነ ሰንበት. Parchment, 220 x 173 x 30 mm, iv + 68 folios, two columns, 20–21 lines, Gə'əz, twentieth century.

IES 02293, Psalter, ዳዊት; Angels Praise Her, ይዌድሰዋ መላእክት ለማርያም. Parchment, 230 x 150 x 58 mm, ii + 137 folios, one column and two columns, 25 lines, Gə'əz, late nineteenth century.

Miniatures:

1. F. i r(ecto): Crude drawing of figures and an angel with sword and scabbard.
2. F. ii v(erso): Crude drawing of an angel with a sword.
3. F. 23r: An angel.

IES 02294, History of the Ethiopian Kings, መጽሐፈ ታሪክ. Parchment, 245 x 210 x 40 mm, ii + 42 folios, two columns, 22 lines, Gə'əz, twentieth century.

IES 02295, Acts of Täklä Haymanot, ገድለ ተክለ ሃይማኖት. Parchment, 255 x 185 x 67 mm, vi + 176 folios, two columns, 26 lines, Gə'əz, twentieth century.

Miniatures:

1. F. iv r(ecto): Täklä Haymanot.

IES 02296, History of the Kings, ታሪክ ነገሥት. Paper, 295 x 205 x 20 mm, 101 folios, one column, 33 lines, Amharic, twentieth century.

IES 02303, Commentary on Mar Yeshaq; ማር ይስሐቅ ትርጓሜ. Parchment and paper, 330 x 215 x 45 mm, i + 231 folios, ff. 1r–65r two columns, ff. 65v–230r one column, 29–32 lines, Gə'əz, twentieth century.

IES 02304, God Reigns, እግዚአብሐር ነግሠ (ነግሥ), ascribed to Zär'a Ya'əqob. Parchment and paper, 215 x 167 x 57 mm, i + 296 folios, ff. 1r–203r two columns, ff. 205r–290v one column, 20 lines in ff. 1r–69r, 41 lines in the rest of the codex, Gə'əz, twentieth century.

Miniatures:

1. F. 73v: Crude drawing of crosses.
2. F. 74r: Crude drawing of a figure.
3. F. 74v: Crude drawing of a figure.
4. F. 143v: Crude drawing of a figure.

IES 02305, Thirty-Six Miracles of Mary, ተአምረ ማርያም. Parchment, 295 x 240 x 30 mm, i + 47 folios, two columns, 21 lines, Gə'əz, nineteenth century.

Miniatures:

1. F. 47r: Crude drawing of a figure.

IES 02307, Vision of Mary, ራዕየ ማርያም. Parchment, 110 x 65 x 30 mm, 48 folios, one column, 15–16 lines, Gə'əz, twentieth century.

IES 02308, Prayer of Mary at Golgotha, ጸሎተ እግዝእትነ ማርያም ዘሰኔ ጎልጎታ. Parchment, 130 x 95 x 30 mm, iv + 35 folios, one column, 11 lines, Gəʿəz, twentieth century.

IES 02309, *Səbḥatä fəqur* hymns, ስብሐተ ፍቁር. Parchment, 100 x 70 x 30 mm, ii + 29 folios, one column, 13–14 lines, Gəʿəz, twentieth century.

IES 02310, Prayer against Terror, ጸሎተ ድንጋጼ። በእንተ ፍቅር ወሰላም; Instruction for Traditional Medicine. Paper, 135 x 100 x 20 mm, v + 94 folios, one column, 12–13 lines, Gəʿəz, Amharic, twentieth century.

Miniatures:

1. F. 5v: Angel of Memros.
2. F. 11v: Box surrounded by four heads, facing the four directions.
3. F. 23v: Winged saint behind a dais.
4. F. 24r: Michael, the Archangel, with a processional cross.
5. F. 33v: Seated saint, with an archangel on either side.
6. F. 35v: John and Mary, with the caption, "He gave John to his mother."
7. F. 37v: Angel with wings outstretched.
8. F. 40v: The Crucifixion.
9. F. 42r: Mount Tabor.
10. F. 45v: Madonna and Child.
11. F. 46r: Yared.
12. F. 48v: Raguel, the Archangel.
13. F. 50r: John the Evangelist.
14. Ff. 56v–58v, 59v, 60v: Talismanic symbols.
15. F. 62r: *Ḥaräg* with face in center.
16. F. 75v: Man standing holding something.
17. F. 85r: Three angels behind a dais.

IES 02314, Image of Saint George, መልክአ ጊዮርጊስ ዘሰዉዳ ሞገስ. Parchment, 100 x 65 x 32 mm, iv + 50 folios, one column, 11 lines, Gəʿəz, twentieth century.

Miniatures:

1. F. 50v: Intertwined rope figure, written in blue ink.

IES 02315, Vision of Mary, ራዕየ ማርያም; Image of Mary, መልክአ ማርያም. Parchment, 110 x 80 x 29 mm, iii + 61 folios, one column, 14 lines, Amharic, twentieth century.

IES 02323, Image of Mary, መልክአ ማርያም; Image of Jesus, መልክአ ኢየሱስ; Image of Gabriel, መልክአ ገብርኤል. Parchment, 140 x 110 x 33 mm, 34 folios, two columns, 17 lines, Gəʿəz, twentieth century.

Miniatures:

1. F. 34r: Angel with a sword.

IES 02329, Prayer of Peter, ጸሎተ ጴጥሮስ; Prayer of Mary at Golgotha, ጸሎተ እግዝእትነ ማርያም ዘሰኔ ጎልጎታ; Anaphora of Our Lady Mary attributed to Cyriacus of Bəhənsa, ቅዳሴ ማርያም. Parchment, 190 x 142 x 55 mm, i + 158 folios, two columns, 16 lines, Gəʿəz, 1874–1926 (mentions the Alexandrian Patriarch Cyril V and Metropolitan Matewos).

IES 02331, Mar Yeshaq or Isaac of Nineveh, ማር ይስሐቅ. Parchment, 195 x 185 x 43 mm, ii + 96 folios, two columns, 30 lines, Gəʿəz, nineteenth century.

Miniatures:

1. F. i r(ecto): Man riding a rooster, with the caption "Thunder and lightening."

2. F. i v(erso): Täklä Haymanot.

3. F. ii r(ecto): Claudius, on horseback, spears "Səndat," the two-tailed man beast.

4. F. ii v(erso): Equestrian saint spearing an ox.

5. F. 95v: An angel.

6. F. 96r: Equestrian saint, Susənyos spearing Wərzəlya.

7. F. 96v: *Abba* Täklä Alpha spears Ǝmmä Wəlud.

IES 02332, Acts of the Apostles, የሐዋርያት ሥራ. Parchment, 165 x 120 x 53 mm, iv + 124 folios, two columns, 16 lines, Amharic, twentieth century.

Miniatures:

1. F. i v(erso): Madonna and Child.
2. F. ii r(ecto): Saint George and the Dragon.
3. F. ii v(erso): The Crucifixion.
4. F. iii r(ecto): The Deposition.
5. F. iii v(erso): Wrapping the body of Jesus in the shroud.
6. F. iv r(ecto): The Entombment of Jesus.
7. F. iv v(erso): The Resurrection of Jesus.
8. F. 123r: The Ascension.
9. F. 123v: Our Lady Mary according to the vision in Revelation 12.
10. F. 124r: Madonna and Child.

IES 02366, Image of Emperor Mənilək II, መልክአ ምኒልክ. Paper, 280 x 220 x 5 mm, 12 folios, one column, French, Gəʿəz.

IES 02371, Lectionary for Passion Week, ግብረ ሕማማት. Parchment, 345 x 260 x 90 mm, ii + 162 folios, three columns, 34–35 lines, Gəʿəz, nineteenth century.

IES 02372, Book of Extreme Unction, መጽሐፈ ቀንዲል. Parchment and paper, 191 x 155 x 28 mm, xi + 39 folios, two columns, 18–19 lines, Gəʿəz, twentieth century.

IES 02376, Gospel of John, ወንጌል ዘዮሐንስ; Book of the Disciples, መጽሐፈ አርድእት; Prayer of Moses which saved him from Pharaoh, ጸሎተ ሙሴ; Image of Gäbrä Krəstos, መልክአ ገብረ ክርስቶስ. Parchment, 205 x 135 x 48 mm, ii + 120 folios, two columns, 18–19 lines, Gəʿəz, nineteenth century.

Miniatures:

1. F. 72v: The Crucifixion of Jesus, effaced.
2. F. 73r: Soldiers at the foot of the cross, effaced.

IES 02377, Anaphora of Our Lady Mary attributed to Cyriacus of Bəhənsa, ቅዳሴ ማርያም; Image of Mary, መልክአ ማርያም; Canticle of the Flower, ማሕሌተ ጽጌ. Parchment, 175 x 115 x 48 mm, iv + 136 folios, two columns, 13 lines, Gəʿəz, 1874–1926 (mentions the Alexandrian Patriarch Cyril V and Metropolitan Matewos).

IES 02378, Mystagogia, ትምህርተ ኀቡዓት; Image of the Praises of Mary, መልክአ ውዳሴ ማርያም; Prayer called *Rəḫuqä Mäʿat*, ርኁቀ መዓት; Praise of the Beloved, ስብሐተ ፍቁር; Prayer of Benediction, ጸሎተ ቡራኪ. Parchment, 100 x 95 x 35 mm, ii + 43 folios, one column, 13–14 lines, Gəʿəz, late nineteenth century.

IES 02379, Prayer of Mary at Golgotha, ጸሎተ እግዝእትነ ማርያም ዘሰኔ ጎልጎታ; Prayer against the Tongue of People, ልሳነ ሰብእ (በእንተ ልሳነ ዘመድ ወባእድ). Parchment, 140 x 105 x 30 mm, iii + 41 folios, two columns, 11–12 lines, Gəʿəz, early twentieth century.

IES 02380, Homiliary in Honor of the Archangel Michael, ድርሳነ ሚካኤል; Image of Mary, መልክአ ማርያም; Image of Jesus, መልክአ ኢየሱስ; Image of the Savior of the World, መልክአ መድኀኔ ዓለም; Image of the Covenant of Mercy, መልክአ ኪዳነ ምሕረት; Image of the Passion Week, መልክአ ሕማማት; Lament of the Virgin, ሰቆቃወ ድንግል; Prayer, "For the sake of the peaceful holy things," በእንተ ቅድሳት ሰላማዊት; Table Prayer, "We beseech you," ሰአልናከ. Parchment, 120 x 90 x 50 mm, ii + 100 folios, two columns, 16 lines, Gəʿəz, 1889–1916 (mentions Metropolitan Peṭros IV [r. 1881– 1916] and Metropolitan Matewos [r. 1889–1926]).

IES 02381, Image of Edom, incomplete, መልክአ ኤዶም; Image of Michael, incomplete, መልክአ ሚካኤል; Image of Saint George, መልክአ ጊዮርጊስ; Image of Gabriel, መልክአ ገብርኤል; Image of John the Baptist, መልክአ ዮሐንስ መጥምቅ; *Asmat* Prayer, incomplete, አስማት; Image of Gäbrä Mänfäs Qəddus, መልክአ ገብረ መንፈስ ቅዱስ; Prayer of the Covenant, ጸሎተ ኪዳን; Angels Praise Her, ይቤድስዋ መላእክት ለማርያም; *Asmat* Prayer, አስማት; Image of Mary, incomplete, ለአዳም ፋሲካሁ; Miracle of Mary, ተአምረ ማርያም. Parchment, 120 x 75 x 40 mm, ii + 64 folios, one column, 16 lines, Gəʿəz, nineteenth century.

IES 02384, Gəʿəz Grammar, ሰዋስወ ግዕዝ. Parchment, 150 x 110 x 39 mm, ii + 53 folios, one column, 22–26 lines, Amharic, Gəʿəz, early twentieth century.

IES 02385, Gate of Penance, አንቀጸ ንስሓ; Vision of Mary, ራዕየ ማርያም. Parchment, 105 x 70 x 35 mm, ii + 72 folios, one column, 12–13 lines, Gəʿəz, twentieth century.

IES 02386, Lectionary Readings from the Gospels. Parchment, 170 x 150 x 42 mm, ii + 64 folios, two columns, 16 lines, Gəʿəz, nineteenth century.

IES 02387, Catholic Epistles and Revelation. Parchment, 190 x 145 x 45 mm, i + 71 folios, two columns, 21–22 lines, Gəʿəz, twentieth century.

IES 02388, Anaphora of Our Lady Mary attributed to Cyriacus of Bəhənsa, ቅዳሴ ማርያም; Absolution of the Son, ፍትሐት ዘወልድ; Praise of the Beloved, ስብሐት ፍቁር; Image of Mary Fasika, ለአዳም ፋሲካሁ; Image of the Icon, መልክአ ሥዕል; Prayer to the Trinity, "Blessing and Praise," ባርኮ ወውዳሴ; Anaphora of Jacob of Serugh, ቅዳሴ ያዕቆብ ዘሥሩግ; God of the Luminaries, እግዚአብሔር ዘብርሃናት; *Asmat* Prayer of the Three Children, አስማት ዘወሀቦሙ እግዚአብሔር ለአናንያ ወአዛርያ ወሚሳኤል; Table Prayer, "We beseech you," ሰአልናክ; Anaphora of the 318 Orthodox Fathers, ቅዳሴ ዘሠለስቱ ምዕት; Greeting to Gäbrä Mänfäs Qəddus, መፍቀሬ ጸሎት ወጸም. Parchment, 200 x 115 x 40 mm, i + 58 folios, two columns, 17–20 lines, Gəʿəz, twentieth century.

IES 02389, Psalter, ዳዊት; Image of the Icon, incomplete, መልክአ ሥዕል; Prayer to Jesus, "I Take Refuge," ተማኅጸንኩ; Sword of Divinity, ሠይፈ መለኮት. Paper, 190 x 120 x 40 mm, ii + 190 folios, one column and two columns, 20 lines, Gəʿəz, late nineteenth/early twentieth century.

Miniatures:

1. F. ii v(erso): King David playing the harp.

IES 02407, In appreciation of *fitawrari* Desta; On the Thirteen Stations of the Cross, in Amharic, ስለ ፲፫ ሕማማተ መስቀል. Parchment, 215 x 165 x 40 mm, ii + 43 folios, two columns, 15–17 lines, Gəʿəz, Amharic, twentieth century.

Miniatures:

1. F. i r(ecto): Portrait of an Ethiopian man, in pencil.
2. F. 42r: Crude drawing of a church.
3. F. 42v: Crude drawing of three faces.
4. F. 43r: Crude drawing of a face.

IES 02408, Homilies of the Lifegiver, arranged for the days of the week, ድርሳነ ማኅየዊ. Parchment, 175 x 135 x 45 mm, iv + 122 folios, two columns, 16 lines, Gəʿəz, 1938 EC = 1945–46 (f. 124r).

IES 02411, Synaxarium, መጽሐፈ ስንክሳር, from a private church in Goǧǧam. Parchment, 350 x 275 x 89 mm, i + 161 folios, three columns, 40 lines, Gəʿəz, 1812 (f. 158v, though the palaeography points to later and the miniatures are clearly modern additions by the same artist who added images to IES 2412–14, 2416).

Miniatures:

1. F. i v(erso): The Holy Trinity surrounded by the Four Living Creatures.
2. F. 3r: The serpent tempting Adam and Eve.
3. F. 6v: Adam and Eve being driven from Eden.
4. F. 11r: The Annunciation.
5. F. 13r: An angel with a sword and processional cross.
6. F. 16v: The Baptism of Jesus.
7. F. 19r: The Nativity.
8. F. 20v: The Flight into Egypt.
9. F. 23r: A group of men with spears point to a donkey's head emerging from the base of a tree.
10. F. 31r: The Holy family with Salome at Mary's feet.
11. F. 33r: Portraits of various animals.
12. F. 41r: Jesus teaching.
13. F. 46v: Jesus teaching.
14. F. 52v: Jesus healing the blind.
15. F. 55r: Jesus raising Lazarus from the dead.
16. F. 60v: A church.
17. F. 69r: The Foot-Washing.
18. F. 73r: The Last Supper.
19. F. 74v: The Garden of Gethsemane.
20. F. 78v: The Arrest of Jesus.

21. F. 81r: The Flogging of Jesus.
22. F. 87r: The Flogging of Jesus.
23. F. 90v: Jesus carrying the cross.
24. F. 96v: Nailing Jesus to the cross.
25. F. 101r: The Crucifixion.
26. F. 103v: Pilate washes his hands.
27. F. 110v: The Deposition.
28. F. 116r: Shrouding the body of Jesus.
29. F. 123v: The Entombment of Jesus.
30. F. 132r: The Resurrection of Jesus.
31. F. 137v: The Risen Christ appears before the disciples.
32. F. 140r: The Ascension.
33. F. 143v: Pentecost.
34. F. 160r: The Risen Christ appears before the disciples.
35. F. 160v: Täklä Haymanot.
36. F. 161r: Gäbrä Mänfäs Qəddus.

IES 02412, Lectionary for Passion Week, ግብረ ሕማማት, a priest called *mämhər* Gäbrä Krəstos gave this codex to the Church of Däbrä Qwəsqwam of Gondär, said to be copied from a manuscript from 1722 EC = 1729–30 (the miniatures are clearly modern additions by the same artist who added images to IES 2411, 2413–14, 2416). Parchment, 351 x 292 x 81 mm, ii + 111 folios, three columns, 30–31 lines, Gəʿəz, twentieth century.

Miniatures:

1. F. i v(erso): Gäbrä Mänfäs Qəddus.
2. F. ii r(ecto): Jesus teaching.
3. F. ii v(erso): Covenant of Mercy.
4. F. 16v: Madonna and Child.
5. F. 21r: The Assumption.
6. F. 26r: Jesus' miracle of the wine at Cana.

7. F. 32v: Jesus teaching.

8. F. 33r: Jesus (left) ministering to a kneeling woman (right).

9. F. 36v: Jesus (center) and the disciples (left) in a dispute with persons (right).

10. F. 37r: The Striking of the Head.

11. F. 42v: Jesus carrying the cross.

12. F. 43r: Jesus being bound to the cross.

13. F. 47v: The Crucifixion.

14. F. 48r: The Resurrection of Jesus.

15. F. 93v: Mary (right) before three persons with canes.

16. F. 94r: Madonna and child.

17. F. 97v: Mary (right) and an angel (center), confront three hostile men (showing one eye, left).

18. F. 98r: Mary and the thirsty dog.

19. F. 99v: Annunciation.

20. F. 102r: Saint George and the Dragon.

21. F. 105v: Four men and three angels.

22. F. 106r: Jesus and the Holy family (in the temple?).

23. F. 110r: Jesus enthroned surrounded by angels.

24. F. 110v: The Entombment of Jesus.

25. F. 111r: Mary and two angels.

IES 02413, Funeral Ritual, መጽሐፈ ግንዘት, said to be copied from a manuscript from 1769 EC = 1776–77. (The miniatures are clearly modern additions by the same artist who added images to IES 2411–12, 2414, 2416). Parchment, 310 x 230 x 70 mm, i + 101 folios, two columns, 29–30 lines, Gəʿəz, Amharic, twentieth century.

Miniatures:

1. F. i v(erso): Madonna and Child.

2. F. 8v: Four saints and three angels.

3. F. 10v: The Holy Trinity surrounded by the four Living Creatures.

4. F. 11r: Three angels and four saints.
5. F. 14v: Mary kneeling, surrounded by four angels.
6. F. 18v: An angel with a sword protects Mary from two men.
7. F. 19r: Joseph and Mary hailed by three people.
8. F. 26v: An angel brings two men to Mary.
9. F. 27r: Mary, Joseph, and an angel.
10. F. 31v: An angel standing on a cloud, holds out a cup to Mary.
11. F. 32r: Mary kneels before an angel.
12. F. 37v: Mary seated before three hostile men.
13. F. 38r: Mary stands before two hostile men.
14. F. 42v: Madonna and Child.
15. F. 43r: Madonna and Child.
16. F. 47v: Mary raises a saint.
17. F. 48r: Jesus surrounded by angels.
18. F. 52r: The Ascension of Jesus.
19. F. 55v: Prayer of Our Lady at Golgotha.
20. F. 56r: Jesus before three women holding jugs on their backs.
21. F. 60r: The miracle of wine at Cana.
22. F. 64v: Jesus and the blind men before healing.
23. F. 65r: Jesus and the blind men after healing.
24. F. 71v: Jesus, enthroned, surrounded by angels.
25. F. 72r: Jesus before a hostile crowd with stones.
26. F. 75v: The Arrest of Jesus.
27. F. 76r: The Binding of Jesus.
28. F. 79v: The Striking of the Head.
29. F. 80r: Jesus carrying the cross.
30. F 83v: The Crucifixion.
31. F. 84r: The Deposition.
32. F. 90v: Wrapping the body of Jesus in the burial shroud.
33. F. 91r: The Resurrection of Jesus.

34. F. 92v: Jesus, surrounded by angels.

35. F. 93r: Mary and two other women.

36. F. 101r: Four women, three angels.

IES 02414, Four Gospels, አርባዕቱ፡ ወንጌል, said to be copied from a manuscript from 1743 EC = 1750–51 (the miniatures are clearly modern additions by the same artist who added images to IES 2411–13, 2416). Parchment, 250 x 210 x 78 mm, ii + 112 folios, two columns, 27–31 lines, Gəʿəz, twentieth century.

Miniatures:

1. F. i v(erso): Madonna and Child.

2. F. ii r(ecto): Our Lady Mary, with angels and men.

3. F. ii v(erso): Two angels and a man.

4. F. 2v: Joachim and Anne are blessed by the Holy Spirit.

5. F. 3r: Presentation of Mary (?).

6. F. 4v: The Visitation (?).

7. F. 5r: Assumption of Mary.

8. F. 8v: Mary and two angels.

9. F. 9r: Mary surrounded by angels.

10. F. 14v: Mary before two men.

11. F. 15r: Mary and the thirsty dog.

12. F. 25r: Mary and two angels.

13. F. 32v: An angel holds a cup to Mary.

14. F. 33r: The Annunciation.

15. F. 40v: Mary before three hostile men.

16. F. 41r: Mary before two hostile men casting stones.

17. F. 49v: Madonna and Child.

18. F. 50r: Mary and the child Jesus.

19. F. 53v: The Ascension.

20. F. 54r: Jesus before Mary.

21. F. 59v: Jesus before two men carrying jugs on their backs.

22. F. 60r: The miracle of the wine at Cana.

23. F. 63v: Jesus before a crowd.

24. F. 64r: Jesus teaching.

25. F. 69v: Jesus enthroned.

26. F. 71v: Jesus before a hostile crowd casting stones.

27. F. 72r: Jesus is bound and led away by a hostile crowd. Mary and John grieve.

28. F. 79v: The Binding of Jesus.

29. F. 80r: The Striking of the Head.

30. F. 91v: The Crucifixion.

31. F. 92r: The Deposition.

32. F. 101v: Wrapping the body of Jesus in the burial shroud.

33. F. 102r: The Resurrection of Jesus.

34. F. 103v: Dormition of the Mother of God.

35. F. 104r: The Assumption of Mary (?).

36. F. 105v: Jesus appears to the disciples.

37. F. 106r: The Assumption of Mary.

IES 02416, Funeral Ritual, መጽሐፈ ግንዘት. Parchment, 220 x 190 x 75 mm, 156 folios, two columns, 15 lines, Gəʿəz, eighteenth century. Tourism Commission number G-IV-447. A note in a later hand states that this manuscript was written in 1778 EC for Däbrä Mäwi Maryam of Goǧǧam (the miniatures are clearly modern additions by the same artist who added images to IES 2411–14). This manuscript was returned to Ethiopia by Sam Fogg.

Miniatures:

1. F. 3r: Three saints.

2. F. 9v: Mary before an angel and a woman.

3. F. 10r: Mary before an angel and a man.

4. F. 15v: Mary before two hostile men.

5. F. 16r: Mary before an angel.

6. F. 23v: Mary before three persons.

7. F. 24r: The Nativity.
8. F. 33v: Mary before two hostile men.
9. F. 34r: Mary before two women.
10. F. 37v: The Annunciation.
11. F. 38r: Mary before two hostile men and a saint.
12. F. 42v: Mary and the boy Jesus with an angel.
13. F. 43r: Jesus at the temple with the elders.
14. F. 49v: The Annunciation.
15. F. 50r: Jesus enthroned before angels.
16. F. 52r: Two angels.
17. F. 59r: An angel between two men.
18. F. 109v: The miracle of the wine at Cana.
19. F. 110r: Jesus healing the blind.
20. F. 115v: Jesus and the woman of Samaria (with a jug on her back, right).
21. F. 116r: Jesus appears to Mary and two disciples.
22. F. 120v: Jesus before two hostile men.
23. F. 121r: The Arrest of Jesus.
24. F. 125v: The Striking of the Head.
25. F. 126r: The Binding of Jesus.
26. F. 127v: The Crucifixion.
27. F. 128r: Wrapping the body of Jesus in the burial shroud.
28. F. 130v: The Resurrection of Jesus.
29. F. 131r: Jesus appears to the disciples.
30. F. 133v: Three saints.
31. F. 134r: Mary with two women (on either side).
32. F. 137r: Gäbrä Mänfäs Qəddus.
33. F. 143r: Two angels standing; two angels in flight.
34. F. 149v: The beheading of John the Baptist (?).
35. F. 150r: Two angels.

36. F. 155v: Mary and another person before an angel.

37. F. 156r: Two saints and an angel.

IES 02417A, Book of Medicine, መጽሐፈ መድኃኒት, from the private collection of *aläqa* Täkäśtä Bərhan. Paper, 315 x 210 x 20 mm, i + 136 folios, one column, 30–31 lines, Gəʿəz, Amharic, mid-twentieth century.

IES 02417B, *Asmat* Prayer for Help in Learning, from the private collection of *aläqa* Täkäśtä Bərhan. Paper, 335 x 210 x 15 mm, i + 133 folios, one column, 31–32 lines, Gəʿəz, Amharic, mid-twentieth century.

IES 02417C, Prayer of Dream, ጸሎት ሕልም; and other *Asmat* Prayers [Satanic], from the private collection of *aläqa* Täkäśtä Bərhan. Paper, 293 x 200 x 15 mm, i + 92 folios, one column, 30 lines, Gəʿəz, Amharic, mid-twentieth century.

IES 02417D, Satanic Prayers, from the private collection of *aläqa* Täkäśtä Bərhan. Paper, 300 x 210 x 20 mm, ii + 96 folios, one column, 31 lines, Gəʿəz, Amharic, mid-twentieth century.

IES 02417E, *Asmat* Prayer against Evil Eye, ጸሎት በእንተ ሕማመ ቡዳ, from the private collection of *aläqa* Täkäśtä Bərhan. Paper, 330 x 220 x 15 mm, ii + 77 folios, one column, 33 lines, Gəʿəz, Amharic, mid-twentieth century.

IES 02417F, Book of Medicine, መጽሐፈ መድኃኒት, from the private collection of *aläqa* Täkäśtä Bərhan. Paper, 300 x 210 x 20 mm, ii + 96 folios, one column, 30 lines, Gəʿəz, Amharic, mid-twentieth century.

IES 02417G, Book of Precious Stones, መጽሐፈ አዕባን, from the private collection of *aläqa* Täkäśtä Bərhan. Paper, 290 x 205 x 16 mm, ii + 50 folios, one column, 30 lines, Gəʿəz, Amharic, mid-twentieth century.

IES 02417H, *Asmat* Prayer against charm, ጸሎት በእንተ መፍትሔ ሥራይ; and other prayers, from the private collection of *aläqa* Täkäśtä Bərhan. Paper, 290 x 205 x 18 mm, i + 34 folios, one column, 29 lines, Gəʿəz, Amharic, mid-twentieth century.

IES 02417I, *Asmat* Prayer for Respect, ጸሎት በእንተ ግርማ ሞገስ; and other prayers, from the private collection of *aläqa* Täkäśtä Bərhan. Paper, 295 x 210 x 19 mm, ii + 96 folios, one column, 29 lines, Gəʿəz, Amharic, mid-twentieth century.

IES 02417J, *Asmat* Prayer for Self Protection, ጸሎት በእንተ ዓቃቢ ርእስ; and other prayers, from the private collection of *aläqa* Täkäśtä Bərhan. Paper, 295 x 205 x 16 mm, ii + 94 folios, one column, 29 lines, Gəʿəz, Amharic, mid-twentieth century.

IES 02417KA, *Asmat* Prayer for Respect and Love, ጸሎት በእንተ ግርማ ሞገስ; and other *Asmat* Prayers, from the private collection of *aläqa* Täkäśtä Bərhan. Paper, 305 x 210 x 18 mm, i + 85 folios, one column, 33-34 lines, Gəʿəz, Amharic, mid-twentieth century.

IES 02417KB, *Asmat* Prayer against an enemy, ጸሎት በእንተ ፀር; and other *Asmat* Prayers, from the private collection of *aläqa* Täkäśtä Bərhan. Paper, 300 x 210 x 15 mm, ii + 96 folios, one column, 29 lines, Gəʿəz, Amharic, mid-twentieth century.

IES 02417LA, *Asmat* Prayer against an enemy, ጸሎት በእንተ ፀር; and other *Asmat* Prayers, from the private collection of *aläqa* Täkäśtä Bərhan. Paper, 320 x 215 x 20 mm, i + 157 folios, one column, 33 lines, Gəʿəz, Amharic, mid-twentieth century.

IES 02417LB, *Asmat* Prayer for Respect and Love, ጸሎት በእንተ ግርማ ሞገስ; and other *Asmat* Prayers, from the private collection of *aläqa* Täkäśtä Bərhan. Paper, 295 x 210 x 14 mm, ii + 95 folios, one column, 29 lines, Gəʿəz, Amharic, mid-twentieth century.

IES 02417N, Excerpt from Book of Flora [Medicine], ከመጽሐፈ ዕፀ ደብዳቤ የተገኘ, from the private collection of *aläqa* Täkäśtä Bərhan. Paper, 295 x 210 x 15 mm, ii + 10 folios, one column, 28 lines, Gəʿəz, Amharic, twentieth century.

IES 02417O, Prayer against the Tongue of People, ጸሎት በእንተ ትከተ ልሳን; and other *Asmat* Prayers, from the private collection of *aläqa* Täkäśtä Bərhan. Paper, 290 x 210 x 16 mm, ii + 96 folios, one column, 28-29 lines, Gəʿəz, Amharic, twentieth century.

IES 02417P, *Asmat* Prayer for Wealth and Appointment, and other *Asmat* Prayers, from the private collection of *aläqa* Täkäśtä Bərhan. Paper, 310 x 210 x 12 mm, ii + 94 folios, one column, 33 lines, Gəʿəz, Amharic, twentieth century.

IES 02439, Gospel of John, ወንጌል ዘዮሐንስ; Revelation, ራዕየ ዮሐንስ. Parchment, 140 x 120 x 95 mm, 155 folios, two columns, 14 lines, Gəʿəz, early sixteenth century.

IES 02440, Image of Mary, መልክአ ማርያም; Image of Jesus, መልክአ ኢየሱስ; Image of Michael, መልክአ ሚካኤል; Image of Gabriel, መልክአ ገብርኤል. Parchment, 135 x 95 x 38 mm, iv + 68 folios, one column, 13 lines, Gəʿəz, twentieth century.

IES 02444, Book of Medicine, መጽሐፈ መድኃኒት. Parchment, 160 x 100 x 50 mm, ii + 154 folios, one column, 26 lines, Amharic, Gəʿəz, late nineteenth century.

Miniatures:

1. Talismanic symbols are found throughout the codex (ff. 56v, 64v, 66v, 67v, 104r, 107v, 108v–109r, 111v–112r, 113v–114r, 139r–140r, 141v).

IES 02445, Book of Tuladan, መጽሐፈ ቱላዳን; *Asmat* Prayers; Mystagogia, ትምህርተ ኅቡዓት; Prayer of the Covenant, ጸሎተ ኪዳን; God of the Luminaries, እግዚአብሔር ዘብርሃናት; Prayer, "For the sake of the peaceful holy things," በእንተ ቅድሳት ሰላማዊት; Anaphora of Our Lord, ቅዳሴ እግዚእ; Image of Mary, መልክአ ማርያም; Image of Jesus, መልክአ ኢየሱስ; Prayer of Mary at Golgotha, ጸሎተ እግዝእትነ ማርያም ዘሰኔ ጎልጎታ. Parchment, 165 x 120 x 50 mm, iv + 116 folios, one column, 18 lines, Gəʿəz, early twentieth century.

Miniatures:

1. F. 29v: Talismanic symbols.

IES 02458, Book of Gəʿəz Poems of Earlier and Later Scholars and Teachers of Ethiopia, handwritten in an exercise book, መጽሐፈ ቅኔ ዘቀደምት ወደኃርት ሊቃውንቲሃ ወማእምራኒሃ ለኢትዮጵያ። ዘአስተጋብአ ብላታ ኃሩይ ወልደ ሥላሴ, by *blatten geta* Ḫəruy Wäldä Śəllase. Paper, 210 x 165 x 57 mm, iv + 287 folios, one column, 20 lines, Gəʿəz, Amharic, twentieth century.

IES 02460, Excerpt from the Beauty of Creation, ሥነ ፍጥረት; On Movable Feasts and Fasting, በእንተ ጾም; Order of Liturgical Yared Hymns for the Whole Year, ሥርዓተ አደራርስ እምዮሐንስ እስከ ዮሐንስ ዘቤተ ልሐይም. Parchment, 165 x 115 x 30 mm, xii + 46 folios, one column, 23–26 lines, Gəʿəz, twentieth century.

IES 02461, Commentary on Our Father, in Amharic, የአቡን ዘበሰማያት ትርጓሜ; Passion of the Cross, በእንተ ሕማገተ መስቀል; Five Pillars of Mystery, አምስቱ አዕማደ ምሥጢር; Story of Mary, ነገረ ማርያም; Miracles of Mary, ተአምረ ማርያም; Vision of Mary, ራዕየ ማርያም. Paper, 230 x 170 x 40 mm, 150 folios, two columns, 23 lines, Gəʿəz, Amharic, twentieth century.

IES 02466, Anaphora of Our Lady Mary attributed to Cyriacus of Bəhənsa, ቅዳሴ ማርያም; Canticle of the Flower, ማሕሌተ ጽጌ; Lament of the Virgin, ሰቆቃወ ድንግል; Image of Saint George, መልክአ ጊዮርጊስ; Hymn to Saint George, "O who is quick for help," ኦ ፍጡን ረድኤት; Image of Gäbrä Mänfäs Qəddus, መልክአ ገብረ መንፈስ ቅዱስ; Brief Catechism on Holy Trinity. Parchment, 130 x 100 x 48 mm, iv + 114 folios, one column, 12-13 lines, Gəʿəz, 1936 (notice of completion f. 116rv mentions the Alexandrian Patriarch John XIX [r. 1928-42], and Metropolitan Qerəllos VI [r. 1929-50]). Double-slip maḥdär.

IES 02467, Synaxarium, መጽሐፈ ስንክሳር, for the first half of the year. Parchment, 356 x 280 x 125 mm, ii + 208 folios, three columns, 39-41 lines, Gəʿəz, 1985-86 EC = 1992-94.

IES 02468, Homiliary in Honor of the Archangel Michael, ድርሳነ ሚካኤል. Parchment, 175 x 135 x 60 mm, ii + 124 folios, two columns, 18 lines, Gəʿəz, twentieth century.

Miniatures:

1. F. ii r(ecto): Michael, the Archangel, Enthroned.

IES 02469, Book of Tuladan, መጽሐፈ ቱላዳን; *Asmat* Prayers. Parchment, 120 x 90 x 38 mm, ii + 54 folios, one column, 13 lines, Gəʿəz, twentieth century.

IES 02470, Prayer to Jesus "Guard me," ኦ እግዚእየ ኢየሱስ ክርስቶስ ዕቀበኒ; Prayer of Mary at Golgotha, ጸሎተ እግዝእትነ ማርያም ዘሰየ ጎልጎታ. Parchment, 153 x 92.5 x 51 mm, ii + 60 folios, one column, 15-16 lines, Gəʿəz, early nineteenth century.

IES 02471, Image of Täklä Haymanot, መልክአ ተክለ ሃይማኖት. Parchment, 150 x 108 x 20 mm, ii + 18 folios, two columns, 14 lines, Gəʿəz, early twentieth century. Single-slip maḥdär.

IES 02479, Acts of *abunä* Tadewos, ገድለ አቡነ ታዴዎስ. Parchment, 205 x 175 x 35 mm, 44 folios, two columns, 19–23 lines, Gəʽəz, eighteenth century.

Miniatures:

1. F. 2r: A king attended by two angels.
2. F. 2v: Madonna and Child.
3. F. 43r: Two angels with swords and scabbards.

IES 02480, Octateuch with marginal mnemonics for the traditional commentary, and Jubilees. Parchment, 230 x 200 x 69 mm, iv + 166 folios, three columns, 35 lines, Gəʽəz, early twentieth century.

Miniatures:

1. F. i r(ecto): The Flight into Egypt.
2. F. 166v: Crude drawing of figures and an angel with a sword.
3. Inside back cover: Crude drawing of a figure.

IES 02481, *Asmat* Prayer against locusts, ጸሎት አንበጣ; *Asmat* Prayer against fire, ጸሎት እሳት; *Asmat* Prayer against theft, ጸሎት በእንተ ማኅስያነ ቤት; *Asmat* Prayer against an enemy, ጸሎት በእንተ ፀር; *Asmat* Prayer against hail and lightning, ጸሎት በረድ ወመብረቅ; and other *Asmat* Prayers. Parchment, 185 x 120 x 38 mm, 48 folios, one column, 17–21 lines, Gəʽəz, late nineteenth century.

IES 02550, Book of Monastic Writings of Mar Yishaq of Nineveh, with marginal mnemonics for andemta, ማር ይስሐቅ. Parchment, 170 x 150 x 78 mm, iii + 184 folios, two columns, 17–18 lines, Gəʽəz, late eighteenth century.

IES 02554, Acts of Täklä Haymanot, ገድለ ተክለ ሃይማኖት; Miracles of Täklä Haymanot, ተአምረ ተክለ ሃይማኖት. Parchment, 295 x 210 x 70 mm, iv + 162 folios, two columns, 25 lines, Gəʽəz, early twentieth century.

Miniatures:

1. F. 159v: Crude drawing of a church.
2. F. 161v: The triumph of the archangel Michael (holding balances) over the devil. The illumination is upside down and written in blue ink.

IES 02569, Synaxarium for the first half of the year, መጽሐፈ ስንክሳር. Parchment, 355 x 280 x 90 mm, ii + 176 folios, three columns, 40 lines, Gəʿəz, twentieth century.

IES 02570, Book of Ṭomar, መጽሐፈ ጦማር; Faith of The Fathers, ሃይማኖተ አበው. Parchment, 375 x 290 x 110 mm, ii + 226 folios, three columns, 31–32 lines, Gəʿəz, 1914 EC = 1921–22 (colophon on frame 227, left).

IES 02571, Funeral Ritual, መጽሐፈ ግንዘት. Parchment, 350 x 260 x 60 mm, i + 93 folios, two columns, 29 lines, Gəʿəz, twentieth century.

IES 02572, Images Collection, መልክአ ጉባኤ. Parchment, 180 x 150 x 60 mm, iv + 121 folios, two columns, 18 lines, Gəʿəz, nineteenth and twentieth centuries, composite.

IES 02573, Missal, መጽሐፈ ቅዳሴ, produced in the Government Scriptorium. Parchment, 285 x 205 x 50 mm, iv + 176 folios, two columns, 21 lines, Gəʿəz, 1941 EC = 1948–49 (page 379 provides specific date; page 86 mentions Emperor Ḫaylä Śəllase, the Alexandrian Patriarch Joseph II, and the Ethiopian Patriarch Basəlyos).

Miniatures:

1. F. 174r: Image of the Host.

IES 02574, Abbreviated Antiphonary for the Whole Year, ድጓ. Parchment, 225 x 180 x 32 mm, ii + 46 folios, two columns, 19 lines, Gəʿəz, twentieth century.

Miniatures:

1. F. i v(erso): Talismanic symbol with a face in the center.
2. F. ii r(ecto): Saint George and the Dragon.
3. F. 3v: A church.
4. F. 4r: Three priests with prayer staffs.
5. F. 43v: A King with a child appearing over his shoulder. To the right two men hold swords upraised.
6. F. 44r: The enthronement of a king by angels.
7. F. 45v: *Abunä* Aragawi of Däbrä Dammo.
8. F. 46r: How Elijah caused rain.

IES 02575, Acts of Gäbrä Mänfäs Qəddus, ገድለ ገብረ መንፈስ ቅዱስ; Miracles of Gäbrä Mänfäs Qəddus, ተአምረ ገብረ መንፈስ ቅዱስ. Parchment, 190 x 165 x 88 mm, i + 168 folios, two columns, 15 lines, Gə'əz, nineteenth century.

Miniatures:

1. F. i v(erso): Michael, the Archangel, Enthroned.

2. F. 168r: Gäbrä Mänfäs Qəddus.

IES 02576, Image of Raphael, መልክአ ሩፋኤል; Five Pillars of Mystery, አምስቱ አዕማደ ምሥጢር; Passion of the Cross, በእንተ ሕማማተ መስቀል. Parchment, 160 x 120 x 40 mm, iv + 89 folios, two columns, 17–19 lines, Gə'əz, twentieth century.

IES 02577, Various Chants. Parchment, 140 x 125 x 67 mm, vi + 121 folios, two columns, 13–15 lines, Gə'əz, nineteenth century and twentieth century, composite.

IES 02578, Five Pillars of Mystery, አምስቱ አዕማደ ምሥጢር. Parchment, 160 x 120 x 38 mm, i + 59 folios, one column, 22 lines, Amharic, twentieth century with added miniatures by the same artists of IES 02579.

Miniatures:

1. F. 13v: Moses receiving a book from heaven.

2. F. 40r: A saint with a book in hand.

3. F. 58v: A saint with arms upstretched.

4. F. 59r: A saint with arms upstretched.

IES 02579, Praises of Mary, in Amharic and Gə'əz in parallel folios, ውዳሴ ማርያም; Gate of Light, in Amharic and Gə'əz in parallel folios, አንቀጸ ብርሃን; Image of Mary, መልክአ ማርያም; Image of Jesus, መልክአ ኢየሱስ. Parchment, 170 x 100 x 30 mm, 56 folios, one column, 19 lines, Gə'əz, Amharic, twentieth century with added miniatures by the same artists of IES 02578.

Miniatures:

1. F. 5v: A saint with arms upstreached.

2. F. 11r: Angel with sword and scabbard.

3. F. 40r: A saint holding a book.

4. F. 55v: A saint.

IES 02580, Gospel of John, in a seventeenth-century hand, ወንጌል ዘዮሐንስ; Gospel of Mark, in a nineteenth-century hand, ወንጌል ዘማርቆስ. Parchment, 180 x 180 x 60 mm, ii + 87 folios, two columns, 19–20 lines, Gəʿəz, seventeenth century and nineteenth century (composite).

IES 02581, Homiliary in Honor of the Archangel Michael, ድርሳነ ሚካኤል. Parchment, 271 x 216 x 40 mm, ii + 76 folios, two columns, 20–23 lines, Gəʿəz, nineteenth century.

Miniatures:

1. F. ii v(erso): Michael, the Archangel.

IES 02582, Gəʿəz Grammar from Gonj, ሰዋስወ፡ ግዕዝ. Parchment, 130 x 90 x 28 mm, i + 28 folios, one column, 20 lines, Gəʿəz, Amharic, nineteenth century.

IES 02591, Gəʿəz–Amharic Vocabulary List of Verbs, ግዕዝ ግሥ. Parchment, 190 x 115 x 35 mm, ii + 52 folios, one column, 25 lines, Gəʿəz, Amharic, early twentieth century.

Miniatures:

1. F. ii v(erso): The Archangel Raguel with a sword and processional cross.

2. F. 31v: Täklä Haymanot.

3. F. 50v: Madonna and Child.

4. F. 52r: Crude drawing of a figure with a cross necklace.

IES 02592, Catechism on the Five Pillars, ቃለ ሃይማኖት. Parchment, 140 x 125 x 35 mm, 50 folios, two columns, 13–14 lines, Gəʿəz, Amharic, late eighteenth century.

IES 02593, Psalter, ዳዊት. Parchment, 185 x 145 x 60 mm, ii + 139 folios, one column and two columns, 23 lines, Gəʿəz, late nineteenth/early twentieth century.

Miniatures:

1. F. i v(erso): Two men pouring beer.
2. F. ii r(ecto): Seven men pouring beer. Caption at the top is illegible.
3. F. ii v(erso): Saint George and the Dragon.
4. F. 138v: An angel with a sword and scabbard.
5. F. 139r: A man holding a book and the devil.

IES 02594, Image of Saint George, መልክአ ጊዮርጊስ; Image of Gäbrä Mänfäs Qəddus, መልክአ ገብረ መንፈስ ቅዱስ; Mystagogia, ትምህርተ ኅቡዓት; Angels Praise Her, ይዌድስዋ መላእክት ለማርያም. Parchment, 130 x 90 x 25 mm, ii + 33 folios, one column, 15 lines, Gəʿəz, twentieth century.

Miniatures:

1. F. i v(erso): The Piercing of Jesus' side.
2. F. ii r(ecto): Madonna and Child.
3. F. ii v(erso): Saint George and the Dragon.
4. F. 20v: How the patron prayed to Gäbrä Mänfäs Qəddus.
5. F. 21r: Gäbrä Mänfäs Qəddus.

IES 02595, *Asmat* Prayers, አስማት. Parchment, 135 x 95 x 20 mm, ii + 30 folios, one column, 17–18 lines, Gəʿəz, twentieth century.

Miniatures:

1. Ff. 29v–30r: Talismanic symbols.

IES 02596, Catechism on the Five Pillars, ቃለ ሃይማኖት; Commentary on the Introductory Rite to the Miracles of Mary, የተአምረ ማርያም መቅድም ትርጓሜ; Commentary on Our Father, የአቡነ ዘበሰማያት ትርጓሜ; Vision of Mary, ራዕየ ማርያም; Five Pillars of Mystery, አምስቱ አዕማደ ምሥጢር. Parchment, 140 x 100 x 70 mm, iv + 184 folios, one column, 17–19 lines, Amharic, twentieth century.

IES 02597, Sword of the Trinity, arranged for the days of the week, ሠይፈ ሥላሴ; Image of the Trinity, መልክአ ሥላሴ; Prayer of Saint Peter, ጸሎተ ጴጥሮስ. Parchment, 180 x 120 x 55 mm, iv + 118 folios, two columns, 17 lines, Gəʿəz, twentieth century.

IES 02598, History of Galla, መጽሐፈ ታሪክ ዘጋላ; History of Ethiopian Kings, መጽሐፈ ታሪክ; Image of Zär'a Ya'əqob, መልክአ ዘርዓ ያዕቆብ. Parchment, 180 x 120 x 30 mm, ii + 108 folios, two columns, 21 lines, Amharic, twentieth century.

Miniatures:

1. F. i r(ecto): A church, in pencil.

IES 02606, Introduction to the Four Gospels, መቅድመ ወንጌል; Four Gospels, አርባዕቱ ወንጌል. Parchment, 295 x 240 x 72 mm, ii + 156 folios, two columns, 24 lines, Gə'əz, twentieth century.

Miniatures:

1. F. 10v: Saint George and the Dragon.
2. F. 11r: How Bogalä Dästa and his wife prayed to Saint George. Signed by the painter Gəra Geta Ǝngəda Säw.

IES 02612, Image of Arägawi/Zä-Mika'el, መልክአ አረጋዊ /ዘሚካኤል; Order of Monastic Life, ሥርዓት ዓሠረ መነኮሳት; Book of Good Works, መጽሐፈ ምግባራት ሠናይት; Book of Spiritual Healing, መጽሐፈ ፈውስ መንፈሳዊ; Admonition for the Priest, ተግሣጽ ዘይደሉ ለካህናት; Order of the Church, ሥርዓት ቤተ ክርስቲያን. Parchment, 265 x 200 x 40 mm, ii + 113 folios, two columns, 26 lines, Gə'əz, late nineteenth century.

IES 02613, Homiliary of the Savior of the World, ድርሳነ መድኃኔ ዓለም. Parchment, 225 x 155 x 40 mm, ii + 64 folios, two columns, 21–22 lines, Gə'əz, twentieth century.

IES 02614, Horologium for the Day, ሰዓታት ዘመዓልት. Parchment, 165 x 155 x 30 mm, i + 38 folios, two columns, 21–22 lines, Gə'əz, twentieth century.

IES 02615, Sword of the Trinity, ሠይፈ ሥላሴ, known in this manuscript as *Zena Nägäromu*, ዜና ነገሮሙ. Parchment, 120 x 90 x 60 mm, i + 148 folios, ff. 1r–81v two columns, ff. 82r–147r one column, 15–16 lines, Gə'əz, twentieth century.

IES 02694, Cycle of Kings, ዐውደ ነገሥት. Parchment, 210 x 170 x 40 mm, ii + 84 folios, ff. 1r–11v one column, ff. 12r–82v two columns, 22–23 lines, Gə'əz, Amharic, twentieth century.

IES 02695, *Asmat* Prayers and Talismanic Symbols, አስማት; Cycle of Kings, ዐውደ ነገሥት. Parchment, 130 x 104 x 33 mm, 87 folios, ff. 1r–10r, 83r–86v one column, ff. 11r–82r two columns, 18 lines, Gəʿəz, Amharic, twentieth century.

Miniatures:

1. Ff. 1v–6r: Talismanic symbols.

IES 02701, Missal, መጽሐፈ ቅዳሴ. Parchment, 265 x 205 x 62 mm, ii + 94 folios, two columns, 24–25 lines, Gəʿəz, twentieth century (mentions Emperor Ḫaylä Śəllase and Patriarch Basəlyos).

IES 02702, Four Gospels, አርባዕቱ ወንጌል. Parchment, 250 x 232 x 56 mm, iii + 128 folios, three columns, 26–36 lines, Gəʿəz, nineteenth century.

IES 02703, Praises of Mary, ውዳሴ ማርያም; Anaphora of Our Lady Mary attributed to Cyriacus of Bəhənsa, ቅዳሴ ማርያም; Hymn to Saint George, "O who is quick for help," አ ፍጡነ ረድኤት. Parchment, 154 x 110 x 40 mm, iii + 85 folios, one column, 11–12 lines, Gəʿəz, twentieth century.

IES 02936, Antiphonary for the Fast of Lent, ጾመ ድጓ. Parchment, 255 x 186 x 40 mm, i + 70 folios, three columns, 24–29 lines, Gəʿəz, late nineteenth century.

Miniatures:

1. F. i v(erso): Saint Yared with a sistrum and prayer staff.
2. F. 69v: The Crucifixion.

IES 02938, *Asmat* Prayer against charm, መፍትሐ ሥራይ. Parchment, 83 x 63 x 23 mm, ii + 58 folios, one column, 11 lines, Gəʿəz, twentieth century.

Miniatures:

1. F. 4v: Nine-box panel with: Angels in boxes 1, 3, 7 and 9; x-shaped patterns in boxes 2, 4, 6 and 8; and a face in box 5.
2. F. 9v: Four-petal pattern.
3. F. 14r: Talismanic symbol with a sun in the center.
4. F. 14v: 12-box panel with faces x-shaped patterns.

5. F. 20v: Talismanic symbol.

6. F. 25r: Talismanic symbol of geometric patterns.

7. F. 28v: Talismanic symbol based on nine-box panel.

8. F. 32r: Twenty-five box panel with an ornate cross in each box, alternating between black and red.

9. F. 36v: A row of crosses.

10. Ff. 53r–54r: Talismanic symbols.

IES 02939, Commentary on Mystagogia, ትምህርተ ኅቡዓት ትርጓሜ; Commentary on Prayer of the Covenant, ጸሎተ ኪዳን ትርጓሜ; Hymn to Saint George, "I Take Refuge with Thee," መልክአ ጊዮርጊስ (ተማኅፀንኩ); *Asmat* Prayer, አስማት. Paper, 216 x 160 x 30 mm, iii + 118 folios, two columns, 21 lines, Gəʿəz, twentieth century.

IES 02940, Prayer of Mary at Golgotha, ጸሎተ እግዝእትነ ማርያም ዘሰኈ ጎልጎታ; Sword of Divinity, ሠይፈ መለኮት. Parchment, 91 x 66 x 21 mm, ii + 42 folios, one column, 13 lines, Gəʿəz, twentieth century.

Miniatures:

1. F. 6r: Madonna and Child.

2. F. 10v: Michael, the Archangel, with sword and scabbard.

IES 02947, God Reigns, እግዚአብሔር ነግሠ (ነግሡ); Images Collection, መልክአ ጉባኤ. Parchment, 180 x 122 x 85 mm, ix + 174 folios, one column, 14 lines, Gəʿəz, twentieth century.

IES 02948, Homiliary in Honor of the Archangel Michael, ድርሳነ ሚካኤል; Image of Michael, መልክአ ሚካኤል; Image of Gabriel, መልክአ ገብርኤል. Parchment, 170 x 164 x 85 mm, ii + 162 folios, two columns, 16–18 lines, Gəʿəz, nineteenth century.

Miniatures:

1. F. 147r: Two angels with swords and scabbards.

IES 02949, Antiphonary for the Fast of Lent, ጸመ ድጓ. Parchment, 183 x 150 x 55 mm, iv + 132 folios, two columns, 17–18 lines, Gəʿəz, 1953–54 EC = 1960–62 (f. 128r).

Miniatures:

1. F. 130v: Crude drawing of an angel with sword and scabbard.

IES 02950, Prayer, "For the sake of the peaceful holy things," በእንተ ቅድሳት ሰላማዊት; Psalter, ዳዊት. Parchment, 171 x 160 x 75 mm, v + 182 folios, one column and two columns, 17–18 lines, Gəʽəz, nineteenth century.

IES 02951, Prayer against the Tongue of People, ልሳነ ሰብእ (በእንተ ልሳነ ዘመድ ወባእድ). Parchment, 94 x 65 x 27 mm, i + 49 folios, one column, 10 lines, Gəʽəz, twentieth century.

IES 02952, Canticle of the Flower, ማሕሌተ ጽጌ. Parchment, 110 x 79 x 29 mm, ii + 50 folios, two columns, 15 lines, Gəʽəz, twentieth century.

IES 02953, Sword of the Trinity, ሠይፈ ሥላሴ; Sword of Divinity, ሠይፈ መለኮት. Parchment, 110 x 106 x 55 mm, iv + 114 folios, one column, 10 lines, Gəʽəz, twentieth century.

IES 02954, Images Collection, መልክአ ጉባዔ. Parchment, 130 x 95 x 35 mm, iv + 58 folios, two columns, 14–15 lines, Gəʽəz, twentieth century.

IES 02955, Funeral Ritual, መጽሐፈ ግንዘት. Parchment, 248 x 186 x 70 mm, iii + 165 folios, two columns, 22 lines, Gəʽəz, early twentieth century.

IES 02956, Prayer of Saint Peter, ጸሎተ ዼጥሮስ; Prayer on the Passion of Christ, ኦእግዚእየ ኢየሱስ ክርስቶስ መድኀን ዓለም ጐልቄ ሕማማቲከ. Parchment, 181 x 136 x 40 mm, ii + 66 folios, two columns, 15–16 lines, Gəʽəz, 1885 EC = 1892–93 (page 120 mentions Emperor Mənilək II and the year 7385 from the Creation of the World) with miniatures added by the same artist of IES 02578–79.

Miniatures:

1. F. 2r: Saint holding orb.
2. F. 24v: Saint standing before hand from heaven.
3. F. 32v: Saint holding a book.
4. F. 64r: Saint holding a book.
5. F. 65r: Saint George and the Dragon.
6. F. 65v: Madonna and Child.

IES 02956A, Prayer of Saint Peter, ጸሎተ ዼጥሮስ, arranged for the days of the week; Treatise on the Trinity, ዜና ሥላሴ. Parchment, 171 x 122 x 45 mm, iv + 109 folios, two columns, 16 lines, Gəʿəz, late nineteenth/early twentieth century. Also known as IES 4680.

Miniatures:

1. F. iv v(erso): An Emperor (Mənilək II?) on a throne holding a book.
2. F. 43r: The Three Youths in the Fiery Furnace rescued by Gabriel.
3. F. 48v: Ornate cross.
4. F. 104r: The Holy Trinity surrounded by the four Living Creatures.
5. F. 105v: The Holy Trinity surrounded by the four living Creatures.
6. F. 106r: The Crucifixion.

IES 02957, Miracles of Saint Michael, ተአምረ ሚካኤል; Angels Praise Her, ይዌድሶ መላእክት ለማርያም; Image of the Icon, መልክአ ሥዕል; Miracles of Mary, ተአምረ ማርያም. Parchment, 235 x 169 x 80 mm, i + 158 folios, two columns, 16 lines, Gəʿəz, nineteenth century with added miniatures dating to the twentieth century.

Miniatures:

1. F. 3v: Michael, the archangel, with sword and scabbard.
2. F. 49r: The Ascension of Jesus.
3. F. 60v: A Gospel writer with pen and parchment.
4. F. 73v: Our Lady Mary with patron.
5. F. 126r: Jesus holding the sacred heart.
6. F. 139v: The Entombment of Jesus.
7. F. 140r: The Crucifixion.
8. F. 157r: The Resurrection of Jesus.
9. Ff. 157v–158r: Crude drawing of figures and an ornate cross.

IES 02958, Miracles of Saint Michael, ተአምረ ሚካኤል; Homiliary in Honor of the Archangel Michael, ድርሳነ ሚካኤል. Parchment, 170 x 165 x 80 mm, i + 135 folios, two columns, 18 lines, Gəʿəz, late eighteenth/early nineteenth century.

Miniatures:

1. F. 40v: The patron, Wäldä Sänbät, prostrate before the angel Michael.

IES 02959, Psalter, ዳዊት. Parchment, 198 x 126 x 54 mm, 166 folios, one column and two columns, 21 lines, Gəʿəz, early twentieth century.

Miniatures:

1. F. 31v: King David playing the harp.
2. F. 165v: Madonna and Child.
3. F. 166r: Two people stand before Mary.

IES 02960, Prayer of the Covenant, ጸሎተ ኪዳን; Rampart of the Cross, ሐጹረ መስቀል; Prayer to the Trinity "I take refuge," ተማኅፀንኩ; Sword of the Trinity, ሠይፈ ሥላሴ; Anaphora of Our Lady Mary attributed to Cyriacus of Bəhənsa, ቅዳሴ ማርያም; Canticle of the Flower, ማኅሌተ ጽጌ; Praise of the Beloved, ስብሐተ ፍቁር; Image of the Savior of the World, መልክአ መድኃኒ ዓለም; Table Prayer, "We beseech you," ሰአልናከ. Parchment, 180 x 128 x 52 mm, 125 folios, two columns, 19 lines, Gəʿəz, 1911 EC (colophon on frame 124; frame 71 mentions the Alexandrian Patriarch Cyril V[r. 1874-1927] and Metropolitan Matewos [r. 1889-1926]) with miniatures added in the second half of the twentieth century.

Miniatures:

1. F. 1v: A king on his throne; two men.
2. F. 2r: The Flight into Egypt.

IES 02961, Four Gospels, አርባዕቱ ወንጌል. Parchment, 295 x 250 x 110 mm, iv + 230 folios, two columns, 20-22 lines, Gəʿəz, twentieth century.

IES 02962, Harp of Praise, አርጋኖነ ውዳሴ; Hymn to Mary, "I Praise Your Grace," እሴብህ ጸጋኪ. Parchment, 200 x 180 x 47 mm, iii + 101 folios, two columns, 18 lines, Gəʿəz, late eighteenth/early nineteenth century. Single-slip maḥdär.

Miniatures:

1. F. iii v(erso): Equestrian saint.

IES 02963, Miracles of *abunä* Zär'a Buruk, ተአምረ አቡነ ዘርኣ ቡሩክ; Image of *abunä* Zär'a Buruk, መልክአ አቡነ ዘርኣ ቡሩክ. Parchment, 210 x 185 x 50 mm, iv + 73 folios, two columns, 20–25 lines, Gəʿəz, nineteenth century.

Miniatures:

1. F. ii v(erso): "Painting of Dämä Krəstos and his wife Maryam Mogäsa."

2. F. iii r(ecto): "Painting of Zär'a Buruk."

IES 02964, *Asmat* Prayer against thief, ጸሎት በእንተ ሌባ ወቀማኛ; Miracle of Jesus, ተአምረ ኢየሱስ; Psalter, ዳዊት; Sword of Divinity, ሠይፈ መለኮት. Parchment, 195 x 186 x 80 mm, iv + 159 folios, one column and two columns, 21 lines, Gəʿəz, nineteenth century.

IES 02965, Homiliary in Honor of the Archangel Gabriel, ድርሳነ ገብርኤል; Image of Gabriel, መልክአ ገብርኤል. Parchment, 272 x 175 x 40 mm, ii + 71 folios, two columns, 22 lines, Gəʿəz, 1907 (frame 68) = 1914–15.

IES 02966, Canticle of the Flower, ማሕሌተ ጽጌ; Lament of the Virgin, ሰቆቃወ ድንግል. Parchment, 125 x 97 x 35 mm, ii + 96 folios, one column, 11–12 lines, Gəʿəz, early twentieth century. EMML 1448.

Miniatures:

1. F. i v(erso): The Striking of the Head.

2. F. ii v(erso): Mary (?) enthroned.

3. F. 3r: A standing saint holding beads and a jug.

4. F. 3v: Saint George and the Dragon.

IES 02967, Missal, መጽሐፈ ቅዳሴ. Parchment, 250 x 190 x 73 mm, ii + 144 folios, two columns, 22 lines, Gəʿəz, 1951–70 (frames 36 and 37 mention Patriarch Basəlyos and Emperor Ḫaylä Śəllase).

IES 02968, Psalter, ዳዊት. Parchment, 145 x 102 x 70 mm, iv + 164 folios, one column and two columns, 23 lines, Gəʿəz, late nineteenth century.

Miniatures:

1. F. 1r: King David playing the harp.

2. F. 8r: King David playing the harp.

3. F. 126r: Two ornate crosses.

4. F. 163v: Ornate cross.

5. There are crude drawings throughout this codex (e.g., ff. iv v[erso], 99r, 111r, 123v, 140v, 164r).

IES 02969, Acts of Gäbrä Mänfäs Qǝddus, ገድለ ገብረ መንፈስ ቅዱስ; Miracles of Gäbrä Mänfäs Qǝddus, ተአምረ ገብረ መንፈስ ቅዱስ; Hymn to Gäbrä Mänfäs Qǝddus, መፍቀሬ ጸሎት ወጾም ኮከበ ገዳም. Parchment, 175 x 170 x 50 mm, 76 folios, two columns, 19 lines, Gǝʿǝz, eighteenth century.

IES 02972, Prayers for the day and the night, ጸሎታት ዘመዓልት ወዘሌሊት; Praises of Mary, ውዳሴ ማርያም, arranged for the days of the week and culminating in Saturday, accompanied with an unknown prayer to Mary; Praise of Mary from the Words of the Prophets, ውዳሴ እምቃለ ነቢያት ዘይትነበብ ላዕለ ማርያም; Prayer on the Sabbath of the Jews, ጸሎት በዕለተ ሰንበተ አይሁድ; Gospel of John, ወንጌል ዘዮሐንስ; Book of Revelation, ራዕየ ዮሐንስ. Parchment, 250 x 175 x 100 mm, 149 folios, two columns, 27–28 lines, Gǝʿǝz, sixteenth century.

IES 02976, Photocopy of four magic scrolls, ክታብ. Paper, 350 x 216 x 3 mm, 19 folios, one column, Gǝʿǝz, nineteenth and twentieth century.

IES 02993, Acts of Gäbrä Mänfäs Qǝddus, ገድለ ገብረ መንፈስ ቅዱስ; Miracles of Gäbrä Mänfäs Qǝddus, ተአምረ ገብረ መንፈስ ቅዱስ. Parchment, 169 x 165 x 65 mm, 130 folios, two columns, 15 lines, Gǝʿǝz, eighteenth century.

IES 02994, Homiliary in Honor of the Archangel Michael, ድርሳነ ሚካኤል. Parchment, 270 x 216 x 65 mm, i + 65 folios, two columns, 21–23 lines, Gǝʿǝz, nineteenth century.

Miniatures:

1. F. i v(erso): Angel with sword and scabbard, with patron, *liqä* Ṭäbäbǝtäldu, below.

2. F. 65v: Angel with sword and scabbard.

IES 02995, Homiliary in Honor of the Archangel Michael, ድርሳነ ሚካኤል, made in the Government Scriptorium. Parchment, 221 x 172 x 70 mm, 168 folios, two columns, 17 lines, Gǝʿǝz, early twentieth century.

Miniatures:

1. F. 166v: Crude drawing of two birds, geometric patterns, and an ornate cross, in blue ink.
2. F. 167v: Crude drawing of a talismanic symbol.

IES 02996, Gospel of John, ወንጌል ዘዮሐንስ; Image of Saint George zä-Säleda Mogäs, መልክአ ጊዮርጊስ ዘሰሉዳ ሞገስ; Image of the Savior of the World, መልክአ መድኃኔ ዓለም; Layman's prayer, in Amharic, አዳምን ከሲኦል ኖኅን ከማየ አይኅ. Parchment, 145 x 103 x 57 mm, iii + 114 folios, two columns, 16–17 lines, Gəʿəz, Amharic, twentieth century.

Miniatures:

1. F. ii v(erso): Crude drawing of a face.
2. F. iii v(erso): Print card of Jesus with the caption "Buona Pasqua" has been glued onto the folio.
3. F. 100v: The Crucifixion.

IES 02997, Gospel of John, ወንጌል ዘዮሐንስ; Instructions about the measurement of shadows for the telling of time for the whole year, ስፍረ ስዓት. Parchment, 152 x 102 x 45 mm, ii + 81 folios, two columns, 17 lines, Gəʿəz, twentieth century.

Miniatures:

1. F. ii v(erso): John the Evangelist.
2. F. 78v: Saint George and the Dragon.
3. F. 79r: Madonna and Child.
4. F. 79v: The Striking of the Head.

IES 02998, Psalter, ዳዊት; On the benefit of the reading of the Gospels, ቃሉ ለወንጌለ ጽድቅ; *Asmat* Prayer for stomach pain, ጸሎት በእንተ ሕማመ ቀርጸት. Parchment, 189 x 125 x 45 mm, iii + 140 folios, one column and two columns, 24 lines, Gəʿəz, twentieth century.

Miniatures:

1. F. 137r: Crude drawing of Madonna and Child.
2. F. 137v: Madonna and Child.
3. F. 138r: The Striking of the Head.

IES 02999, Psalter, ዳዊት; Image of David, መልክአ ዳዊት; with a mirror niche containing a mirror. Parchment, 140 x 107 x 56 mm, ii + 149 folios, one column and two columns, 22–24 lines, Gəʿəz, twentieth century.

Miniatures:

1. F. ii r(ecto): Madonna and Child.
2. F. 146v: Crude drawing of a dog.
3. F. 148r: Crude drawing of animals.
4. F. 148v: Crude drawing of the Crucifixion.
5. F. 149r: Crude drawing of the piercing of Jesus' side.

IES 03000, *Asmat* Prayers, አስማት. Parchment, 123 x 90 x 30 mm, vi + 66 folios, two columns, 14 lines, Gəʿəz, twentieth century.

Miniatures:

1. F. iv r(ecto): A snake in a tree, in blue ink.
2. F. v r(ecto): Man standing and holding beads, in blue ink.
3. F. 2r: An angel and the tendril of a plant.
4. Ff. 3v–4r: Talismanic symbols.
5. F. 7r: Nine-box panel with a face and x-shaped patterns.
6. F. 9r: Angel with sword and scabbard and a three-box panel.
7. F. 16v: An angel with a sword and a talismanic symbol.
8. F. 19r: A fifteen-box panel with faces in boxes.
9. F. 19v: A talismanic symbol and a five-box panel with faces in boxes 1–4.
10. F. 22r: Talismanic symbols.
11. F. 24v: Two weeping men.
12. F. 26v: A talismanic symbol.
13. F. 27v: Talismanic symbols and an ornate cross with a figure on either side.
14. F. 30r: An angel with sword and scabbard.
15. F. 30v: A talismanic symbol based on a nine-box panel with faces.

16. F. 34v: A talismanic symbol based on a nine-box pattern and a figure between two demons.

17. F. 35v: An angel with a sword.

18. F. 39r: A talismanic symbol based on a nine-box pattern.

19. F. 39v: Seven faces in a panel.

20. F. 42r: A talismanic symbol based on a nine-box pattern.

21. F. 44v: Three faces in a panel.

22. F. 48r: Seven faces in a panel.

23. F. 50r: A talismanic symbol based on a nine-box pattern.

IES 03001, *Asmat* Prayers, አስማት; Image of Saint Raguel, መልአክ ራጉኤል. Parchment, 107 x 75 x 26 mm, ii + 40 folios, one column, 14 lines, Gəʿəz, twentieth century.

Miniatures:

1. F. 1r: An angel with sword and scabbard.

2. F. 3r: An angel.

3. F. 4r: Text inside boxes.

4. F. 4v: Two snakes devouring each other, text written inside the circle of their bodies.

5. F. 6r: Two snakes devouring each other, text written inside the circle of their bodies.

6. F. 6v: Text inside boxes.

7. F. 9r: Angel with sword and scabbard. Four intertwined snakes above.

8. F. 11r: Text inside boxes.

9. F. 11v: Two snakes devouring each other, text written inside the circle of their bodies.

10. F. 14r: Two snakes devouring each other, text written inside the circle of their bodies.

11. F. 14v: Text inside boxes.

12. F. 16r: The Holy Trinity surrounded by the four Living Creatures.

13. F. 16v: Two snakes devouring each other, text written inside the circle of their bodies with the Lamb with Cross in the center.

14. F. 19r: The angel Raguel.
15. F. 19v: Two snakes devouring each other, text written inside the circle of their bodies.
16. F. 21v: Text inside boxes.
17. F. 22r: Two snakes devouring each other, text written inside the circle of their bodies.
18. F. 23v: Two snakes devouring each other, text written inside the circle of their bodies, with the Lamb with Cross in the center.
19. F. 24r: Text inside boxes.
20. F. 27r: Four-headed bird.
21. F. 39r: Talismanic symbols.

IES 03002, *Asmat* Prayers, አስማት. Parchment, 110 x 90 x 14 mm, i + 26 folios, one column, 10–13 lines, Gəʿəz, twentieth century.

Miniatures:

1. F. 4r: An angel.
2. F. 5r: An angel.
3. F. 6r: Two snakes devouring each other, text written inside the circle of their bodies, with the Lamb with Cross in the center.
4. F. 8v: The angel Raguel.
5. F. 14r: Angel with sword and scabbard.
6. F. 14v: Man with arms upstretched.
7. F. 15r: Four-headed bird.
8. F. 18r: Lion.
9. F. 19v: Madonna and Child.
10. F. 21r: Two snakes (Leviatian) devouring each other, with the Lamb with Cross in the center.

IES 03004, Greeting to Stephen, ሰላም ለከ መክብብ ሰማዕታት እዕላፍ; Image of the Icon, መልክአ ሥዕል; One Miracle of Mary, ተአምረ ማርያም. Parchment, 114 x 85 x 18 mm, 40 folios, one column, 12–16 lines, Gəʿəz, nineteenth century and twentieth century with eighteenth-century miniatures (composite).

Miniatures:

1. F. 4r: Covenant of Mercy with patron in proskynesis.
2. F. 5v: *Abba* Abib.
3. F. 6v: "How they stoned Ǝstifanos."
4. F. 9r: Abraham, Isaac, and Jacob.
5. F. 10r: Gäbrä Mänfäs Qǝddus.
6. F. 11r: Täklä Haymanot.
7. F. 12r: The Crucifixion.
8. F. 13r: The Striking of the Head.
9. F. 14r: Saint George and the Dragon.
10. F. 16r: "Saint Eusebius, Son of the Governor of Syria."
11. F. 17v: How the patron prostrated himself to Mary.
12. F. 18r: Madonna and Child.
13. F. 19v: Joseph and Salome.
14. F. 20r: Flight into Egypt.
15. F. 22r: The Holy Trinity surrounded by the four Living Creatures.
16. F. 23v: The Entry into Jerusalem.

IES 03005, *Asmat* Prayer against the bandit, ጸሎት በእንተ ቀማኛ ወለወንበዴ; Psalter, ዳዊት. Parchment, 180 x 126 x 52 mm, iv + 134 folios, one column and two columns, 24–25 lines, Gǝ'ǝz, twentieth century.

Miniatures:

1. F. i r(ecto): Angel with sword and scabbard.
2. F. i v(erso): Saint George and the Dragon.
3. F. ii r(ecto): Täklä Haymanot.
4. F. ii v(erso): The Baptism of Jesus.
5. F. iii v(erso): "Our Father, teacher Ewosṭatewos, preacher of Ethiopia."
6. F. iv r(ecto): King David playing the harp.
7. F. iv v(erso): Saint with prayer beads.
8. F. 133r: How Lalibäla prayed.

9. F. 133v: Madonna and Child.

10. F. 134r: Gäbrä Mänfäs Qəddus.

11. F. 134v: Equestrian saint.

IES 03006, Homiliary in Honor of the Archangel Michael, ድርሳነ ሚካኤል, incomplete; Acts of *Abba* Kiros, ገድለ ኪሮስ (inserted within the Homiliary in Honor of Michael). Parchment, 190 x 158 x 63 mm, i + 115 folios, two columns, 18–19 lines, Gəʿəz, eighteenth century.

Miniatures:

1. F. i v(erso): Michael (upper left), *Abba* Zärʾa Buruk, the devil (below).

2. F. 56r: Gäbrä Mänfäs Qəddus, the Archangel Gabriel, *abunä* Kiros.

3. F. 57v: Madonna and Child.

IES 03007, Cycle of Kings, ዐውደ ነገሥት, with 19 charts. Parchment, 197 x 125 x 45 mm, ii + 83 folios, two columns, 21–23 lines, Gəʿəz, twentieth century.

IES 03010, Homiliary in Honor of the Archangel Michael, ድርሳነ ሚካኤል. Parchment, 300 x 260 x 80 mm, ii + 132 folios, two columns, 18 lines, Gəʿəz, late eighteenth/early nineteenth century.

Miniatures:

1. F. 131r: Madonna and Child.

2. F. 131v: Saint George (drawing).

3. F. 132v: Saint George and the Dragon (drawing).

IES 03075, Faith of The Fathers, ሃይማኖተ አበው. Parchment, 340 x 270 x 90 mm, iv + 182 folios, three columns, 33 lines, Gəʿəz, late nineteenth/early twentieth century. EMML 756.

IES 03076, Funeral Ritual, መጽሐፈ ግንዘት, owned by *Eččäge* Gäbrä Śəllase. Parchment, 350 x 245 x 80 mm, ii + 134 folios, two columns, 27 lines, Gəʿəz, early twentieth century. EMML 757.

Miniatures:

1. Ff. 133v–134v: Crude drawings.

IES 03077, Psalter, ዳዊት. Parchment, 211 x 150 x 76 mm, ii + 198 folios, one column and two columns, 17–18 lines, Gəʿəz, nineteenth century.

Miniatures:

1. F. ii r(ecto): An angel with sword and scabbard.

IES 03078, Homiliary of the Lifegiver, ድርሳነ ማኅየዊ, a gift of *grazmač* Dänägäṭu to the Qäranyo Church. Parchment, 260 x 200 x 80 mm, ii + 166 folios, two columns, 17 lines, Gəʿəz, 1924 EC = 1931–32 (f. 162v mentions Emperor Ḫaylä Śəllase). EMML 771.

IES 03079, Sixty-Nine Miracles of Jesus, ተአምረ ኢየሱስ. Parchment, 280 x 230 x 60 mm, i + 104 folios, two columns, 23–26 lines, Gəʿəz, nineteenth century.

IES 03080, Missal, መጽሐፈ ቅዳሴ. Parchment, 233 x 188 x 70 mm, i + 98 folios, two columns, 23 lines, Gəʿəz, 1881–89 (f. 22v mentions Bishop Luqas [r. 1881–89]; f. 23r mentions Emperor Yoḥannəs IV [r. 1872–89] and Metropolitan Ṗeṭros IV [r. 1881–1916]).

Miniatures:

1. F. 98r: Image of the Host.

IES 03081, Book of Ezra, መጽሐፈ እዝራ; Book of Second Ezra, excerpt from Prayer of the Covenant (f. 44r). Parchment, 194 x 165 x 83 mm, 119 folios, two columns, 20–21 lines, Gəʿəz, late sixteenth/early seventeenth century.

IES 03082, Acts of Gäbrä Mänfäs Qəddus, ገድለ ገብረ መንፈስ ቅዱስ; Miracles of Gäbrä Mänfäs Qəddus, ተአምረ ገብረ መንፈስ ቅዱስ. Parchment, 238 x 191 x 61 mm, ii + 113 folios, two columns, 18–22 lines, Gəʿəz, 1918 EC = 1925–26.

IES 03083, Acts of Gäbrä Mänfäs Qəddus, ገድለ ገብረ መንፈስ ቅዱስ; Miracles of Gäbrä Mänfäs Qəddus, ተአምረ ገብረ መንፈስ ቅዱስ. Parchment, 220 x 187 x 85 mm, vi + 164 folios, two columns, 15–17 lines, Gəʿəz, late nineteenth century.

Miniatures:

1. Inside front cover: Crude drawing of a figure and a face.

IES 03084, Image of Gabriel, መልክአ ገብርኤል; Harp of Praise, አርጋኖን ውዳሴ, arranged for the days of the week, each day followed by the Praise of Mary for the Day and a Miracle of Mary, ተአምረ ማርያም; Image of Mary, መልክአ ማርያም አምሳለ ስቴ ወይን መጥለሊ.; Hymn to Mary, "In heaven and on earth," በሰማይ ወበምድር. Parchment, 200 x 175 x 75 mm, iii + 178 folios, two columns, 16 lines, Gəʿəz, eighteenth century.

IES 03085, Unidentified Prayer; Harp of Praise, አርጋኖን ውዳሴ, arranged for the days of the week; On the benefit of reading the Gospels (in a later hand), ወዘያነብብ ወንጌለ ዘእንበለ አዕርፎ. Parchment, 230 x 210 x 63 mm, v + 129 folios, two columns, 16–17 lines, Gəʿəz, late eighteenth/early nineteenth century.

IES 03086, Missal, መጽሐፈ ቅዳሴ. Parchment, 255 x 195 x 75 mm, iii + 134 folios, two columns, 21–22 lines, Gəʿəz, 1889–1917 (f. 43r mentions Metropolitan Ṗeṭros IV [r. 1881–1917] and Metropolitan Matewos [r. 1889–1926]).

IES 03087, Missal, መጽሐፈ ቅዳሴ. Parchment, 255 x 185 x 79 mm, ii + 132 folios, two columns, 20–21 lines, Gəʿəz, 1946–56 (f. 31v mentions Emperor Iyoʾas II and the Alexandrian Patriarch Joseph II [1946–56]; only the latter is clear evidence of the time frame based on the manuscript's paleography).

IES 03088, Epistles of Paul, lacking the Book of Hebrews, መልእክታተ ጳውሎስ. Parchment, 189 x 176 x 53 mm, ii + 106 folios, two columns, 17 lines, Gəʿəz, early twentieth century.

IES 03089, Collection of Prayers, መጽሐፈ ጸሎት; Image of Mary, መልክአ ማርያም; Image of the Covenant of Mercy, መልክአ ኪዳነ ምሕረት. Parchment, 141 x 105 x 40 mm, iv + 91 folios, two columns, 12–13 lines, Gəʿəz, 1937 EC = 1944–45 (f. 76v).

IES 03090, Homiliary in Honor of the Archangel Michael, ድርሳነ ሚካኤል; Image of Michael, መልክአ ሚካኤል. Parchment, 205 x 145 x 50 mm, ii + 122 folios, two columns, 20 lines, Gəʿəz, early twentieth century.

Miniatures:

1. F. i v(erso): The archangel Michael triumphs over the devil and his demons.
2. F. ii r(ecto): The archangel Michael with two patrons below.

IES 03091, Harp of Praise, አርጋኖን ውዳሴ, arranged for the days of the week. Parchment, 185 x 165 x 65 mm, ii + 164 folios, two columns, 15–16 lines, Gəʿəz, eighteenth century.

IES 03097, Synaxarium, for the first half of the year, መጽሐፈ ስንክሳር. Parchment, 355 x 277 x 109 mm, ii + 198 folios, two columns, 34–35 lines, Gəʿəz, nineteenth century.

Miniatures:

1. Inside front cover: Crude drawing of a horse.

2. F. i r(ecto): Crude drawing of two horses.

3. F. 89v: Crude drawing of a figure with a processional cross.

IES 03098, Miracles of Mary, ተአምረ ማርያም; Miracles of Jesus, ተአምረ ኢየሱስ. Parchment, 313 x 285 x 73 mm, iv + 120 folios, three columns, 26 lines, Gəʿəz, eighteenth century.

IES 03099, Lectionary for Passion Week, ግብረ ሕማማት. Parchment, 330 x 170 x 90 mm, i + 177 folios, three columns, 27–28 lines, Gəʿəz, early twentieth century.

IES 03100, Miracles of Mary, ተአምረ ማርያም, belonging to *däǧǧazmač* Gäbrä Śəllase. Parchment, 360 x 293 x 117 mm, ix + 240 folios, three columns, 28 lines, Gəʿəz, 1905 EC (colophon on f. 234v, mentions Emperor Mənilək II).

Miniatures:

1. F. 240v: Ornate cross, in blue ink.

IES 03101, Miracles of Jesus, ተአምረ ኢየሱስ. Parchment, 310 x 230 x 80 mm, vi + 152 folios, two columns, 22 lines, Gəʿəz, late nineteenth century.

Miniatures:

1. F. iii r(ecto): Madonna and Child, faintly in pencil.

2. F. iv r(ecto): The Crucifixion, faintly in pencil.

IES 03102, Synaxarium, መጽሐፈ ስንክሳር, for the second half of the year. Parchment, 360 x 275 x 79 mm, ii + 144 folios, three columns, 39 lines, Gəʿəz, early nineteenth century.

IES 03103, Canticle of the Flower, **ማሕሌተ ጽጌ**; Anaphora of Our Lady Mary attributed to Cyriacus of Bəhənsa, **ቅዳሴ ማርያም**. Parchment, 165 x 112 x 42 mm, 74 folios, two columns, 14 lines, Gəʿəz, 1889–1926 (f. 50r mentions Metropolitan Matewos [r. 1889–1926]) with miniatures by a twentieth-century hand.

Miniatures:

1. F. 45r: Madonna and Child.
2. F. 45v: Jesus pointing toward Lazarus (?).
3. F. 46r: Equestrian saint.
4. F. 46v: Joachim and Anne with the white dove.
5. F. 48v: The Crucifixion.
6. F. 72v: Our Lady Mary with saints on either side.
7. F. 73r: The Holy Trinity surrounded by the four Living Creatures.

IES 03104, Miracles of Mary, **ተአምረ ማርያም**; Miracles of Jesus, **ተአምረ ኢየሱስ**. Parchment, 190 x 145 x 47 mm, iii + 99 folios, two columns, 14–15 lines, Gəʿəz, twentieth century.

Miniatures:

1. Ff. iii rv: Crude drawing of figures.
2. F. 99v: Crude drawing of figures.

IES 03105, Image of the Praises of Mary, **መልክአ ውዳሴ ማርያም**; Gospel of John, **ወንጌል ዘዮሐንስ**. Parchment, 121 x 90 x 40 mm, iv + 120 folios, two columns, 15 lines, Gəʿəz, early twentieth century. Single-slip maḫdär.

Miniatures:

1. F. iv r(ecto): Madonna and Child, in pencil.

IES 03106, Gəʿəz Grammar (second part), **ሰዋሰው፡ ግዕዝ** on the conjugation of the verb; Psalter, **ዳዊት**; Psalter of the Virgin, **መዝሙረ ድንግል**; Gəʿəz Grammar (first part), **ሰዋሰው፡ ግዕዝ** on the conjugation of the verb. Parchment, 214 x 180 x 75 mm, ii + 196 folios, one column and two columns, 21 lines, Gəʿəz, seventeenth century.

Miniatures:

1. F. 67v: Crude drawing of a face.
2. F. 69r: Two birds.

IES 03144, Pauline Epistles, Corinthians through Hebrews, መልእክታተ ጳውሎስ; Book of Acts, ግብረ ሐዋርያት, incomplete at the end. Parchment, 209 x 175 x 45 mm, 75 folios, two columns, 22 lines, Gəʿəz, late eighteenth century.

IES 03145, School Chants, sometimes called የቃል ትምህርት. Parchment, 162 x 150 x 40 mm, 81 folios, two columns, 15 lines, Gəʿəz, early nineteenth century.

IES 03146, *Zəmmare* Chants, ዝማሬ. Parchment, 173 x 145 x 50 mm, iii + 111 folios, two columns, 21 lines, Gəʿəz, 1926 EC = 1933–34 (f. 1r, which also mentions Emperor Ḥaylä Śəllase, Metropolitan Qerəllos VI, etc.).

IES 03147, Psalter, ዳዊት; Psalter of the Virgin, መዝሙረ ድንግል, with extended introduction; Praises of Mary, ውዳሴ ማርያም, is interwoven with Image of the Praises of Mary, መልክአ ውዳሴ ማርያም; *Asmat* Prayer for help in learning. Parchment, 220 x 215 x 70 mm, iii + 191 folios, one column and two columns, 21 lines, Gəʿəz, late seventeenth/early eighteenth century.

IES 03148, Prayer, "For the sake of peaceful holy things, በእንተ ቅድሳት ሰላማዊት; Rampart of the Cross, ሐጹረ መስቀል; Canticle of the Flower, ማሕሌተ ጽጌ. Parchment, 120 x 82 x 25 mm, iv + 56 folios, one column, 15 lines, Gəʿəz, early twentieth century.

IES 03149, *Zəmmare* Chants, ዝማሬ; *Mäwaśəʾət* Chants, መዋሥዕት. Parchment, 205 x 184 x 36 mm, ii + 67 folios, three columns, 29 lines, Gəʿəz, twentieth century.

Miniatures:

1. F. i r(ecto): Multiple *haräg* patterns in black ink.
2. F. ii v(erso): Multiple *haräg* patterns in black ink.

IES 03150, Psalter, ዳዊት. Parchment, 163 x 120 x 60 mm, ii + 148 folios, one column and two columns, 20–22 lines, Gəʿəz, early twentieth century.

IES 03151, Image of the Passion of the Cross, መልክአ ሕማማት መስቀል; God Reigns, እግዚአብሐር ነግሠ, ascribed to Zärʾa Yaʿəqob, incomplete at the end. Parchment, 163 x 112 x 28 mm, i + 21 folios, two columns, 18–19 lines, Gəʿəz, early twentieth century.

IES 03152, Antiphonary for the Fast of Lent, ጾመ ድጓ. Parchment, 182 x 161 x 38 mm, ii + 64 folios, three columns, 22 lines, Gəʿəz, early twentieth century.

Miniatures:

1. F. 64r: Crude drawing of a figure and ornate crosses.

IES 03153, Catholic Epistles, ስብዓቱ መልእክታት, bound in disorder. Parchment, 228 x 160 x 32 mm, i + 33 folios, two columns, 22–24 lines, Gəʿəz, twentieth century.

Miniatures:

1. F. 33r: Crude drawing of the Lion of Judah.

IES 03154, Miracles of Mary, ተአምረ ማርያም. Parchment, 223 x 194 x 45 mm, ii + 71 folios, two columns, 21–22 lines, Gəʿəz, twentieth century.

Miniatures:

1. F. 30r: Crude drawing of a face.
2. F. 45v: Crude drawing of two figures.
3. F. 46r: Crude drawing of a figure.
4. Inside back cover: Crude drawing of a figure.

IES 03155, Images Collection, መልክአ ጉባኤ. Parchment, 126 x 86 x 45 mm, iv + 88 folios, one column, 10–11 lines, Gəʿəz, twentieth century.

Miniatures:

1. F. i r(ecto): Crude drawing of a face.
2. F. iv r(ecto): Madonna and Child.
3. F. 87v: Crude drawing of an angel and a figure with a sword.

IES 03156, Psalter, ዳዊት. Parchment, 173 x 153 x 64 mm, ii + 157 folios, one column and two columns, 19–20 lines, Gəʿəz, nineteenth century.

IES 03157, Mystery of Communion, ምሥጢረ ቁርባን; Excerpt of Sword of Divinity, ሰይፈ መለኮት, by a later hand; Gospel of Mark, ወንጌል ዘማርቆስ; Sword of Divinity, ሰይፈ መለኮት. Parchment, 92 x 90 x 42 mm, iv + 94 folios, two columns, 11 lines, Gəʿəz, eighteenth century.

Miniatures:

1. F. 94v: Crude drawing of figures and a cross.

IES 03158, Wisest of the Wise, ጠቢበ ጠቢባን. Parchment, 102 x 90 x 40 mm, iv + 80 folios, two columns, 8 lines, Gəʿəz, late eighteenth century.

IES 03159, Hymn to the Savior of the World called "Host of His Angels," ሠራዊተ መላእክቲሁ, with musical notation; Harp of Praise, አርጋኖነ ውዳሴ. Parchment, 180 x 160 x 50 mm, ii + 128 folios, two columns, 17–18 lines, Gəʿəz, eighteenth century.

IES 03160, Acts of *abba* Kiros, ገድለ ኪሮስ; Image of *abba* Kiros, መልክአ አባ ኪሮስ. Parchment, 180 x 130 x 43 mm, ii + 64 folios, two columns, 16 lines, Gəʿəz, twentieth century.

Miniatures:

1. F. i v(erso)–ii r(ecto): Crude drawing of crosses.

IES 03161, Psalter, ዳዊት. Parchment, 200 x 184 x 90 mm, 200 folios, one column and two columns, 21 lines, Gəʿəz, eighteenth century.

IES 03162, Psalter, ዳዊት; additional copy of Song of Songs, in later hand; *Asmat* Prayer against sharp pain, ጸሎት በእንተ ውግአት. Parchment, 220 x 189 x 75 mm, ii + 174 folios, one column and two columns, 18–20 lines, Gəʿəz, eighteenth century.

Miniatures:

1. F. i r(ecto): Drawing of *abunä* Barlaam and Josaphat.

2. F. ii r(ecto): Crude drawing of a face.

3. F. ii v(erso): Two equestrian saints.

IES 03163, Harp of Praise, አርጋኖነ ውዳሴ. Parchment, 180 x 160 x 53 mm, i + 140 folios, two columns, 16 lines, Gəʿəz, late eighteenth/early nineteenth century.

IES 03164, Anaphora of the Apostles, ቅዳሴ ሐዋርያት; Anaphora of Our Lord, ቅዳሴ እግዚእ; Anaphora of Our Lady Mary attributed to Cyriacus of Bəhənsa, ቅዳሴ ማርያም; Anaphora of Epiphanius, ቅዳሴ ኤጲፋንዮስ; Anaphora of Dioscorus, ቅዳሴ ዲዮስቆሮስ; Anaphora of John Chrysostom, ቅዳሴ ዮሐንስ አፈ ወርቅ; Anaphora of Jacob of Serugh, ቅዳሴ ያዕቆብ ዘሥሩግ; Anaphora of John, Son of Thunder, ቅዳሴ ዮሐንስ ወልደ ነጉድጓድ; Anaphora of the 318 Orthodox Fathers, ቅዳሴ ዘሠለስቱ ምዕት; Anaphora of Athanasius, ቅዳሴ አትናቴዎስ; Anaphora of Gregory, brother of Basil, ቅዳሴ ጎርጎርዮስ እኀወ ባስልዮስ; Anaphora of Gregory, the second, ቅዳሴ ጎርጎርዮስ ካልዕ, incomplete at the end. Parchment, 155 x 140 x 60 mm, 122 folios, two columns, 14–15 lines, Gəʿəz, 1937–42 (f. 16v and passim mention the Alexandrian Patriarch John XIX [r. 1928–42] and bishop *abba* Marqos bishop of Eritrea and Tigray [1937–60]).

IES 03165, Psalter, ዳዊት with three charts of the feast days covering the years from 1956–2011 EC. Parchment, 210 x 150 x 63 mm, v + 171 folios, one column and two columns, 21 lines, Gəʿəz, ca. 1956 = 1963–64 (f. 167r mentions Emperor Ḫaylä Śəllase and Bishop Gäbrəʾel).

Miniatures:

1. F. ii v(erso): "How Antiochus told Maccabees to sacrifice to his gods." "How the king became angry and cut off his head and put his wife into the fire."
2. F. iii r(ecto): "How Maccabees said he would die for his faith and refused to sacrifice to the gods."
3. F. v r(ecto): King David playing the harp.
4. F. 149v: Madonna and Child.
5. F. 170r: An angel with sword and scabbard.

IES 03166, Image of Mary, መልክአ ማርያም; Image of Jesus, መልክአ ኢየሱስ; Image of the Praises of Mary, መልክአ ውዳሴ ማርያም. Parchment, 109 x 93 x 33 mm, i + 45 folios, one column, 12–16 lines, Gəʿəz, twentieth century.

IES 03173, Excerpts from the Antiphonary for the Whole Year, ድጓ. Parchment, 235 x 152 x 16 mm, 46 folios, two columns, 30–31 lines, Gəʿəz, twentieth century.

IES 03477, Lectionary for Passion Week, ግብረ ሕማማት. Parchment, 363 x 290 x 95 mm, iv + 168 folios, three columns, 28 lines, Gəʿəz, 1889–1913 (f. 42r mentions Emperor Mənilək II; f. 142v mentions Metropolitan Matewos and Atənatewos).

Miniatures:

1. F. iii r(ecto): Saint George and the Dragon, in blue ink.

IES 03478, Funeral Ritual, መጽሐፈ ግንዘት. Parchment, 282 x 240 x 63 mm, ii + 150 folios, two columns, 24 lines, Gəʿəz, late nineteenth/early twentieth century.

Miniatures:

1. F. i r(ecto): Crude drawing of angels and figures.

2. F. i v(erso): Gäbrä Mänfäs Qəddus.

3. F. ii v(erso): The Holy Trinity surrounded by the four Living Creatures.

IES 03479, Synaxarium for the second half of the year, መጽሐፈ ስንክሳር. Parchment, 380 x 280 x 95 mm, iv + 181 folios, three columns, 35 lines, Gəʿəz, 1929 EC = 1936–37 (dated colophon on f. 179v) with miniatures by a later hand.

Miniatures:

1. F. ii r(ecto): Saint George and the Dragon.

2. F. iii r(ecto): Madonna and Child.

3. F. 178v: An angel and Gäbrä Mänfäs Qəddus.

4. F. 179r: The Crucifixion.

IES 03480, Funeral Ritual, መጽሐፈ ግንዘት. Parchment, 262 x 210 x 112 mm, 138 folios, two columns, 24 lines, Gəʿəz, nineteenth century.

IES 03481, Homiliary in Honor of the Archangel Michael, ድርሳነ ሚካኤል. Parchment, 204 x 157 x 44 mm, 86 folios, two columns, 22 lines, Gəʿəz, early twentieth century.

Miniatures:

1. F. 86v: Crude drawing of a figure.

IES 03482, Psalter, ዳዊት, incomplete, twentieth century paintings over text. Parchment, 226 x 175 x 70 mm, ii + 146 folios, one column and two columns, 20 lines, Gəʿəz, nineteenth century with twentieth-century miniatures.

Miniatures:

1. Inside front cover: The Crucifixion, badly effaced.
2. F. i v(erso): Madonna and Child.
3. F. 139v: The Nativity.
4. F. 140v: God gives a book case to a kneeling saint while an angel blows a ram's horn.
5. F. 141v: Mary Magdalene washes Jesus' feet.
6. F. 142v: Mary Enthroned.
7. F. 143v: Saint George and the Dragon.
8. F. 144v: The Piercing of Jesus' side.
9. F. 145v: The Resurrection of Jesus.
10. F. 146v: The Holy Trinity surrounded by the four Living Creatures.

IES 03483, Homiliary in Honor of the Archangel Michael, ድርሳነ ሚካኤል. Parchment, 240 x 210 x 60 mm, viii + 112 folios, two columns, 18 lines, Gəʿəz, twentieth century.

Miniatures:

1. F. iii v(erso): Archangel Michael with sword and scabbard with the souls of saints on his wings.
2. F. iv r(ecto): Archangel Michael with sword, faces two people.
3. F. vii v(erso): Archangel Michael defeats the devil for two saints.
4. F. viii r(ecto): The devil argues with a man; the archangel Michael protects above.

IES 03484, Synaxarium for the first half of the year, መጽሐፈ ስንክሳር. Parchment, 340 x 265 x 97 mm, ii + 188 folios, three columns, 38–40 lines, Gəʿəz, twentieth century.

IES 03487, *Praises for God*, hymnbook published by the Church of Mäsärätä Krəstos. Paper, 240 x 170 x 10 mm, i + 81 folios, Amharic, 1961 EC = 1968–69.

IES 03488, Musical Transcription for Praises of Mary and Antiphonary for the Season of Lent, written in Western musical notation by Ṗawlos Badma. Paper, 276 x 216 x 6 mm, i + 14 folios, Gəʿəz, 1927 EC = 1935–36.

IES 03507, Image of Mary, መልክአ ማርያም; Image of Michael, መልክአ ሚካኤል; Image of Gabriel, መልክአ ገብርኤል; Image of Saint George, መልክአ ጊዮርጊስ; Image of Gäbrä Mänfäs Qəddus, መልክአ ገብረ መንፈስ ቅዱስ, incomplete at the end; Prayer of Mary at Bartos, ባርቶስ; Prayer of Saint Peter, ጸሎተ ጴጥሮስ; Image of the Praises of Mary, መልክአ ውዳሴ ማርያም; Vision of Mary, ራዕየ ማርያም. Parchment, 164 x 116 x 40 mm, 79 folios, two columns, 24–27 lines, Gəʿəz, early twentieth century.

IES 03582, Photocopy of a manuscript from Däbrä Libanos, Treatise on the Trinity, ዜና ሥላሴ (pp. 1–134), arranged for the days of the week; Book of Life and Mercy, መጽሐፈ ሕይወት ወምሕረት (pp. 134–266), arranged for the months of the year; Thirty-Eight Miracles of the Trinity, ተአምረ ሥላሴ (pp. 267–421); Hymn to the Trinity, "I Worship," እስግድ ለህላዌክሙ (pp. 423–42). Paper, 300 x 215 x 32 mm, i + 225 folios, two columns, 17 lines, Amharic, twentieth century.

IES 03592, Photocopy of manuscript containing the Brief History of *abunä* Täklä Haymanot; The Acts of Adam and Eve, ገድለ አዳም ወሔዋን, arranged for the months of the year; History of the Queen of the East, ታሪክ ዘንግሥተ አዜብ. Paper, 305 x 220 x 15 mm, i + 96 folios, two columns, 29 lines, Gəʿəz, 1973 EC = 1980–81.

IES 03593, Hymn to Mary called Praise of the Harp, ዕንዚራ ስብሐት; Portal of Light, ኖጣተ ብርሃን; published texts from Paris, Bibliothèque nationale de France, MSS Eth. d'Abbadie 121 and Eth. d'Abbadie 235, photocopy. Paper, 220 x 305 x 15 mm, i + 73 folios, one column, Gəʿəz, late twentieth century.

IES 03653, Psalter, ዳዊት. Parchment, 165 x 125 x 70 mm, ii + 152 folios, one column and two columns, 22–25 lines, Gəʿəz, late nineteenth/early twentieth century.

IES 03654, Psalter, ዳዊት. Parchment, 150 x 115 x 50 mm, ii + 133 folios, one column and two columns, 24 lines, Gəʿəz, twentieth century.

Miniatures:

1. F. i v(erso): Crude drawing of a horse.
2. F. ii v(erso): Crude drawing of a figure and a face.
3. F. 133r: Crude drawing of a figure.
4. F. 133v: Crude drawing of an equestrian saint.

IES 03655, Psalter, ዳዊት. Parchment, 105 x 110 x 75 mm, i + 217 folios, one column and two columns, 14 lines, Gəʿəz, eighteenth century.

Miniatures:

1. F. 141v: Drawing of two crosses and a circle in red and black ink.
2. F. 217v: Crude drawing of two figures.

IES 03656, Psalter, ዳዊት. Parchment, 169 x 145 x 70 mm, i + 182 folios, one column and two columns, 18 lines, Gəʿəz, late seventeenth/early eighteenth century.

Miniatures:

1. F. i v(erso): An angel with sword and scabbard.

IES 03657, Psalter, ዳዊት. Parchment, 165 x 120 x 65 mm, ii + 143 folios, one column and two columns, 24 lines, Gəʿəz, late nineteenth century.

IES 03658, Psalter, ዳዊት, with mirror in a niche in the inside back cover. Parchment, 185 x 120 x 70 mm, ii + 152 folios, one column and two columns, 22–25 lines, Gəʿəz, early nineteenth century.

Miniatures:

1. F. i v(erso): Crude drawing of two kings.
2. F. ii r(ecto): King David playing the harp.
3. F. ii v(erso): Crude drawing of a figure.

IES 03659, Horologium for the Night, ሰዓታት ዘሌሊት. Parchment, 120 x 90 x 50 mm, v + 48 folios, one column, 12–14 lines, Gəʿəz, twentieth century.

Miniatures:

1. F. i v(erso): An angel with sword and scabbard.
2. F. V r(ecto): A figure.

IES 03660, Missal, መጽሐፈ ቅዳሴ; Anaphora of Our Lady Mary attributed to Cyriacus of Bəhənsa, ቅዳሴ ማርያም. Parchment, 97 x 67 x 33 mm, ii + 41 folios, one column, 12 lines, Gəʿəz, 1881–1916 (the Metropolitan Qerəllos VI and the Metropolitan Ṗeṭros IV mentioned on ff. 3rv).

IES 03661, Psalter, ዳዊት; Angels Praise Her, ይዌድስዎ መላእክት ለማርያም. Parchment, 193 x 130 x 55 mm, ii + 129 folios, one column and two columns, 27 lines, Gəʿəz, early twentieth century.

Miniatures:

1. F. 127: Angel with sword and scabbard.

IES 03662, Psalter, ዳዊት. Parchment, 180 x 125 x 75 mm, iv + 160 folios, one column and two columns, 21 lines, Gəʿəz, twentieth century.

IES 03663, Psalter, ዳዊት; Hymn to God from the Praise of the Beloved (ስብሐተ ፍቁር) called, "O, Father, Help us for the Sake of Jesus," አ አብ በእንተ ኢየሱስ ርድአነ; Image of the Praises of Mary, መልክአ ውዳሴ ማርያም. Parchment, 170 x 115 x 70 mm, ii + 149 folios, one column and two columns, 26–27 lines, Gəʿəz, twentieth century.

Miniatures:

1. F. 149r: Madonna and Child.
2. F. 149v: Crude drawing of a cross.
3. Inside back cover: Crude drawing of a figure.

IES 03664, Psalter, ዳዊት; Nicene Creed (f. i r); Constantinople Creed (ff. i r and ii v); *Asmat* Prayer against Demons, "I will Call the Kings of the Land;" Hymn to Mary, "I will Praise Thy Grace," እሴብህ ጸጋኪ. Parchment, 180 x 120 x 63 mm, iv + 158 folios, one column and two columns, 23 lines, Gəʿəz, twentieth century.

IES 03665, Wisest of the Wise, ጠቢበ ጠቢባን. Parchment, 130 x 92 x 35 mm, ii + 60 folios, one column, 11 lines, Gəʿəz, early twentieth century.

IES 03666, Psalms 1–43, ዳዊት. Parchment, 165 x 120 x 25 mm, 34 folios, one column, 21 lines, Gəʿəz, twentieth century.

IES 03667, Psalter, ዳዊት; written with unjustified margins; *Asmat* Prayer against snake, ጸሎተ ዓርዌ ምድር. Parchment, 155 x 105 x 75 mm, ii + 156 folios, one column, 17–20 lines, Gəʿəz, twentieth century.

IES 03668, Prayer of Mary at Golgotha, ጸሎተ እግዝእትነ ማርያም ዘሰነ ጎልጎታ; Mystagogia, ትምህርተ ኅቡአት; Excerpt from Hymn to Mary, "Passover for Adam," ለአዳም ፋሲካሁ; Excerpt from the Gospel of John (19:25–27). Parchment, 90 x 73 x 30 mm, ii + 42 folios, one column, 13 lines, Gəʿəz, nineteenth century.

IES 03669, Psalter, ዳዊት. Parchment, 195 x 145 x 70 mm, iv + 172 folios, one column and two columns, 20–21 lines, Gəʿəz, early twentieth century.

IES 03670, Psalter, ዳዊት. Parchment, 197 x 173 x 70 mm, ii + 173 folios, one column and two columns, 20 lines, Gəʿəz, nineteenth century.

IES 03671, *Ziq* Chants, መጽሐፈ ዚቅ, incomplete at beginning and end. Parchment, 185 x 145 x 40 mm, 41 folios, two columns, 23–24 lines, Gəʿəz, eighteenth century.

IES 03672, *Ziq* Chants, መጽሐፈ ዚቅ; Mystagogia, ትምህርተ ኅቡአት; *Asmat* Prayer against the Evil Eye, ጸሎት በእንተ ዓይን. Parchment, 203 x 172 x 30 mm, iv + 32 folios, three columns, 35–38 lines, Gəʿəz, late eighteenth/early nineteenth century.

IES 03673, Psalter, ዳዊት; Catechism on the Five Pillars, ቃለ ሃይማኖት. Parchment, 170 x 155 x 55 mm, 159 folios, one column and two columns, 17–19 lines, Gəʿəz, late eighteenth/early nineteenth century.

Miniatures:

1. F. 159v: Crude drawing of two crosses.

IES 03674, Funeral Ritual, መጽሐፈ ግንዘት. Parchment, 185 x 180 x 70 mm, 143 folios, two columns, 16–18 lines, Gəʿəz, late eighteenth century.

IES 03675, Psalter, ዳዊት, incomplete at the end (missing final quire). Parchment, 155 x 105 x 50 mm, iv + 140 folios, one column and two columns, 24 lines, Gəʿəz, nineteenth century.

Miniatures:

1. F. ii v(erso): A saint with scabbard reads from Psalm 102, "Hear me, O Lord."
2. F. iii r(ecto): Crude drawing of man with processional cross.

IES 03676, Psalter, ዳዊት. Parchment, 140 x 140 x 95 mm, i + 172 folios, one column and two columns, 17–19 lines, Gəʿəz, eighteenth century.

Miniatures:

1. F. 172r: Crude drawing of a figure.

IES 03677, Fragment of a Psalter, ዳዊት, including Psalms 1–72. Parchment, 163 x 148 x 26 mm, iv + 50 folios, one column, 19–20 lines, Gəʿəz, late eighteenth/early nineteenth century.

IES 03678, Acts of Gäbrä Mänfäs Qəddus, ገድለ ገብረ መንፈስ ቅዱስ; Miracles of Gäbrä Mänfäs Qəddus, ተአምረ ገብረ መንፈስ ቅዱስ, rebound in some disorder at the end. Parchment, 190 x 160 x 60 mm, 84 folios, two columns, 16 lines, Gəʿəz, late eighteenth century.

IES 03679, Missal, መጽሐፈ ቅዳሴ; Angels Praise Her, ይቤድስዋ መላእክት ለማርያም; Excerpt from the Gospels; Excerpt from the Missal. Parchment, 180 x 180 x 75 mm, v + 157 folios, two columns, 18 lines, Gəʿəz, 1730–55 (f. 32r mentions Emperor Yoḥannəs II, d. 1761; f. 32v and 33r mention Emperor Iyasu II [r. 1730–55]).

IES 03680, Psalter, ዳዊት; Hymn to Mary, "I Praise Thy Grace" እሴብሀ ጸጋኪ; Excerpt of the Image of Edom, መልክአ ኤዶም (f. 150r). Parchment, 160 x 145 x 70 mm, ii + 150 folios, one column and two columns, 20–22 lines, Gəʿəz, seventeenth and late eighteenth centuries (composite).

Miniatures:

1. F. ii r(ecto): Crude drawing of a figure.
2. F. ii v(erso): Crude drawing of crosses.
3. F. 149v: Crude drawing of figures.

IES 03697, Psalter, ዳዊት, incomplete at the beginning and end. Parchment, 125 x 130 x 80 mm, 181 folios, one column and two columns, 17–18 lines, Gəʿəz, eighteenth century.

IES 03698, Psalter, ዳዊት, incomplete at the beginning and end. Parchment, 140 x 110 x 40 mm, i + 93 folios, one column, 26 lines, Gəʿəz, late nineteenth century.

IES 03699, Psalter, ዳዊት, incomplete at the beginning and end. Parchment, 220 x 195 x 60 mm, 124 folios, one column, 22 lines, Gəʿəz, late eighteenth century.

IES 03700, Psalter, ዳዊት, with Psalter of the Virgin, መዝሙረ ድንግል. Parchment, 208 x 200 x 90 mm, ii + 205 folios, one column and two columns, 20 lines, Gəʿəz, eighteenth century.

IES 03701, Gospel of John, ወንጌል ዘዮሐንስ. Parchment, 160 x 120 x 40 mm, ii + 82 folios, two columns, 15 lines, Gəʿəz, late nineteenth century.

Miniatures:

1. F. i r(ecto): Crude drawing of an equestrian saint.
2. F. i v(erso): Crude drawing of a bird.
3. F. ii r(ecto): Crude drawing of a bird.

IES 03702, Image of the Icon, መልክአ ሥዕል. Parchment, 120 x 85 x 30 mm, 45 folios, one column, 15–16 lines, Gəʿəz, late nineteenth/early twentieth century.

IES 03703, Psalter, ዳዊት. Parchment, 155 x 120 x 53 mm, ii + 158 folios, one column and two columns, 21 lines, Gəʿəz, twentieth century.

Miniatures:

1. F. i r(ecto): Crude drawing of an ornate cross.

IES 03704, Horologium for the Night, ሰዓታት ዘሌሊት. Parchment, 190 x 130 x 55 mm, 78 folios, two columns, 24 lines, Gəʿəz, early twentieth century.

Miniatures:

1. F. 75r: Crude drawing of two faces.
2. F, 78v: Crude drawing of two faces.

IES 03705, Psalter, ዳዊት; *Asmat* Prayer after the birth of a child, አስማተ ጸሎተ ዕጹባት; Prayer of the Covenant, ጸሎተ ኪዳን; Hymn to Mary, "I prostrate before you," እሰግድ ለኪ. Parchment, 165 x 180 x 80 mm, 176 folios, one column and two columns, 19 lines, Gəʿəz, early nineteenth century.

Miniatures:

1. F. 49v: Crude drawing of a figure.

2. F. 59v: Crude drawing of a figure.

3. F. 122v: Crude drawing of an ornate cross.

4. F. 172r: Crude drawing of the Crucifixion.

IES 03706, List of the Missions of the Archangel Michael; List of the Feast Days of the Apostles and Evangelists and Saint Mary; Book of the Disciples, መጽሐፈ አርድእት. Parchment, 110 x 75 x 45 mm, v + 74 folios, one column, 14–15 lines, Gəʿəz, late nineteenth century.

Miniatures:

1. F. i v(erso): Crude drawing of a cross.

2. F. iv v(erso): A man, partially erased.

3. F. 74r: Crude drawing of Madonna and Child.

IES 03707, Harp of Praise, አርጋኖን ውዳሴ. Parchment, 180 x 170 x 70 mm, iii + 188 folios, two columns, 14–16 lines, Gəʿəz, seventeenth century.

IES 03708, Psalter, ዳዊት; *Asmat* Prayer against headache, ጸሎት በእንተ ፍልጸተ ርእስ; *Asmat* Prayer against snake, ጸሎት ዓርዌ ምድር; *Asmat* Prayer against miscarriage. Parchment, 205 x 180 x 65 mm, i + 154 folios, one column and two columns, 20 lines, Gəʿəz, 1708–11, Colophon on folio 152v mentions Emperor Tewoflos (r. 1708–11).

IES 03709, *Ziq* Chants, መጽሐፈ ዚቅ. Parchment, 130 x 105 x 55 mm, iv + 136 folios, two columns, 15 lines, Gəʿəz, twentieth century.

IES 03710, Gospel of John, ወንጌል ዘዮሐንስ; Reward for reading the Gospel and Psalter regularly, extended version; Image of Michael, መልክአ ሚካኤል; Image of Gabriel, መልክአ ገብርኤል; *Asmat* Prayer for Protection, ጸሎት በእንተ ዓቃቤ ርእስ; *Asmat* Prayer against Evil Eye,

ጸሎት በእንተ ዓይነ ጥላ. Parchment, 155 x 100 x 45 mm, ii + 121 folios, two columns, 17 lines, Gəʿəz, early twentieth century.

IES 03711, Psalter, ዳዊት. Parchment, 135 x 100 x 50 mm, ii + 145 folios, one column and two columns, 25 lines, Gəʿəz, twentieth century.

Miniatures:

1. F. ii v(erso): Crude drawing of a man and a king.

IES 03712, Psalter, ዳዊት, incomplete at the end. Parchment, 190 x 160 x 90 mm, iii + 148 folios, one column, 19 lines, Gəʿəz, nineteenth century.

Miniatures:

1. F. ii r(ecto): Crude drawing of crosses and a figure.

2. F. iii r(ecto): Crude drawing of an equestrian saint.

IES 03713, Missal, መጽሐፈ ቅዳሴ. Parchment, 103 x 73 x 26 mm, ii + 39 folios, one column, 12 lines, Gəʿəz, 1881–87 (the Metropolitan Matewos and the Metropolitan Ṗeṭros IV mentioned on f. 3v).

Miniatures:

1. F. ii r(ecto): Crude drawing of a standing person.

IES 03714, Hymn to Mary, "Mary, Glorified, Rainbow of Noah," ማርያም ስብሕት ቀስተ መሐላሁ ለኖኅ; Angels Praise Her, ይዌድስዋ መላእክት ለማርያም; Harp of Praise, አርጋኖነ ውዳሴ; Hymn to Mary, "Hail Mary," በሀኪ ማርያም. Parchment, 155 x 130 x 85 mm, iii + 220 folios, two columns, 15 lines, Gəʿəz, seventeenth century. Single-slip maḥdär.

IES 03715, Gospel of John, ወንጌል ዘዮሐንስ. Parchment, 107 x 80 x 30 mm, v + 81 folios, two columns, 17 lines, Gəʿəz, twentieth century.

Miniatures:

1. F. 80v: Print folio from another work with an image of the Crucifixion has been stitched onto the folio.

2. F. 81r: Print folio from another work with an image of Madonna and Child has been stitched onto the folio.

IES 03716, Image of Michael, መልክአ ሚካኤል, incomplete at end; Gospel of John, ወንጌል ዘዮሐንስ; Image of Michael, መልክአ ሚካኤል; Image of Michael, መልክአ ሚካኤል, conclusion. Parchment, 155 x 120 x 40 mm, iv + 87 folios, two columns, 14 lines, Gəʿəz, twentieth century.

IES 03717, Psalter, ዳዊት, incomplete at the end. Parchment, 150 x 125 x 50 mm, ii + 133 folios, one column, 20–21 lines, Gəʿəz, twentieth century.

IES 03721, Psalter, ዳዊት, incomplete at the beginning and end. Parchment, 140 x 135 x 75 mm, 169 folios, one column and two columns, 19 lines, Gəʿəz, nineteenth century.

IES 03722, Psalter, ዳዊት. Parchment, 135 x 95 x 60 mm, iii + 178 folios, one column and two columns, 20 lines, Gəʿəz, early twentieth century.

IES 03723, Psalter, ዳዊት. Parchment, 185 x 138 x 40 mm, ii + 146 folios, one column and two columns, 23–24 lines, Gəʿəz, twentieth century.

Miniatures:

1. F. i r(ecto): Crude drawing of a figure.

IES 03724, Image of Jesus, መልክአ ኢየሱስ (incipit, ሰላም ለዝክረ ስምከ በመጽሐተ መስቀል ዘተለክዓ); Anaphora of Our Lady Mary attributed to Cyriacus of Bəhənsa, ቅዳሴ ማርያም. Parchment, 125 x 90 x 32 mm, i + 44 folios, one column, 13–14 lines, Gəʿəz, 1874–1927 (f. 18rv mentions the Alexandrian Patriarch Cyril V [r. 1874–1927] and a bishop *Abba* Yəsḥäq).

Miniatures:

1. F. 12v: The Crucifixion.

2. F. 13v: Madonna and Child.

3. F. 14v: The Archangel Michael, with a processional cross and a handkerchief. There is a demon laying at his feet.

IES 03725, Hymn to Christ, "For the sake of your Trinity, በእንተ ሥላሴከ; Praise of the Beloved, ስብሐተ ፍቁር; *Asmat* Prayer against an enemy, ጸሎት በእንተ ፀር; Image of the Praises of Mary, መልክአ ውዳሴ ማርያም; *Asmat* Prayer for Help in Learning; Image of Gabriel, መልክአ

ገብርኤል; Gəʿəz Alphabet; Book of Hours of *Abba* Giyorgis, መጽሐፈ ሰዓታት ዘባ ጊዮርጊስ; Prayer of Repentance, ጸሎተ ንስሐ, from the book of Missal; Book of Hours of *Abba* Giyorgis, መጽሐፈ ሰዓታት ዘአባ ጊዮርጊስ, continued. Parchment, 112 x 120 x 65 mm, i + 92 folios, two columns, 12–14 lines, Gəʿəz, late nineteenth century.

Miniatures:

1. F. 89v: Interlocking four-cornered geometric patterns.

2. F. 90v: Interlocking four-cornered geometric patterns.

IES 03726, Psalter, ዳዊት. Parchment, 160 x 120 x 86 mm, 143 folios, one column, 22–24 lines, Gəʿəz, twentieth century.

Miniatures:

1. F. 65r: A box with an x-shaped pattern within it.

IES 03727, Three Miracles of Mary, ተአምረ ማርያም (ff. 1r–17r); Prayer of Mary at Golgotha, ጸሎተ እግዝእትነ ማርያም ዘሰኔ ጎልጎታ (ff. 17v–35r). Parchment, ca. 159 x 117 x 45 mm, ii + 37 folios, two columns, 18 lines, Gəʿəz, twentieth century.

IES 03728, Psalter, ዳዊት. Parchment, 165 x 160 x 90 mm, ii + 164 folios, one column and two columns, 19–20 lines, Gəʿəz, eighteenth century.

IES 03730, Homiliary of the Savior of the World, ድርሳነ መድኃኔ ዓለም. Parchment, 210 x 170 x 65 mm, iv + 100 folios, two columns, 20 lines, Gəʿəz, early twentieth century.

Miniatures:

1. F. 95v: The Striking of the Head.

IES 03731, Psalter, ዳዊት; Excerpt of Hymn to Mary, "All hosts of heaven glorify you," ኩሎሙ ሠራዊተ ሰማያት. Parchment, 173 x 155 x 68 mm, 182 folios, one column and two columns, 19 lines, Gəʿəz, eighteenth century. Double-slip maḥdär.

Miniatures:

1. Inside back cover: Crude drawing of an ornate cross.

IES 03732, Psalter, ዳዊት. Parchment, 180 x 120 x 53 mm, i +132 folios, one column and two columns, 26 lines, Gəʿəz, early twentieth century. Single-slip maḥdär.

Miniatures:

1. F. 11v: Crude drawing of a face.

IES 03733, Image of John the Baptist, መልክአ ዮሐንስ መጥምቅ; Image of Gäbrä Mänfäs Qəddus, መልክአ ገብረ መንፈስ ቅዱስ; Image of Gabriel, መልክአ ገብርኤል; Image of Mary, መልክአ ማርያም; Image of the Savior of the World, መልክአ መድኃኔ ዓለም. Parchment, 124 x 98 x 33 mm, i + 41 folios, one column, 15 lines, Gəʿəz, twentieth century. Single-slip maḥdär.

IES 03734, Anaphora of Our Lady Mary attributed to Cyriacus of Bəhənsa, ቅዳሴ ማርያም; Prayer of the Covenant, ጸሎተ ኪዳን; God of the Luminaries, እግዚአብሔር ዘብርሃናት. Parchment, 115 x 85 x 31 mm, ii + 47 folios, one column, 14 lines, Gəʿəz, twentieth century.

Miniatures:

1. F. i r(ecto): Crude drawing of a face, in black ink.
2. F. 44v: Crude drawing of a man holding a rod, with a bird behind, in black ink.
3. F. 45r: Crude drawing of two people, in black ink.

IES 03735, Prayer of Mary at Golgotha, ጸሎተ እግዝእትነ ማርያም ዘዴ ጎልጎታ; Mystagogia, ትምህርተ ኅቡዓት; Prayer to Jesus Christ, "In the Name of God, the Beginning," በስመ እግዚአብሔር ቀዳማዊ; Asmat Prayer Against Disease, (= Asmat Prayer of the Archangel Michael which is written on his left and right wings, often included in Dersana Mikaʾel in the month of Ḫədar, and Asmat Prayer of the Seven Archangels). Parchment, 95 x 73 x 35 mm, ii + 51 folios, one column, 12 lines, Gəʿəz, nineteenth century. Double-slip maḥdär.

Miniatures:

1. F. ii v(erso): Crude drawing of a figure.
2. F. 47v: An angel with sword and scabbard.
3. F. 49r: Talismanic symbol based on a nine-box panel with a face in the center.

4. F. 50v: Crude drawing of an angel.

5. F. 51r: Crude drawing of a figure.

IES 03736, *Asmat* Prayer against the evil eye with the story of Jesus and the Disciples at the Sea of Tiberias, ጸሎተ ንድራ; Image of Jesus, መልክአ ኢየሱስ. Parchment, 93 x 61 x 24 mm, iv + 24 folios, one column, 12–13 lines, Gəʿəz, twentieth century.

Miniatures:

1. F. i r(ecto): Crude drawing of a figure.

2. F. ii r(ecto): Talismanic symbol based on a nine-box panel with a face in the center.

3. F. iv r(ecto): Crude drawing of an ornate cross.

IES 03737, Image of the Trinity, መልክአ ሥላሴ; Absolution of the Son, ፍትሐት ዘወልድ. Parchment, 125 x 98 x 16 mm, ii + 20 folios, one column, 15 lines, Gəʿəz, early twentieth century.

IES 03738, Psalter, ዳዊት. Parchment, 135 x 122 x 75 mm, i + 174 folios, one column and two columns, 20–22 lines, Gəʿəz, late eighteenth century.

IES 03739, Psalter, ዳዊት (without Praises of Mary and Gate of Light). Parchment, 110 x 95 x 77 mm, i + 192 folios, one column, 17–20 lines, Gəʿəz, twentieth century.

Miniatures:

1. There are crude drawings of faces in blue ink throughout the codex.

IES 03740, Psalter, ዳዊት. Parchment, 185 x 152 x 97 mm, 180 folios, one column and two columns, 19 lines, Gəʿəz, early nineteenth century.

IES 03741, Psalter, ዳዊት; Image of the Praises of Mary, መልክአ ውዳሴ ማርያም. Parchment, 160 x 145 x 73 mm, i + 187 folios, one column and two columns, 19 lines, Gəʿəz, late eighteenth century.

IES 03742, Hymn to Sebastian, "Greeting to your hands which were bound behind your back," ሰላምታ ዘሰብስትያኖስ; Psalter, ዳዊት; brief medicinal instruction. Parchment, 145 x 105 x 60 mm, i + 138 folios, one column and two columns, 20–22 lines, Gəʿəz, nineteenth century.

Miniatures:

1. F. 138v: Crude drawing of the Crucifixion.

IES 03743, Psalter, ዳዊት, incomplete after the 11th Biblical Canticle. Parchment, 140 x 113 x 45 mm, ii + 106 folios, one column, 24 lines, Gəʽəz, nineteenth century.

Miniatures:

1. F. i v(erso): Crude drawing of King David playing the harp.

IES 03744, Psalter, ዳዊት. Parchment, 170 x 150 x 60 mm, 130 folios, one column and two columns, 19–20 lines, Gəʽəz, eighteenth century.

Miniatures:

1. F. 115v: Crudely drawn four-corner patterns.

IES 03745, Psalter, ዳዊት. Parchment, 150 x 140 x 70 mm, 181 folios, one column and two columns, 14–16 lines, Gəʽəz, eighteenth century.

IES 03746, Psalter, ዳዊት, incomplete at the beginning. Parchment, 150 x 135 x 60 mm, 161 folios, one column and two columns, 19 lines, Gəʽəz, nineteenth century.

Miniatures:

1. F. 141v: Four boxes with x-shaped patterns inside of them.

IES 03747, Image of the Praises of Mary, መልክአ ውዳሴ ማርያም; Psalter, ዳዊት, missing Psalms 1 and 2. Parchment, 180 x 170 x 75 mm, ii + 156 folios, one column and two columns, 17–19 lines, Gəʽəz, nineteenth century.

IES 03748, *Asmat* Prayers, አስማት. Parchment, 62 x 45 x 20 mm, iii + 25 folios, one column, 11–12 lines, Gəʽəz, twentieth century.

IES 03749, Image of Saint George, መልክአ ጊዮርጊስ; Nicene Creed, ጸሎተ ሃይማኖት; Prayer against the Tongue of People, ልሳነ ሰብእ (በእንተ ልሳነ ዘመድ ወባእድ). Parchment, 90 x 75 x 20 mm, 46 folios, one column, 10–11 lines, Gəʽəz, twentieth century.

IES 03750, *Asmat* Prayer which the Disciples received from the Lord; Psalms of Christ, መዝሙረ ዳዊት ምስለ መዝሙረ ክርስቶስ; Hymn to

Jesus Christ, "You are the River of Love, the King of Glory," ሙሓዘ ፍቅር አንተ ወንጉሥ ስብሐት; (previously unknown) Image of Jesus, መልክአ ኢየሱስ (incipit: ሰላም ለህላዌከ እምቅድመ ዓለማት ዘሀሎ); Hymn to Jesus, ምክሐ ምእመናን, authored by *aläqa* Taye; Image of the Savior of the World, መልክአ መድኃኔ ዓለም. Parchment, 165 x 140 x 40 mm, 83 folios, two columns, 21 lines, Gəʿəz, twentieth century.

Miniatures:

1. Ff. 80v–81v: Crude drawing of figures, in blue ink.

IES 03751, Psalter, ዳዊት; Collection of Concluding Hymns of the Miracles of Mary, መርገፍ ዘተአምረ ማርያም, incomplete at the beginning and end; (previously unknown) Image of Mary, መልክአ ማርያም. Parchment, 150 x 140 x 87 mm, i + 199 folios, one column and two columns, 16 lines, Gəʿəz, nineteenth century.

Miniatures:

1. F. 127v: Crude drawing of ornate crosses.
2. F. 148r: Crude drawing of an ornate cross.
3. F. 185v: Crude drawing of an ornate cross.

IES 03752, List of Days when the Anaphora is to be read; Anaphora of Our Lady Mary, ቅዳሴ ማርያም; Angels Praise Her, ይዌድሰዋ መላእክት ለማርያም; Image of the Passion of the Cross, መልክአ ሕማማት መስቀል; Instructions to the Priest for Conducting the Mass, ሥርዓት ዘይደሉ ለዝንቱ መል(እ)ክተ ምሥጢር. Parchment, 132 x 104 x 39 mm, vi + 61 folios, one column, 9–16 lines, Gəʿəz, Mäskäräm 17, 1937 EC (f. 38r).

IES 03753, About the Moveable Feasts; Commentary on Church Order; Psalter, ዳዊት, with extensive marginal notes; *Asmat* Prayer against the evil eye with the story of Jesus and the Disciples at the Sea of Tiberias, ጸሎተ ንድራ; Commentary on Mystagogia, ትምህርተ ኅቡዓት ትርጓሜ. Parchment, 200 x 143 x 55 mm, ii + 148 folios, one column and two columns, 22–23 lines, Gəʿəz, dated 7,382 Year of the World = 1882 (f. 145).

IES 03754, *Asmat* Prayers, አስማት. Parchment, 90 x 50 x 20 mm, 40 folios, one column, 16 lines, Gəʿəz, twentieth century.

IES 03755, Gəʿəz Grammar, ሰዋስወ፡ ግዕዝ. Parchment, 134 x 112 x 10 mm, 32 folios, two columns, 16 lines, Gəʿəz, early twentieth century.

IES 03756, Gospel of John, ወንጌል ዘዮሐንስ, with a leaf from a fifteenth century manuscript bound at the end. Parchment, 152 x 137 x 39 mm, 57 folios, two columns, 17–18 lines, Gəʿəz, nineteenth and fifteenth centuries.

IES 03797, Photocopy of a Commentary on the Fifteen Biblical Canticles. Paper, 300 x 210 x 10 mm, 78 folios, two columns, 36 lines, Geez, early twentieth century.

IES 04094, *Ethiopic New Testament*, published by Thomas Pell Platt (Lipsiae, 1899). Paper, 237 x 160 x 30 mm, iv + 227 folios, one column, 33 lines, Gəʿəz, 1899.

IES 04096, *Ethiopic Book of Solomon and Book of Siraq*, published in 1917. Paper, 275 x 223 x 23 mm, iv + 186 folios, two columns, 38 lines, Gəʿəz, Amharic, 1917.

IES 04138, Code of Kings, ፍትሐ ነገሥት. Parchment, 320 x 270 x 74 mm, iv + 105 folios, three columns, 33–34 lines, Gəʿəz, 1887 EC = 1894–95 (f. 102r gives the date).

IES 04175, Loose folio from a manuscript, painted with illuminations depicting the Council of Nicaea, painted in the so-called Second Gondarene Style. Parchment, 260 x 161 x 1 mm, 1 folio, eighteenth century.

Miniatures:

1. Ff. 1rv: The Council of Nicaea.

IES 04178, Book of Medicine, መጽሐፈ መድኃኒት, copied in 1930 from manuscripts in the British Museum. Paper, 163 x 105 x 40 mm, ii + 338 folios, one column, 19 lines, Amharic, 1930 EC = 1937–38.

IES 04179, Image of the Trinity, መልክአ ሥላሴ; *Asmat* Prayers; Praises of Mary, ውዳሴ ማርያም; Image of the Praises of Mary, መልክአ ውዳሴ ማርያም (dates of celebration of different saints in front). Parchment, 237 x 103 x 46 mm, 99 folios, one column, 23–24 lines, Gəʿəz, eighteenth century.

Miniatures:

1. F. 11r: An angel.
2. F. 11v: Crude drawing of a figure.

3. F. 12v: Crude drawing of a figure.

4. F. 97r: Crude drawing of an ornate cross and figures.

5. F. 97v: Crude drawing of figures.

6. F. 99r: Crude drawing of figures and faces.

7. F. 99v: Crude drawing of an ornate cross.

IES 04192, Photocopy of a manuscript dated 1880 EC = 1887–88, containing the History of the Order of the Palace of Ethiopian Kings; Commentary on the Book of Ezekiel, ትርጓሜ ሕዝቅኤል; Theological Treatise on the Unctionist Controversy in the time of Emperor Susənyos. Paper, 222 x 306 x 17 mm, i + 100 folios, two columns, 39–46 lines, Gəʿəz, 1880 EC = 1887–88 (f. 26r).

IES 04219, Pictures of a twentieth-century manuscript of the Bandlet of Righteousness, ልፋፈ ጽድቅ, sent to Professor Pankhurst for review from Mr. George Mendenhall. Paper, 280 x 220 x 3 mm, ii + 21 folios, one column, 9–10 lines, Gəʿəz, twentieth century.

Miniatures:

1. F. 2r: Two angels with swords and scabbards.

2. F. 21r: Angel with sword and scabbard.

IES 04229, Psalter, ዳዊት. Parchment, 160 x 140 x 71 mm, 174 folios, one column and two columns, 19–20 lines, Gəʿəz, nineteenth century. Double-slip maḥdär.

IES 04230, Psalter, ዳዊት. Parchment, 192 x 188 x 63 mm, i + 164 folios, one column and two columns, 17 lines, Gəʿəz, late eighteenth century. Single-slip maḥdär.

Miniatures:

1. F. 130v: A cross in red and black ink.

IES 04231, Homiliary in Honor of the Archangel Michael, ድርሳነ ሚካኤል, made in the Government Scriptorium. Parchment, 230 x 178 x 52 mm, ii + 102 folios, two columns, 20 lines, Gəʿəz, twentieth century.

Miniatures:

1. F. ii v(erso): Michael, the Archangel.

IES 04236, Homiliary in Honor of the Archangel Michael, ድርሳነ ሚካኤል. Parchment, 185 x 127 x 63 mm, ii + 154 folios, two columns, 18 lines, Gəʽəz, twentieth century.

IES 04237, Mission of Saint Michael; Psalter, ዳዊት; Excerpt from the Gospel of Matthew about the Ten Virgins. Parchment, 153 x 147 x 66 mm, ii + 167 folios, one column and two columns, 18–19 lines, Gəʽəz, nineteenth century.

IES 04238, Image of John the Baptist, መልክአ ዮሐንስ መጥምቅ; Canticle of the Flower, ማሕሌተ ጽጌ; Lament of the Virgin, ሰቆቃወ ድንግል; Anaphora of Our Lady Mary attributed to Cyriacus of Bəhənsa, ቅዳሴ ማርያም; Instructions about the measurement of shadows for the telling of time for the whole year, ስፍረ ስዓት. Parchment, 140 x 110 x 39 mm, iv + 96 folios, two columns, 15 lines, Gəʽəz, twentieth century (f. 69r mentions the Metropolitan Qerəllos VI).

Miniatures:

1. F. i r(ecto): Ornate cross, in pencil.
2. F. i v(erso): An angel, in pencil.

IES 04239, Praise of the Beloved, ስብሐተ ፍቁር; Prayer of Moses which saved him from Pharaoh, ጸሎተ ሙሴ. Parchment, 124.5 x 86 x 23 mm, i + 31 folios, one column, 16 lines, Gəʽəz, twentieth century.

IES 04241, Psalter, ዳዊት, missing Praises of Mary and Gate of Light, said to be taken from Maqdala during the siege by R. Napier; purchased in England by Andrew Heavens and Amber Henshaw and donated to the IES. Parchment, 151 x 110 x 50 mm, 106 folios, one column, 17–19 lines, Gəʽəz, twentieth century.

IES 04249, Psalter, ዳዊት. Parchment, 174 x 135 x 45 mm, iii + 124 folios, one column and two columns, 23–24 lines, Gəʽəz, twentieth century.

Miniatures:

1. F. iii v(erso): Image of the host.

IES 04250, Image of Ewosṭatewos, መልክአ ኤዎስጣቴዎስ; Psalter, ዳዊት; Greeting to Saint George, ሰላም ለከ ጊዮርጊስ; Greeting to the Saints; List of the days of the year on which heaven is open to receive prayers, ርኅወ ሰማይ. Parchment, 156 x 146 x 68 mm, iii + 156 folios, one column and two columns, 19 lines, Gəʿəz, eighteenth century.

Miniatures:

1. Crude drawings of crosses are found throughout the codex.

IES 04251, Psalter, ዳዊት. Parchment, 170 x 114 x 58 mm, i + 158 folios, one column and two columns, 20–22 lines, Gəʿəz, late nineteenth century.

IES 04252, Psalter, ዳዊት, incomplete at the beginning and the end. Parchment, 170 x 146 x 58 mm, 140 folios, one column and two columns, 20 lines, Gəʿəz, nineteenth century.

IES 04253, Psalter, ዳዊት. Parchment, 160 x 152 x 65 mm, i + 180 folios, one column and two columns, 19 lines, Gəʿəz, late eighteenth/early nineteenth century.

IES 04254, Praise of the Beloved, ስብሐተ ፍቁር; Psalter, ዳዊት; Lament of the Virgin, ሰቆቃወ ድንግል; Hymn to Mary, "In heaven and on earth," በሰማይ ወበምድር. Parchment, 180 x 151 x 75 mm, iv + 171 folios, one column and two columns, 21 lines, Gəʿəz, eighteenth century.

IES 04255, Psalter, ዳዊት, in disorder at the end. Parchment, 162 x 128 x 87 mm, 172 folios, one column and two columns, 20 lines, Gəʿəz, late eighteenth/early nineteenth century.

IES 04256, Introduction to the Miracles of Mary; Excerpt from 1 Corinthians 15 and 1 Thessalonians 4; Horologium for the Day, ስዓታት ዘመዓልት. Parchment, 140 x 117 x 46 mm, i + 107 folios, two columns, 16 lines, Gəʿəz, early nineteenth century.

Miniatures:

1. F. i v(erso): A man with arms upraised, in black ink.

IES 04257, Psalter, ዳዊት. Parchment, 164 x 132 x 55 mm, ii + 128 folios, one column and two columns, 24 lines, Gəʿəz, nineteenth century.

Miniatures:

1. F. 128r: *Däbtära* Amära on horseback.
2. F. 128v: Madonna and Child.

IES 04258, Antiphonary for the Whole Year, ድጓ, incomplete at the beginning and the end. Parchment, 181 x 146 x 30 mm, 23 folios, two columns, 24–25 lines, Gəʿəz, eighteenth century.

IES 04259, Funeral Ritual, መጽሐፈ ግንዘት, incomplete at the end. Parchment, 260 x 200 x 42 mm, iii + 57 folios, two columns, 28–29 lines, Gəʿəz, nineteenth century.

Miniatures:

1. Inside back cover: Crude drawing of figures.

IES 04260, Homiliary in Honor of the Archangel Michael, ድርሳነ ሚካኤል. Parchment, 140 x 109 x 35 mm, ii + 66 folios, two columns, 19 lines, Gəʿəz, nineteenth century.

Miniatures:

1. F. i v(erso): Crude drawing of a figure.

2. F. ii r(ecto): Crude drawing of several churches.

3. F. ii v(erso): Crude drawing of an ornate cross.

IES 04261, Image of the Praises of Mary, መልክአ ውዳሴ ማርያም (excerpt from Sunday); Psalter, ዳዊት; *Asmat* Prayer against snake, ጸሎት ኃቤ ምድር; bound with loose leaves at the end, including a leaf from an early fifteenth century manuscript, containing the Gate of Repentance, አንቀጸ ንስሐ. Parchment, 200 x 190 x 80 mm, ii + 165 folios, one column and two columns, 20–22 lines, Gəʿəz, late eighteenth/early nineteenth century, with a folio from the early fifteenth century.

IES 04262, Psalter, ዳዊት. Parchment, 180 x 135 x 60 mm, iv + 119 folios, one column and two columns, 21–25 lines, Gəʿəz, nineteenth century with twentieth-century miniatures.

Miniatures:

1. F. ii v(erso): Madonna and Child.

2. F. iii r(ecto): The Crucifixion with a prostrate man with a hand cross before the cross.

IES 04263, Psalter, ዳዊት. Parchment, 182 x 114 x 60 mm, ii + 140 folios, one column and two columns, 21–27 lines, Gəʿəz, twentieth century.

Miniatures:

1. F. 140r: Three crosses, in red ink.

IES 04264, Praise of the Beloved, ስብሐተ ፍቁር; Psalter, ዳዊት; Lament of the Virgin, ሰቆቃወ ድንግል; Hymn to Mary, "In heaven and on earth," በሰማይ ወበምድር, second set of images of IES 4254. Parchment, 185 x 162 x 70 mm, iv + 171 folios, one column and two columns, 21 lines, Gəʿəz, eighteenth century.

IES 04265, God of the Luminaries, እግዚአብሔር ዘብርሃናት; Psalter, ዳዊት. Parchment, 157 x 123 x 57 mm, ii + 144 folios, one column and two columns, 24–25 lines, Gəʿəz, early twentieth century.

IES 04266, Psalter, ዳዊት. Parchment, 165 x 150 x 67 mm, ii + 160 folios, one column and two columns, 18 lines, Gəʿəz, nineteenth century.

Miniatures:

1. F. 160r: Crude drawing of Saint George and the Dragon.

IES 04267, Psalter, ዳዊት. Parchment, 155 x 137 x 83 mm, i + 187 folios, one column and two columns, 17 lines, Gəʿəz, late seventeenth century.

Miniatures:

1. F. 162v: Crude drawing of a face.
2. F. 171r: Crude drawing of two figures.
3. F. 185v: Crude drawing of an ornate cross.

IES 04268, Psalter, ዳዊት. Parchment, 180 x 155 x 70 mm, i + 162 folios, one column and two columns, 20 lines, Gəʿəz, nineteenth century.

Miniatures:

1. F. i v(erso): A figure, partially erased.
2. F. 162v: Crude drawing of a figure.

IES 04269, Mystagogia, ትምህርተ ኅቡዓት; Psalter, ዳዊት. Parchment, 182 x 120 x 57 mm, iv + 146 folios, one column and two columns, 24 lines, Gəʿəz, early twentieth century.

Miniatures:

1. F. 145v: The Holy Trinity.
2. F. 146r: Madonna and Child with a man in proskynesis.

IES 04270, Psalter, ዳዊት; Excerpt of the Wisest of the Wise, ጠቢበ ጠቢባን. Parchment, 160 x 142 x 65 mm, ii + 170 folios, one column and two columns, 20 lines, Gəʿəz, early eighteenth century.

IES 04271, Psalter, ዳዊት. Parchment, 177 x 120 x 70 mm, i + 153 folios, one column and two columns, 20–22 lines, Gəʿəz, twentieth century.

Miniatures:

1. F. i r(ecto): Crude drawing of a figure.
2. F. i v(erso): Madonna and Child.
3. F. 153v: Crude drawing of a figure.

IES 04272, Image of Mary's Entrance in the Temple, መልክአ ማርያም (በዓታ ለማርያም); Psalter, ዳዊት. Parchment, 160 x 117 x 52 mm, ii + 190 folios, one column and two columns, 17–20 lines, Gəʿəz, twentieth century.

IES 04273, Psalter, ዳዊት; Prayer to Jesus Christ, "O My Lord, My God and My Savior," ኦ እግዚእየ ወአምላኪየ ወመድኃኒነ(የ) ኢየሱስ ክርስቶስ. Parchment, 174 x 165 x 69 mm, 175 folios, one column and two columns, 19 lines, Gəʿəz, eighteenth century.

IES 04274, Psalter, ዳዊት. Parchment, 137 x 104 x 65 mm, ii + 140 folios, one column and two columns, 20 lines, Gəʿəz, early twentieth century.

IES 04275, Psalter, ዳዊት. Parchment, 195 x 150 x 72 mm, 165 folios, one column and two columns, 19–21 lines, Gəʿəz, twentieth century.

IES 04276, Absolution of the Son, ፍትሐት ዘወልድ (in a twentieth century hand, before and after the Psalter); Psalter, ዳዊት, in early nineteenth-century hand, with missing sections supplied from a hand of the twentieth century. Parchment, 168 x 149 x 73 mm, ii + 155 folios, one column and two columns, 19 lines, Gəʿəz, early nineteenth/twentieth century (composite).

IES 04277, Antiphonary for the Whole Year, ድጓ, with musical notation. Parchment, 188 x 130 x 39 mm, iii + 105 folios, two columns, 21 lines, Gəʿəz, twentieth century.

IES 04278, Psalter, ዳዊት. Parchment, 165 x 140 x 57 mm, iii + 158 folios, one column and two columns, 20 lines, Gəʿəz, eighteenth century.

Miniatures:

1. F. i r(ecto): Crude drawing of a figure.

IES 04279, Mystery of the Trinity, ምሥጢረ ሥላሴ; Anaphora of Our Lady Mary, ቅዳሴ ማርያም; Image of the Savior of the World, መልክአ መድኃኔ ዓለም. Parchment, 127 x 92 x 33 mm, iv + 42 folios, one column, 13 lines, Gəʿəz, twentieth century.

IES 04280, Psalter, ዳዊት. Parchment, 220 x 198 x 70 mm, v + 162 folios, one column and two columns, 20 lines, Gəʿəz, late eighteenth century.

Miniatures:

1. F. i v(erso): Crude drawing of a figure and a horse.
2. F. ii r(ecto): Crude drawing of Saint George and the Dragon.

IES 04281, Image of the Passion of the Cross, መልክአ ሕማማት መስቀል; Prayer of the Covenant, ጸሎተ ኪዳን; Supplication, መስተብቁዕ; Litany, ሊጦን, arranged for the days of the week; Missal, መጽሐፈ ቅዳሴ. Parchment, 226 x 180 x 63 mm, ii + 120 folios, two columns, 19 lines, Gəʿəz, 1682–1706 (ff. 29rv mention the Alexandrian Patriarch John XVI [r. 1676–1718] and the Ethiopian Metropolitan Marqos IV [r. 1689–1716]; f. 35r mentions Emperor Iyasu I, [r. 1682–1706]).

IES 04282, Psalter, ዳዊት. Parchment, 205 x 154 x 75 mm, ii + 174 folios, one column and two columns, 18–19 lines, Gəʿəz, early twentieth century.

Miniatures:

1. F. i v(erso): Crude drawing of a face.
2. F. ii r(ecto): Crude drawing of an angel with a sword, an animal, and a figure.
3. F. 35v: Crude drawing of a figure.

IES 04283, Psalter, ዳዊት. Parchment, 215 x 155 x 65 mm, 178 folios, one column and two columns, 19 lines, Gəʿəz, late eighteenth/early nineteenth century.

Miniatures:

1. F. 98r: An angel (marginal drawing).

2. F. 114r: A man (marginal drawing).

3. F. 163v: Crude drawing of a face.

4. F. 175r: Crude drawing of a face.

5. Ff. 176v–177r: Two angels (marginal drawing).

IES 04284, Fragment of the Book of Ṭomar, መጽሐፈ ጦማር. Parchment, 198 x 171 x 29 mm, i + 20 folios, two columns, 20 lines, Gəʿəz, nineteenth century.

IES 04285, Instructions for Blessing and Pointing the Host, ሥርዓት ቡራኬ ወእማሬ; Gospel of John, ወንጌል ዘዮሐንስ; Calendar of the Conception, Birth, and Baptism of Jesus, made in the Government Scriptorium. Parchment, 168 x 115 x 47 mm, iii + 101 folios, two columns, 17 lines, Gəʿəz, early twentieth century.

IES 04286, Psalms 1 and 2; *Asmat* Prayer; Psalter, ዳዊት; Angels Praise Her, ይዌድስዋ መላእክት ለማርያም; Image of Saint Raguel, መልክአ ሩጉኤል, with *Asmat* Prayer; *Asmat* Prayer "Vanquisher of the Enemy," ጸሎት በእንተ መግረሬ ጸር; made in the Government Scriptorium. Parchment, 146 x 102 x 57 mm, iv + 167 folios, one column and two columns, 23 lines, Gəʿəz, twentieth century.

Miniatures:

1. F. 166v: Crude drawing of an ornate cross.

IES 04287, Psalter, ዳዊት. Parchment, 151 x 111 x 62 mm, ii + 181 folios, one column and two columns, 18 lines, Gəʿəz, twentieth century.

IES 04288, Lists of holy days of Saints and Feasts; Book of Hours of *Abba* Giyorgis, መጽሐፈ ሰዓታት ዘአባ ጊዮርጊስ; God Reigns, እግዚአብሔር ነግሠ, ascribed to Zärʾa Yaʿəqob. Parchment, 144 x 115 x 43 mm, iii + 77 folios, two columns, 17 lines, Gəʿəz, late nineteenth/early twentieth century.

IES 04289, Prayer of the Covenant, ጸሎተ ኪዳን; Litany, ሊጦን, arranged for the days of the week; Supplication, መስተብቁዕ; Absolution of the Son, ፍትሐት ዘወልድ; Beginning of the Introduction to the Miracles of Mary, መቅድመ ተአምረ ማርያም ዘሙዓልቃ; Mystagogia, ትምህርተ ኅቡዓት; Image of the Praises of Mary, መልክአ ውዳሴ ማርያም; Prayer of Mary at Golgotha, ጸሎተ እግዝእትነ ማርያም ዘሰኔ ጎልጎታ; Conclusion to the Introduction to the Miracles of Mary, መቅድም ተአምረ ማርያም ዘሙዓልቃ. Parchment, 166 x 119 x 40 mm, i + 59 folios, two columns, 15–16 lines, Gəʿəz, 1930–974 (f. 14v mentions Emperor Ḥaylä Śəllase).

IES 04290, Psalter, ዳዊት. Parchment, 146 x 100 x 50 mm, i + 154 folios, one column and two columns, 17–18 lines, Gəʿəz, twentieth century.

Miniatures:

1. F. i v(erso): A holy man.

2. F. 152r: Crude drawing of faces.

3. F. 152v: A holy man holding a handkerchief.

IES 04291, Book of Hours of *Abba* Giyorgis, መጽሐፈ ሰዓታት ዘአባ ጊዮርጊስ. Parchment, 124 x 84 x 30 mm, ii + 51 folios, one column, 19–20 lines, Gəʿəz, twentieth century.

IES 04292, Abbreviated Antiphonary for the Whole Year, ድጓ, with musical notation. Parchment, 163 x 145 x 32 mm, 56 folios, two columns, 17–20 lines, Gəʿəz, twentieth century.

IES 04293, Psalter, ዳዊት. Parchment, 178 x 115 x 56 mm, ii + 152 folios, one column and two columns, 24–25 lines, Gəʿəz, twentieth century. Double-slip maḥdär.

Miniatures:

1. F. ii r(ecto): A print card of the Crucifixion with the caption "Gesu Crocifisso" has been glued onto the folio.

IES 04294, Funeral Ritual, መጽሐፈ ግንዘት. Parchment, 211 x 165 x 37 mm, ii + 56 folios, two columns, 21 lines, Gəʿəz, late nineteenth/early twentieth century.

IES 04295, Psalter, ዳዊት; Image of the Praises of Mary, መልክአ ውዳሴ ማርያም; One Miracle of Mary, ተአምረ ማርያም. Parchment, 135 x 88 x 38 mm, iv + 187 folios, one column and two columns, 18–19 lines, Gəʿəz, twentieth century. Single-slip maḥdär.

Miniatures:

1. F. ii v(erso): "A blessed man" reads from a Psalter held by a servant.

2. F. iii r(ecto): "A blessed woman" faces the man, opposite.

IES 04296, Psalter, ዳዊት; Ten Commandments, ዐሥርቱ ትእዛዛት (Exodus 20); List of the Twelve Apostles; List of the Books of the Bible, ኍልቆ መጻሕፍት ቅዱሳት; Image of Jesus, መልክአ ኢየሱስ; Sword of Divinity, ሠይፈ መለኮት. Parchment, 205 x 177 x 91 mm, 191 folios, one column and two columns, 19 lines, Gəʿəz, seventeenth century.

IES 04297, Computus, ባሕረ ሐሳብ. Parchment, 155 x 115 x 31 mm, 66 folios, two columns, 18–22 lines, Gəʿəz, twentieth century.

Miniatures:

1. F. 23r: Crude drawing of a face.

2. F. 59v: Crude drawing of an angel.

IES 04298, *Asmat* Prayer against Evil Eye, ጸሎት በእንተ ሕማም ቡዳ; Excerpt from Sword of the Trinity, ሠይፈ ሥላሴ; Prayer to the Trinity, " I Beseech You, Father, Son, and Holy Spirit," ተማኅጸንኩ ብከሙ አብ ወወልድ ወመንፈስ ቅዱስ; Sword of the Trinity, ሠይፈ ሥላሴ; Image of the Trinity, መልክአ ሥላሴ. Parchment, 124 x 83 x 53 mm, ix + 77 folios, one column, 16 lines, Gəʿəz, twentieth century.

Miniatures:

1. F. ii r(ecto): The Holy Trinity.

2. F. ii v(erso): Madonna and Child.

3. F. viii v(erso): The Holy Trinity.

IES 04299, *Asmat* Prayers, ክታብ. Parchment, 132 x 10 cm, two strips, one column, Gəʿəz, twentieth century. Copied for ወለተ ገብርኤል.

Miniatures:

- Three miniatures: (a) angel with sword and scabbard; (b) ornate cross surrounded by four angels; and (c) multi-box panel.

IES 04300, *Asmat* Prayers, ክታብ. Parchment, 143 x 10 cm, two strips, two columns, Gəʿəz, twentieth century. Space for a name was left blank.

Miniatures:

- Two miniatures: (a) angel with sword and scabbard; and (b) angel with sword and scabbard.

IES 04301, *Asmat* Prayers, ክታብ. Parchment, 180 x 11 cm, three strips, one column, Gəʿəz, early twentieth century. Copied for ወለተ ጊዮርጊስ.

Miniatures:

- Three miniatures: (a) angel with sword and hand cross; (b) multi-box panel; and (c) talismanic symbol.

IES 04302, *Asmat* Prayers, ክታብ. Parchment, 74 x 10.5 cm, one strip, one column, Gəʿəz, twentieth century. The original name was erased and replaced with ኪዳን ማርያም.

Miniatures:

- One miniature: (a) ornate cross with a figure on either side.

IES 04303, *Asmat* Prayers, ክታብ. Parchment, 145 x 9 cm, three strips, one column, Gəʿəz, twentieth century. Copied for ወለተ ጊዮርጊስ.

Miniatures:

- One miniature: (a) talismanic symbol.

IES 04304, *Asmat* Prayers, ክታብ. Parchment, 126 x 7 cm, two strips, one column, Gəʿəz, early twentieth century. Copied for ገብረ ማርያም and ወለተ ሥላሴ.

Miniatures:

- Two miniatures: (a) angel with sword and scabbard; and (b) talismanic symbol.

IES 04305, *Asmat* Prayers, ከታብ. Parchment, 138 x 9 cm, two strips, one column, Gəʻəz, twentieth century. Copied for መለተ እግዚእ.

Miniatures:

- One miniature: (a) talismanic symbol.

IES 04306, *Asmat* Prayers, ከታብ. Parchment, 207 x 5 cm, three strips, one column, Gəʻəz, twentieth century. Copied for መለተ ጊዮርጊስ, replaced with መለተ ማርያም ገብሬ.

Miniatures:

- Four miniatures: (a) angel with sword and scabbard; (b) man with spear and handkerchief; (c) figure (demon?) pierced by a spear; and (d) talismanic symbol.

IES 04307, *Asmat* Prayers, ከታብ. Parchment, 56 x 8.5 cm, one strip, one column, Gəʻəz, early twentieth century. No owner was mentioned.

Miniatures:

- One miniature: (a) figure, badly faded.

IES 04308, *Asmat* Prayers, ከታብ. Parchment, 108 x 11 cm, two strips, one column, Gəʻəz, twentieth century. Copied for ተስፋ ማርያም and ጽጌ ሚካኤል.

Miniatures:

- Three miniatures: (a) two ornate crosses; (b) two ornate crosses; and (c) ornate cross.

IES 04309, *Asmat* Prayers, ከታብ. Parchment, 164 x 9.5 cm, three strips, one column, Gəʻəz, twentieth century. Copied for ገብረ መስቀል.

IES 04310, *Asmat* Prayers, ከታብ. Parchment, 85 x 10 cm, one strip, one column, Gəʻəz, nineteenth century. Copied for ሀብተ ጊዮርጊስ ገብረ ሥላሴ.

Miniatures:

- Two miniatures: (a) talismanic symbol surrounded by eyes; and (b) talismanic symbol.

IES 04311, *Asmat* Prayers, ከታብ. Parchment, 180 x 10.5 cm, two strips, one column, Gəʿəz, twentieth century. Original name was erased and replaced with ወለተ ኪዳን and ወለተ ሚካኤል.

Miniatures:

- Three miniatures: (a) multi-box panel; (b) ornate cross of four faces; and (c) three ornate crosses.

IES 04312, *Asmat* Prayers, ከታብ. Parchment, 189 x 11 cm, three strips, two columns, Gəʿəz, early twentieth century. Copied for ወለተ ማርያም.

Miniatures:

- Three miniatures: (a) angel with sword and scabbard; (b) talismanic symbol surrounded by figures; and (c) ornate cross with a figure on either side.

IES 04313, *Asmat* Prayers, ከታብ. Parchment, 146 x 9 cm, three strips, one column, Gəʿəz, twentieth century. Copied for ወለተ ኢየሱስ እታዮ እት አዮ.

Miniatures:

- Two miniatures: (a) talismanic symbol; and (b) ornate cross.

IES 04314, *Asmat* Prayers, ከታብ. Parchment, 74 x 11.5 cm, one strip, two columns, Gəʿəz, twentieth century. The name of the patron is illegible (ወለተ. . .).

Miniatures:

- One miniature: (a) ornate cross with a figure on either side.

IES 04315, *Asmat* Prayers, ከታብ. Parchment, 176 x 10.5 cm, three strips, one column, Gəʿəz, twentieth century. Copied for ወለተ ማርያም.

Miniatures:

- Three miniatures: (a) angel with sword and scabbard; (b) ornate cross with a figure on either side; and (c) talismanic symbol.

IES 04316, *Asmat* Prayers, ከታብ. Parchment, 74 x 10.5 cm, one strip, one column, Gəʿəz, twentieth century. Copied for ወልደ ገብማ.

IES 04317, *Asmat* Prayers, ክታብ. Parchment, 154 x 15.5 cm, two strips, two columns, Gəʿəz, twentieth century. Copied for ወለተ ኪዳን.

Miniatures:

- Two miniatures: (a) angel with sword and scabbard and figure on either side; and (b) three figures.

IES 04318, *Asmat* Prayers, ክታብ. Parchment, 182 x 10 cm, three strips, one column, Gəʿəz, late nineteenth century. Original patron's name was replaced with ገብረ ማርያም ወለተ ሥላሴ.

Miniatures:

- One miniature: (a) angel with sword and scabbard.

IES 04319, *Asmat* Prayers, ክታብ. Parchment, 76 x 9.5 cm, one strip, two columns, Gəʿəz, twentieth century. Copied for ወርቄቱ.

Miniatures:

- One miniature: (a) talismanic symbol.

IES 04320, *Asmat* Prayers, ክታብ. Parchment, 80 x 16 cm, one strip, two columns, Gəʿəz, twentieth century. Copied for ወለተ ኪዳን.

Miniatures:

- One miniature: (a) ornate cross with a figure on either side.

IES 04321, *Asmat* Prayers, ክታብ. Parchment, 163 x 11 cm, three strips, one column, Gəʿəz, late nineteenth century. Copied for ወለተ ገብርኤል.

Miniatures:

- Three miniatures: (a) angel with sword and scabbard; (b) talismanic symbol; and (c) talismanic symbol.

IES 04322, *Asmat* Prayers, ክታብ. Parchment, 107 x 9 cm, two strips, one column, Gəʿəz, twentieth century. Original owner's name was erased and replaced with ማሪራ.

Miniatures:

- One miniature: (a) angel with sword and scabbard.

IES 04323, *Asmat* Prayers, ክታብ. Parchment, 184 x 10 cm, three strips, one column, Gəʿəz, nineteenth century. Copied for ወለተ ገብርኤል, replaced in some places with ወለተ ኢየሱስ.

Miniatures:

- Three miniatures: (a) talismanic symbol; (b) talismanic symbol; and (c) talismanic symbol.

IES 04324, *Asmat* Prayers, ክታብ. Parchment, 54 x 7.5 cm, one strip, one column, Gəʿəz, twentieth century. Original name has been erased (ወለተ. . .) and replaced in a later hand with ወለተ መድኅን and the name ወለተ ዚደን ደስ written on the back of the scroll.

Miniatures:

- One miniature: (a) talismanic symbol.

IES 04325, *Asmat* Prayers, ክታብ. Parchment, 109 x 9 cm, two strips, one column, Gəʿəz, twentieth century. Copied for ወለተ ገብርኤል with ወለተ ቃለ አብ written in a later hand.

Miniatures:

- Two miniatures: (a) angel with sword and scabbard; and (b) talismanic symbol.

IES 04326, *Asmat* Prayers, ክታብ. Parchment, 153 x 7 cm, three strips, one column, Gəʿəz, twentieth century. Copied for ያልጋነሽ. See IES 04340.

Miniatures:

- Three miniatures: (a) angel; (b) angel; and (c) angel.

IES 04327, *Asmat* Prayers, ክታብ. Parchment, 160 x 8 cm, three strips, one column, Gəʿəz, twentieth century. Original name was erased and replaced with ወለተ ስኂነ ሥላሴ.

IES 04328, *Asmat* Prayers, ክታብ. Parchment, 75 x 9.5 cm, one strip, two columns, Gəʿəz, twentieth century. Copied for ወለተ ማርያም ወርቂቱ.

IES 04329, *Asmat* Prayers, ክታብ. Parchment, 170 x 8 cm, three strips, one column, Gəʿəz, twentieth century. Original name erased and replaced with ወለተ ተድሉ መድህን.

Miniatures:

- Three miniatures: (a) angel; (b) talismanic symbol, and (c) multi-box panel.

IES 04330, *Asmat* Prayers, ክታብ. Parchment, 50 x 9 cm, one strip, one column, Gəʿəz, twentieth century. No owner was mentioned.

Miniatures:

- One miniature: (a) angel with sword and scabbard.

IES 04331, *Asmat* Prayers, ክታብ. Parchment, 146 x 8 cm, three strips, one column, Gəʿəz, twentieth century. Copied for ኀብ ሪቱ ወለተ ማርያም.

Miniatures:

- Three miniatures: (a) angel with sword and scabbard; (b) talismanic symbol; and (c) talismanic symbol.

IES 04332, *Asmat* Prayers, ክታብ. Parchment, 69 x 8 cm, one strip, one column, Gəʿəz, twentieth century. Original name was erased and replaced with an illegible name.

Miniatures:

- One miniature: (a) multi-box panel.

IES 04333, *Asmat* Prayers, ክታብ. Parchment, 75 x 4.5 cm, one strip, one column, Gəʿəz, twentieth century. No owner was mentioned.

Miniatures:

- One miniature: (a) geometric design.

IES 04334, *Asmat* Prayers, ክታብ. Parchment, 90 x 9.5 cm, three strips, one column, Gəʿəz, early twentieth century. Space for a name is left blank.

Miniatures:

- Two miniatures: (a) ornate cross with a figure on either side; and (b) angel with sword and scabbard.

IES 04335, *Asmat* Prayers, ክታብ. Parchment, 149 x 8.8 cm, three strips, one column, Gəʿəz, twentieth century. Copied for ወለተ ስንበት ጥሩ.

IES 04336, *Asmat* Prayers, ክታብ. Parchment, 174 x 8 cm, three strips, one column, Gəʿəz, twentieth century. Copied for ኪዳን ማርያም.

Miniatures:

- Four miniatures: (a) angel with sword and scabbard; (b) ornate cross; (c) talismanic symbol; and (d) talismanic symbol.

IES 04337, *Asmat* Prayers, ክታብ. Parchment, 175 x 10 cm, three strips, two columns, Gəʿəz, twentieth century. Copied for ወልደ ሐዋርያት.

Miniatures:

- Three miniatures: (a) angel with sword and scabbard; (b) talismanic symbol; and (c) two ornate crosses.

IES 04338, *Asmat* Prayers, ክታብ. Parchment, 58 x 12 cm, one strip, one column, Gəʿəz, twentieth century. Copied for ወለተ ኪዳን.

Miniatures:

- Two miniatures: (a) multi-box panel; and (b) ornate cross.

IES 04339, *Asmat* Prayers, ክታብ. Parchment, 68 x 12 cm, one strip, one column, Gəʿəz, early twentieth century. Copied for ዓመተ ዮሐንስ and later replaced in some places with ገብረ ማርያም.

IES 04340, *Asmat* Prayers, ክታብ. Parchment, 140 x 6 cm, three strips, one column, Gəʿəz, twentieth century. Copied for ያልጋ. See IES 04326.

Miniatures:

- Three miniatures: (a) angel; (b) angel; and (c) angel.

IES 04341, *Asmat* Prayers, ክታብ. Parchment, 96 x 11 cm, two strips, one column, Gəʿəz, twentieth century. Copied for ወልደ ገćማ.

IES 04342, *Asmat* Prayers, ክታብ. Parchment, 158 x 7.8 cm, three strips, one column, Gəʿəz, twentieth century. Copied for ንግሥተ ማርያም.

Miniatures:

- Two miniatures: (a) angel with sword and scabbard; and (b) talismanic symbol.

IES 04343, *Asmat* Prayers, ክታብ. Parchment, 159 x 9 cm, three strips, one column, Gəʿəz, twentieth century. Copied for ገብረ ሕይወት.

Miniatures:

- Four miniatures: (a) talismanic symbol; (b) talismanic symbol; (c) talismanic symbol; and (d) talismanic symbol.

IES 04344, *Asmat* Prayers, ከታብ. Parchment, 58 x 10 cm, one strip, one column, Gəʿəz, twentieth century. No owner was mentioned.

Miniatures:

- One miniature: (a) angel.

IES 04345, *Asmat* Prayers, ከታብ. Parchment, 53 x 10 cm, one strip, one column, Gəʿəz, twentieth century. Copied for አመተ ጻድቃን.

Miniatures:

- One miniature: (a) angel.

IES 04346, *Asmat* Prayers, ከታብ. Parchment, 76 x 12 cm, one strip, one column, Gəʿəz, twentieth century. Copied for ወልደ ጊዮርጊስ.

IES 04347, *Asmat* Prayers, ከታብ. Parchment, 153 x 7.5 cm, three strips, one column, Gəʿəz, twentieth century. Copied for ማረች and ወለተ ማርያም.

Miniatures:

- Two miniatures: (a) angel; and (b) angel.

IES 04348, *Asmat* Prayers, ከታብ. Parchment, 180 x 9.5 cm, four strips, one column, Gəʿəz, early twentieth century. Copied for ወለተ ጊዮርጊስ, replaced with ወለተ መድህን.

Miniatures:

- Three miniatures: (a) angel with sword and scabbard; (b) king with two figures; and (c) talismanic symbol.

IES 04349, *Asmat* Prayers, ከታብ. Parchment, 68.5 x 6.5 cm, one strip, one column, Gəʿəz, twentieth century. Copied for ወለተ ሥላሴ.

Miniatures:

- One miniature: (a) angel with sword and scabbard.

IES 04350, *Asmat* Prayers, ካታብ. Parchment, 102 x 10 cm, two strips, one column, Gəʿəz, early twentieth century. Copied for ኃይለ ማርያም.

Miniatures:

- Two miniatures: (a) talismanic symbol; and (b) talismanic symbol.

IES 04351, *Asmat* Prayers, ካታብ. Parchment, 89 x 10.5 cm, one strip, one column, Gəʿəz, nineteenth century. Copied for ሀብት ጊዮርጊስ ገብረ ሥላሴ.

Miniatures:

- Two miniatures: (a) four eyes; and (b) ornate cross.

IES 04352, *Asmat* Prayers, ካታብ. Parchment, 78 x 9 cm, one strip, one column, Gəʿəz, twentieth century. Copied for ገብረ መስቀል.

IES 04353, *Asmat* Prayers, ካታብ. Parchment, 172 x 11 cm, three strips, one column, Gəʿəz, twentieth century. Copied for ዓመተ ሚካኤል.

Miniatures:

- Three miniatures: (a) two angels with swords and scabbards; (b) talismanic symbol surrounded by four faces; and (c) two angels with swords and scabbards.

IES 04354, *Asmat* Prayers, ካታብ. Parchment, 71 x 10 cm, one strip, one column, Gəʿəz, twentieth century. Copied for ወለተ ኪዳን.

IES 04355, *Asmat* Prayers, ካታብ. Parchment, 134 x 10 cm, three strips, one column, Gəʿəz, twentieth century. Original patron's name was replaced with ወለተ አብርሃ.

Miniatures:

- Three miniatures: (a) talismanic symbol; (b) talismanic symbol; and (c) talismanic symbol.

IES 04356, *Asmat* Prayers, ካታብ. Parchment, 170 x 10 cm, three strips, one column, Gəʿəz, twentieth century. Copied for ወለተ ማርያም.

Miniatures:

- Three miniatures: (a) angel with sword and scabbard; (b) multi-box panel; and (c) talismanic symbol.

IES 04357, *Asmat* Prayers, ከታብ. Parchment, 123 x 8 cm, two strips, one column, Gəʻəz, twentieth century. Copied for ወለተ መድኅን ወለተ ሥላሴ.

Miniatures:

- Two miniatures: (a) angel with sword and scabbard; and (b) talismanic symbol.

IES 04358, *Asmat* Prayers, ከታብ. Parchment, 79 x 10 cm, one strip, one column, Gəʻəz, twentieth century. Copied for አመተ ጸድቃን.

Miniatures:

- One miniature: (a) person spearing a demon.

IES 04359, *Asmat* Prayers, ከታብ. Parchment, 176 x 7.5 cm, three strips, one column, Gəʻəz, nineteenth century. Copied for ያልጋኒሽ, erased and replaced with ወለተ ማርያም.

Miniatures:

- Two miniatures: (a) person; and (b) talismanic symbol.

IES 04360, *Asmat* Prayers, ከታብ. Parchment, 106 x 10 cm, two strips, one column, Gəʻəz, twentieth century. Copied for ወለተ ዮሐንስ ማርሸኛ.

Miniatures:

- One miniature: (a) angel.

IES 04361, *Asmat* Prayers, ከታብ. Parchment, 66 x 10 cm, one strip, one column, Gəʻəz, twentieth century. Copied for አመተ ሚካኤል, erased and replaced with a name that is not sufficiently legible.

Miniatures:

- Three miniatures: (a) two figures by a lion; (b) talismanic symbol; and (c) two figures beside a talismanic symbol.

IES 04362, *Asmat* Prayers, ከታብ. Parchment, 66 x 10 cm, two strips, one column, Gəʻəz, late nineteenth century. Copied for ወለተ ሥላሴ, replaced with ወለተ ማርያም.

Miniatures:

- One miniature: (a) three ornate crosses.

IES 04363, *Asmat* Prayers, ክታብ. Parchment, 187 x 8 cm, two strips, one column, Gəʿəz, twentieth century. Copied for ወለተ ተክለ ሃይማኖት.

Miniatures:

- One miniature: (a) talismanic symbol.

IES 04364, *Asmat* Prayers, ክታብ. Parchment, 129 x 5.5 cm, three strips, one column, Gəʿəz, twentieth century. Space for a name was left blank.

Miniatures:

- Three miniatures: (a) angel with sword and scabbard; (b) multi-box panel; and (c) angel.

IES 04365, *Asmat* Prayers, ክታብ. Parchment, 150 x 7 cm, three strips, one column, Gəʿəz, twentieth century. The name ወለተ መስቀል was written in a later hand.

Miniatures:

- One miniature: (a) angel with sword and scabbard.

IES 04366, *Asmat* Prayers, ክታብ. Parchment, 172 x 8.5 cm, three strips, one column, Gəʿəz, twentieth century. Copied for ጣሂሩ.

Miniatures:

- Two miniatures: (a) angel with sword, and (b) talismanic symbol.

IES 04367, *Asmat* Prayers, ክታብ. Parchment, 160 x 8 cm, three strips, one column, Gəʿəz, twentieth century. Copied for ወለተ ሥላሴ.

Miniatures:

- Two miniatures: (a) angel with sword and scabbard; and (b) multi-box panel.

IES 04368, *Asmat* Prayers, ክታብ. Parchment, 177 x 9.5 cm, three strips, one column, Gəʿəz, twentieth century. Copied for ወለተ ጸድቃን.

Miniatures:

- Two miniatures: (a) angel with sword; and (b) multi-box panel.

IES 04369, *Asmat* Prayers, ከታብ. Parchment, 172 x 5 cm, three strips, one column, Gəʿəz, twentieth century. Original patron's name was erased and replaced with ገብረ ጻድቅ.

Miniatures:

- Three miniatures: (a) multi-box panel; (b) multi-box panel; and (c) ornate cross.

IES 04370, *Asmat* Prayers, ከታብ. Parchment, 197 x 8 cm, three strips, one column, Gəʿəz, twentieth century. Copied for አበቦች ወለተ ሥላሴ.

Miniatures:

- Four miniatures: (a) talismanic symbol; (b) talismanic symbol; (c) geometric design; and (d) multi-box panel.

IES 04371, *Asmat* Prayers, ከታብ. Parchment, 67 x 9.1 cm, one strip, one column, Gəʿəz, early twentieth century. No owner was mentioned.

Miniatures:

- One miniature: (a) talismanic symbol.

IES 04372, *Asmat* Prayers, ከታብ. Parchment, 135 x 8.5 cm, three strips, one column, Gəʿəz, twentieth century. Copied for ወለተ ስንበት.

Miniatures:

- One miniature: (a) talismanic symbol.

IES 04373, *Asmat* Prayers, ከታብ. Parchment, 110 x 6.7 cm, two strips, one column, Gəʿəz, twentieth century. Copied for ገብረ ሚካኤል.

Miniatures:

- Two miniatures: (a) angel with sword and scabbard; and (b) ornate cross.

IES 04374, *Asmat* Prayers, ከታብ. Parchment, 178 x 8.5 cm, three strips, one column, Gəʿəz, twentieth century. Copied for ፍጤማ.

Miniatures:

- Two miniatures: (a) angel with sword; and (b) talismanic symbol.

IES 04375, *Asmat* Prayers, ከታብ. Parchment, 118 x 7.5 cm, two strips, one column, Gəʿəz, twentieth century. Copied for ወለተ ተክለ ሃይማኖት.

Miniatures:

- Two miniatures: (a) angel with sword and scabbard; and (b) ornate cross with a figure on either side.

IES 04376, *Asmat* Prayers, ከታብ. Parchment, 75.3 x 15.5 cm, three strips, three columns, Gəʿəz, twentieth century. Copied for ኃይለ ኢየሱስ.

IES 04377, *Asmat* Prayers, ከታብ. Parchment, 99 x 11.5 cm, two strips, one column, Gəʿəz, twentieth century. Original patron's name was erased and replaced with ኪዳን ማርያም.

Miniatures:

- One miniature: (a) two ornate crosses, a person, and a person holding a hand cross.

IES 04378, *Asmat* Prayers, ከታብ. Parchment, 119.5 x 11.5 cm, two strips, one column, Gəʿəz, twentieth century. Copied for ወለተ ሥላሴ, later replaced with ወለተ ማርያም.

Miniatures:

- Two miniatures: (a) multi-box panel; and (b) angel with sword and scabbard.

IES 04379, *Asmat* Prayers, ከታብ. Parchment, 78 x 8.5 cm, two strips, one column, Gəʿəz, twentieth century. Original patron's name was erased and replaced with a name that is not sufficiently legible.

Miniatures:

- Two miniatures: (a) talismanic symbol; and (b) talismanic symbol.

IES 04380, *Asmat* Prayers, ከታብ. Parchment, 82 x 8.5 cm, one strip, one column, Gəʿəz, early twentieth century. Space for a name was left blank.

Miniatures:

- Two miniatures: (a) equestrian saint spearing a figure (demon?); and (b) angel.

IES 04381, *Asmat* Prayers, ክታብ. Parchment, 187 x 9.5 cm, three strips, one column, Gəʿəz, twentieth century. Copied for ወለተ ሥላሴ ሐረጉ.

Miniatures:

- Three miniatures: (a) angel with sword and scabbard; (b) talismanic symbol; and (c) ornate cross with a face in the center.

IES 04382, *Asmat* Prayers, ክታብ. Parchment, 105 x 9.8 cm, two strips, one column, Gəʿəz, twentieth century. Copied for ወልደ ሥላሴ.

Miniatures:

- Two miniatures: (a) talismanic symbol; and (b) talismanic symbol.

IES 04383, *Asmat* Prayers, ክታብ. Parchment, 191.5 x 5.5 cm, three strips, one column, Gəʿəz, twentieth century. Copied for ወለተ ዮሐንስ.

Miniatures:

- Three miniatures: (a) angel with sword and scabbard; (b) talismanic symbol surrounded by four eyes; and (c) talismanic symbol.

IES 04384, *Asmat* Prayers, ክታብ. Parchment, 72 x 9.5 cm, one strip, one column, Gəʿəz, twentieth century. Copied for ወለተ መድኅን.

Miniatures:

- One miniature: (a) angel with sword and scabbard.

IES 04385, *Asmat* Prayers, ክታብ. Parchment, 71 x 11 cm, one strip, one column, Gəʿəz, twentieth century. Copied for ዓመተ ዮሐንስ.

Miniatures:

- One miniature: (a) angel with sword and scabbard.

IES 04386, *Asmat* Prayers, ክታብ. Parchment, 109 x 11 cm, three strips, two columns, Gəʿəz, twentieth century. Copied for አመተ ማርያም.

Miniatures:

- Two miniatures: (a) ornate cross with a figure on either side; and (b) fragment of a talismanic symbol.

IES 04387, *Asmat* Prayers, ከታብ. Parchment, 66 x 8.5 cm, one strip, one column, Gəʿəz, twentieth century. Copied for ወለተ ማርያም.

IES 04388, *Asmat* Prayers, ከታብ. Parchment, 90 x 9.5 cm, one strip, one column, Gəʿəz, twentieth century. Copied for ኃይለ ማርያም.

Miniatures:

- One miniature: (a) angel with sword and scabbard.

IES 04389, *Asmat* Prayers, ከታብ. Parchment, 155 x 10 cm, three strips, one column, Gəʿəz, twentieth century. Original patron's name was erased and replaced with ወለተ ገብርኤል.

Miniatures:

- Two miniatures: (a) angel with sword and scabbard; and (b) talismanic symbol.

IES 04390, *Asmat* Prayers, ከታብ. Parchment, 155 x 9 cm, two strips, one column, Gəʿəz, twentieth century. Space for a name was left blank.

Miniatures:

- Three miniatures: (a) angel with sword and scabbard; (b) ornate cross; and (c) angel with sword and scabbard.

IES 04391, *Asmat* Prayers, ከታብ. Parchment, 97 x 11.5 cm, one strip, one column, Gəʿəz, twentieth century. Copied for ወለተ ኪዳን.

Miniatures:

- One miniature: (a) geometric design.

IES 04392, *Asmat* Prayers, ከታብ. Parchment, 60 x 9.5 cm, one strip, one column, Gəʿəz, late nineteenth/early twentieth century. The name is not sufficiently legible (ወለተ መ. . .).

Miniatures:

- One miniature: (a) talismanic symbol.

IES 04393, *Asmat* Prayers, ከታብ. Parchment, 213 x 9 cm, four strips, one column, Gəʿəz, twentieth century. Copied for ፍጢማ.

Miniatures:

- One miniature: (a) lion.

IES 04394, *Asmat* Prayers, ክታብ. Parchment, 135 x 8 cm, three strips, one column, Gəʿəz, twentieth century. Copied for አርኡ.

Miniatures:

- Two miniatures: (a) angel; and (b) a face.

IES 04395, *Asmat* Prayers, ክታብ. Parchment, 146 x 8 cm, three strips, one column, Gəʿəz, twentieth century. Copied for አልጋነሽ ሥርጉተ ሥላሴ.

Miniatures:

- One miniature: (a) talismanic symbol.

IES 04396, *Asmat* Prayers, ክታብ. Parchment, 134 x 8.6 cm, three strips, one column, Gəʿəz, twentieth century. Copied for ድርብ ድርብ.

Miniatures:

- Three miniatures: (a) angel with sword and scabbard; (b) angel with hand cross; and (c) talismanic symbol.

IES 04397, *Asmat* Prayers, ክታብ. Parchment, 168 x 8.5 cm, three strips, one column, Gəʿəz, twentieth century. Copied for ፉጢግ.

Miniatures:

- Two miniatures: (a) talismanic symbol, and (b) angel.

IES 04398, *Asmat* Prayers, ክታብ. Parchment, 203 x 10 cm, three strips, one column, Gəʿəz, twentieth century. Copied for አመተ ኢየሱስ.

Miniatures:

- Four miniatures: (a) angel; (b) talismanic symbol; (c) talismanic symbol; and (d) angel.

IES 04399, *Asmat* Prayers, ክታብ. Parchment, 70 x 6 cm, one strip, one column, Gəʿəz, twentieth century. Name is not sufficiently legible.

IES 04400, *Asmat* Prayers, ከታብ. Parchment, 153 x 8.5 cm, three strips, one column, Gəʿəz, twentieth century. No owner was mentioned.

Miniatures:

- Three miniatures: (a) angel; (b) angel; and (c) talismanic symbol.

IES 04401, *Asmat* Prayers, ከታብ. Parchment, 72 x 11.1 cm, one strip, one column, Gəʿəz, twentieth century. Original patron's name was erased and replaced with ዓመተ ዮሐንስ.

Miniatures:

- One miniature: (a) multi-box panel.

IES 04402, *Asmat* Prayers, ከታብ. Parchment, 71 x 10 cm, one strip, one column, Gəʿəz, twentieth century. Copied for አመተ ጸድቃን.

Miniatures:

- One miniature: (a) talismanic symbol.

IES 04403, *Asmat* Prayers, ከታብ. Parchment, 217 x 10 cm, three strips, one column, Gəʿəz, twentieth century. Copied for ዮሐንስ ሐጽጉ.

Miniatures:

- Three miniatures: (a) angel with sword and scabbard; (b) talismanic symbol; and (c) ornate cross.

IES 04404, *Asmat* Prayers, ከታብ. Parchment, 192 x 9 cm, three strips, one column, Gəʿəz, twentieth century. Copied for ወለተ ሚካኤል, erased and replaced with ወለተ ኪዳን.

Miniatures:

- Three miniatures: (a) angel with sword and scabbard; (b) talismanic symbol; and (c) talismanic symbol.

IES 04405, *Asmat* Prayers, ከታብ. Parchment, 210 x 10 cm, three strips, one column, Gəʿəz, twentieth century. Copied for ወለተ ኢየሱስ and ወለተ መድኃን.

Miniatures:

- Three miniatures: (a) angel with sword and scabbard; (b) king and a demon; and (c) talismanic symbol.

IES 04406, *Asmat* Prayers, ከታብ. Parchment, 160 x 9.5 cm, two strips, one column, Gəʿəz, twentieth century. Copied for መለተ ኢየሱስ.

Miniatures:

- Three miniatures: (a) angel; (b) cross; and (c) geometric design.

IES 04407, *Asmat* Prayers, ከታብ. Parchment, 187 x 8 cm, four strips, one column, Gəʿəz, twentieth century. Copied for ወልደ ትንግሌ.

Miniatures:

- Three miniatures: (a) angel with sword and scabbard; (b) talismanic symbol; and (c) person with sword and hand cross.

IES 04408, *Asmat* Prayers, ከታብ. Parchment, 74 x 10 cm, two strips, one column, Gəʿəz, twentieth century. Original owner's name was erased and replaced with መለተ ጸድቃን, the name አመተ ኢየሱስ ጥሩየ was written later in a different ink.

Miniatures:

- One miniature: (a) multi-box panel.

IES 04409, *Asmat* Prayers, ከታብ. Parchment, 160 x 9.5 cm, three strips, one column, Gəʿəz, twentieth century. Copied for መለተ ገብርኤል.

Miniatures:

- Four miniatures: (a) angel with sword and scabbard; (b) talismanic symbol; (c) multi-box panel; and (d) ornate cross with a figure on either side.

IES 04410, *Asmat* Prayers, ከታብ. Parchment, 191 x 7.5 cm, three strips, one column, Gəʿəz, twentieth century. Copied for መለተ እግዚእ መለተዝጉ.

Miniatures:

- Four miniatures: (a) angel with sword and scabbard; (b) multi-box panel; (c) multi-box panel; and (d) cross.

IES 04411, *Asmat* Prayers, ከታብ. Parchment, 150 x 7.5 cm, three strips, one column, Gəʿəz, twentieth century. Space for a name was left blank.

Miniatures:

- Three miniatures: (a) talismanic symbol; (b) angel with sword and scabbard; and (c) talismanic symbol.

IES 04412, *Asmat* Prayers, ከታብ. Parchment, 127 x 6 cm, three strips, one column, Gəʿəz, twentieth century. Copied for ወለተ ስንበት ትረጎ.

Miniatures:

- Three miniatures: (a) geometric design; (b) geometric design; and (c) geometric design.

IES 04413, *Asmat* Prayers, ከታብ. Parchment, 138 x 9 cm, three strips, one column, Gəʿəz, twentieth century. Copied for ኃይለ ሥላሴ.

Miniatures:

- Three miniatures: (a) fragment of an angel; (b) talismanic symbol; and (c) angel with sword and scabbard.

IES 04414, *Asmat* Prayers, ከታብ. Parchment, 178 x 9 cm, three strips, one column, Gəʿəz, twentieth century. Copied for ወለተ ጸድቃን መብራህቲ.

Miniatures:

- Three miniatures: (a) angel with sword; (b) multi-box panel; and (c) ornate cross.

IES 04415, *Asmat* Prayers, ከታብ. Parchment, 160 x 4.5 cm, two strips, one column, Gəʿəz, twentieth century. Copied for ሚካኤል.

Miniatures:

- Two miniatures: (a) multi-box panel; and (b) talismanic symbol.

IES 04416, *Asmat* Prayers, ከታብ. Parchment, 195 x 10 cm, three strips, one column, Gəʿəz, twentieth century. Space for a name was left blank.

Miniatures:

- Three miniatures: (a) angel with sword and scabbard; (b) two figures; and (c) ornate cross with a figure on either side.

IES 04417, *Asmat* Prayers, ከታብ. Parchment, 220 x 9 cm, three strips, one column, Gəʿəz, twentieth century. Name of original patron was erased.

Miniatures:

- Two miniatures: (a) two angels; and (b) angel with sword and scabbard.

IES 04418, *Asmat* Prayers, ከታብ. Parchment, 32 x 9.5 cm, one strip, one column, Gəʿəz, twentieth century. No owner was mentioned.

Miniatures:

- One miniature: (a) ornate cross with a figure on either side.

IES 04419, *Asmat* Prayers, ከታብ. Parchment, 57 x 10 cm, two strips, one column, Gəʿəz, twentieth century. Copied for ወለተ ኢየሱስ ስኒን.

Miniatures:

- One miniature: (a) ornate cross.

IES 04420, *Asmat* Prayers, ከታብ. Parchment, 149 x 7 cm, three strips, one column, Gəʿəz, twentieth century. Copied for ተንዲ, replaced with ንግር.

Miniatures:

- Two miniatures: (a) figure with sword and scabbard; and (b) talismanic symbol.

IES 04421, *Asmat* Prayers, ከታብ. Parchment, 115 x 10 cm, two strips, one column, Gəʿəz, twentieth century. The name of the original patron was erased and replaced with ወለተ ገብርኤል.

Miniatures:

- Two miniatures: (a) talismanic symbol; and (b) cross.

IES 04422, *Asmat* Prayers, ከታብ. Parchment, 89 x 8 cm, two strips, one column, Gəʿəz, twentieth century. Copied for ወለተ ሚካኤል.

Miniatures:

- Two miniatures: (a) talismanic symbol, and (b) angel with a sword.

IES 04423, *Asmat* Prayers, ክታብ. Parchment, 69 x 7.8 cm, one strip, one column, Gəʿəz, twentieth century. The name of the original patron was erased and replaced with ወለተ መድኅን.

IES 04424, *Asmat* Prayers, ክታብ. Parchment, 38 x 10 cm, one strip, one column, Gəʿəz, twentieth century. Copied for ወለተ ትንሣኤ.

Miniatures:

- One miniature: (a) talismanic symbol.

IES 04425, *Asmat* Prayers, ክታብ. Parchment, 123 x 9.5 cm, three strips, one column, Gəʿəz, twentieth century. Copied for ወለተ ማርያም.

IES 04426, *Asmat* Prayers, ክታብ. Parchment, 44 x 10 cm, one strip, one column, Gəʿəz, twentieth century. The name of the original patron was erased and the replacement is not sufficiently legible.

IES 04427, *Asmat* Prayers, ክታብ. Parchment, 73 x 9.5 cm, three strips, one column, Gəʿəz, twentieth century. The name ወለተ ጼድቃን was added in a later hand.

Miniatures:

- One miniature: (a) multi-box panel.

IES 04428, *Asmat* Prayers, ክታብ. Parchment, 170 x 12 cm, three strips, one column, Gəʿəz, twentieth century. Copied for ወለተ ሚካኤል.

Miniatures:

- Three miniatures: (a) angel with sword and hand cross; (b) talismanic symbol surrounded by four eyes; and (c) ornate cross.

IES 04429, *Asmat* Prayers, ክታብ. Parchment, 187 x 10 cm, three strips, one column, Gəʿəz, twentieth century. Copied for ወለተ ሚካኤል, replaced with ወለተ ሥላሴ in some places.

Miniatures:

- Three miniatures: (a) angel with sword; (b) talismanic symbol; and (c) ornate cross with a face in the center.

IES 04430, *Asmat* Prayers, ክታብ. Parchment, 175 x 9 cm, three strips, one column, Gəʿəz, twentieth century. Copied for ፐሩ ወለተ ስንበት.

Miniatures:

- One miniature: (a) angel with sword and scabbard.

IES 04431, *Asmat* Prayers, ክታብ. Parchment, 133 x 9 cm, three strips, one column, Gəʿəz, twentieth century. Copied for ወለተ ሥላሴ and ወለተ ማርያም.

Miniatures:

- Three miniatures: (a) angel with sword and scabbard; (b) crowned figure with a spear pointing at a demon; and (c) talismanic symbol with a lion's face in the center.

IES 04432, *Asmat* Prayers, ክታብ. Parchment, 103 x 10 cm, two strips, one column, Gəʿəz, twentieth century. The name of the original patron was erased and replaced with ወለተ ኪዳን ወርት.

Miniatures:

- One miniature: (a) talismanic symbol.

IES 04433, *Asmat* Prayers, ክታብ. Parchment, 183 x 7.5 cm, three strips, one column, Gəʿəz, twentieth century. Copied for ገብረ ሕይወት (ገብረ ኅይወት).

Miniatures:

- Three miniatures: (a) angel with a sword; (b) ornate cross; and (c) ornate cross with a figure on either side.

IES 04434, *Asmat* Prayers, ክታብ. Parchment, 192 x 8.5 cm, three strips, one column, Gəʿəz, twentieth century. The name አመተ ሥላሴ was added in a later hand.

Miniatures:

- Four miniatures: (a) angel with sword and scabbard; (b) multi-box panel; (c) ornate cross with a figure on either side; and (d) talismanic symbol.

IES 04435, *Asmat* Prayers, ክታብ. Parchment, 182 x 8.5 cm, four strips, one column, Gəʿəz, twentieth century. Copied for ወልደ ዮሐንስ.

Miniatures:

- Four miniatures: (a) angel; (b) talismanic symbol; (c) talismanic symbol; and (d) angel with a sword.

IES 04436, *Asmat* Prayers, ከታብ. Parchment, 156 x 9 cm, three strips, one column, Gəʽəz, twentieth century. Copied for ወለተ ጸድቃን, erased and replaced with ወለተ ኢየሱስ.

Miniatures:

- Three miniatures: (a) angel with sword and scabbard; (b) talismanic symbol; and (c) multi-box panel.

IES 04437, *Asmat* Prayers, ከታብ. Parchment, 137 x 8 cm, three strips, one column, Gəʽəz, twentieth century. Copied for አመተ ማርያም.

Miniatures:

- Two miniatures: (a) multi-box panel; and (b) figure with a sword.

IES 04438, *Asmat* Prayers, ከታብ. Parchment, 147 x 8.8 cm, three strips, one column, Gəʽəz, twentieth century. Copied for የብርንል.

IES 04439, *Asmat* Prayers, ከታብ. Parchment, 137 x 7.5 cm, two strips, one column, Gəʽəz, twentieth century. Copied for ሸቀም.

Miniatures:

- Three miniatures: (a) angel; (b) angel; and (c) angel.

IES 04440, *Asmat* Prayers, ከታብ. Parchment, 115 x 9.5 cm, two strips, one column, Gəʽəz, twentieth century. The name of the original patron was erased and replaced with ወለተ አብርሃ ጽዮን.

IES 04441, *Asmat* Prayers, ከታብ. Parchment, 53.5 x 9 cm, one strip, one column, Gəʽəz, twentieth century. Copied for ወለተ እግዚእ.

Miniatures:

- One miniature: (a) fragment of a figure.

IES 04442, *Asmat* Prayers, ከታብ. Parchment, 139 x 8 cm, two strips, one column, Gəʽəz, twentieth century. Space for a name was left blank.

Miniatures:

- Three miniatures: (a) angel with sword and scabbard; (b) talismanic symbol; and (c) angel with sword and scabbard.

IES 04443, *Asmat* Prayers, ክታብ. Parchment, 85 x 9 cm, two strips, one column, Gəʿəz, twentieth century. Copied for ውጢቱ ወለተ ኢየሱስ.

Miniatures:

- Two miniatures: (a) ornate cross with two faces on either side; and (b) three figures.

IES 04444, *Asmat* Prayers, ክታብ. Parchment, 65 x 9.5 cm, two strips, one column, Gəʿəz, twentieth century. The name of the original patron was erased and replaced with ወለተ ጻድቃን. The name ፕሩየ አመተ ኢየሱስ was written in the miniature.

Miniatures:

- One miniature: (a) angel with sword and scabbard.

IES 04445, *Asmat* Prayers, ክታብ. Parchment, 186 x 7.5 cm, three strips, one column, Gəʿəz, early twentieth century. Copied for ወለተ ሚካኤል ግይቱ.

Miniatures:

- Three miniatures: (a) angel with sword and scabbard; (b) talismanic symbol; and (c) ornate cross.

IES 04446, *Asmat* Prayers, ክታብ. Parchment, 152 x 9 cm, three strips, one column, Gəʿəz, twentieth century. Copied for ወለተ ወል ወልተ ሃና ዘነበች.

Miniatures:

- Three miniatures: (a) angel with sword and scabbard; (b) multi-box panel; and (c) figure.

IES 04447, *Asmat* Prayers, ክታብ. Parchment, 120 x 9 cm, two strips, one column, Gəʿəz, twentieth century. Copied for ወለተ ማርያም ትኩነሽ.

Miniatures:

- Two miniatures: (a) figure; and (b) multi-box panel.

IES 04448, *Asmat* Prayers, ክታብ. Parchment, 157 x 6.8 cm, two strips, one column, Gəʿəz, twentieth century. Copied for ወለተ ማርያም.

Miniatures:

- Three miniatures: (a) angel with sword and scabbard; (b) talismanic symbol; and (c) multi-box panel.

IES 04449, *Asmat* Prayers, ክታብ. Parchment, 74 x 4 cm, one strip, one column, Gəʿəz, twentieth century. Copied for አስካለ ማርያም.

IES 04450, *Asmat* Prayers, ክታብ. Parchment, 180 x 8 cm, three strips, one column, Gəʿəz, twentieth century. The name of the original patron was erased (አመተ ማርያም?) and replaced with አመተ ሚካኤል.

Miniatures:

- Four miniatures: (a) angel with sword and scabbard; (b) ornate cross with a figure on either side; (c) talismanic symbol; and (d) talismanic symbol.

IES 04451, *Asmat* Prayers, ክታብ. Parchment, 200 x 10 cm, four strips, one column, Gəʿəz, twentieth century. Copied for ወለተ ትንሣኤ.

IES 04486, Photocopy of twentieth-century manuscript containing *Asmat* Prayer against the enemies of the soul and the flesh. Paper, 300 x 220 x 12 mm, 71 folios, one column, 7–11 lines, Gəʿəz, twentieth century.

IES 04488, Photocopy of Asmara Gəʿəz New Testament, with an insert of the Book of Isaiah in Tigrinya. Paper, 300 x 220 x 40 mm, ii + 296 folios, one column and two columns, 30 lines, Gəʿəz, Tigrinya, 1912 EC = 1919–20.

IES 04539, Mar Yeshaq or Isaac of Nineveh, ማር ይስሐቅ. Parchment, 270 x 197 x 66 mm, 92 folios, two columns, 31 lines, Gəʿəz, early twentieth century.

IES 04540, Homiliary in Honor of the Archangel Michael, ድርሳን ሚካኤል. Parchment, 220 x 174 x 45 mm, ii + 95 folios, two columns, 18 lines, Gəʿəz, late eighteenth/early nineteenth century.

Miniatures:

1. F. i r(ecto): Crude drawing of a figure.
2. F. ii v(erso): An angel with sword and scabbard.
3. F. 94v: Crude drawing of crosses.
4. F. 95r: The archangel Michael seated on a throne with a patron prostrate before him.
5. F. 95v: The Crucifixion.

IES 04541, Homiliary on the Lifegiver, ድርሳነ ማኅየዊ. Parchment, 224 x 166 x 42 mm, iv + 94 folios, two columns, 19 lines, Gəʿəz, twentieth century.

IES 04542, Vision of Mary, ራዕየ ማርያም, in Amharic; Prayer of the Covenant, ጸሎተ ኪዳን; Horologium for the Night, ሰዓታት ዘሌሊት. Parchment, 156 x 124 x 41 mm, ii + 61 folios, two columns, 17 lines, Amharic, Gəʿəz, twentieth century.

IES 04543, Concluding Hymns from the Miracles of Mary; Introductory Hymn from the Miracles of Jesus; Psalter, ዳዊት. Parchment, 136 x 94 x 50 mm, iv + 131 folios, one column and two columns, 25–26 lines, Gəʿəz, twentieth century.

IES 04544, Beauty of Creation, ሥነ ፍጥረት, in Amharic; Gəʿəz Grammar, ሰዋሰው፣ ግዕዝ; *Asmat* Prayer, አስማት; Commentary on Our Father, in Amharic, የአቡነ ዘበሰማያት ትርጓሜ; Order of Liturgical Blessings, ሥርዓተ ቡራኬ. Parchment, 142 x 101 x 50 mm, iv + 122 folios, two columns, 20 lines, Amharic, Gəʿəz, early twentieth century.

IES 04545, Treatises on the Computus. Parchment, 125 x 100 x 22 mm, ii + 24 folios, one column, 10 lines, Amharic, twentieth century.

IES 04546, Treatises on the Computus. Parchment, 152 x 120 x 29 mm, 31 folios, one column, 14–16 lines, Amharic, twentieth century.

IES 04547, Image of Michael, መልክአ ሚካኤል; Image of the Passion of the Cross, መልክአ ሕማማት መስቀል. Parchment, 105 x 75 x 30 mm, 32 folios, one column, 9–10 lines, Gəʿəz, twentieth century.

IES 04556, Acts of Täklä Haymanot, ገድለ ተክለ ሃይማኖት; Miracles of Täklä Haymanot, ተአምረ ተክለ ሃይማኖት; Image of Täklä Haymanot,

መልክአ ተክለ ሃይማኖት, made in the Government Scriptorium. Parchment, 299 x 245 x 76 mm, iv + 172 folios, two columns, 23–26 lines, Gəʿəz, twentieth century.

IES 04557, Missal, መጽሐፈ ቅዳሴ, with musical notation, made in the Government Scriptorium. Parchment, 270 x 205 x 53 mm, ii + 140 folios, two columns, 22 lines, Gəʿəz, twentieth century. Double-slip maḥdär.

IES 04592, Published copy of Psalter, ዳዊት. Paper, 175 x 120 x 25 mm, i + 220 folios, one column, 22 lines, Gəʿəz, 1939 EC = 1946–47.

IES 04600, Photocopy of early twentieth-century manuscripts containing Homiliary in Honor of Zion, in Amharic and Gəʿəz. Paper, 220 x 300 x 30 mm, 234 folios, two columns, 29 lines, Amharic, Gəʿəz, early twentieth century.

IES 04608, Photocopy of an autograph of a Gəʿəz Grammar in French. Paper, 180 x 240 x 10 mm, 40 folios, one column, Gəʿəz, French, twentieth century.

IES 04620, Law of the Kings, ፍትሐ ነገሥት, donated to the IES by Tekalign Gedamu. Parchment, 286 x 211 x 90 mm, ii + 180 folios, two columns, 29–41 lines, Gəʿəz, early twentieth century.

IES 04677, Psalter, ዳዊት; Angels Praise Her, ይዌድሰዋ መላእክት ለማርያም. Parchment, 216 x 150 x 65 mm, iv + 166 folios, one column and two columns, 21 lines, Gəʿəz, late nineteenth/early twentieth century.

IES 04679, Horologium for the Night, ሰዓታት ዘሌሊት. Parchment, 147 x 100 x 37 mm, ii + 60 folios, one column, 15 lines, Gəʿəz, early twentieth century.

Miniatures:

1. F. i v(erso): Crude drawing of a cross.
2. F. 59v: Crude drawing of a cross.
3. F. 60r: Crude drawing of a wheel.

IES 04680, Prayer of Saint Peter, ጸሎት ጴጥሮስ; Sword of the Trinity, ሠይፈ ሥላሴ, arranged for days of the week, made in the Government Scriptorium. Parchment, 142 x 104 x 46 mm, iv + 109 folios, two columns, 15–16 lines, Gəʿəz, early twentieth century. Also known as IES 2956A.

Miniatures:

1. F. iv v(erso): A King (Mənilək?) on a throne holding a book.
2. F. 43r: The Three Youths in the Fiery Furnace rescued by Gabriel.
3. F. 48v: Ornate cross.
4. F. 105v: The Holy Trinity surrounded by the four Living Creatures and a patron in proskynesis.
5. F. 106r: The Crucifixion.

IES 04682, Psalter, ዳዊት; Image of John the Baptist, መልከአ ዮሐንስ መጥምቅ. Parchment, 175 x 117 x 56 mm, ii + 158 folios, one column and two columns, 23 lines, Gəʿəz, early twentieth century.

Miniatures:

1. F. ii r(ecto): Crude drawing of an ornate cross.
2. F. 135r: Crude drawing of an equestrian saint.

IES 04683, Psalter, ዳዊት. Parchment, 150 x 134 x 65 mm, ii + 188 folios, one column and two columns, 15–17 lines, Gəʿəz, late eighteenth/early nineteenth century.

IES 04684, Miracles of Mary, ተአምረ ማርያም. Parchment, 175 x 131 x 30 mm, ii + 33 folios, two columns, 17 lines, Gəʿəz, early twentieth century.

IES 04685, Psalter, ዳዊት. Parchment, 170 x 155 x 60 mm, i + 148 folios, one column and two columns, 19–21 lines, Gəʿəz, nineteenth century.

Miniatures:

1. F. 146v: Crude drawing of a figure.

IES 04686, *Asmat* Prayers, አስማት. Parchment, 135 x 100 x 35 mm, 62 folios, one column, 15 lines, Gəʿəz, twentieth century.

IES 04687, Missal, መጽሐፈ ቅዳሴ, with musical notation. Parchment, 163 x 145 x 35 mm, i + 71 folios, two columns, 15–16 lines, Gəʿəz, 1889–1913 (f. 44r mentions Emperor Mənilək II).

IES 04688, Psalter, ዳዊት. Parchment, 135 x 105 x 55 mm, iv + 155 folios, one column and two columns, 23 lines, Gəʽəz, early twentieth century.

Miniatures:

1. F. iii v(erso): An angel with sword and scabbard, badly faded.

2. F. 154r: Madonna and Child.

IES 04689, Missal, መጽሐፈ ቅዳሴ. Parchment, 135 x 127 x 28 mm, i + 84 folios, two columns, 14 lines, Gəʽəz, early nineteenth century.

Miniatures:

1. Crude drawings are found throughout the codex (e.g., ff. 10r, 11r–12r, 65rv, 66v–67r, 68r).

IES 04690, Psalter, ዳዊት, with a rejected leaf from a nineteenth-century manuscript at the end. Parchment, 206 x 155 x 88 mm, ii + 172 folios, one column and two columns, 19 lines, Gəʽəz, twentieth century.

Miniatures:

1. F. 124v: Ornate cross.

IES 04691, Image of Täklä Haymanot, መልክአ ተክለ ሃይማኖት; Prayer of Mary at Golgotha, ጸሎተ እግዝእትነ ማርያም ዘሰኔ ጎልጎታ; Mystagogia, ትምህርተ ኅቡዓት; Image of Edom, መልክአ ኤዶም; Image of the Christian Sabbath, መልክአ ሰንበተ ክርስቲያን; Hymn to Saint George, "Come, come, come, George," ነዓ ነዓ ነዓ ጊዮርጊስ. Parchment, 169 x 154 x 20 mm, ii + 34 folios, two columns, 15–17 lines, Gəʽəz, twentieth century.

IES 04692, Psalter, ዳዊት. Parchment, 154 x 149 x 80 mm, ii + 188 folios, one column and two columns, 16–17 lines, Gəʽəz, late eighteenth/ early nineteenth century.

IES 04693, Vision of Mary, ራዕየ ማርያም. Parchment, 149 x 136 x 20 mm, i + 35 folios, two columns, 17 lines, Gəʽəz, late eighteenth century.

IES 04696, Images of the Trinity, Jesus, the Savior of the World, Täklä Haymanot, Gäbrä Mänfäs Qəddus, Saint George, Mary of Zion, Mary, Adome, Almighty God (arranged for the days of the week), Trinity (arranged for the days of the week), Michael, Gabriel; Prayer to defeat devils (arranged for the days of the week); Prayer to defeat the evil eye; Image of Mary. Parchment, 297 x 224 x 66 mm, iii + 129 folios, two columns, 21 lines, Gəʽəz, twentieth century.

IES 05445, Pauline Epistles, መልእክታተ ጳውሎስ; Catholic Epistles, ሰብዓቱ መልእክታት (አጠቃላይ መልእክታት). Parchment, 191 x 183 x 63 mm, vii + 106 folios, two columns, 20–22 lines, Gəʽəz, eighteenth century.

IES 05446, Acts of Lalibäla, ገድለ ላሊበላ. Paper, 220 x 160 x 20 mm, i + 146 folios, one column, 22 lines, Amharic, late twentieth century.

IES 05447, Photocopy of twentieth-century manuscript containing Amharic Words. Paper, 290 x 210 x 25 mm, 175 folios, one column, 26 lines, Gəʽəz, 1901 EC.

IES 05449, Miracles of Jesus, ተአምረ ኢየሱስ; Book of Ṭomar, መጽሐፈ ጦማር. Parchment, 240 x 212 x 76 mm, iii + 148 folios, two columns, 20–24 lines, Gəʽəz, nineteenth century.

IES 05474, Psalter, ዳዊት. Parchment, 159 x 107 x 64 mm, ii + 204 folios, one column and two columns, 20–21 lines, Gəʽəz, 1906 EC = 1913–14 (f. 202r). Double-slip maḥdär.

Miniatures:

1. F. 204v: Crude drawing of figures and faces.

IES 05475, Gospel of John, ወንጌል ዘዮሐንስ; Image of the Trinity, መልክአ ሥላሴ; Image of the Savior of the World, መልክአ መድኃኔ ዓለም; Image of Jesus, መልክአ ኢየሱስ; Image of Mary, መልክአ ማርያም, made in the Government Scriptorium. Parchment, 160 x 112 x 46 mm, iv + 114 folios, two columns, 20 lines, Gəʽəz, twentieth century. Double-slip maḥdär.

IES 05476, Homiliary in Honor of the Archangel Michael, ድርሳነ ሚካኤል. Parchment, 214 x 169 x 48 mm, ii + 95 folios, two columns, 18 lines, Gəʽəz, twentieth century.

Miniatures:

1. F. 1r: The Archangel Michael standing with a person on either side. "His eyes are like the dove; his vestment is like the lightening. Verdant of Gold, Mikaʼel the knowledgeable."

2. F. 6v: Michael, the Archangel.

IES 05477, Psalter, ዳዊት; Angels Praise Her, ይዌድስዋ መላእክት ለማርያም. Parchment, 123 x 100 x 70 mm, ii + 185 folios, one column and two columns, 18 lines, Gə'əz, twentieth century. Single-slip maḥdär.

IES 05478, Book of Faith, መጽሐፈ ሃይማኖት. Parchment, 160 x 110 x 24 mm, ii + 25 folios, one column, 25–26 lines, Amharic, early twentieth century.

Miniatures:

    1. F. ii v(erso): Crude drawing of a figure.

IES 05479, *Ziq* Chants, መጽሐፈ ዚቅ, with musical notation. Parchment, 162 x 120 x 30 mm, ii + 52 folios, two columns, 21–23 lines, Gə'əz, twentieth century.

IES 05480, Praise of the Beloved, ስብሐተ ፍቁር; Excerpts of Rampart of the Cross, ሐጹረ መስቀል. Parchment, 99 x 62 x 25 mm, ii + 24 folios, one column, 19 lines, Gə'əz, early twentieth century.

IES 05481, Image of the Trinity, መልክእ ሥላሴ; Image of the Savior of the World, መልክእ መድኃኔ ዓለም. Paper and parchment, 100 x 60 x 30 mm, ii + 58 folios, one column, 11 lines, Gə'əz, twentieth century.

IES 05482, Mystagogia, ትምህርተ ኅቡዓት. Parchment, 55 x 40 x 13 mm, i + 25 folios, one column, 10 lines, Gə'əz, twentieth century.

IES 05483, Bandlet of Righteousness, ልፋፈ ጽድቅ. Parchment, 65 x 50 x 20 mm, 32 folios, one column, 11 lines, Gə'əz, twentieth century.

Miniatures:

    1. F. 31r: Ornate cross and geometric design (drawing).

    2. F. 31v: Sun and moon, with stars falling from the sky (drawing).

    3. F. 32r: Angel with two swords (drawing).

IES 05484, Image of John the Baptist, መልክእ ዮሐንስ መጥምቅ; Excerpt of Image of Phanuel, መልክእ ፋኑኤል; *Asmat* Prayer of Saint Michael; *Asmat* Prayer for binding demons. Parchment, 110 x 55 x 16 mm, i + 28 folios, one column, 16–17 lines, Gə'əz, twentieth century.

IES 05485, Image of Michael, መልክእ ሚካኤል; Image of Gabriel, መልክእ ገብርኤል; Image of Saint George, መልክእ ጊዮርጊስ; Image of Gäbrä

Mänfäs Qəddus, መልክአ ገብረ መንፈስ ቅዱስ. Parchment, 159 x 114 x 20 mm, 30 folios, two columns, 15–18 lines, Gəʿəz, twentieth century.

Miniatures:

1. F. 30r: Crude drawing of a figure.
2. F. 30v: Ornate cross.

IES 05486, Gate of Light, አንቀጸ ብርሃን. Parchment, 148 x 112 x 6 mm, 10 folios, two columns, 14 lines, Gəʿəz, twentieth century.

IES 05487, Wisest of the Wise, ጠቢበ ጠቢባን. Parchment, 108 x 86 x 26 mm, ii + 28 folios, one column, 14–15 lines, Gəʿəz, late nineteenth century.

IES 05488, Anaphora of the Apostles, ቅዳሴ ሐዋርያት; Anaphora of Dioscorus, ቅዳሴ ዲዮስቆሮስ; Anaphora of Our Lady Mary attributed to Cyriacus of Bəhənsa, ቅዳሴ ማርያም. Parchment, 179 x 162 x 40 mm, iii + 55 folios, two columns, 19–21 lines, Gəʿəz, 1865–1913 (ff. 16r, 19v, etc., mentions Emperor Mənilək II).

Miniatures:

1. F. ii r(ecto): Crude drawing of a figure with a sword and scabbard.
2. F. ii v(erso): Crude drawing of an angel and a figure.

IES 05522, Synaxarium, መጽሐፈ ስንክሳር. Parchment, 335 x 305 x 75 mm, i + 149 folios, three columns, 37–38 lines, Gəʿəz, late eighteenth/early nineteenth century.

IES 05523, Prayer of Saint Peter, ጸሎተ ጴጥሮስ; Prayer of the Twelve Disciples, ጸሎተ ዘ፲ወ፪ አርድእት; *Asmat* Prayer of the Three Children, አስማት ዘወሀቦሙ እግዚአብሔር ለአናንያ ወአዛርያ ወሚሳኤል; *Asmat* Prayer, "I Beseech You Lest I die Early," ተማኅጸንኩ ከመ ኢይሙት ዘእንበለ ጊዜየ, made in the Government Scriptorium. Parchment, 132 x 90 x 44 mm, ii + 87 folios, one column, 15 lines, Gəʿəz, early twentieth century. Double-slip maḥdär.

IES 05524, Sword of the Trinity, ሠይፈ ሥላሴ; Image of the Trinity, መልክአ ሥላሴ. Parchment, 160 x 95 x 40 mm, iii + 98 folios, two columns, 14–16 lines, Gəʿəz, twentieth century.

IES 05525, Acts of Gäbrä Mänfäs Qəddus, ገድለ ገብረ መንፈስ ቅዱስ; Miracles of Gäbrä Mänfäs Qəddus, ተአምረ ገብረ መንፈስ ቅዱስ; Image of Gäbrä Mänfäs Qəddus, መልክአ ገብረ መንፈስ ቅዱስ, possibly made in the Government Scriptorium. Parchment, 300 x 220 x 70 mm, ii + 107 folios, two columns, 20–22 lines, Gəʿəz, early twentieth century. Double-slip maḥdär.

IES 05526, *Asmat* Prayers, ከታብ. Parchment, 176 x 10 cm, three strips, one column, Gəʿəz, twentieth century. Copied for ወለተ ቂርቆስ ዘረቱ.

Miniatures:

- Three miniatures: (a) angel with sword and scabbard; (b) angel with sword and scabbard; and (c) ornate cross.

List of Manuscripts by IES Shelf Mark

IES 00001	IES 00026	IES 00051
IES 00002	IES 00027	IES 00052
IES 00003	IES 00028	IES 00053
IES 00004	IES 00029	IES 00054
IES 00005	IES 00030	IES 00055
IES 00006	IES 00031	IES 00056
IES 00007	IES 00032	IES 00057
IES 00008	IES 00033	IES 00058
IES 00009	IES 00034	IES 00059
IES 00010	IES 00035	IES 00060
IES 00011	IES 00036	IES 00061
IES 00012	IES 00037	IES 00062
IES 00013	IES 00038	IES 00063
IES 00014	IES 00039	IES 00064
IES 00015	IES 00040	IES 00065
IES 00016	IES 00041	IES 00066
IES 00017	IES 00042	IES 00067
IES 00018	IES 00043	IES 00068
IES 00019	IES 00044	IES 00069
IES 00020	IES 00045	IES 00070
IES 00021	IES 00046	IES 00071
IES 00022	IES 00047	IES 00072
IES 00023	IES 00048	IES 00073
IES 00024	IES 00049	IES 00074
IES 00025	IES 00050	IES 00075

IES 00076	IES 00124	IES 00163
IES 00077	IES 00125	IES 00164
IES 00078	IES 00126	IES 00165
IES 00079	IES 00127	IES 00166
IES 00080	IES 00128	IES 00167
IES 00081	IES 00129	IES 00168
IES 00082	IES 00130	IES 00169
IES 00083	IES 00131	IES 00170
IES 00084	IES 00132	IES 00171
IES 00085	IES 00133	IES 00172
IES 00088	IES 00134	IES 00173
IES 00089	IES 00135	IES 00174
IES 00090	IES 00136	IES 00175
IES 00091	IES 00136A	IES 00176
IES 00092	IES 00136B	IES 00177
IES 00093	IES 00137	IES 00178
IES 00094	IES 00138	IES 00179
IES 00095	IES 00139	IES 00180
IES 00096	IES 00140	IES 00181
IES 00097	IES 00141	IES 00182
IES 00098	IES 00142	IES 00184
IES 00099	IES 00144	IES 00185
IES 00100	IES 00145	IES 00186
IES 00101	IES 00146	IES 00190
IES 00102	IES 00147	IES 00191
IES 00103	IES 00148	IES 00192
IES 00104	IES 00149	IES 00193
IES 00105	IES 00150	IES 00194
IES 00106	IES 00151	IES 00195
IES 00107	IES 00152	IES 00196
IES 00108	IES 00153	IES 00197
IES 00109	IES 00154	IES 00198
IES 00115	IES 00155	IES 00199
IES 00116	IES 00156	IES 00200
IES 00117	IES 00158	IES 00201
IES 00118	IES 00159	IES 00202
IES 00119	IES 00160	IES 00203
IES 00122	IES 00161	IES 00209
IES 00123	IES 00162	IES 00210

List of Manuscripts by IES Shelf Mark   265

IES 00212	IES 00252	IES 00372
IES 00213	IES 00253	IES 00373
IES 00214	IES 00254	IES 00374
IES 00216	IES 00278	IES 00375
IES 00217	IES 00292	IES 00377
IES 00218	IES 00293	IES 00378A
IES 00219	IES 00294	IES 00378B
IES 00220	IES 00295	IES 00378C
IES 00221	IES 00296	IES 00379
IES 00222	IES 00297	IES 00380A
IES 00223	IES 00298	IES 00380B
IES 00224	IES 00312	IES 00381
IES 00225	IES 00313	IES 00382
IES 00226	IES 00314A	IES 00383
IES 00227	IES 00314B	IES 00385
IES 00228	IES 00314C	IES 00386
IES 00229	IES 00315	IES 00387
IES 00230	IES 00316	IES 00388
IES 00231	IES 00317	IES 00392
IES 00232	IES 00318	IES 00393
IES 00233	IES 00321	IES 00394
IES 00234	IES 00322	IES 00395
IES 00235	IES 00323	IES 00396
IES 00236	IES 00324	IES 00397
IES 00237	IES 00325	IES 00398
IES 00238	IES 00326	IES 00400
IES 00239	IES 00327	IES 00401
IES 00240	IES 00329	IES 00402
IES 00241	IES 00330	IES 00403
IES 00242	IES 00333	IES 00404
IES 00243	IES 00345	IES 00405
IES 00244A	IES 00348	IES 00406
IES 00245	IES 00350	IES 00407
IES 00246	IES 00351	IES 00408
IES 00247	IES 00355	IES 00409
IES 00248	IES 00357	IES 00410
IES 00249	IES 00358	IES 00411
IES 00250	IES 00361	IES 00412
IES 00251	IES 00371	IES 00413

IES 00414	IES 00458	IES 00498
IES 00415	IES 00459	IES 00499
IES 00416	IES 00460	IES 00500
IES 00417	IES 00461	IES 00501
IES 00419	IES 00462	IES 00502
IES 00420	IES 00463	IES 00503
IES 00421A	IES 00464	IES 00504
IES 00421B	IES 00466	IES 00505
IES 00421C	IES 00467	IES 00506
IES 00422	IES 00468	IES 00507
IES 00424	IES 00469	IES 00508
IES 00425	IES 00470	IES 00509
IES 00426	IES 00471	IES 00510
IES 00427	IES 00472	IES 00511
IES 00428	IES 00473	IES 00512
IES 00429A	IES 00474	IES 00513
IES 00430	IES 00475	IES 00514
IES 00431	IES 00476	IES 00515
IES 00434	IES 00477	IES 00516
IES 00435	IES 00478	IES 00517
IES 00436	IES 00479	IES 00518
IES 00439	IES 00480	IES 00519
IES 00440	IES 00481	IES 00520
IES 00441	IES 00482	IES 00521
IES 00442	IES 00483	IES 00522
IES 00443	IES 00484	IES 00523
IES 00444	IES 00485	IES 00524
IES 00445	IES 00486	IES 00525
IES 00446	IES 00487	IES 00526
IES 00447	IES 00488	IES 00527
IES 00448	IES 00489	IES 00528
IES 00450	IES 00490	IES 00529
IES 00451	IES 00491	IES 00530
IES 00452	IES 00492	IES 00531
IES 00453	IES 00493	IES 00532
IES 00454	IES 00494	IES 00533
IES 00455	IES 00495	IES 00534
IES 00456	IES 00496	IES 00535
IES 00457	IES 00497	IES 00536

List of Manuscripts by IES Shelf Mark   267

IES 00537	IES 00576	IES 00615
IES 00538	IES 00577	IES 00616
IES 00539	IES 00578	IES 00617
IES 00540	IES 00579	IES 00618
IES 00541	IES 00580	IES 00618B
IES 00542	IES 00581	IES 00619
IES 00543	IES 00582	IES 00620
IES 00544	IES 00583	IES 00621
IES 00545	IES 00584	IES 00622
IES 00546	IES 00585	IES 00623
IES 00547	IES 00586	IES 00624
IES 00548	IES 00587	IES 00625
IES 00549	IES 00588	IES 00626
IES 00550	IES 00589	IES 00627
IES 00551	IES 00590	IES 00628
IES 00552	IES 00591	IES 00629
IES 00553	IES 00592	IES 00630
IES 00554	IES 00593	IES 00631
IES 00555	IES 00594	IES 00632
IES 00556	IES 00595	IES 00633
IES 00557	IES 00596	IES 00634
IES 00558	IES 00597	IES 00635
IES 00559	IES 00598	IES 00636
IES 00560	IES 00599	IES 00637
IES 00561	IES 00600	IES 00638
IES 00562	IES 00601	IES 00639
IES 00563	IES 00602	IES 00640
IES 00564	IES 00603	IES 00641
IES 00565	IES 00604	IES 00642
IES 00566	IES 00605	IES 00643
IES 00567	IES 00606	IES 00644
IES 00568	IES 00607	IES 00645
IES 00569	IES 00608	IES 00646
IES 00570	IES 00609	IES 00649
IES 00571	IES 00610	IES 00650
IES 00572	IES 00611	IES 00651
IES 00573	IES 00612	IES 00652
IES 00574	IES 00613	IES 00653
IES 00575	IES 00614	IES 00654

IES 00655	IES 00697	IES 00738
IES 00656	IES 00698	IES 00739
IES 00657	IES 00699	IES 00740
IES 00658	IES 00700	IES 00741
IES 00659	IES 00701	IES 00743
IES 00660	IES 00702	IES 00744
IES 00661	IES 00703	IES 00745
IES 00662	IES 00704	IES 00746
IES 00663	IES 00705	IES 00747
IES 00664	IES 00706A	IES 00748
IES 00665	IES 00706B	IES 00749
IES 00666	IES 00707	IES 00750
IES 00667	IES 00708	IES 00751
IES 00668	IES 00709	IES 00752
IES 00669	IES 00710	IES 00753
IES 00670	IES 00711	IES 00754
IES 00671	IES 00712	IES 00755
IES 00672	IES 00714	IES 00756
IES 00673	IES 00715	IES 00757
IES 00674	IES 00716	IES 00758
IES 00675	IES 00717	IES 00759
IES 00677	IES 00718	IES 00760
IES 00679	IES 00719	IES 00761
IES 00680	IES 00720	IES 00762
IES 00681	IES 00721	IES 00763
IES 00682	IES 00722	IES 00764
IES 00683	IES 00723	IES 00765
IES 00684	IES 00724	IES 00766
IES 00685	IES 00725	IES 00767
IES 00686	IES 00726	IES 00768
IES 00687	IES 00727	IES 00770
IES 00688	IES 00728	IES 00772
IES 00690	IES 00729	IES 00776
IES 00691	IES 00730	IES 00777
IES 00692	IES 00731	IES 00778
IES 00693	IES 00732	IES 00779
IES 00694	IES 00735	IES 00780
IES 00695	IES 00736	IES 00781
IES 00696	IES 00737	IES 00782

List of Manuscripts by IES Shelf Mark 269

IES 00783	IES 00991	IES 01035
IES 00784	IES 00992	IES 01036
IES 00785	IES 00994	IES 01037
IES 00786	IES 00995	IES 01038
IES 00787	IES 00996	IES 01039
IES 00788	IES 00998	IES 01040
IES 00789	IES 00998A	IES 01041
IES 00790	IES 00999	IES 01042
IES 00791	IES 00999A	IES 01043
IES 00792	IES 00999B	IES 01044
IES 00793	IES 01000	IES 01045
IES 00795	IES 01001	IES 01046
IES 00796	IES 01002	IES 01047
IES 00836	IES 01003	IES 01048
IES 00837	IES 01004	IES 01049
IES 00838	IES 01011	IES 01051
IES 00842A	IES 01012	IES 01052
IES 00842B	IES 01013	IES 01053
IES 00844	IES 01014	IES 01054
IES 00845A	IES 01015	IES 01055
IES 00845B	IES 01016	IES 01056
IES 00846	IES 01017	IES 01057
IES 00849	IES 01018	IES 01058
IES 00852	IES 01019	IES 01064
IES 00853	IES 01020	IES 01065
IES 00854	IES 01021	IES 01066
IES 00855	IES 01022	IES 01067
IES 00856	IES 01023	IES 01068
IES 00874	IES 01024	IES 01080
IES 00876	IES 01025	IES 01081
IES 00877	IES 01026	IES 01082
IES 00879	IES 01027	IES 01083
IES 00977	IES 01028	IES 01084
IES 00984	IES 01029	IES 01085
IES 00985	IES 01030	IES 01087
IES 00986	IES 01031	IES 01089
IES 00988	IES 01032	IES 01125
IES 00989	IES 01033	IES 01126.1
IES 00990	IES 01034	IES 01126.2

IES 01130	IES 01402	IES 01743
IES 01133	IES 01555	IES 01744
IES 01136	IES 01556	IES 01745
IES 01137	IES 01557	IES 01747
IES 01148	IES 01558	IES 01759
IES 01213	IES 01559	IES 01760
IES 01214	IES 01560	IES 01763
IES 01243	IES 01561	IES 01765
IES 01255	IES 01562	IES 01766
IES 01256	IES 01563	IES 01767
IES 01268	IES 01564	IES 01768
IES 01276	IES 01565	IES 01774
IES 01279	IES 01566	IES 01777
IES 01280	IES 01572	IES 01778
IES 01285	IES 01573	IES 01779
IES 01288	IES 01579	IES 01780
IES 01291	IES 01591	IES 01781
IES 01305	IES 01609	IES 01782
IES 01315	IES 01617	IES 01800
IES 01316	IES 01624	IES 01801
IES 01322	IES 01625	IES 01807
IES 01326	IES 01626	IES 01816
IES 01340	IES 01627	IES 01818A
IES 01342	IES 01631	IES 01818B
IES 01348	IES 01633	IES 01820
IES 01350	IES 01642	IES 01821
IES 01368	IES 01667	IES 01823
IES 01373	IES 01668	IES 01824
IES 01377	IES 01672	IES 01825
IES 01381A	IES 01732	IES 01826
IES 01381B	IES 01733–34	IES 01827
IES 01382	IES 01735–36	IES 01830
IES 01383	IES 01736	IES 01832
IES 01384	IES 01737	IES 01841
IES 01397	IES 01738	IES 01842
IES 01398	IES 01739	IES 01890
IES 01399	IES 01740	IES 01908
IES 01400	IES 01741	IES 01918
IES 01401	IES 01742	IES 01919

List of Manuscripts by IES Shelf Mark 271

IES 01920	IES 02178	IES 02303
IES 01921	IES 02180	IES 02304
IES 01930	IES 02181	IES 02305
IES 01939	IES 02182	IES 02307
IES 01959	IES 02183	IES 02308
IES 01983	IES 02184	IES 02309
IES 01992	IES 02185	IES 02310
IES 01996	IES 02187	IES 02314
IES 01998	IES 02188	IES 02315
IES 02000	IES 02189	IES 02323
IES 02032	IES 02190	IES 02329
IES 02055	IES 02193	IES 02331
IES 02073	IES 02199	IES 02332
IES 02081	IES 02203	IES 02366
IES 02083	IES 02204	IES 02371
IES 02084	IES 02205	IES 02372
IES 02137	IES 02209	IES 02376
IES 02138	IES 02210	IES 02377
IES 02145	IES 02211	IES 02378
IES 02146	IES 02212	IES 02379
IES 02147	IES 02213	IES 02380
IES 02148	IES 02228	IES 02381
IES 02149	IES 02243	IES 02384
IES 02150	IES 02244	IES 02385
IES 02151	IES 02256	IES 02386
IES 02152	IES 02257	IES 02387
IES 02153A	IES 02260	IES 02388
IES 02153B	IES 02261	IES 02389
IES 02153C	IES 02263	IES 02407
IES 02153D	IES 02268	IES 02408
IES 02154	IES 02269	IES 02411
IES 02157	IES 02282	IES 02412
IES 02158	IES 02283	IES 02413
IES 02159	IES 02291	IES 02414
IES 02160	IES 02292	IES 02416
IES 02161	IES 02293	IES 02417A
IES 02166	IES 02294	IES 02417B
IES 02167	IES 02295	IES 02417C
IES 02168	IES 02296	IES 02417D

IES 02417E	IES 02577	IES 02957
IES 02417F	IES 02578	IES 02958
IES 02417G	IES 02579	IES 02959
IES 02417H	IES 02580	IES 02960
IES 02417I	IES 02581	IES 02961
IES 02417J	IES 02582	IES 02962
IES 02417KA	IES 02591	IES 02963
IES 02417KB	IES 02592	IES 02964
IES 02417LA	IES 02593	IES 02965
IES 02417LB	IES 02594	IES 02966
IES 02417N	IES 02595	IES 02967
IES 02417O	IES 02596	IES 02968
IES 02417P	IES 02597	IES 02969
IES 02439	IES 02598	IES 02972
IES 02440	IES 02606	IES 02976
IES 02444	IES 02612	IES 02993
IES 02445	IES 02613	IES 02994
IES 02458	IES 02614	IES 02995
IES 02460	IES 02615	IES 02996
IES 02461	IES 02694	IES 02997
IES 02466	IES 02695	IES 02998
IES 02467	IES 02701	IES 02999
IES 02468	IES 02702	IES 03000
IES 02469	IES 02703	IES 03001
IES 02470	IES 02936	IES 03002
IES 02471	IES 02938	IES 03004
IES 02479	IES 02939	IES 03005
IES 02480	IES 02940	IES 03006
IES 02481	IES 02947	IES 03007
IES 02550	IES 02948	IES 03010
IES 02554	IES 02949	IES 03075
IES 02569	IES 02950	IES 03076
IES 02570	IES 02951	IES 03077
IES 02571	IES 02952	IES 03078
IES 02572	IES 02953	IES 03079
IES 02573	IES 02954	IES 03080
IES 02574	IES 02955	IES 03081
IES 02575	IES 02956	IES 03082
IES 02576	IES 02956A	IES 03083

List of Manuscripts by IES Shelf Mark   273

IES 03084	IES 03165	IES 03675
IES 03085	IES 03166	IES 03676
IES 03086	IES 03173	IES 03677
IES 03087	IES 03477	IES 03678
IES 03088	IES 03478	IES 03679
IES 03089	IES 03479	IES 03680
IES 03090	IES 03480	IES 03697
IES 03091	IES 03481	IES 03698
IES 03097	IES 03482	IES 03699
IES 03098	IES 03483	IES 03700
IES 03099	IES 03484	IES 03701
IES 03100	IES 03487	IES 03702
IES 03101	IES 03488	IES 03703
IES 03102	IES 03507	IES 03704
IES 03103	IES 03582	IES 03705
IES 03104	IES 03592	IES 03706
IES 03105	IES 03593	IES 03707
IES 03106	IES 03653	IES 03708
IES 03144	IES 03654	IES 03709
IES 03145	IES 03655	IES 03710
IES 03146	IES 03656	IES 03711
IES 03147	IES 03657	IES 03712
IES 03148	IES 03658	IES 03713
IES 03149	IES 03659	IES 03714
IES 03150	IES 03660	IES 03715
IES 03151	IES 03661	IES 03716
IES 03152	IES 03662	IES 03717
IES 03153	IES 03663	IES 03721
IES 03154	IES 03664	IES 03722
IES 03155	IES 03665	IES 03723
IES 03156	IES 03666	IES 03724
IES 03157	IES 03667	IES 03725
IES 03158	IES 03668	IES 03726
IES 03159	IES 03669	IES 03727
IES 03160	IES 03670	IES 03728
IES 03161	IES 03671	IES 03730
IES 03162	IES 03672	IES 03731
IES 03163	IES 03673	IES 03732
IES 03164	IES 03674	IES 03733

IES 03734	IES 04241	IES 04287
IES 03735	IES 04249	IES 04288
IES 03736	IES 04250	IES 04289
IES 03737	IES 04251	IES 04290
IES 03738	IES 04252	IES 04291
IES 03739	IES 04253	IES 04292
IES 03740	IES 04254	IES 04293
IES 03741	IES 04255	IES 04294
IES 03742	IES 04256	IES 04295
IES 03743	IES 04257	IES 04296
IES 03744	IES 04258	IES 04297
IES 03745	IES 04259	IES 04298
IES 03746	IES 04260	IES 04299
IES 03747	IES 04261	IES 04300
IES 03748	IES 04262	IES 04301
IES 03749	IES 04263	IES 04302
IES 03750	IES 04264	IES 04303
IES 03751	IES 04265	IES 04304
IES 03752	IES 04266	IES 04305
IES 03753	IES 04267	IES 04306
IES 03754	IES 04268	IES 04307
IES 03755	IES 04269	IES 04308
IES 03756	IES 04270	IES 04309
IES 03797	IES 04271	IES 04310
IES 04094	IES 04272	IES 04311
IES 04096	IES 04273	IES 04312
IES 04138	IES 04274	IES 04313
IES 04175	IES 04275	IES 04314
IES 04178	IES 04276	IES 04315
IES 04179	IES 04277	IES 04316
IES 04192	IES 04278	IES 04317
IES 04219	IES 04279	IES 04318
IES 04229	IES 04280	IES 04319
IES 04230	IES 04281	IES 04320
IES 04231	IES 04282	IES 04321
IES 04236	IES 04283	IES 04322
IES 04237	IES 04284	IES 04323
IES 04238	IES 04285	IES 04324
IES 04239	IES 04286	IES 04325

IES 04326	IES 04365	IES 04404
IES 04327	IES 04366	IES 04405
IES 04328	IES 04367	IES 04406
IES 04329	IES 04368	IES 04407
IES 04330	IES 04369	IES 04408
IES 04331	IES 04370	IES 04409
IES 04332	IES 04371	IES 04410
IES 04333	IES 04372	IES 04411
IES 04334	IES 04373	IES 04412
IES 04335	IES 04374	IES 04413
IES 04336	IES 04375	IES 04414
IES 04337	IES 04376	IES 04415
IES 04338	IES 04377	IES 04416
IES 04339	IES 04378	IES 04417
IES 04340	IES 04379	IES 04418
IES 04341	IES 04380	IES 04419
IES 04342	IES 04381	IES 04420
IES 04343	IES 04382	IES 04421
IES 04344	IES 04383	IES 04422
IES 04345	IES 04384	IES 04423
IES 04346	IES 04385	IES 04424
IES 04347	IES 04386	IES 04425
IES 04348	IES 04387	IES 04426
IES 04349	IES 04388	IES 04427
IES 04350	IES 04389	IES 04428
IES 04351	IES 04390	IES 04429
IES 04352	IES 04391	IES 04430
IES 04353	IES 04392	IES 04431
IES 04354	IES 04393	IES 04432
IES 04355	IES 04394	IES 04433
IES 04356	IES 04395	IES 04434
IES 04357	IES 04396	IES 04435
IES 04358	IES 04397	IES 04436
IES 04359	IES 04398	IES 04437
IES 04360	IES 04399	IES 04438
IES 04361	IES 04400	IES 04439
IES 04362	IES 04401	IES 04440
IES 04363	IES 04402	IES 04441
IES 04364	IES 04403	IES 04442

IES 04443	IES 04592	IES 05447
IES 04444	IES 04600	IES 05449
IES 04445	IES 04608	IES 05474
IES 04446	IES 04620	IES 05475
IES 04447	IES 04677	IES 05476
IES 04448	IES 04679	IES 05477
IES 04449	IES 04680	IES 05478
IES 04450	IES 04682	IES 05479
IES 04451	IES 04683	IES 05480
IES 04486	IES 04684	IES 05481
IES 04488	IES 04685	IES 05482
IES 04539	IES 04686	IES 05483
IES 04540	IES 04687	IES 05484
IES 04541	IES 04688	IES 05485
IES 04542	IES 04689	IES 05486
IES 04543	IES 04690	IES 05487
IES 04544	IES 04691	IES 05488
IES 04545	IES 04692	IES 05522
IES 04546	IES 04693	IES 05523
IES 04547	IES 04696	IES 05524
IES 04556	IES 05445	IES 05525
IES 04557	IES 05446	IES 05526

IES Manuscripts Microfilmed in the EMML Project

EMML 0003 = IES 0439, 53
EMML 0004 = IES 0496, 61
EMML 0005 = IES 0377, 45
EMML 0006 = IES 0001, 1
EMML 0007 = IES 0002, 1
EMML 0008 = IES 0003, 1
EMML 0009 = IES 0005, 1
EMML 0010 = IES 0010, 4
EMML 0394 = IES 00762, 110
EMML 0401 = IES 00754, 109
EMML 0454 = IES 0760, 93
EMML 0461 = IES 00795, 115
EMML 0592 = IES 0781, 95
EMML 0622 = IES 0783, 96
EMML 0624 = IES 00780, 112
EMML 0625 = IES 0782, 96
EMML 0630 = IES 0989, 101
EMML 0633 = IES 00735, 105
EMML 0634 = IES 00736, 106
EMML 0635 = IES 01022, 123
EMML 0703 = IES 00740, 106
EMML 0707 = IES 0838, 98
EMML 0708 = IES 00738, 106
EMML 0756 = IES 03075, 195
EMML 0757 = IES 03076, 195
EMML 0771 = IES 03078, 195
EMML 0795 = IES 00766, 111
EMML 0799 = IES 00776, 112
EMML 0837 = IES 00779, 112
EMML 0839 = IES 01015, 122
EMML 0933 = IES 00759, 110
EMML 1152 = IES 00752, 108
EMML 1153 = IES 00753, 108–109
EMML 1283 = IES 0004, 1
EMML 1284 = IES 0006, 2
EMML 1285 = IES 0008, 4
EMML 1286 = IES 0011, 4
EMML 1287 = IES 0017, 5
EMML 1288 = IES 0018, 5
EMML 1289 = IES 0014, 4
EMML 1290 = IES 0015, 5
EMML 1291 = IES 0012, 4
EMML 1292 = IES 0019, 5
EMML 1293 = IES 1293, 4
EMML 1294 = IES 0016, 5
EMML 1295 = IES 0013, 4
EMML 1296 = IES 0009, 4
EMML 1297 = IES 0034, 7
EMML 1298 = IES 0030, 7
EMML 1299 = IES 0031, 7

EMML 1300 = IES 0032, 7
EMML 1301 = IES 0033, 7
EMML 1302 = IES 0029, 7
EMML 1303 = IES 0038, 8
EMML 1304 = IES 0028, 6
EMML 1305 = IES 0035, 7
EMML 1306 = IES 0026, 6
EMML 1307 = IES 0021, 5
EMML 1308 = IES 0036, 8
EMML 1309 = IES 0022, 6
EMML 1310 = IES 0023, 6
EMML 1311 = IES 0037, 8
EMML 1312 = IES 0024, 6
EMML 1313 = IES 0020, 5
EMML 1314 = IES 0039, 8
EMML 1315 = IES 0027, 6
EMML 1316 = IES 0025, 6
EMML 1333 = IES 0049, 9
EMML 1334 = IES 0041, 8
EMML 1335 = IES 0047, 9
EMML 1336 = IES 0048, 9
EMML 1337 = IES 0053, 10
EMML 1338 = IES 0054, 10
EMML 1339 = IES 0052, 10
EMML 1340 = IES 0046, 9
EMML 1341 = IES 0051, 10
EMML 1342 = IES 0045, 9
EMML 1343 = IES 0043, 9
EMML 1344 = IES 0040, 8
EMML 1345 = IES 0050, 9
EMML 1346 = IES 0044, 9
EMML 1347 = IES 0042, 8
EMML 1348 = IES 0091, 17
EMML 1349 = IES 0060, 11
EMML 1349 = IES 0091, 17
EMML 1350 = IES 0070, 12
EMML 1351 = IES 0057, 11
EMML 1352 = IES 0066, 12
EMML 1353 = IES 0064, 11
EMML 1354 = IES 0061, 11

EMML 1355 = IES 0072, 12
EMML 1356 = IES 0055, 10
EMML 1357 = IES 0062, 11
EMML 1358 = IES 0069, 12
EMML 1359 = IES 0068, 12
EMML 1360 = IES 0056, 10
EMML 1361 = IES 0067, 12
EMML 1362 = IES 0071, 12
EMML 1363 = IES 0059, 11
EMML 1364 = IES 0065, 11
EMML 1366 = IES 0088, 16
EMML 1367 = IES 0096, 18
EMML 1369 = IES 0085, 16
EMML 1370 = IES 0093, 17
EMML 1371 = IES 0090, 17
EMML 1372 = IES 0101, 18
EMML 1373 = IES 0080, 16
EMML 1374 = IES 0089, 17
EMML 1375 = IES 0100, 18
EMML 1376 = IES 0084, 16
EMML 1377 = IES 0102, 19
EMML 1378 = IES 0097, 18
EMML 1379 = IES 0079, 15
EMML 1380 = IES 0092, 17
EMML 1381 = IES 0081, 16
EMML 1382 = IES 0078, 15
EMML 1383 = IES 0082, 16
EMML 1384 = IES 0083, 16
EMML 1385 = IES 0098, 18
EMML 1386 = IES 0108, 20
EMML 1387 = IES 0104, 19
EMML 1388 = IES 0109, 20
EMML 1389 = IES 0116, 21
EMML 1390 = IES 0106, 20
EMML 1391 = IES 0107, 20
EMML 1392 = IES 0117, 21
EMML 1393 = IES 0118, 21
EMML 1396 = IES 0119, 21
EMML 1397 = IES 0115, 20
EMML 1399 = IES 0174, 27

IES Manuscripts Microfilmed in the EMML Project

EMML 1400 = IES 0193, 29
EMML 1401 = IES 0175, 27
EMML 1402 = IES 0177, 28
EMML 1403 = IES 0176, 27
EMML 1404 = IES 0182, 28
EMML 1405 = IES 0194, 30
EMML 1406 = IES 0184, 29
EMML 1407 = IES 0244A, 36
EMML 1408 = IES 0244A, 36
EMML 1409 = IES 0209, 31
EMML 1410 = IES 0216, 32
EMML 1411 = IES 0254, 38
EMML 1412 = IES 0292, 38
EMML 1413 = IES 0297, 38
EMML 1414 = IES 0240, 36
EMML 1421 = IES 0212, 31
EMML 1422 = IES 0247, 37
EMML 1423 = IES 0214, 32
EMML 1424 = IES 0296, 38
EMML 1425 = IES 0248, 37
EMML 1426 = IES 0245, 37
EMML 1427 = IES 0250, 37
EMML 1428 = IES 0249, 37
EMML 1436 = IES 0246, 37
EMML 1437 = IES 0223, 33
EMML 1438 = IES 0210, 31
EMML 1439 = IES 0213, 31
EMML 1448 = IES 02966, 187
EMML 1462 = IES 0322, 41
EMML 1463 = IES 0373, 44
EMML 1464 = IES 0358, 43
EMML 1465 = IES 0350, 42
EMML 1466 = IES 0321, 41
EMML 1467 = IES 0327, 42
EMML 1468 = IES 0355, 43
EMML 1469 = IES 0318, 41
EMML 1470 = IES 0324, 41
EMML 1471 = IES 0357, 43
EMML 1472 = IES 0323, 41
EMML 1473 = IES 0326, 42

EMML 1474 = IES 0330, 42
EMML 1475 = IES 0317, 41
EMML 1476 = IES 0345, 42
EMML 1477 = IES 0316, 41
EMML 1478 = IES 0222, 33
EMML 1483 = IES 0387, 46
EMML 1484 = IES 0400, 47
EMML 1485 = IES 0401, 47
EMML 1486 = IES 0385, 46
EMML 1487 = IES 0422, 51
EMML 1489 = IES 0388, 46
EMML 1491 = IES 0378A, 45
EMML 1491 = IES 0378B, 45
EMML 1492 = IES 0395, 47
EMML 1493 = IES 0393, 47
EMML 1494 = IES 0394, 47
EMML 1495 = IES 0397, 47
EMML 1496 = IES 0377, 45
EMML 1497 = IES 0402, 47
EMML 1498 = IES 0398, 47
EMML 1499 = IES 0381, 45
EMML 1500 = IES 0378B, 45
EMML 1500 = IES 0378C, 45
EMML 1501 = IES 0383, 46
EMML 1502 = IES 0386, 46
EMML 1503 = IES 0426, 52
EMML 1505 = IES 0425, 52
EMML 1506 = IES 0424, 52
EMML 1507 = IES 0428, 52
EMML 1508 = IES 0427, 52
EMML 1510 = IES 0439, 53
EMML 1511 = IES 0417, 50
EMML 1512 = IES 0440, 53
EMML 1513 = IES 0420, 50
EMML 1514 = IES 0419, 50
EMML 1515 = IES 0681, 83
EMML 1516 = IES 0467, 57
EMML 1517 = IES 0468, 57
EMML 1518 = IES 0688, 84
EMML 1519 = IES 0469, 57

EMML 1519 = IES 0470, 57
EMML 1520 = IES 0685, 83
EMML 1521 = IES 0682, 83
EMML 1523 = IES 0699, 85
EMML 1524 = IES 0494, 61
EMML 1525 = IES 0471, 57
EMML 1526 = IES 0441, 53
EMML 1527 = IES 0691, 84
EMML 1528 = IES 0443, 54
EMML 1529 = IES 0444, 54
EMML 1530 = IES 0464, 57
EMML 1531 = IES 0675, 82
EMML 1532 = IES 0692, 84
EMML 1533 = IES 0683, 83
EMML 1534 = IES 0497, 62
EMML 1535 = IES 0686, 83
EMML 1536 = IES 0462, 56
EMML 1537 = IES 0492, 61
EMML 1538 = IES 0493, 61
EMML 1539 = IES 0460, 56
EMML 1540 = IES 0495, 61
EMML 1541 = IES 0442, 53
EMML 1542 = IES 0687, 83
EMML 1543 = IES 0995, 102
EMML 1544 = IES 01018, 122
EMML 1548 = IES 01016, 122
EMML 1549 = IES 0708, 86
EMML 1550 = IES 0706A, 86
EMML 1551 = IES 0706B, 86
EMML 1553 = IES 0697, 84
EMML 1554 = IES 0709, 86
EMML 1555 = IES 0704, 85
EMML 1556 = IES 0710, 86
EMML 1556 = IES 0712, 86
EMML 1556 = IES 0714, 86
EMML 1556 = IES 0717, 87
EMML 1556 = IES 0718, 87
EMML 1556 = IES 0719, 87
EMML 1556 = IES 0720, 87

EMML 1557 = IES 0705, 85
EMML 1558 = IES 0702, 85
EMML 1559 = IES 0703, 85
EMML 1560 = IES 0700, 85
EMML 1561 = IES 0701, 85
EMML 1562 = IES 0696, 84
EMML 1568 = IES 0694, 84
EMML 1569 = IES 0724, 88
EMML 1570 = IES 0725, 88
EMML 1571 = IES 0695, 84
EMML 1572 = IES 0737, 90
EMML 1573 = IES 0723, 87
EMML 1581 = IES 0730, 89
EMML 1582 = IES 0731, 89
EMML 1583 = IES 0732, 89
EMML 1584 = IES 0693, 84
EMML 1585 = IES 0728, 88
EMML 1591 = IES 0743, 90
EMML 1592 = IES 0751, 92
EMML 1593 = IES 0741, 90
EMML 1594 = IES 0758, 93
EMML 1595 = IES 0739, 90
EMML 1596 = IES 0757, 93
EMML 1597 = IES 0764, 94
EMML 1598 = IES 0755, 93
EMML 1692 = IES 0777, 95
EMML 1693 = IES 0788, 97
EMML 1694 = IES 0787, 97
EMML 1695 = IES 0791, 97
EMML 1696 = IES 0789, 97
EMML 1697 = IES 0790, 97
EMML 1699 = IES 0796, 98
EMML 2344 = IES 0852, 99
EMML 3766 = IES 0999, 102
EMML 7454 = IES 2189, 133
Foliated with numbers in blue ink, but no EMML number is visible, IES 00785, 00994, 01068

List of Dated or Datable Codices

1505–6: IES 439

1630–1705: IES 429A

1682–92 (mentions Emperor Iyasu I and Metropolitan Sinoda): IES 98, 373

1682–1706 (mentions Patriarch Yoḥannəs XVI, Metropolitan Marqos IV, and Emperor Iyasu): IES 4281

1682–1788 (mentions an Emperor Iyasu): IES 105

1708–11 (mentions Emperor Tewoflos): IES 3708

1730–55 (mentions Emperor Iyasu II): IES 3679

1755–69 (mentions Emperor Iyo'as I): IES 62

1779–96 (mentions Emperor Takla Giyorgis [r. 1779–1800], Metropolitan Yosab II [Yosab II 1770–1801], and Patriarch Yoḥannəs [1769–96]): IES 212

1780/81 (=1773 EC): IES 2145

1812: IES 2411

1837/38 (=1830 EC): IES 986

1841–67 (mentions Metropolitan Sälama): IES 33

1843: IES 1832

1847–55 (copied for Ḫaylä Mäläkot, father of Mənilək II): IES 37

1865–1913 (mentions Emperor Mənilək II): IES 27, 35, 240, 788, 5488

1868: IES 396

1868–89: IES 842A

1868–1905 (mentions Emperor Mənilək II): IES 2146

1874: IES 323

1874–1926 (mentions *Abba* Matewos and Patriarch Cyril V of Alexandria): IES 1055, 2329, 2377

1874–1926 (mentions Patriarch Cyril V of Alexandria): IES 3724

1881–82: IES 175

1881–87 (mentions Metropolitan Ṗeṭros IV and Metropolitan Matewos): IES 249, 3713

1881–89 (mentions Bishop Luqas, Emperor Yoḥannəs IV, and Metropolitan Ṗeṭros IV): IES 3080

1881–1926 (mentions Metropolitan Matewos): IES 64

1882 (mentions 7,382 Year of the World): IES 3753

1885/56 (=7378 AM): IES 89, 397

1887/88 (=1880 EC): IES 4192

1889–1913 (mentions Emperor Menilek II, Metropolitan Matewos and Atənatewos): IES 3477, 4687

1889–1913 (mentions Emperor Menilek II, Metropolitan Ṗeṭros IV, and Metropolitan Matewos): IES 762

1889–1917 (mentions Metropolitans Ṗeṭros IV and Matewos): IES 2380, 3086

1889–1926 (mentions Metropolitan Matewos): IES 3103

1889–1926 (mentions Alexandrian Patriarch Cyril V and Metropolitan Matewos): IES 786, 1055

1890/91 (=1883 EC): IES 9, 79

1892/93 (=1885 EC, mentions Menilek II and the year 7385): IES 2956

1894/95 (=1887 EC): IES 25, 4138

1899: IES 4094

1899–1900: IES 44

1903: IES 701

1904: IES 91

List of Dated or Datable Codices 283

1905/6 (=1898 EC): IES 1397, 1398

1908 (=1901 EC): IES 5447

1908–14 (=1901–07 EC): IES 2187

1909 (twentieth year of the reign of Menilek II): IES 7, 70, 325, 358

Nov. / Dec. 1912 (=Ḫədar 1905): IES 20

1910 (=1902 EC): IES 787

1911–13: IES 324

1912/13 (=1905 EC): IES 2185, 3100

1913: IES 380B

1913/14 (=1906 EC): IES 5474

1913–16 (mentions Lej Iyasu): IES 1034

1913–26 (mentions Metropolitan Matewos): IES 30

1914/5 (=1907 EC): IES 47, 2965

1916–30 (mentions Empress Zäwditu): IES 60, 63, 2147

1917: IES 4096

1918: IES 677

1918/19 (=1911 EC): IES 1983

1918/19 (=1911 EC, mentions Alexandrian Patriarch Cyril V and Metropolitan Matewos): IES 2960

1919/20 (=1912 EC): IES 49, 355, 4488

1920–35 (=1913–28 EC): IES 1384

1921/22 (=1914 EC): IES 2269, 2570

1922/23 (=1915 EC): IES 460

1925/26 (=1918 EC): IES 3082

1927/28 (=1920 EC): IES 1213

1929: IES 745, 748

1930: IES 329

1930–62 (mentions Ḫaylä Śəllase, and Empress Manan): IES 244A

1930–74: (mentions Emperor Ḫaylä Śəllase): IES 61, 247, 322, 743, 766, 1939, 4289

1931/32 (=1924 EC): IES 193, 417, 3078

1932/33 (=1925 EC): IES 419

1933/34 (=1926 EC): IES 3146

1934: IES 699

1934/35 (=1927 EC): IES 77, 1383

1935 (=1927 EC): IES 216, 702, 705

1935/36 (=1928 EC): IES 395, 2268, 3488

1936 (=1928 EC): IES 731, 2466

1936/37 (=1929 EC): IES 3479

1937/38 (=1930 EC): IES 4178

1937–42: IES 3164

1938/39 (=1931 EC): IES 400

1939: IES 738

1939/40 (=1932 EC): IES 29

1941: IES 714

1941–50: IES 24

1941–65 (=1934–57 EC): IES 1243

1941–73 (=1934–65 EC): IES 1322

1942: IES 700

1942–66 (=1935–58 EC): IES 1285

1944/45 (=1937 EC): IES 3089

July 24, 1945 (=*Mäskäräm* 17, 1937 EC): IES 3752

1945/46 (=1938 EC): IES 38, 1609, 1733–34, 2408

1946/47 (=1939 EC): IES 2138, 4592

1946–56 (mentions Alexandrian Patriarch Joseph II): IES 3087

1948/49 (=1941 EC): IES 2573

1949: IES 162

November 24, 1950: IES 57

1951–56 (mentions Metropolitan Basəlyos and Alexandrian Metropolitan Joseph II): IES 1920

List of Dated or Datable Codices   285

1951–70 (mentions Metropolitan Basəlyos and Emperor Haylä Śəllase): IES 2967

1952/53 (=1945 EC): IES 317, 999

1952–54: IES 326

1952–68 (=1945–60 EC): IES 1288

1954/55 (=1947 EC): IES 984

1955: IES 712

1955/56 (=1948 EC): IES 704, 1739

1955–57: IES 136

1956/57 (=1949 EC): IES 388

1958: IES 374

1960–61: IES 132

1960–62 (=1953–54 EC): IES 2949

1961: IES 251, 252, 253, 746, 750

1961–62: IES 124, 134, 135

1962: IES 131

1962/63 (=1955 EC): IES 1326

1963: IES 125

1963/64 (=1956 EC): IES 424, 425, 426, 427, 428, 1316, 3165

1963–71 (=1956–63 EC): IES 1559

1964–66 (=1957–59 EC): IES 1268

1967–68 (1960 EC): IES 2203

1970–78 (=1963–70 EC): IES 1557

1964 (=1957 EC): IES 2, 3, 1377

1965: IES 312, 431

1965/66 (=1958 EC): IES 1566

1965/73 (=1958–65 EC): IES 1558

1966–67 (=1959 EC): IES 768, 1126.1, 1126.2

1967 (=1959 EC): IES 185, 717, 1214

1967–68: IES 196, 197

1967–80 (=1960–72 EC): IES 1556

1968: IES 198, 199, 200, 202, 203, 243, 708, 710

1968/69 (=1961 EC): IES 209, 3487

1968–72: IES 720

1969 (=1961 EC): IES 201, 241, 298, 313, 314A, 314B, 314C, 719, 772

1969–70 (=1962 EC): IES 1350

1970: IES 348, 726, 727

1970–73 (=1963–65 EC): IES 1555

1971 (=1963 EC): IES 351, 361, 715, 718

1972 (=1965 EC): IES 372, 374, 379, 421A–C, 685, 709, 711, 716

1972–73 (=1965 EC): IES 1631

1973–74 (=1966 EC): IES 767

1974–75 (=1967 EC): IES 849, 999A, 999B, 1667, 1668

1975: IES 466

1975–76 (=1968 EC): IES 1841

1976–77 (=1969 EC): IES 998, 998A

1977–80 (=1970–72 EC): IES 1624

1979: IES 123

1979/80 (=1972 EC): IES 1617

1980/81 (=1973 EC): IES 3592

1980/82 (=1973 EC): IES 1642

1986/87 (=1979 EC): IES 1992

1992–94 (=1985–86 EC): IES 2467

1996/97 (=1889 EC): IES 210

List of Undated Codices

Fourteenth Century

Late fourteenth/early fifteenth century: IES 377, 679

Fifteenth Century

Early fifteenth century: IES 695, 4261 (rejected leaf)

Fifteenth century: IES 294, 392, 461, 837, 1830 (composite), 3756 (rejected leaf)

Late fifteenth century: IES 74, 242, 722

Late fifteenth/early sixteenth century: IES 436, 721

Sixteenth Century

Early sixteenth century: IES 496, 2439

Sixteenth century: IES 21 (composite), 723, 777 (composite), 2972

Late sixteenth century: IES 1049

Late sixteenth/early seventeenth century: IES 3081

Sixteenth/seventeenth century: IES 777 (composite)

Seventeenth Century

Early seventeenth century: IES 444 (composite)

Seventeenth century: IES 16 (composite), 71 (composite), 76 (composite), 84, 102, 214 (composite), 318, 687, 791, 796, 1305, 2084, 2580 (composite), 3106, 3680 (composite), 3707, 3714, 4296

Late seventeenth century: IES 4267

288 List of Undated Codices

Late seventeenth/early eighteenth century: IES 2032, 3147, 3656

Seventeenth/eighteenth century: IES 32, 36, 692, 782, 783, 790, 995

Eighteenth Century

Early eighteenth century: IES 6, 54, 103, 989, 1039, 4270

Eighteenth century: IES 10, 16 (composite), 21 (composite), 22, 34, 40, 41, 42, 50, 55, 59, 66, 104, 107, 174, 176, 177, 182, 315, 350, 398, 422, 440, 441, 444 (composite), 724, 725, 730, 852, 1002, 1064, 1672, 1781, 1816, 1823, 1824, 1827 (composite), 2148, 2416, 2479, 2969, 2993, 3006, 3084, 3091, 3098, 3157, 3159, 3161, 3162, 3655, 3671, 3676, 3697, 3700, 3728, 3731, 3744, 3745, 4175, 4179, 4250, 4254, 4258, 4264, 4273, 4278, 5445

Late eighteenth century: IES 75, 76 (composite), 99, 472, 854, 1038, 1830 (composite), 2550, 2592, 3144, 3158, 3674, 3678, 3680 (composite), 3699, 3738, 4230, 4280, 4693

Late eighteenth/early nineteenth century: IES 73, 2958, 2962, 3010, 3085, 3163, 3672, 3673, 3677, 4253, 4255, 4261, 4283, 4540, 4683, 4692, 5522

Eighteenth/nineteenth century: IES 26, 106, 163, 1399, 2157

Nineteenth Century

Early nineteenth century: IES 17, 100, 184, 383, 497, 1012, 1041, 2153A, 2470, 3102, 3145, 3658, 3705, 3740, 4256, 4276 (composite), and 4689

Nineteenth century: IES 8, 12, 15, 19, 21 (composite), 39, 45, 46, 51, 56, 58, 65, 67, 78, 90, 92, 101, 115, 118, 130, 194, 214 (composite), 248, 250, 296, 297, 402, 443, 691, 729, 735, 740, 753, 755, 764, 780, 781, 789, 1011, 1016, 1021, 1022, 1023, 1027, 1046, 1056, 1065, 1373, 1400, 1401, 1626, 1627, 1779, 1818A, 1818B, 1826, 1827 (composite), 1842, 1930, 2149, 2160, 2182, 2211, 2282, 2283, 2305, 2331, 2371, 2376, 2381, 2386, 2572 (composite), 2575, 2577 (composite), 2580 (composite), 2581, 2582, 2702, 2948, 2950, 2957, 2963, 2964, 2994, 3004 (composite), 3077, 3079, 3097, 3156, 3480, 3482, 3668, 3670, 3675, 3712, 3721, 3735, 3741, 3743, 3746, 3747, 3751, 3756, 4229, 4237, 4252, 4257, 4259, 4260, 4262, 4266, 4268, 4284, 4685, 5449

Late nineteenth century: IES 81, 109, 129, 141, 330, 690, 693, 736, 792, 836, 842B, 844, 845A, 845B, 846, 853, 994, 1028, 1044, 1045, 1402, 1759, 1918, 2293, 2378, 2444, 2481, 2612, 2936, 2968, 3083, 3101, 3657, 3698, 3701, 3706, 3725, 4251, 5487

Late nineteenth/early twentieth century: IES 1, 94, 760, 855, 1057, 2158, 2167, 2389, 2593, 2956A, 3075, 3478, 3653, 3660, 3702, 4288, 4294, 4677

Nineteenth/twentieth century: IES 14, 28, 52, 117, 401, 464, 468, 471, 493, 675, 686, 694, 757, 2166

Twentieth Century

Early twentieth century: IES 43, 80, 83, 93, 95, 108, 136A, 136B, 139, 173, 213, 222, 316, 333, 357, 495, 499, 683, 751, 752, 754, 776, 784, 785, 786, 838, 856, 992, 996, 1040, 1043, 1068, 1084, 1085, 1137, 1255, 1256, 1565, 1825, 1959, 2151, 2188, 2189, 2210, 2291, 2379, 2384, 2445, 2471, 2480, 2554, 2591, 2955, 2959, 2966, 2995, 3076, 3088, 3090, 3099, 3105, 3148, 3150, 3151, 3152, 3481, 3507, 3661, 3665, 3669, 3704, 3710, 3722, 3730, 3732, 3737, 3755, 3797, 4265, 4269, 4274, 4282, 4285, 4539, 4544, 4600, 4620, 4679, 4680, 4682, 4684, 4688, 5478, 5480, 5523, 5525

Twentieth century: IES 3, 5, 11, 18, 23, 31, 48, 53, 68, 69, 71 (composite), 72, 82, 85, 88, 96, 97, 116, 119, 126, 127, 128, 133, 137, 138, 140, 142, 152, 153, 160, 161, 223, 245, 246, 254, 278, 292, 321, 327, 345, 371, 385, 386, 387, 393, 394, 420, 434, 435, 442, 462, 463, 467, 469, 470, 492, 494, 498, 681, 682, 684, 688, 696, 697, 703, 706A, 706B, 728, 732, 737, 739, 741, 744, 747, 749, 756, 758, 759, 761, 763, 765, 770, 778, 779, 793, 795, 874, 977, 985, 988, 990, 991, 1001, 1013, 1014, 1015, 1017, 1018, 1019, 1020, 1024, 1025, 1026, 1029, 1030, 1031, 1032, 1033, 1035, 1036, 1037, 1042, 1047, 1048, 1051, 1052, 1053, 1054, 1058, 1066, 1067, 1080, 1081, 1082, 1087, 1130, 1148, 1276, 1279, 1280, 1315, 1342, 1382, 1625, 1633, 1732, 1735-36, 1736, 1737, 1738, 1740, 1741, 1742, 1743, 1744, 1745, 1747, 1760, 1763, 1765, 1766, 1767, 1768, 1774, 1777, 1778, 1780, 1782, 1807, 1820, 1821, 1827 (composite), 1890, 1919, 1921, 1996, 2000, 2055, 2073, 2081, 2083, 2137, 2150, 2152, 2153B, 2153C, 2153D, 2154, 2159, 2161, 2168, 2178, 2180, 2181, 2183, 2184, 2190, 2193, 2199, 2204, 2205, 2212, 2213, 2228, 2243, 2244, 2256, 2257, 2260, 2261, 2263, 2292, 2294, 2295, 2296, 2303, 2304, 2307, 2308, 2309, 2310, 2314,

2315, 2323, 2332, 2372, 2385, 2387, 2388, 2407, 2412, 2413, 2414, 2440, 2458, 2460, 2461, 2468, 2469, 2569, 2571, 2572 (composite), 2574, 2576, 2577 (composite), 2578, 2579, 2594, 2595, 2596, 2597, 2598, 2606, 2613, 2614, 2615, 2694, 2695, 2701, 2703, 2938, 2939, 2940, 2947, 2951, 2952, 2953, 2954, 2961, 2996, 2997, 2998, 2999, 3000, 3001, 3002, 3004 (composite), 3005, 3007, 3104, 3149, 3153, 3154, 3155, 3160, 3166, 3173, 3483, 3484, 3582, 3654, 3659, 3662, 3663, 3664, 3666, 3667, 3703, 3709, 3711, 3715, 3716, 3717, 3723, 3724, 3726, 3727, 3733, 3734, 3736, 3739, 3748, 3749, 3750, 3754, 4219, 4231, 4236, 4238, 4239, 4241, 4249, 4263, 4271, 4272, 4275, 4276 (composite), 4277, 4279, 4286, 4287, 4290, 4291, 4292, 4293, 4295, 4297, 4298, 4486, 4541, 4542, 4543, 4545, 4546, 4547, 4556, 4557, 4608, 4686, 4690, 4691, 4696, 5475, 5476, 5477, 5479, 5481, 5482, 5483, 5484, 5485, 5486, 5524

Mid twentieth century: IES 13, 1136, 1340, 1348, 1368, 1381A, 1381B, 1560, 1561, 1562, 1563, 1564, 1572, 1573, 1579, 1591, 2417

Late twentieth century: IES 154, 378A, 378B, 378C, 876, 877, 879, 1000, 1003, 1004, 1083, 1089, 1125, 1133, 1291, 1908, 3593, 5446

List of Dates of the Magic Scrolls

Eighteenth Century

Eighteenth century: IES 165

Late eighteenth century: IES 407

Late eighteenth/early nineteenth century: IES 192, 410

Eighteenth/nineteenth century: IES 195

Nineteenth Century

Early nineteenth century: IES 156, 164, 171

Nineteenth century: IES 155, 158, 159, 178, 179, 186, 191, 236, 238, 382, 403, 445, 446, 447, 451, 452, 454, 455, 456, 458, 640, 672, 2976, 4310, 4323, 4351, 4359

Late nineteenth century: IES 190, 217, 21, 229, 234, 235, 237, 295, 485, 651, 665, 4318, 4321, 4362

Late nineteenth/early twentieth century: IES 167, 180, 406, 4392

Twentieth Century

Early twentieth century: IES 145, 170, 172, 181, 224, 225, 239, 293, 408, 457, 476, 477, 500, 516, 522, 581, 621, 642, 664, 666, 669, 4301, 4304, 4307, 4312, 4334, 4339, 4348, 4350, 4371, 4380, 4445

1950–75: IES 168

Twentieth century: IES 144, 146, 147, 148, 149, 150, 151, 166, 169, 218, 219, 220, 226, 227, 228, 230, 231, 232, 233, 404, 405, 409, 411, 412, 413, 414, 415, 416, 448, 450, 453, 475, 478, 479, 480, 483, 486, 490, 491, 501, 502, 503, 504, 505, 506, 507, 508, 509, 510, 511, 512, 513,

514, 515, 517, 518, 519, 520, 521, 523, 524, 525, 526, 527, 528, 529, 530, 531, 532, 533, 534, 535, 536, 537, 538, 539, 540, 541, 542, 543, 544, 545, 546, 547, 548, 549, 550, 551, 552, 553, 554, 555, 556, 557, 558, 559, 560, 561, 562, 563, 564, 565, 566, 567, 568, 569, 570, 571, 572, 573, 574, 575, 576, 577, 578, 579, 580, 582, 583, 584, 585, 586, 587, 588, 589, 590, 591, 592, 593, 594, 595, 596, 597, 598, 599, 600, 601, 602, 603, 604, 605, 606, 607, 608, 609, 610, 611, 612, 613, 614, 615, 616, 617, 618B, 619, 620, 622, 623, 624, 625, 626, 627, 628, 629, 630, 631, 632, 633, 634, 635, 636, 637, 638, 639, 641, 643, 644, 645, 646, 649, 650, 652, 653, 654, 655, 656, 657, 658, 659, 660, 661, 662, 663, 667, 668, 670, 673, 674, 680, 698, 1998, 2976, 4299, 4300, 4302, 4303, 4305, 4306, 4308, 4309, 4311, 4313, 4314, 4315, 4316, 4317, 4319, 4320, 4322, 4324, 4325, 4326, 4327, 4328, 4329, 4330, 4331, 4332, 4333, 4335, 4336, 4337, 4338, 4340, 4341, 4342, 4343, 4344, 4345, 4346, 4347, 4349, 4352, 4353, 4355, 4356, 4357, 4358, 4360, 4361, 4363, 4364, 4365, 4366, 4367, 4368, 4369, 4370, 4372, 4373, 4374, 4375, 4376, 4377, 4378, 4379, 4381, 4382, 4383, 4384, 4385, 4386, 4387, 4388, 4389, 4390, 4391, 4393, 4394, 4395, 4396, 4397, 4398, 4399, 4400, 4401, 4402, 4403, 4404, 4405, 4406, 4407, 4408, 4409, 4410, 4411, 4412, 4413, 4414, 4415, 4416, 4417, 4418, 4419, 4420, 4421, 4422, 4423, 4424, 4425, 4426, 4427, 4428, 4429, 4430, 4431, 4432, 4433, 4434, 4435, 4436, 4437, 4438, 4439, 4440, 4441, 4442, 4443, 4444, 4446, 4447, 4448, 4449, 4450, 4451, 5526

Late twentieth century: IES 459, 473, 474, 481, 482, 484, 487, 488, 489

Plates

Plate 1. IES 4, ff. iv v(erso)–1r

Plate 2. IES 7, ff. 34v–35r

Plate 3. IES 7, ff. 48v–49r

Plate 4. IES 7, ff. 49v–50r

Plate 5. IES 7, ff. 50v–51r

Plate 6. IES 7, ff. 16v–17r

Plate 7. IES 73, front cover

Plate 8. IES 73, back cover

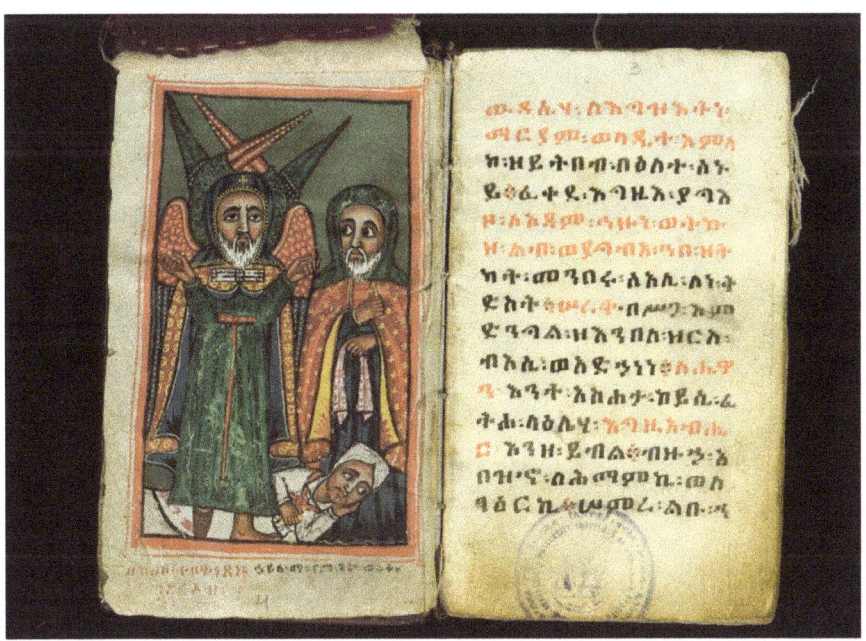

Plate 9. IES 73, ff. ii v(erso)–1r

298 Plates

Plate 10. IES 73, ff. 109v–110r

Plate 11. IES 74, ff. i v(erso)–1r

Plate 12. IES 74, ff. 124v–125r

Plate 13. IES 34, inside front cover–1r

Plate 14. IES 34, ff. 226v–inside back cover

Plate 15. IES 103, ff. iv v(erso)–1r

Plate 16. IES 103, ff. 26v–27r

Plate 17. IES 103, ff. 67v–68r

302   Plates

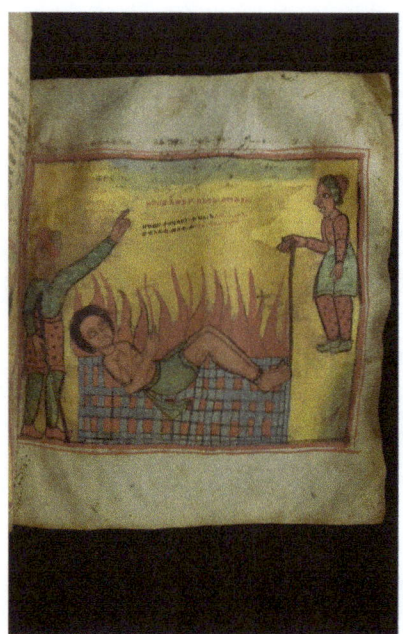

Plate 18. IES 105, f. 6r

Plate 19. IES 105, f. 5v

Plate 20. IES 242, ff. 2v–3r

Plate 21. IES 242, ff. 3v–4r

Plate 22. IES 242, ff. 75v–76r

Plate 23. IES 242, f. 161r

Plate 24. IES 722, ff. 75r

Plate 25. IES 721, ff. 2v–3r

Plate 26. IES 721, ff. 85v–86r

Plate 27. IES 721, ff. 174v–175r

Plate 28. IES 723, ff. ii v(erso)–1r

Plate 29. IES 723, ff. 6v–7r

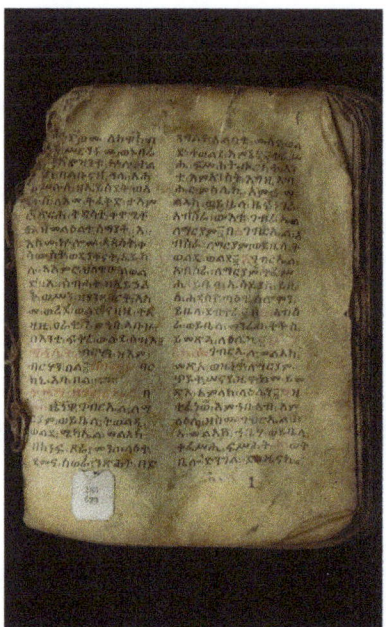

Plate 30. IES 679, f. 1r

Plate 31. IES 679, spine

Plate 32. IES 496, ff. 14v–15r

Plate 33. IES 496, f. 43v

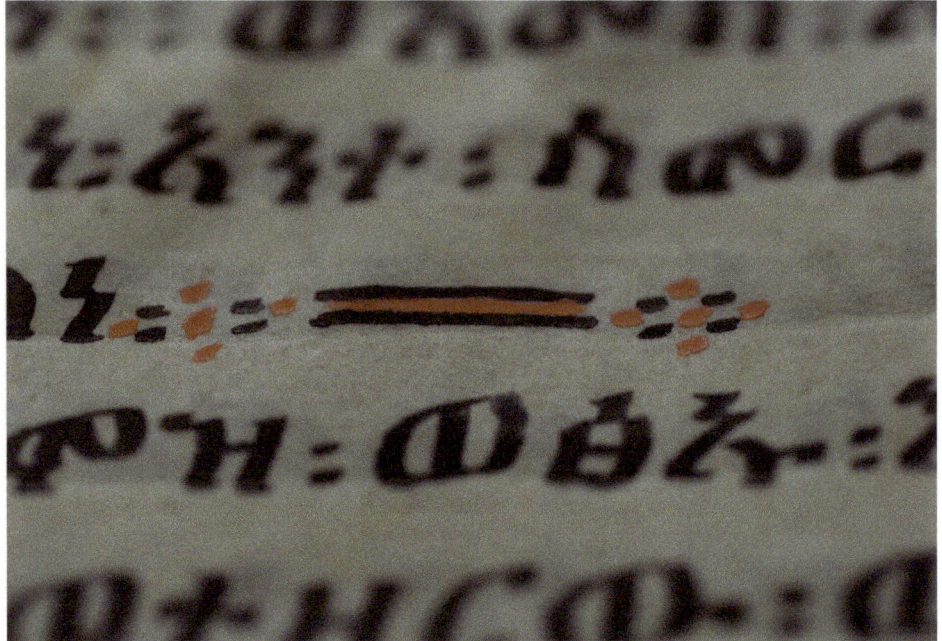

Plate 34. IES 496, f. 43v

Plate 35. IES 496, f. 43v

Plate 36. IES 496, ff. 70v–71r

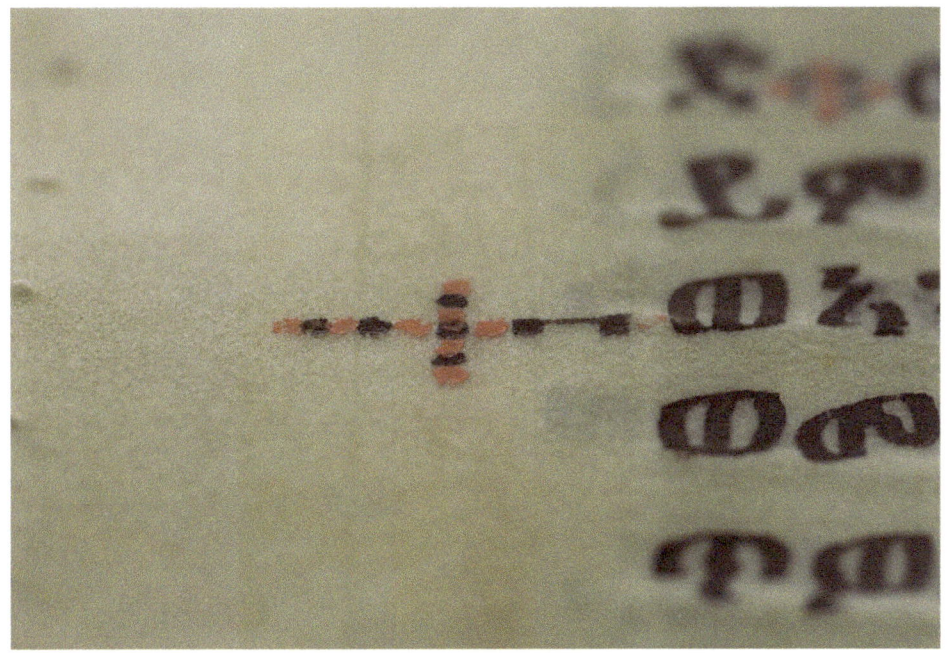

Plate 37. IES 496, f. 70v

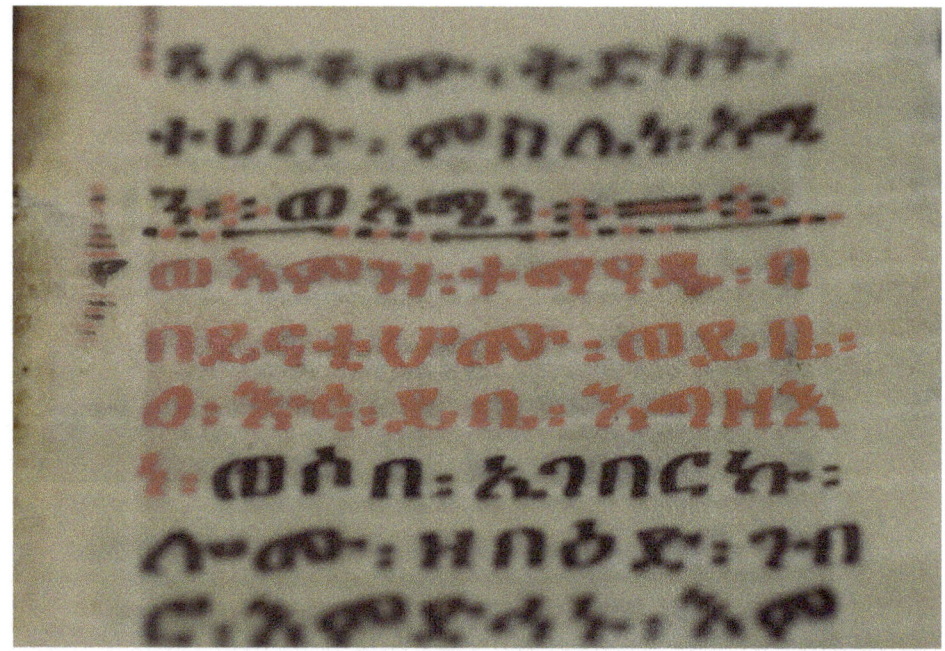

Plate 38. IES 496, f. 71r

Plate 39. IES 496, f. 102r

Plate 40. IES 496, f. 89v

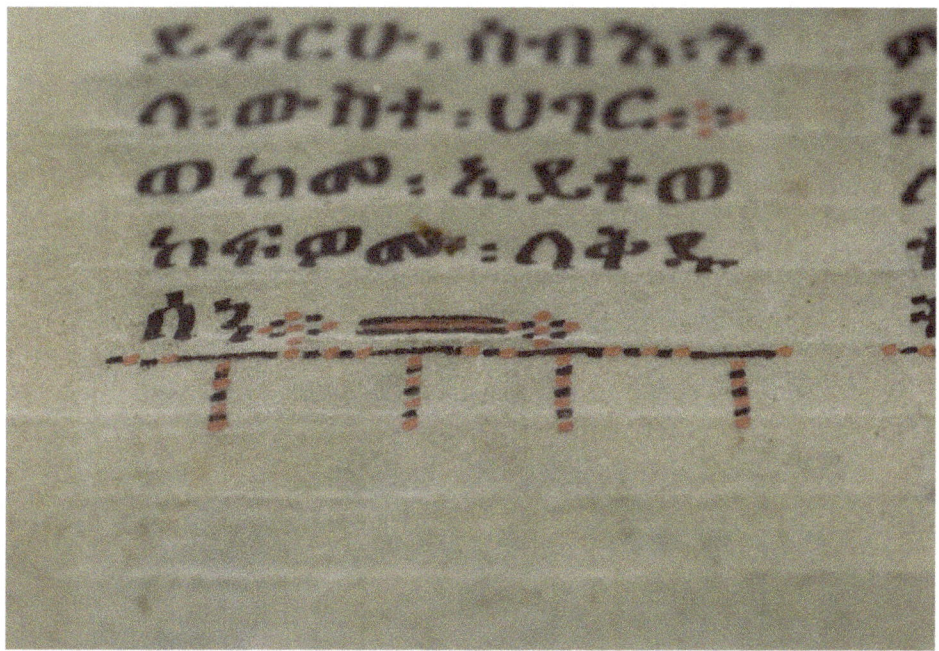

Plate 41. IES 496, f. 89v

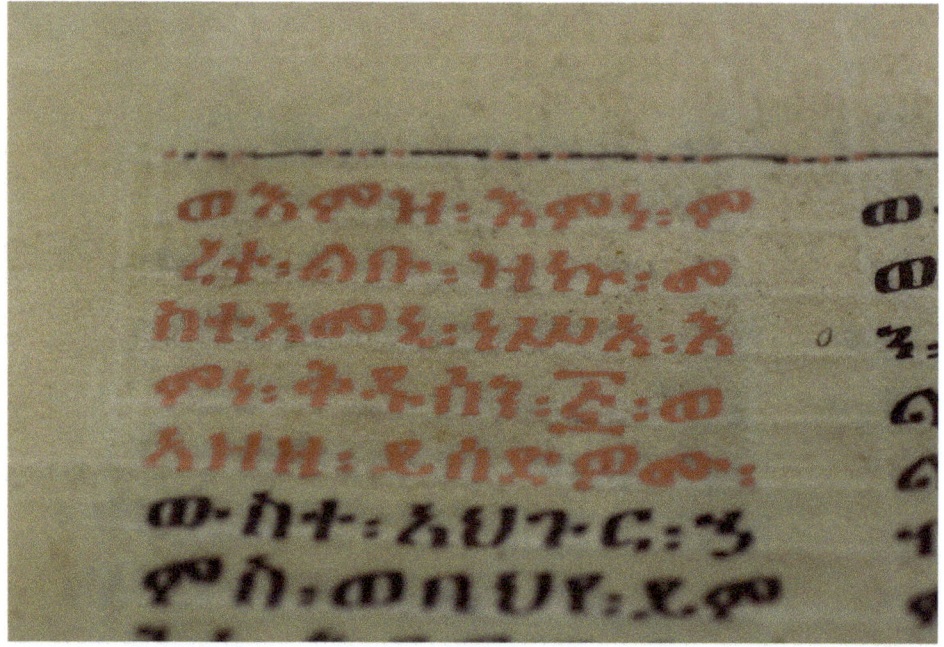

Plate 42. IES 496, f. 89v

Index of Major Works in the Codices

Absolution of the Son, 104, 123, 146, 157, 163, 215, 224, 227
Acts of
    Abib, 12
    Adam and Eve, 204
    Apostles, Apocryphal, 25
    Arsema of Armenia, 152
    Bula, *abba*, 12
    Däbrä Dammo, Holy Fathers and Brothers who dwelt at, 74
    Fiqṭor, saint, 136
    Gäbrä Krəstos, 157
    Gäbrä Mänfäs Qəddus, 57, 64, 125, 177, 187, 194, 208, 261
    George, saint, 21, 22, 65, 152
    John of the East, 12
    John the Baptist, 12
    Kiros, *abba*, 193, 200
    Lalibäla, 258
    Mäbʿa Ṣəyon, *abunä*, 153
    Mark the Evangelist, 152
    Märqorewos, 148
    Näʾakkwəto Läʾab, 14
    Nob, *abba*, 54
    Tadewos, *abunä*, 175
    Täklä Haymanot, 133, 152, 158, 175, 254
    Tärbu, *abunä*, 14, 104
    Zärʾa Buruk, *abunä*, 142
Admonition, 147, 156
    for the Priest, 180

Alexander, Life of, 132
Alphabet, Gəʿəz, 213
Anaphora of
    318 Orthodox Fathers, 163, 201
    Apostles, 201, 260
    Athanasius the Apostolic, 201
    Dioscorus, 201, 260
    Epiphanius, 201
    Gregory, brother of Basil, 201
    Gregory, the second, 201
    Jacob of Serugh, 163, 201
    John Chrysostom, 201
    John Son of Thunder, 201
    Our Lady Mary, 8, 15, 21, 22, 26, 44, 46, 60, 108, 109, 113, 126, 129, 146, 155, 157, 160, 162, 163, 174, 181, 185, 197, 201, 206, 212, 214, 217, 220, 225, 260
    Our Lord, 21, 104, 123, 173, 201
    When the Anaphora is to be read, 217
Angels Praise Her, 1, 2, 8, 15, 16, 26, 37, 60, 108, 123, 151, 157, 162, 179, 184, 206, 208, 211, 217, 226, 255, 259
Antiphonary
    Fast of Lent, 14, 16, 24, 29, 38, 68, 121, 181, 182, 199
    abbreviated, 14
    excerpts, 29
    Rules of Chanting, 26

Antiphonary (cont.)
    Whole Year, 50, 115, 118, 149, 154, 202, 222, 225
        abbreviated, 74, 99, 149, 150, 176, 227
        excerpts, 202
        introduction, 115
Apostles, List of the Twelve, 228
Arero People, History, 111
Aslət, book of, 141
Asmat Prayers, 14, 16, 17, 21, 27, 28, 29, 30, 31, 32, 33, 34, 35, 36, 38, 39, 40, 41, 42, 43, 44, 45, 46, 47, 50, 51, 55, 56, 58, 59, 60, 65, 66, 67, 68, 71, 72, 73, 74, 75, 76, 77, 78, 79, 80, 81, 82, 83, 84, 85, 86, 87, 88, 89, 90, 91, 92, 93, 94, 95, 96, 97, 98, 99, 101, 106, 107, 108, 109, 117, 119, 122, 126, 128, 141, 142, 143, 146, 147, 150, 156, 162, 163, 171, 172, 173, 174, 175, 179, 181, 182, 186, 188, 189, 190, 191, 192, 198, 200, 206, 207, 210, 212, 214, 215, 216, 217, 218, 222, 226, 228, 229, 230, 231, 232, 233, 234, 235, 236, 237, 238, 239, 240, 241, 242, 243, 244, 245, 246, 247, 248, 249, 250, 251, 252, 253, 254, 256, 259, 260, 261
    after birth of a child, 210
    against
        Bandit, 192
        Charm, 126, 128, 171, 181
        demons, 28, 206
        Disease, 214
        Enemies of the soul and the flesh, 253
        Enemy, 128, 172, 175, 212
        Epilepsy and Legewon, 28
        Epilepsy, Legewon, and the Evil Eye, 28
        Evil Eye, 27, 171, 207, 210, 215, 217, 228
        Fire, 175
        Hail and Lightning, 175
        Headache, 210
        Locust, 175
        medicine man, 141
        Miscarriage, 210
        sharp pain, 200
        Snake, 207, 210, 222
        Thief, 175, 186
    for
        Angels, 214
        Appointment, 172
        binding demons, 27, 259
        drowning demons, 28
        Help in learning, 171, 198, 212
        Love, 172
        Michael, 214
        Protection, 210
        protection of the shinbone, 28
        Respect, 171, 172
        Self Protection, 172
        Stomach pain, 188
        Wealth, 172
    Future Telling, 74
    I Beseech You Lest I die Early, 260
    Jesus and the Disciples at the Sea of Tiberias, 215, 217
    of
        Angels, 122
        Michael, 28, 119, 214, 259
        Thomas the Apostle, 50
        Three Children, 163, 260
    Vanquisher of the Enemy, 226
Asosa, History, Geography, and Culture, 36

Bandlet of Righteousness, 29, 109, 141, 153, 154, 155, 219, 259
Baptism
    Book of Christening, 9, 12, 50, 54
    Book of the Jar, 112, 115
    Discourse, in Amharic, 14, 36
Beauty of Creation, 8, 10, 57, 105, 141, 157, 173, 254
    excerpt, 173
Beni Sangul, History, Geography, and Culture, 36

Bible
  1–4 Kings, 34, 114
    commentary, 114
  Acts of the Apostles, 34, 161
  Asmara Gəʿəz New Testament, 253
  Baruch, 103, 138
  Catholic Epistles, 34, 114, 163, 199, 258
    commentary, 2
  Chronicles, 134
  Daniel, 64, 134
    additions, 64
    commentary, 156
    Susanna, 64
  Ecclesiastes, 131, 134
  Ecclesiasticus, 114
  Epistles, 163
  Ezekiel, 103, 134
    commentary, 219
  Ezra, 139, 194
  Ezra, Second, 194
  First Corinthians 15
    excerpts, 221
  First Thessalonians 4, 221
  Genesis, 133, 138
    commentary, 20
  Gospel of John, 8, 12, 23, 106, 108, 109, 111, 112, 125, 126, 157, 161, 172, 178, 187, 188, 197, 207, 209, 210, 211, 212, 218, 226, 258
    excerpt, 207
    fragment, 64
  Gospel of Mark, 113, 178, 200
  Gospel of Matthew, 139
    excerpt, 220
    introduction, 119
  Gospels, 44, 54, 68, 125, 143, 168, 180, 181, 185
    Benefit of reading the Gospels, 188, 195
    excerpt, 208
    introduction, 143, 180
    Reward for reading the Gospel and Psalter regularly, 210
  Haylä Səllase Bible, 20
    New Testament, 134
  Hebrews, 137
  Isaiah, 138
    commentary, 113
    excerpts, 103
    in Tigrinya, 253
  Jeremiah, 103, 138
  Job, 134
  Joshua, 138
  Judith, 139
  Lamentations, 103
  List of the books, 228
  Maccabees, 103, 114, 134, 201
  Maccabees, First, 103, 114
  Maccabees, Second, 103, 114
  Maccabees, Third, 103, 114
  Minor Prophets, 22, 134
  New Testament, printed, 134, 218
  Octateuch, 46, 133, 175
    commentary, 46, 113
  Pauline Epistles, 34, 114, 133, 195, 198, 258
    commentary, 2, 133
  Proverbs, 131, 134, 156
  Psalms, 138
    1–72, 208
    1–43, 207
    1–2, 216, 226
    8, 137
    118–120, 117
  Revelation, 15, 34, 114, 146, 163, 172, 187
    commentary, 2
  Sirach, 114, 138, 141
    commentary, 153
    printed, 218
  Solomonic Books, printed, 218
  Song of Songs, 131, 138, 200
    fragment, 137
  Ten Commandments, 228
  Tobit, 139
  Wisdom of Solomon, 131, 134
Biblical Canticles
  Commentary, 218
Biography of
  Alula, *ras*, 55
  Arʾaya, *ras*, 117
  ʾƎnbaqom, *aläqa*, 136
  Ǝśate Täkätaläw, *nägadras*, 148
  Gugsa Wäle, *ras*, 116, 120

Biography of (cont.)
   Mogäs Däräso, *märigeta qes*, 103
   Täsämä, *aläqa*, 137
   Täšomä Šänquṭ, *däǧǧazmač*, 120
   Wäldä Mika'el, *ras*, 137
Borana People, History, 111

Calendar
   Conception, Birth, and Baptism of Jesus, 226
   Days the Heavens are Open to Receive Prayer, 155
   Feast Days of the Apostles, Evangelists, and Saint Mary, 210
   Feast Days of the Church Year, 106, 146
   Holy Days of Saints and Feasts, 226
   Measurement of shadows for the telling of time, 188, 220
Canticle of Mary, 100
Canticle of the Flower, 9, 113, 124, 162, 174, 183, 185, 186, 197, 198, 220
Catechism, 9, 111, 128
   Catholic Church, 101
   Five Pillars, 178, 179, 207
   Orthodox Faith, 141
   Trinity, 174
Catholic Church
   Catechism, 101
   History in Ethiopia, 135
   Prayer book, 118
Chants, 177
   Arba'ət, 74
   Aryam, 74, 155
   'Əzəl, 146
   Greek Orthodox Church for the feast days of Ḥaylä Śəllase, 103
   Mästägabə', 74
   Mäwaśə'ət, 123, 125, 156, 198
   Mäzmur, 13
   Mə'raf, 13
   Resurrection of the Dead, 104
   Śäläst, 74
   School, 12, 14, 125, 147, 198
   Zəmmare, 16, 198
   Ziq, 40, 106, 110, 124, 153, 156, 207, 210, 259
Christening, Book of, 9, 12, 50, 54
Chronicle of
   1868–1875, 116
   'Amdä Ṣəyon, 69
   Ethiopian rulers up to Ḥaylä Śəllase, 147
   Mənilək II, 101
   Täklä Giyorgis and Yoḥannəs IV, 140
   Tewodros II, 22, 51, 99
   Yoḥannes I, 57
Church among Gentiles, 133
Church, Order of, 180
Code of Kings, 34, 46, 56, 124, 218
   commentary, 56, 153
Commemoration of Gäbrä Mänfäs Qəddus, 64
Commemoration of the Savior of the World, 101
Commentary, Gə'əz
   Anaphora, 114
   Biblical Canticles, 218
   Chronicles, 1–2, 114
   Church Order, 217
   Code of Kings, 56, 153
   Daily Prayer, 107, 108, 143, 154
   Daniel, 156
   Ecclesiasticus, 114
   Enoch, 113
   Ezekiel, 144, 219
   Ezra, 114
   Gospel, Six Words of the Gospel, 107, 108
   Gospel of Matthew, 131
   Horologium, 108
   Introductory Rite to the Miracles of Mary, 99, 179
   Isaiah, 114
   Jeremiah, 114
   Jubilees, 113, 114
   Kings, 1–3, 114
   Kings, 1–4, 114
   Law of Kings, 139
   Maccabees, 1–3, 114
   Mar Yeshaq, 158
   Mystagogia, 182, 217
   New Testament, 14

Index of Major Works in the Codices 319

Octateuch, 46, 113, 175
Prayer of the Covenant, 182
Sirach, 153
Six Words of the Gospel, 107, 108
Symbols, 22
Ten Commandments, 107, 108
Commentary, Amharic
   Anaphora of Our Lady Mary by Cyriacus, 60
   Catholic Epistles, 2
   Covenant of the Morning, 51
   Ezekiel, 144, 219
   Genesis, 20
   Introductory Rite to the Miracles of Mary, 22, 52, 179
   Law of Kings, 102
   Mar Yeshaq, 1
   Opening Prayer, 104
   Our Father, 22, 174, 179, 254
   Pauline Epistles, 2, 133
   Praises of Mary, 60
   Psalter, 45
   Revelation, 2
Computus
   Baḥärä Ḥasab, 12, 52, 57, 114, 121, 153, 155, 228
   Märḥä ʾəwwer, 22
   treatise, 254
   Who Is the Author?, 131
Confession, book of, 115, 122, 154
Constitution of Imperial Government, 139
Covenant of Gäbrä Mänfäs Qəddus, 23
Creation and Its Way, 121

Creed
   Constantinople, 206
   Nicaean, 206, 216
Cycle of Kings, 20, 47, 119, 142, 150, 180, 181, 193

Dead, Book of the, 14
Desta, Appreciation of *fitawrari*, 163
Dictionary 27, 46, 57, 102, 104, 105, 140
   Amharic-English, 46
   Amharic-Oromiffa, 73
   English-Afar, 44
   Ethiopic-Latin, 57
   Gəʿəz, 102, 140

Gəʿəz Glossary, 7, 21, 39, 55, 119
Gəʿəz-Amharic Vocabulary List of Verbs, 178
Gidole, 105
Gondär Dialect, 52
Gurage-English, 27
Harari, 27
Konso, 104
Sidamo-English, 27
Word Lists, 47
Didascalia, 154
Disciples, book of, 24, 56, 106, 127, 150, 161, 210
Discourses
   Baptism, in Amharic, 14
   Christian Life, 36
   Creation of Nature, in Amharic, 14
   Faith and Commandments, 14
   Reading with attention, in Amharic, 14
Dolors, Five, 69
Drawings, book of, 28

Education, Traditional Church, 102
Enoch, 56, 98, 138
   commentary, 113
Extreme Unction, book of, 161

Faith of the Fathers, 34, 132, 136, 176, 193
Faith, book of, 259
Feast days
   Apostles, Evangelists, and Saint Mary, 210
   Church Year, 106
   Holy Days of Saints and Feasts, 226
   Importance of celebrating the feasts of Saint Michael, 7
   Moveable Feasts, 173, 217
   Five Pillars of Mystery, 8, 45, 57, 105, 119, 122, 141, 149, 157, 174, 177, 179
   Catechism, 178, 179, 207
Fountain of Blood, 149
Funeral Ritual, 10, 11, 108, 117, 166, 169, 176, 183, 193, 202, 207, 222, 227
   abbreviated, 57
Furqan, 150

Gäbrä Mäsqäl, The Slave, 27
Galla, History, 69, 99, 116, 130, 180
Gate of Belief, 99
Gate of Light, 8, 15, 16, 17, 100, 112, 143,
    157, 177, 215, 220, 260
Gate of Penance, 163
Genealogy
    Ethiopian Emperors, Amharic, 157
    Ethiopian Kings from Queen of
        Sheba to Emperor
        Dəlnaʿod, 132
    Ethiopian Monasticism, 106
    Ethiopian rulers through Iyasu II,
        148
    Fathers, 157
    Täklä Haymanot, 133
Glory of Kings, 99, 153
God of the Luminaries, 123, 127, 146,
    163, 173, 214, 223
God Reigns, 100, 105, 117, 158, 182,
    199, 226
Golgotha, 121, 126, 155, 159, 160, 162,
    167, 173, 174, 182, 207,
    213, 214, 227, 257
Good Works, book of, 180
Government Scriptorium
    Business of the Scriptorium, 133
    Codex made in, 1, 44, 107, 119, 131,
        139, 152, 154, 176, 187,
        219, 226, 255, 258, 260,
        261
    Establishment of the Scriptorium,
        147
    Letters to Imperial Special Treasury,
        133
    Log Book
        Books assigned to scribes, 133
        Parchment and ink, 134
        Parchment and Materials
            Needed, 132
        Parchment Income and
            Expense, 131
        Parchment Projects, 132
        Parchment Receipt Book, 131
        Transfer of skins from the
            palace butcher to the
            Scriptorium, 132

Grammar
    A critical review of M. Chaîne,
        Grammaire éthiopienne,
        103
    Ethiopian Languages, 47
    Gəʿəz, 7, 8, 14, 39, 41, 51, 55, 99,
        102, 117, 119, 122, 127,
        136, 140, 141, 144, 162,
        178, 197, 217, 254, 255
        from Gonj, 178
        in French, 255
    Language Teaching and Curricula in
        Traditional Education of
        the Ethiopian Orthodox
        Church, 102
Greeting to
    Afnin, 64, 65
    Christian Sabbath, 57
    Church, 57, 106
    Ǝbäyä Dəngəl, 65
    Ǝḫətä Krəstos, 65
    Gäbrä Mänfäs Qəddus, 163
    Gabriel, 64
    George, 105, 220
    Guardian Angel, 57, 74
    Michael, 106
    Phanuel, 64
    Raphael, 64
    Saints, 110, 220
    Sachiel, 64
    Savior of the World, 110
    Stephen, 191
    Your Acts, 126

Ḥaräg tərgwame, 102
Harp of Praise, 2, 9, 24, 47, 50, 114, 121,
    124, 149, 152, 185, 195,
    196, 200, 201, 210, 211
Ḥawi, 138, 142, 154
Ḥaylä Śəllase, emperor
    Accomplishments of the Emperor
        for the Ethiopian
        Orthodox Church, 132
Healing, Spiritual, 113, 126, 180
Hikar, book of, 142
History, 130
    Alula, *ras*, 55
    Arero and Borana People, 111

Index of Major Works in the Codices   321

Baffana, 148
Dessie, 100
Elyas, *abba*, 140
Emperors Täklä Giyorgis and
  Yoḥannəs IV, 116
Ethiopia, 9, 46, 99, 100, 153
Ethiopia, in Tigrinya, 51
Ethiopian Kings, 158, 180
Order of the Palace, 219
Exile, 120
Ezekiel, 99
Galla, 99, 116, 130, 180
Galla, Amharic, 69
Goǧǧam, 46
Iyasu I, 100
King Susənyos to King Mənilək II,
  136
Kings, 50, 53, 153, 158
Kings of Ethiopia, 157
Kings of Gamo, 126
Lasta Kings, 47
Mənilək I to Mənilək II, 153
Monasticism, 29
Näsibu Zäʾamanuʾel, *däǧǧazmač*, 39
Oromo, 29, 34, 55
Oromo People, 130
Queen of the East, 204
Religious Controversies in Ethiopia,
  99
Roman Catholic Church in Ethiopia,
  135
Saint Stephen and all his Disciples, 74
Shewa, 153
Shoan Dynasty, 111
Täklä Haymanot, 99, 204
Wəqaw, *däǧǧazmač abba*, 57
Yoḥannəs IV, 51
History, Geography, and Culture of the
  Region of Asosa Beni
  Sangul, 36
Homiliary in Honor of
  Elijah, 10
  Gabriel, 11, 186
  George, 10
  Michael, 10, 11, 13, 52, 114, 122,
    124, 129, 155, 162, 174,
    178, 182, 184, 187, 193,
    195, 202, 203, 219, 220,
    222, 253, 258
  Sabbath of the Church, 112, 116,
    157
  Savior of the World, 122, 142, 154,
    180, 213
  Zion, 255
Homilies
  Basil, 54
  Ephrem, 139
  Ephrem on Abraham and Sarah, 54
  Evagrius of Pontes, 25
  Jacob of Serugh, 64
    How Abraham offered his son,
      139
  Lifegiver, 69, 105, 164, 194, 254
  Religious Education and Guidance,
    9
  Religious Education and Guidance,
    in Amharic, 10
  Zärʾa Yaʿəqob, emperor, 105
  Zechariah, life of, 148
Horologium
  commentary, 108
  excerpts, 108
  For the Day, 16, 106, 180, 221
  For the Night, 10, 16, 22, 65, 106,
    110, 112, 143, 206, 209,
    254, 255
  excerpts, 17, 29, 155
Host, Instructions for Blessing and
  Pointing, 226
Human Anatomy, Book of, 108
Hymn, 150
  from
    Horologium, 100
    Miracles of Jesus, 254
    Miracles of Mary, 143, 217, 254
    Praise of the Beloved, 206
  Liturgical, Yared, 173
  Məqnay, 155
  Səbḥatä fəqur, 159
  to
    Apostles, 17
    Claudius, 16
    Covenant of Mercy, 16
    Ezekiel, 99
    Gäbrä Mänfäs Qəddus, 187

322 *Index of Major Works in the Codices*

Hymn, to (cont.)
    Gälawdewos, 16
    George, 105
        Come, come, come, George, 257
        Finisher of the Acts, 143
        I take Refuge with Thee, 182
        O, who is quick for help, 119, 174, 181
    God
        God of the Ancient Time, 8
        O, Father, Help us for the Sake of Jesus, 206
    Jesus, 69, 217
        For the sake of your Trinity, 212
        O, for the sake of us, 61
        You are the River of Love, the King of Glory, 217
    Mary, 9, 106, 111
        All hosts of heaven glorify you, 213
        For She is Glorious, 8
        Glorified, Rainbow of Noah, 211
        Hail Mary, 211
        I Praise Thy Grace, 112, 208
        I prostrate before you, 210
        I Worship Thee, 8, 112
        In heaven and on earth, 100, 195, 221, 223
        Passover for Adam, 207
        Praise of the Harp, 204
        Rejoice, Mary, Virgin in mind and body, 16
        with the saints, 9
        Your Lamentation, 107, 108
    Savior of the World, Host of His Angels, 200
    Sebastian, Greeting to your hands which were bound behind your back, 215
    Trinity, 143, 204
        I Worship, 50, 204

Icons, book of, 2
Image of
    Abib, 12
    Adome, 257
    Anne, Mother of Mary, 16, 119
    Apostles, 9
    Arägawi, 112, 180
    Arsema of Armenia, 152
    Assumption, 2, 16, 112, 129, 143
    Bula, 12
    Christian Sabbath, 100, 117, 131, 257
    Claudius, 112
    Collection, 11, 31, 176, 182, 183, 199
    Covenant of Mercy, 2, 50, 162, 195
    Creatures, Four, 24
    Cross, 105
    David, 189
    Edom, 130, 162, 208, 257
    Elijah, 10, 113
    Eucharist, 155
    Ewosṭatewos, 220
    Gäbrä Krəstos, 21, 157, 161
    Gäbrä Mänfäs Qəddus, 44, 51, 57, 64, 131, 162, 174, 179, 204, 214, 261
    Gabriel, 2, 13, 44, 117, 143, 154, 160, 162, 173, 182, 186, 195, 204, 210, 212, 214, 259
    Gälawdewos, 112
    Gate of Light, 112, 157
    George, 2, 7, 12, 14, 28, 44, 69, 105, 110, 112, 119, 126, 128, 144, 159, 162, 174, 179, 188, 204, 216, 259
    George zä-Säleda Mogäs, 188
    God, 257
    Guardian Angel, 74, 104, 122, 154
    Ḥaylä Səllase, 27
    Icon, 16, 61, 144, 163, 184, 191, 209
    Jesus, 2, 12, 44, 110, 112, 117, 123, 129, 131, 144, 160, 162, 173, 177, 201, 212, 215, 217, 228, 258
    John, 149, 154
    John Son of Thunder, 145
    John the Baptist, 12, 61, 162, 214, 220, 256, 259
    Kiros, *abba*, 200
    Lalibäla, 122
    Mary, 12, 44, 65, 100, 110, 112, 117, 123, 129, 160, 162, 173, 177, 195, 201, 204, 214, 217, 258

Mary Fasika, 163
Mary of Edom, 130, 162, 208, 257
Mary of Zion, 119, 257
Mary's Entrance in the Temple, 224
Mənilək II, 161
Michael, 2, 10, 14, 16, 22, 23, 44, 50,
    117, 123, 128, 143, 162,
    173, 182, 195, 204, 210,
    212, 254, 259
Michael and Gabriel, 119
Näʾakkwəto Läʾab, 122
Paraclete, 126
Passion of the Cross, 126, 199, 217,
    225, 254
Passion Week, 155, 162
Paul, 21
Peter, 21
Peter, Patriarch, 29
Phanuel, 28, 44, 64, 100, 259
Praises of Mary, 8, 16, 112, 146, 157,
    162, 197, 198, 201, 204,
    206, 212, 215, 216, 218,
    222, 227, 228
Raguel, 53, 145, 148, 190, 226
Raphael, 24, 44, 127, 131, 177
Samuʾel, *abba*, 154
Saṭnaʾel, 56
Savior of the World, 105, 126, 144,
    162, 185, 188, 214, 217,
    225, 257, 258, 259
Täklä Haymanot, 14, 24, 44, 106,
    144, 156, 174, 254, 257
Tewodros, 149
Trinity, 14, 28, 73, 179, 215, 218,
    228, 258, 259, 260
Victory of Obedience, 119
Walatta Giyorgis, 27
Yəmrəḥannä Krəstos, 74, 122
Zä-Mikaʾel, 112, 180
Zärʾa Buruk, *abunä*, 186
Zärʾa Yaʿəqob, Amharic, 180
Zechariah, 148
Zena Marqos, 143
Imperial Government Constitution, 139

Inventory
    Addis Ababa Churches, 61
    Aksum, 63, 64
    Bägemdər and Səmen Provinces, 117

Däbrä Dima, 38
Däbrä Marqos, 38
Däbrä Marqos, Bəčäna Giyorgis,
    Yäräz Mikaʾel, and Yätäb
    Gäbrä Mänfäs Qəddus,
    38
Däbrä Ṣəmmuna, 38
Däbrä Warq, 38
Dima Giyorgis, 38
Manuscripts of the Institute of
    Ethiopian Studies, 130
Moret District, 52
Museum of the University of Zurich,
    54
Saint Stephen dei Mori, Roma, 63
Wolaita Sodo Museum, 55
Wollamo Sodu Regional Museum,
    111
Isaac of Nineveh, 1, 160, 253

Japanese Religion and Culture, 153
Jesus
    At the Cross of Jesus Christ, 108
    Conception, Birth, and Baptism, 226
    Explanations of, 104
    Number of the Sufferings of Christ,
    104
Jokes by Täkle of Wašära, 103
Journey to Heaven, 12
Jubilees, 56, 64, 175
    commentary, 113, 114

Quran, Amharic translation, 132, 141
Kəbrä Nägäśt, 99

Lament of the Virgin, 112, 155, 162,
    174, 186, 220, 221, 223
Law of Kings, 68, 139, 255
    commentary, 102, 139
Lectionary for, 100
    Ecclesiastical Feasts and Festivals,
    141
    Passion Week, 128, 161, 165, 196,
    202
    Readings from the Gospels, 163
    Weeks after Pentecost, 134
Lessons on Christian Religion, 105

Letters
  between Metropolitan Matewos and
      abba Andreas, 115
  Debates on Faith, 101
  Ḥaylä Maryam Lämma, *däǧǧazmač*,
      68
  Imperial Special Treasury
      from Government
      Scriptorium, 133
  Ministry of Pen to the Ministry of
      Treasury, 138
  Yoḥannǝs IV, 115, 116
Life and Mercy, book of, 204
Light, book of, 143
Litany, 69, 104, 106, 225, 227
Literature
  Gǝʿǝz Books, list of, 130
  Gǝʿǝz Literature, 118
Liturgical Blessings, Order of, 254

Mar Yeshaq, 1, 160, 253
  commentary, 158
Martyrdom of George, 21
Mary, Story of, 174
Medical
  Book of Flora, 172
  Book of Medicine, 56, 119, 171, 173,
      218
  Herb Treatments, 32
  Medicinal instruction, 215
  Plants that are medicine, 103
  Prescriptions and formulae, 45
  Remedies against Sorcery, 32
  Traditional Medicine, 159
Michael, mission of, 220
Miracles of
  Aragawi, 106
  Ewosṭatewos, 61
  Gäbrä Mänfäs Qǝddus, 44, 57, 61,
      64, 106, 125, 177, 187,
      194, 208, 261
  Gabriel, 13
  George, 10, 11, 12, 21, 44, 61, 65,
      106, 129, 152
  Jesus, 11, 110, 111, 118, 140, 155,
      194, 196, 197, 258
    hymn, 254
  John of the East, 12

Mark the Evangelist, 152
Mary, 10, 11, 14, 22, 44, 47, 52, 61,
    104, 105, 106, 108, 110,
    111, 118, 121, 127, 158,
    174, 184, 196, 197, 199,
    213, 256
  commentary, 22, 52, 99, 179
  concluding hymns, 143, 217, 254
  excerpts, 217
  introduction, 100, 108, 221, 227
Michael, 13, 44, 61, 155, 184
Näʾakkwǝto Läʾab, 14
Phanuel, 44
Qäwǝsṭos, 61
Raphael, 24
Samuʾel, *abba*, 154
Täklä Haymanot, 44, 61, 175, 254
Trinity, 106, 204
Zärʾa Buruk, *abunä*, 186
Missal, 15, 23, 39, 45, 109, 110, 111, 124,
    176, 181, 186, 194, 195,
    206, 211, 213, 225, 255,
    256, 257
  excerpt, 208
Mister Insatiable and Mister Vanity, 121
Monastic Orders
  Advice and Admonition, 156
  Monastic Life, 180
  Monastic Orders of Pachomius, 25
  Monastic Rules and Conduct, 68
  Order of Monastic Life, 106, 180
Monasticism
  Genealogy, 106
  History, 29
Music
  Folk Songs, in Amharic, 39
  Songs by Beggars about riches, 64
Mystagogia, 72, 104, 114, 123, 128, 146,
    162, 173, 179, 207, 214,
    223, 227, 257, 259
  Catechesis, 14
  commentary, 182, 217
  printed, 151
Mystery of
  Communion, 200
  Incarnation, 32, 52
  Sky, 99
  Trinity, 32, 155, 225

Nablis, 119
Net of Solomon, 115, 127, 128
Novel, 28

Order of the Church, 104
Order of the Church of Däbrä Marqos, Goǧǧam, 134
Orthodox Faith, 124

Paphnutius on his Visit to the Ascetics, 54
Passion of the Cross, 57, 174, 177
Pearl of Great Price, 112
Petition, 8, 143, 148, 152
Philosophers, book of, 156
Philosophy, 130, 143
    Zär'a Ya'əqob, 128
Philoxenus of Mabbug, 25
Pillars of Mystery, 8, 45, 57, 105, 119, 122, 141, 149, 157, 174, 177, 179
Pillars of Wisdom of the Old and New Testaments, 27
Poetry
    in Amharic, 28, 99, 102, 103, 111, 135, 136, 137, 157
    Culture, 137
    Praise of Mənilək II, 157
    Religious, 137
    Rhyming Composition, 103
    The King and the Crown, 56
    in Gə'əz, 103, 111, 135, 136, 138, 173
    Fənotä qəne, 12
    Heroism of *ras* Alula, 147
    Methods, 27
    Qəne, 63
    Qəne Jokes, 103
    in Gurage, 68
Portal of Light, 204
Praise, 16
Praises of
    Basəlyos, 155
    Beloved, 61, 65, 143, 162, 163, 185, 206, 212, 220, 221, 223, 259
    God, 8, 11, 74, 139, 204
    Haylä Śəllase, 155

Lord, 54
Mary, 8, 12, 14, 15, 16, 17, 20, 46, 100, 108, 112, 143, 146, 157, 181, 187, 198, 204, 215, 218, 220
    commentary, 60
    in Amharic, 108, 177
    Mənilək II, 157
Trinity, 121
Prayer, 8, 9, 14, 30, 31, 46, 47, 104, 147, 171, 172, 195
    against
        charm, 73
        demons, 27, 28
        Terror, 159
        Tongue of People, 30, 162, 172, 183, 216
    Covenant of the Morning, 14, 15, 16, 22, 104, 108, 114
        Commentary, 51
    Daily, 107, 108, 143, 154
    Day and Night, 187
    End Times, 147
    Entering the Church, 143
    for
        Haylä Śəllase, 15
        Iyo'as I, 15
        Matewos, metropolitan, 10, 15
        Mənilək II, 11
        Mornings, Evenings, and Communion, 108
        Sälama, metropolitan, 11
        Undoing Charm, 153
    For the sake of the peaceful holy things, 123, 162, 173, 183
    I beseech you by God, the Father, 154
    I Praise God, 154
    in Amharic, 8
    Intercessory Prayer of Basil Bishop of Caesarea, 107, 108
    Interpretation of the letters of the Hebrew Alphabet, 104
    Layman, 188
    Litanical, 106
    Magico-Religious, 45
    O, Lord Jesus Christ, Son of the Living God, 154

Prayer (cont.)
  of
    blatten geta Maḫtämä Śəllase Wäldä Mäsqäl, 107, 108
    Benediction, 162
    Catholic Church, 118
    Covenant, 123, 139, 151, 154, 162, 173, 185, 210, 214, 225, 227, 254
      commentary, 182
      excerpt, 194
      printed, 150
    Dəmeṭros and *abunä* Sälama for Long Life and Repentance, 156
    Dream, 171
    Elderly, 8
    Ephrem the Syrian, 104, 108
    Forgiveness of Sin, 143
    Incense, 15
    Laity, O Lord Save Me, Thou Who Saved, 8
    Maḫtämä Śəllase Wäldä Mäsqäl, *blatten geta*, 107, 108
    Mary at Bartos, 46, 143, 204
    Mary at Golgotha, 121, 126, 155, 159, 160, 162, 173, 174, 182, 207, 213, 214, 227, 257
    Moses, 155, 161, 220
    Peter, 120, 126, 144, 150, 160, 179, 183, 184, 204, 255, 260
    Repentance, 213
    Supplication for the Departed, 157
    Twelve Disciples, 260
  Passion of Christ, 183
  Rəḫuqä Mä'at, 162
  Sabbath of the Jews, 187
  Satanic, 171
  Secret names that God gave to Michael, 10
  Service Granting Diaconate Orders, 31
  Table, 108, 155, 162, 163, 185
  We Beseech You, 108, 155, 162, 163, 185
  to
    Afnin, 64
    bind demons, 64
    defeat devils, 258
    defeat the evil eye, 258
    Gabriel, 64
    God, 8
    God, in Amharic, 8
    Jesus, 154, 155
      For the sake of Your Trinity, 17, 61, 143
      Guard me, 174
      I Take Refuge, 163
      In the name of God, 214
      O My Lord, My God and My Savior, 224
      O, Who Descended, 17
    Mary, 155
      All the Hosts of Heaven Glorify You, 155
      O my Lady, Mary, Sanctify Me with Your Sanctity, 14
    Peter, 260
    Phanuel, 64
    Raguel, 64
    Raphael, 64
    Sachiel, 64
    Trinity, 21
      Blessing and Praise, 163
      composed for Ḥaylä Śəllase, 21
      I Beseech You, Father, Son, and Holy Spirit, 228
      I take refuge, 185
Precious Stones, book of, 171
Priestly Duties
  Instructions for Blessing and Pointing the Host, 226
  Instructions for Conducting the Mass, 217
Proverbs, in Amharic, 28
Psalms of Christ, 216

Psalter, 1, 7, 8, 9, 13, 16, 17, 20, 21, 24,
    26, 35, 37, 44, 52, 57, 60,
    106, 107, 110, 111, 112,
    113, 115, 116, 120, 123,
    124, 125, 127, 131, 138,
    147, 148, 149, 151, 157,
    163, 178, 183, 185, 186,
    188, 189, 192, 194, 197,
    198, 200, 201, 203, 205,
    206, 207, 208, 209, 210,
    211, 212, 213, 214, 215,
    216, 217, 219, 220, 221,
    222, 223, 224, 225, 226,
    227, 228, 254, 255, 256,
    257, 258, 259
  commentary, 45
  excerpt, 117
  fragment, 131, 208
  in Amharic, 152
  of the Virgin, 106, 116, 197, 198, 209
  published, 255
  text copied from the end, 137
Qəne, 12
Qerəllos, 122, 136, 148

Rampart of the Cross, 143, 154, 185, 198
  excerpts, 259
Records
  Alexandrian Bishops, 153
  Caliphates, 153
  Church Vestments and Gifts to the
      Priests in Axum, 134
  Colophon, 140, 143
  Ethiopian Emperors, 157
  Notes, Transactions, and Wills, 135
  Persons cured by *mämhər* Wäldä
      Tənsa'e Gəzaw, 28
  Persons healed and assisted by
      Saint Gabriel and Saint
      Michael, 54
  Persons healed by exorcism by
      mämhər Wäldä Tənsa'e
      Gəzaw, 28, 29
Responsibility of the Church towards
    Youth, 103
Rise of Mohamad Grañ, 156
Ritual, Book of the Jar, 112, 115

Scriptural readings for night hours, 107
Senodos, 68, 141
Shepherd of Hermes, 31
Shoan Dynasty History, 111
Spiritual Healing, 113, 126, 180
Stations of the Cross, 163
Stories in Amharic, 28
Sun, book of, 27
Supplication, 8, 143, 148, 152, 225, 227
Sword of Divinity, 127, 130, 163, 182,
    183, 186, 200, 228
  excerpt, 200
Sword of the Trinity, 21, 45, 143, 155,
    179, 180, 183, 185, 228,
    255, 260
  excerpt, 228
Synaxarium, 1, 147, 164, 174, 176, 196,
    202, 204, 260

Testaments of the Patriarchs, 54
Tewodros, Historical Tragedy about
    Tewodros, 118
Thanksgiving, 16
Ṭomar, 176, 258
  fragment, 226
Treasure of Faith, 100
Treatises
  Advice, book of, 51
  Defense of the teaching on the
      oneness of the nature of
      Christ, 52
  Faith of the Earlier Fathers, 101
  Learn Religion, Do Good Deeds, 36
  Mäṣḥafä estegubu', in Amharic, 10
  on
      Computus, 52, 254
      Prayer Beads, 147
      Trinity, 122, 184, 204
      Trinity and Incarnation, 114
      Unctionist Controversy, 219
Treatises (cont.)
  Revive Faith by Embarrassing
      Catholicism, 50
  Theological, 60
  What Should Christians Do During
      the Mass, 64
Treaty of 1843, 144

Trinity
    On the, 108
    Story of, 21
Tuladan, 142, 154, 173, 174

Unction, book of, 122

Victory of Obedience, 119
Vision of
    Ləbnä Dəngəl, 99
    Mary, 141, 158, 160, 163, 174, 179, 204, 254, 257
        in Amharic, 12
    Sinoda, 14

Wax and Gold, 28
Window on Heaven, 147
Wisest of the Wise, 14, 144, 200, 207, 260
    excerpt, 224
Writings of ʿAlämayyähu Mogäs, 102

Zodiak, Path of, 147

Index of Miniatures

Aaron, 49
Abali, equestrian saint, 48
Abib, *abba*, 48, 192
    Martyrdom, 17
Abraham, 49, 54, 151, 192
    and Sarah, 146
Abrəham, *abunä*, 107
Abunafer, 54
Adam and Eve
    Driven from Eden, 164
    Tempted by the Serpent, 164
Akädäma, 5
Akalä Wäld, *mämhər*, 1
Alexander, archbishop, 49
Alexis, 49
Amära, *däbtära*, 221
Ammonius, 49
Andrew, Martyrdom, 19
Angel, 2, 4, 5, 6, 10, 13, 25, 26, 34, 41, 50, 54, 56, 107, 109, 119, 128, 140, 141, 143, 151, 157, 159, 160, 164, 166, 167, 168, 169, 170, 171, 175, 176, 177, 179, 187, 189, 190, 191, 192, 194, 199, 201, 202, 203, 205, 206, 218, 219, 220, 253, 257
    crude drawing, 17, 20, 23, 24, 34, 41, 50, 107, 109, 110, 114, 117, 123, 124, 157, 183, 199, 202, 214, 215, 225, 226, 228, 257, 259, 260
    on magic scroll, 29, 30, 31, 32, 33, 34, 35, 36, 38, 40, 41, 42, 43, 44, 47, 58, 59, 60, 65, 66, 67, 71, 72, 73, 75, 77, 78, 79, 80, 81, 82, 83, 84, 85, 86, 88, 89, 90, 91, 92, 93, 94, 95, 96, 97, 98, 99, 101, 110, 112, 113, 114, 117, 123, 124, 125, 129, 148, 150, 152, 181, 182, 183, 185, 229, 230, 231, 232, 233, 234, 235, 236, 237, 238, 239, 240, 241, 242, 243, 244, 245, 246, 247, 248, 249, 250, 251, 252, 253, 254, 261
    playing with children, 5
    protecting a sheep, 5
    reaching down to a king, 19
    rescuing Philip, 25
    riding a horse, 6, 54
    saving a lion, 6
    s. also, Gabriel, Michael, Phanuel, Raguel, Raphael
Animal, 164
Bat, 145
Cat, 4
Crow, 3
    crude drawing, 189, 225
Dog, 3, 7, 166, 168
    crude drawing, 189
Dove, 197
Eagle, 4

Index of Miniatures

Animal (cont.)
    Elephant, 5
    Fish, 5
    Fox, 3, 5, 6
    Frog, 4, 53
    Goat, 5
    Groundhogs, 5
    Horse, 3, 4, 6, 20, 123, 205
        crude drawing, 21, 34, 126, 196, 225
    Hyena, 6
    Lamb, 145
    Leopard, 5, 145
    Lion, 4, 5, 6, 21, 41, 43, 54, 109, 145, 191, 238, 244
    Monkey, 6, 7
    Mouse, 3
    Ox, 5
    Pig, 5
    Rooster, 160
    Scorpion, 6
    Serpent, 3
    Sheep, 5, 6
    Snake, 4, 5, 6, 35, 53, 88, 145, 189, 190, 191
    Turtle, 4, 5
    Whale, 5
    Winged Creature, 86
Anne, 2, 168, 197
Anthony, 17
Antiochus, 201
Apostles, 18, 44, 48, 49, 110
Aragawi, *abunä*, 176
Arius, 49
Ark of the Covenant, 1
Aron, *abba*, 49
Arsenius, 49
Awsabyos, equestrian saint, 48

Bahəran, 52, 129
Balance, 153
Barlaam, *abunä*, 200
Bartholomew
    Martyrdom, 20
Beer, 179
Behnam, equestrian saint, 48
Bird, 3, 5, 7, 73, 82, 198, 214
    caught in snare, 2
    crude drawing, 113, 188, 209
    four-headed, 53, 145, 191
Birutawit, 70
Blind man, 3
Bogalä Dästa, 180
Box, 190, 191
Building, 6
Bula, *abba*, 17

Canon Tables, 112
Children, 4, 5, 6, 7
Church, 39, 164, 176, 180
    crude drawing, 24, 149, 163, 175, 222
Church Fathers, 49
Claudius, equestrian saint, 160
Constantine, emperor, 49
Council of Nicaea, 218
Covenant of Mercy, 49
Cross, 7, 10, 11, 13, 15, 39, 58, 104, 107, 109, 111, 115, 144, 148, 150, 152, 154, 158, 182, 184, 187, 189, 196, 200, 206, 207, 208, 210, 211, 219, 220, 221, 223, 254, 255, 256, 257, 259
    crude drawing, 11, 20, 109, 112, 114, 121, 124, 148, 158, 184, 188, 199, 200, 206, 207, 208, 209, 210, 211, 213, 215, 217, 219, 221, 222, 223, 226, 254, 255, 256
    on magic scroll, 29, 30, 31, 32, 33, 34, 35, 36, 40, 41, 42, 43, 44, 46, 59, 65, 66, 67, 74, 75, 76, 77, 78, 79, 80, 81, 82, 83, 84, 85, 86, 87, 88, 89, 91, 92, 93, 94, 95, 96, 97, 98, 99, 101, 107, 109, 229, 230, 231, 232, 234, 235, 237, 238, 240, 241, 242, 243, 244, 245, 246, 247, 248, 249, 250, 252, 253, 256, 257, 261
Crude drawing, 187, 193, 257
    face, 9, 15, 35, 68, 100, 107, 109, 111, 113, 117, 118, 120, 121, 124, 138, 148, 188, 194, 198, 199, 200, 205, 209, 214, 215, 219, 223, 225, 226, 227, 228, 258

Index of Miniatures 331

figure, 2, 9, 17, 20, 21, 24, 30, 34, 35, 45, 68, 73, 74, 100, 101, 107, 111, 113, 114, 118, 120, 121, 122, 123, 124, 126, 127, 138, 141, 142, 148, 152, 157, 158, 175, 178, 188, 194, 196, 198, 199, 200, 205, 208, 209, 211, 214, 215, 219, 223, 225, 226, 227, 228, 258, 260
   geometric design, 234, 240
   talismanic symbol, 117, 188
   wheel, 255
Crucifixion, 2, 17, 19, 26, 37, 48, 62, 71, 101, 107, 121, 126, 145, 146, 159, 161, 165, 166, 167, 169, 170, 181, 184, 188, 192, 196, 197, 202, 203, 211, 212, 222, 227, 254, 256
   crude drawing, 120, 189, 210, 216
Cup of Life, 37
Cyricus, 49

Däbrä Dammo, 176
Däbrä Ṣəyon, 152
Dämä Krəstos, 186
Daniel, 49
David, 2, 21, 26, 37, 49, 52, 60, 123, 146, 163, 185, 186, 192, 201, 205
   and Goliath, 37
   crude drawing, 205, 216
   birth of Christ revealed, 37
Demon, 62, 190, 195, 212
   on magic scroll, 59, 66, 230, 238, 245, 250
Devil, 5, 6, 52, 129, 175, 179, 193, 195
   arguing with a man, 203
   bound, 37
   capturing men in a cage of thorns, 2
   mating with a hyena, 5
   sitting on a man, 6
   slain by sheep with cross, 5
   attempting to burn a church, 4
Dignitary, 26

Donor Portrait, 25, 37, 71, 187, 254
   before Gäbrä Mänfäs Qəddus, 179
   before Jesus, 62
   before Mark, 152
   before Mary, 26, 37, 184, 192
   before Michael, 49, 185, 195, 254
   before Raphael, 127
   before Saint George, 48
   before Trinity, 48, 256
   Ḥaylä Mäläkot, 11
   Wäldä Mädḫan, 11

Elder, 2
Elijah, 146
   Being fed by the raven, 16
   Causing rain, 176
Ǝnbaqom, 49
Equestrian saint, 8, 18, 50, 69, 141, 151, 156, 185, 193, 197, 200
   Abali, 48
   Awsabyos, 48
   Behnam, 48
   crude drawing, 17, 74, 116, 147, 154, 205, 209, 211, 256
   Fasiladas, 48
   Filatäwos, 48
   Fiqṭor, 48
   Gälawdewos, 48
   Mercury, 48
   Nääkweto Lääb, 25
   on magic scroll, 31, 46, 97, 241
   Sebastian, 48
   Tewodros, 48
   Tewodros Masəriqawi, 48
   Yosṭos, 48
   s. also, George
Ǝstifanos, 192
Ethiopia stretches out her hand to God, 37
Eusebius, 192
Ewosṭatewos, *abunä*, 17, 25, 48, 192
   Travelling to Armenia, 19, 63
Exodus
   Children of Israel Rejoice, 37
   Destruction of the Egyptian Army in the Red Sea, 37
Eyes, 33, 40, 59, 67, 96, 230, 237, 242, 249
Ezra, 146

Index of Miniatures

Face 45, 159, 190
    on magic scroll, 109, 111, 148, 242
    s. also, Crude drawing
Farmer, 7
Fasiladas, equestrian saint, 48
Father, 4
Figure
    on magic scroll, 30, 31, 32, 33, 40, 48, 52, 77, 82, 87, 110, 190, 203, 208, 210, 211, 212, 218, 222, 224, 230, 232, 238, 241, 246, 250, 251, 252, 254, 256, 259, 260
    s. also, Crude drawing
Filatäwos, equestrian saint, 48
Fiqṭor, equestrian saint, 48
Flower, 37
    drawing, 118

Gäbrä Mänfäs Qəddus, 17, 23, 24, 48, 53, 57, 60, 62, 68, 147, 165, 170, 177, 179, 192, 193, 202
    on magic scroll, 43, 46
Gäbrä Mäsqäl, king, 115
Gäbrä Ṣəyon, 140
Gabriel, archangel, 61, 112, 184
    on magic scroll, 55
    Rescuing the three Hebrew children, 184, 256
Gälawdewos, equestrian saint, 48
gänna, 48
Geometric design, 39, 104, 118, 182, 188, 213, 259
    on magic scroll, 66, 79, 83, 84, 85, 87, 90, 92, 93, 96, 97, 234, 240, 243, 246, 247, 259
George, equestrian saint, 48
    Martyrdom, 17, 69, 70, 71
    Spearing the Dragon, equestrian saint, 1, 17, 18, 23, 25, 26, 48, 52, 55, 63, 68, 70, 109, 121, 123, 127, 129, 147, 151, 161, 166, 176, 179, 180, 183, 186, 188, 192, 193, 202, 203
    crude drawing, 223, 225
    on magic scroll, 47

Gəra Geta Ǝngəda Säw, 180
God the Father, 61, 146, 203
    Ancient of Days, 10, 18, 127, 129
Golgotha, 167
Goliath and David, 37

Ḥaylä Śəllase, emperor, 37
Hermit, 37
Herod, 49
Hezekiah, 49
Holy Family, 164, 166
Holy Spirit, 25, 168
Horsemen of Revelation 6, 4
Host, 45, 104, 107, 109, 176, 194, 220
Hyssop branch, 4

Isaac, 49, 192
Israelite Children, 49
Israelites eating Mana, 37
Iyasu I, emperor, 48, 49
Iyasus Mo'a, 140

Jacob, 49, 192
James, 25
    Martyrdom, 19
Jesus, 144, 166, 197
    Anastasis, 19, 62
    Arrest, 18, 62, 164, 167, 170
    Ascension, 19, 62, 161, 165, 167, 168, 184
    At the temple, 170
    Baptism, 18, 61, 164, 192
    before Annas, 18
    before King Herod, 19
    before Pilate, 19
    before the High Priest, 19
    Betrayal by Judas, 18
    Blessing a man, 16
    Carrying the cross, 18, 37, 62, 165, 166, 167
    Deposition, 19, 62, 161, 165, 167, 169
    Enthroned, 166, 167, 169, 170
    Entombment, 19, 62, 161, 165, 166, 184
    Entry into Jerusalem, 192
    Flagellation, 18, 19, 62
    Flight into Egypt, 2, 18, 164, 175, 185, 192

Index of Miniatures   333

Flogging, 165
Foot Washing, 18, 164
Garden of Gethsemane, 164
Giving key to Peter, 21
Healing the blind, 164, 170
Holding the Sacred Heart, 184
Kidanä Məhrät, 18, 49, 165, 192
Last Supper, 18, 127, 164
Lifting Peter, 144
Mary Magdalene washing his feet, 203
Ministering to a woman, 166
Miracle at Cana, 165, 167, 169, 170
Mocking, 18, 19
Nailing to the cross, 19, 62, 165, 166
Nativity, 18, 48, 61, 164, 170, 203
On Mount Tabor, 159
Raising Lazarus, 164
Resurrection, 161, 165, 166, 167, 169, 170, 171, 184, 203
Samaritan woman, 170
Second Coming, 19, 24, 62
Striking of the Head, 62, 71, 105, 145, 166, 167, 169, 170, 186, 188, 192
Teaching, 164, 165, 166, 169
Temptation, 18, 61
Wrapped in Shroud, 62, 161, 167, 169, 170
s. also, Crucifixion
Joachim, 168, 197
John, Evangelist, 15, 45, 109, 125, 146, 154, 159, 169, 188
with an evil man, 19
John the Baptist
Beheading, 49, 63, 170
Jonah, 49
Josaphat, 200
Joseph, 48, 167, 192
Josiah, 49
Julitta, 49

King, 7, 24, 175, 176, 185
crude drawing, 205, 211
in a fire, 71
on magic scroll, 36, 59, 245, 261
King of Egypt, 6
Kiros, *abba*, 48, 49

Kiros, *abunä*, 193

Lalibäla, emperor, 192
Lamb of God, 53, 91, 145, 190, 191
Lazarus, 197
Ləbnä Dəngəl, emperor, 1
Lion of Judah, 32
crude drawing, 199
Luke, Evangelist, 25, 45, 125

Maccabees, 201
Madonna and Child, 2, 8, 10, 12, 16, 17, 18, 23, 25, 26, 44, 48, 52, 53, 55, 68, 104, 105, 109, 112, 115, 116, 121, 123, 125, 126, 127, 129, 131, 143, 145, 146, 147, 151, 152, 153, 155, 156, 157, 159, 161, 165, 166, 167, 168, 175, 178, 179, 182, 183, 185, 188, 189, 191, 192, 193, 196, 197, 199, 201, 202, 203, 206, 211, 212, 221, 222, 224, 228, 257
crude drawing, 13, 22, 24, 39, 45, 188, 210
drawing, 116
s. also, Mary
Man (unidentified), 159, 163, 168, 169, 210
arms upstretched, 191
bitten by snake, 4
chasing a rabbit, 3
climbing a tree, 3
climbing through window, 5
cutting off finger, 4
drawing water, 5
falling off cliff, 4
holding book, 147, 179, 228
holding cup, 4
holding handkerchief, 227, 230
holding jug, 168
holding prayer beads, 189
holding spear, 164, 230
holding sword, 4, 176
holding telescope, 6
measuring, 6

Man (unidentified) (cont.)
　pouring beer, 179
　riding rooster, 160
　searching, 5
　seated by a Psalter, 26
　stingy, 6
　wise, 4, 5
　writing, 6
Man-Beast, 6, 160
Mark, Evangelist, 25, 49, 125, 152
　Martyrdom, 20
Martyrdom of
　Abib, *abunä*, 17
　Andrew, 19
　Apostle, 25
　Bartholomew, 20
　Bula, *abba*, 17
　Ǝstifanos, 192
　George, 17, 70, 71
　James, 19, 25
　John the Baptist, 49, 63, 170
　Luke, 25
　Mark, 20, 25
　Matthew, 20, 25
　Matthias, 20, 25
　Nathaniel, 20
　Paul, 19
　Paul of Egypt, 17
　Saint (unidentified), 20
　Sebastian, 49
　Stephen, 49
　Thaddeus, 20
　Thomas, 20, 25, 50
Mary, 48, 151, 159, 164, 166, 167, 168, 169, 170, 171, 186, 192, 197, 203
　Annunciation, 2, 18, 61, 164, 166, 168, 170
　Appearing as a white bird, 62
　Assumption, 17, 165, 168, 169
　At Däbrä Mäṭmaq, 48
　At Däbrä Qwǝsqwam, 48
　At Golgotha, 168
　Delivering a soul, 62
　Dormition, 169
　Flight into Egypt, 2, 18, 164, 175, 185, 192
　Kidanä Mǝhrät, 18, 49, 165, 192
　Presentation to Temple, 48, 140, 168
　raising a saint, 167
　Surrounded by the four Living Creatures, 37
　Weeping, 71
　s. also, Madonna and Child
Maryam Mogäsa, 186
Matthew, Evangelist, 25, 44, 125
　Martyrdom, 20
Matthias, 25
　Martyrdom, 20
Medicine, 5, 6
Memros, 159
Mǝnilǝk II, emperor, 22, 183, 256
Mercurius, equestrian saint, 48
Michael, archangel, 11, 26, 49, 52, 112, 129, 159, 174, 177, 178, 182, 184, 185, 188, 193, 195, 203, 212, 219, 254, 258
　Defeating the devil, 129, 175, 195, 203
　Delivering souls, 129
　on magic scroll, 55
　Protecting a man, 203
　Raising the dead, 129
　Releasing captives, 129
　Rescuing Saint Euphemia, 129
Monastery, 151
Monk, 151
Moon, 259
Moses, 115
　Receiving the law, 49, 1177
Multi-box panel, 181, 182, 189, 190
　on magic scroll, 31, 32, 33, 35, 36, 38, 40, 41, 43, 44, 58, 59, 65, 67, 68, 72, 74, 75, 79, 80, 81, 82, 84, 85, 87, 88, 89, 90, 91, 92, 93, 94, 95, 98, 229, 231, 234, 235, 237, 239, 240, 241, 245, 246, 247, 249, 250, 251, 252, 253

Nääkweto Lääb, emperor, 25
Näṣärä Ab, *abba*, 17
Nathaniel
　Martyrdom, 20
Nero, emperor, 19
Nicaean Council, 218

Index of Miniatures 335

Nine Saints, 48
Nob, *abba*, 54

Painter, 151
Paralyzed man, 3
Paul
    Martyrdom, 19
Paul of Egypt
    Martyrdom, 17
Paul of Thebes, 49
Pentecost, 25, 165
Peter, 146
    Blessed by Jesus, 144
    Lifted up by Jesus, 144
    Martyrdom, 19
Phanuel, archangel, 33, 55
Philip, 25
    Angel rescuing Philip's dead body, 19
Philosopher, 3, 4, 5
Pilate, 19, 62, 65
Pishoy, 49
Plant, 189
Prayer Staff
    crude drawing, 148
Priest, 48, 49, 151, 176
Printed Card
    Jesus, 105, 188
    Crucifixion, 107, 211, 227
    Madonna and Child, 105, 131, 153, 155, 211
    Sebastian, 131
Prophet, 18

Raguel, archangel, 22, 53, 55, 145, 159, 178, 191
Romna, 146
Raphael, archangel, 127

Sacred being surrounded by wild creatures, 3
Saint, 2, 12, 17, 18, 48, 49, 126, 143, 151, 159, 166, 167, 169, 170, 171, 186, 197, 203
    crude drawing, 156
    holding a book, 127, 129, 177, 178, 183
    holding a jug, 186
    holding an orb, 183
    holding prayer beads, 192
    holding a rod with a fish, 129
    holding a scabbard, 208
    Receiving a blessing, 71
Salome, 48, 49, 192
Samaritan, Good, 3
Samson, 52
Samuʽel, *abba*, 48
    on magic scroll, 32
    riding a lion, 18, 46
Scribe, 1, 142, 151, 184
Sebastian, equestrian saint, 48
    printed card, 131
    Martyrdom of, 49
Səndat, 160
Shenute, 49
Shepherd, 3
Simeon the Stylite, 49
Solomon, 17, 49, 52, 115, 146
    on magic scroll, 33, 55, 66
Star, 51, 56, 259
Stoning, 25
Sun, 181, 259
Susənyos, equestrian saint, 160
    on magic scroll, 36, 42, 67

Tabot, 1
Täklä Alpha, *abba*
    spearing Əmmä Wəlud, 160
Täklä Əstifanos, 25
Täklä Haymanot, *abunä*, 17, 19, 23, 25, 48, 49, 63, 68, 140, 158, 160, 165, 178, 192
Talismanic symbol, 39, 45, 56, 117, 128, 150, 152, 156, 159, 173, 176, 179, 181, 182, 189, 190, 191, 214, 215
    crude drawing, 117, 188
    on magic scroll, 29, 30, 31, 33, 34, 35, 36, 40, 41, 42, 43, 44, 47, 55, 58, 59, 60, 65, 67, 68, 72, 73, 75, 76, 77, 78, 79, 80, 81, 82, 83, 84, 85, 86, 87, 88, 89, 90, 91, 92, 93, 97, 99, 215, 229, 232, 233, 234, 235, 236, 238, 239, 240, 241, 243, 244, 245, 246, 247, 251, 252, 253
Temple of Jerusalem, 2, 37, 140, 170
Tewodros, equestrian saint, 48, 140

Tewodros Masəriqawi, equestrian saint, 48
Tewogolos, 146
Thaddeus
    Martyrdom, 20
The three Hebrew children, 49, 184, 256
Thieves, 3, 6
Thomas, 25
    Carrying his flayed skin, 20, 50
Town Council, 7
Tree, 3, 4, 5
Trinity, 2, 54, 61, 73, 145, 151, 164, 166, 184, 190, 192, 197, 202, 203, 224, 228, 256
    on magic scroll, 73

Wäldä Maryam, 152
Wäldä Mäsqäl Tariku, *bitwäddäd*, 107

War, 7
Wheel
    crude drawing, 255
Woman, 51, 69, 166, 169, 170, 228
    attempting to enter town council, 7
    before Madonna and Child, 152
    nursing a baby, 2
    of Samaria, 170

Yared, 15, 16, 115, 146, 159, 181
Yoḥannəs Hasir, 49
Yoḥannəs, *abunä*, 107
Yoḥannəs, emperor, 49
Yosṭos, equestrian saint, 48

Zä-Iyasus, keeper of hours, 140
Zä-Kərstos Täsfanä, keeper of hours, 140
Zär'a Buruk, *abba*, 186, 192

Index of Names and Places in the Codices

Abrəham, *abunä*, 107
ʿAlämayyähu Mogäs, 27, 28, 102, 103
Alula, *ras*, 55, 147
Amära, *däbtära*, 221
ʿAmdä Ṣəyon, emperor, 69
Andreas, *abba*, 115
Anduʿaläm Mulaw, 53
Arʾaya, *ras*, 117
Asfaw Täsäma Wärqe, *grazmač*, 116, 120
Asmara, 253
Atənatewos, 202
Aṭme, *aläqa*, 34, 55
Aksum, 63, 64, 99, 134

Badəmma Yaläw, *qes*, 57
Baffana, 148
Bägemdər, 117
Bahəry, *abba*, 130
Bakawlé, 104
Bäkurä Ṣəyon Ṭəlahun, 111
Bar Kidanä Məhrät, monastery, 130
Barlaam, *abunä*, 200
Basəlyos, patriarch, 125, 146, 155, 176,
    181, 186
Bəčäna, 135
Bəčäna Giyorgis, 38
Bender, Marvin Lionel, 47
Black, Paul, 104, 105
Bogalä Dästa, 180
Boyd, S. Dempster, 64

Chaîne, M., 103
Chojnacki, S., 118

Cowley, R., 52
Curtopassi, Jacopo, 57
Cyril V, patriarch of Alexandria, 113,
    126, 160, 162, 185, 212

Däbrä Bərhan Śəllase, 53
Däbrä Dammo, 74, 176
Däbrä Dima, 38
Däbrä Libanos, 204
Däbrä Marqos, 38, 134
Däbrä Mäwi Maryam, 169
Däbrä Məṭmaq, 48
Däbrä Qwəsqwam, 18, 48, 165
Däbrä Ṣəmmuna, 38
Däbrä Ṣəyon, 152
Däbrä Wärq, 38, 135
Dämä Krəstos, 186
Dänägäṭu, *grazmač*, 194
Dästa Täklä Wäld, 140
Dəlnaʿod, emperor, 132
Deresa, *fitawrari*, 121
Dessie, 100
Desta, *fitawrari*, 163
Dima Giyorgis, 38
Dima, monastery, 142

Elyas, *abba*, 140
Ǝnbaqom Qalä Wäld, *aläqa*, 69, 99, 111
Ǝnbaqom, *aläqa*, 49, 135, 136, 137
Ǝndrəyas, *abba*, 101
Erlich, Haggai, 55
Ǝśäte Täkätäläw, *nägadras*, 148

Fleming, Harold, 47

Gäbrä Krəstos, *mämhər*, 165
Gäbrä Mädḫən, *aläqa*, 118
Gäbrä Mäsqäl Täsfaye, *mämhər*, 47
Gäbrä Mikaʾel Gərmu, 51
Gäbrä Śəllase Wäldä Arägay, *ṣäḥafe ṭəʾəzaz*, 101
Gäbrä Śəllase, *däǧǧazmač*, 196
Gäbrä Śəllase, *ečäge*, 193
Gäbrəʾel, bishop, 201
Galla, 69, 99, 116, 130, 180
Gamo, 126
Gännätä Maryam, 47
Gärima Täfärra, *ato*, 53
Gəra Geta Ǝngəda Säw, 180
Gidole, 105
Giusto da Urbino, 57
Goǧǧam, 38, 46, 99, 131, 134, 135, 142, 164, 169
Gondär, 52, 53, 165
Gugsa Wäle, ras, 116, 120

Harar, 27, 118
Ḥaylä Mäläkot, 11, 137
Ḥaylä Maryam Lämma, *däǧǧazmač*, 68
Ḥaylä Śəllase, emperor, 15, 20, 27, 37, 45, 50, 103, 111, 130, 131, 133, 134, 136, 147, 155, 176, 181, 186, 194, 198, 201, 227
Heavens, Andrew, 220
Henshaw, Amber, 220
Ḥeruy Wäldä Śəllase, *blatten geta*, 63, 173
Holy Trinity Theological College, 131

Iyasu I, emperor, 23, 48, 49, 54, 100, 225
Iyasu II, emperor, 148, 208
Iyasu, emperor, 25
Iyoʾas I, emperor, 15
Iyoʾas II, emperor, 195

John XVI, patriarch of Alexandria, 225
John XIX, patriarch of Alexandria, 174, 201
Josaphat, 200
Joseph II, patriarch of Alexandria, 146, 176, 195

Kaffa, 99
Kane, Thomas, 46
Kaśa, *däǧǧazmač*, 116
Kəfle Giyorgis, *mämhər*, 140
Kidana Maryam Gäbrä Ḥəywot, *mämhər*, 131
Kidanä Wäld Kəfle, *aläqa*, 101, 102, 117, 140, 144
Kirubel Bäšah, 121
Konso, 104, 105
Krəstos Haräyo, 47

Lämläm, *aläqa*, 116
Iyasu, *ləǧ*, king, 124
Ləsanä Wärq Gäbrä Giyorgis Gäbrä Śəlase, *märigeta*, 147
Leslau, Wolf, 27
Littmann, Enno, 51
Luqas, bishop, 194

Mäbaʾa Ṣəyon, *abunä*, 142
Maḫtämä Śəllase Wäldä Mäsqäl, *blatten geta*, 107, 108
Mäkwännən, *bitwäddäd*, 149
Mäləʾakä Bərhan, 153
Manan, empress, 45
Maqdala, 220
Marqos, *abba*, 133, 201
Marqos, bishop, 150
Marqos IV, metropolitan, 225
Märsəʿe Ḥazän Wäldä Qirqos, *blatten*, 120, 130
Maryam Mogäsa, 186
Mäsärätä Krəstos, church, 204
Mäse Qosəṭin, 137
Matewos, metropolitan, 10, 15, 46, 101, 110, 113, 115, 126, 160, 162, 185, 195, 197, 202, 211
Mekibib Zeleke, 54
Memros, 159
Mendenhall, George, 219
Mənilək I, king, 153
Mənilək II, emperor, 10, 11, 16, 22, 44, 101, 110, 114, 136, 144, 149, 153, 157, 161, 183, 184, 196, 202, 256, 260

Index of Names and Places in the Codices   339

Mika'el, king, 129
Mogäs Däräso, *märigeta qes*, 103
Mohamad Grañ, 156
Moret District, 52

Napier, R., 220
Näṣärä Ab, *abba*, 17
Näsibu Zä'amanu'el, *däǧǧazmač*, 39
Nəguśənna Zäwdu, 56

Oromo, 29, 34, 55, 130
Otto, Shako, 104, 105

Pankhurst, Richard, 219
Parker, Enid, 44
Pawlos Badma, 204
Peṭros IV, metropolitan, 46, 110, 162, 194, 195, 206, 211
Platt, Thomas Pell, 218

Qäranyo, church, 194
Qəddus Giyorgis, church, 142
Qerəllos VI, metropolitan, 154, 174, 198, 206, 220

Raunib, 54

Śahəle Täkaləñ, 120
Saint Stephen dei Mori, church, 63
Sälama, metropolitan, 11
Sartori, P. Gabriele, 68
Səmen, 117
Shoa, 111
Sinoda, metropolitan, 23, 54
Sirak Fekade Sellasie, 57
Susənyos, emperor, 136, 219

Ṭäbäbətäldu, *liqä*, 187
Täkäśtä Bərhan, *aläqa*, 171, 172
Täklä Ǝstifanos, 25
Täklä Giyorgis, emperor, 39, 116, 140
Täklä Giyorgis II, emperor, 50
Täklä Haymanot, 14, 23, 24, 44, 48, 61, 63, 68, 106, 133, 140, 144, 152, 156, 158, 160, 165, 174, 175, 178, 192, 254, 257

Täklä Haymanot, *abunä*, 17, 19, 25, 49, 204
Täklä Haymanot, king, 99, 133
Täkle of Wašära, 103
Täsäma, *aläqa*, 137
Täsfa Śəllase Mogäs, 130
Tašomä Šänquṭ, *däǧǧazmač*, 120
Teme, *aläqa*, 116
Tewodros II, emperor, 22, 51, 99, 118
Tewoflos, emperor, 210

Van Meter, Bruce and Barbie, 55, 111
Victoria, Queen of Britain, 144

Wäldä Maryam, *aläqa*, 22, 152
Wäldä Mäsqäl Tariku, *bitwäddäd*, 107
Wäldä Mika'el, *ras*, 137
Wäldä Sänbät, 185
Wäldä Tənsa'e Gəzaw, *mämhər*, 28, 29
Wänago Mənčəle, 137
Wašära, 103
Wəqaw, *däǧǧazmač abba*, 57
Wolaita Sodo Museum, 55
Wollamo Sodu Regional Museum, 111
Wollo, 129
Woynna Kidanä Məḥrät, monastery, 135

Yäräz Mika'el, 38
Yätäb Gäbrä Mänfäs Qəddus, 38
Yəkunno Amlak, 69
Yəsḥäq, *abba*, 212
Yoḥannəs, *abunä*, 107
Yoḥannəs I, emperor, 49, 57
Yoḥannəs II, emperor, 208
Yoḥannəs IV, emperor, 51, 115, 116, 140, 194
Yoḥannəs, patriarch, 39
Yosab II, metropolitan, 39

Zännäb, *däbtära*, 51, 99
Zär'a Ya'əqob, emperor, 65, 105, 117, 128, 158, 180, 199, 226
Zär'a Buruk, 142, 186, 193
Zäwditu, empress, 10, 15, 149
Zurich, University of, 54

Index of Names of Owners in the Magic Scrolls

ኅብ ሪቱ፡ ወለተ፡ ማርያም፡, 234
ኃብት፡ ማርያም፡ ዶቃ፡, 86
ሀብተ፡ ጊዮርጊስ፡ ገብረ፡ ሥላሴ፡, 230, 237
ኃይለ፡ ሚካኤል፡, 35
ኃይለ፡ ሚካኤል፡ ተክለ፡, 89
ኃይለ፡ ማርያም፡, 30, 237, 243
ኃይለ፡ ማርያም፡ (ኃይሉ፡), 78
ኃይለ፡ ሥላሴ፡ ኃይሉ፡, 73
ኃይለ፡ ኢየሱስ፡, 241
ኃይለ፡ እግዚአብሔር፡, 36
ኃይለ፡ ጊዮርጊስ፡, 90
ኒሩተ፡ ሥላሴ፡ ደስታ፡, 66
ለማ፡, 93
ለማ፡ ገብረ፡ ጻድቅ፡, 79
ለተ፡ ገብርኤል፡ ዓለምነሽ፡, 90
ላህያ፡ ድንግል፡, 67
ልጅ፡ ተክለ፡ መድኃን, 95
መልክአ፡ ማርያም፡, 36
መስፍን፡ አየለ፡, 86
መንገሻ፡, 72
ሙሉነህ፡ ኃይለ፡ መርያም፡, 93
ሚካኤል፡, 247
ማረች፡, 236
ማርያም፡ እናኑ፡, 83
ሰሎሞን፡ ክፍለ፡ ማርያም፡, 76
ሰበነ፡ ጊዮርጊስ፡, 97
ሰይፈ፡ ሥላሴ፡, 84
ሣህለ፡ ሥላሴ፡, 97
ስለሺ፡, 75
ሥላሴ፡, 55
ስመኝ፡, 81
ሥራሐ፡ ድንግል፡, 31
ርግበ፡ ዳዊት፡, 36

ሮማን፡, 72
ሸቀም፡, 251
ሺፈራው፡ ገብረ፡ ተክለሃይማኖት፡, 75
ቀነኒ፡ ኃይለ፡ ማርያም፡, 79, 85
ቄስ፡ የሻነው፡ አፈወርቅ፡, 95
በቀለች፡, 88
በየን፡ ወልደ፡ ሐዋርያት፡, 80
በየኔ፡, 86
በግጹ፡ አበቡ፡, 89
ብሥራተ፡ ማርያም፡, 34
ገብረ፡ ጊዮርጊስ፡ የሻነው፡, 73
ገብረ፡ ጻድቅ፡, 89, 91, 240
ብርሃነ፡ ሚካኤል፡, 82
ብዙነሽ፡ (ወለተ፡ ሐና፡), 81
ብዙነሽ፡ ወለተ፡ ማርያም፡, 79
ቦጋለች፡ (ወለተ፡ ጻድቅ፡), 84
ቦጋለች፡ አስካለ፡ ሥላሴ፡, 89
ተሊላ፡, 75
ተስፋ፡ ማርያም፡, 29, 230
ተስፋ፡ ሥላሴ፡, 34
ተረጨ፡ አካለ፡ ወልድ፡, 96
ተሾመ፡ ተፈራ፡ (አክሊለ፡ ማርያም፡), 80
ተክልኝ፡, 88
ተክለ፡ ሃይማኖት፡, 46
ተክለ፡ ሚካኤል፡, 46
ተክለ፡ ማርያም፡, 94
ተክለ፡ ወልድ፡ ማሞ፡, 96
ተክለ፡ ጊዮርጊስ፡, 72
ተክለ፡ ጊዮርጊስ፡ ተክሉ፡, 91
ተክለሃይማኖት፡ (ሺፈራው፡), 75
ተንዲ፡, 248
ተጠምቀ፡ መድኃን፡, 66
ቱራ፡ ገብረ፡ ሚካኤል፡, 93

Index of Names of Owners in the Magic Scrolls

ታከለ፡ (ኃይለ፡ ሚካኤል፡), 69
ታዬ፡ ቀጸለ ጊዮርጊስ፡, 93
ታፈሰ፡ ኃይለ፡ ኢየሱስ፡, 88
ንግሥተ፡ ማርያም፡, 58, 235
ንግሥተ፡ አዜብ፡, 40
ንግሥቴ፡ ንግሥተ፡, 67
ንግር፡, 248
አሌሉዓያ፡ ማርያም፡, 86
አልጋሽ፡ ሥርጉተ፡ ሥላሴ፡, 244
አመተ፡ ሚካኤል፡, 238, 253
አመተ፡ ማርያም፡, 101, 242, 251, 253
አመተ፡ ሥላሴ፡, 250
አመተ፡ ኢየሱስ፡, 38, 59, 244
አመተ፡ ኢየሱስ፡ ጥሩየ፡, 246
አመተ፡ ዮሐንስ፡ በሃብታ፡, 67
አመተ፡ ጸድቃን፡, 59, 236, 238, 245
አሰበ፡, 92
አሰን፡, 33
አሰገደች፡ ጽጌ፡ ማርያም፡, 80
አሰፋ፡ ገብረ፡ ሚካኤል፡, 93
አሥራተ፡ ማርያም፡ ከበበ፡, 75, 90
አስካለ፡ ማርያም፡, 80, 82, 253
አርአያ፡ ሥላሴ፡, 95
አርጉ፡, 244
አበበች፡, 89
አበበች፡ ወለተ፡ ሚካኤል፡, 83
አበበች፡ ወለተ፡ ማርያም፡, 92
አበበች፡ ወለተ፡ ሥላሴ፡, 240
አቦየ፡ ገብረ፡ እግዚአብሔር፡, 55
አባ፡ ማንፀን፡ እዳየሱስ፡, 31
አክሊሉ፡ ሰማዕት፡, 95
አክሊሉ፡ ገብረ፡ ሚካኤል፡, 79
አውላቸው፡ ወልድ፡ መደህን፡, 84
አየለች፡ አስካለ፡ ማርያም፡, 95
አጥናፉ፡ ገብረ፡ ሥላሴ፡, 85
አጸደ፡ ማርያም፡ (ሎሚ፡), 79
አጸደ፡ ማርያም፡ ወርቅነሽ፡, 89
አጽመ፡ ጊዮርጊስ፡, 81
ዓመተ፡ ሚካኤል፡, 237
ዓመተ፡ ማርያም፡, 60, 67, 90, 96
ዓመተ፡ ማርያም፡ ወርቂቱ፡, 82
ዓመተ፡ ዮሐንስ፡, 66, 235, 242, 245
ዓስካለ፡ ማርያም፡ (ፋናየ፡), 76
ዓቢየ፡ እግዚእ፡, 58
ዓፀደ፡ ማርያም፡, 78, 94
ዓጸደ፡ ማርያም፡ ከበቡሽ፡, 94
ዓፀደ፡ ማርያም፡ ወርቅነሽ፡, 73, 91
እንተ፡ ገብርኤል፡ (ይሻረጋ፡), 83

እንተ፡ ማርያም፡, 82
እንተ፡ ጊዮርጊስ፡ ምንትዋብ፡, 88
እልፉ፡, 72
እሴተ፡ ማርያም፡, 90
እሸቱ፡ ገብረ፡ ማርያም፡, 92
እሸቲ፡ ገብረ፡ ማርያም፡, 85
እትአለምሁ፡, 77
ከበደ፡, 87
ከበደ፡ (ገብረ፡ ኢየሱስ፡), 80
ኪዳነ፡ ማርያም፡, 35
ኪዳን፡ ማርያም፡, 229, 235, 241
ክበበ፡ ፀሐይ፡, 76, 87
ክንፈ፡ ሚካኤል፡, 82
ክንፈ፡ ገብርኤል፡, 80
ወለተ፡ ሐርገወይን፡, 58
ወለተ፡ ሐና፡, 32
ወለተ፡ ሃይማኖት፡, 41, 46
ወለተ፡ ሕይወት፡, 30, 32, 33, 41, 96, 98
ወለተ፡ ሕይወት፡ ገብረ፡ ሕይወት፡, 43
ወለተ፡ መስቀል፡, 239
ወለተ፡ መድህን፡, 236
ወለተ፡ መድህን፡ መነን፡, 93
ወለተ፡ መድህን፡ መንን፡, 86
ወለተ፡ መድጎን፡, 58, 66, 233, 242, 245, 249
ወለተ፡ መድጎን፡ እተነስ፡, 90
ወለተ፡ መድጎን፡ ወለተ፡ ሥላሴ፡, 238
ወለተ፡ ሙሴ፡, 43, 65
ወለተ፡ ሚካኤል፡, 42, 66, 67, 73, 80, 96, 231, 245, 248, 249
ወለተ፡ ሚካኤል፡ ይሓላየ፡, 33
ወለተ፡ ሚካኤል፡ ግሀቱ፡, 252
ወለተ፡ ማርያም፡, 32, 36, 40, 42, 43, 59, 60, 66, 92, 97, 231, 236, 237, 238, 241, 243, 249, 250, 253
ወለተ፡ ማርያም፡ (ሌንሴ፡), 84
ወለተ፡ ማርያም፡ (በቀለች፡), 84
ወለተ፡ ማርያም፡ (ብዙዓለም፡), 77
ወለተ፡ ማርያም፡ (ጣይቱጌጢቱ፡), 78
ወለተ፡ ማርያም፡ ሻሼ፡, 88
ወለተ፡ ማርያም፡ በቀለች፡, 91
ወለተ፡ ማርያም፡ ቡላቂት፡, 78
ወለተ፡ ማርያም፡ ትኮነሽ፡, 252
ወለተ፡ ማርያም፡ አበበች፡, 88
ወለተ፡ ማርያም፡ ወርቂቱ፡, 233
ወለተ፡ ማርያም፡ ዘርጊ፡, 95
ወለተ፡ ማርያም፡ ገብሬ፡, 230

Index of Names of Owners in the Magic Scrolls

ወለተ፡ ሰጊነ፡ ሥላሴ፡, 233
ወለተ፡ ሰማዕት፡ አለማየሁ፡, 92
ወለተ፡ ሰንበት፡, 98, 240
ወለተ፡ ሰንበት፡ በሻዱ፡, 92
ወለተ፡ ሰንበት፡ ትረጕ፡, 247
ወለተ፡ ሰንበት፡ የብልጫ፡, 87
ወለተ፡ ሰንበት፡ ደልደዋ፡, 85
ወለተ፡ ሰንበት፡ ጥሩ፡, 234
ወለተ፡ ሴት፡, 35
ወለተ፡ ሥለሴ፡, 229
ወለተ፡ ሥላሲ፡ ጥሩነሽ፡, 88
ወለተ፡ ሥላሴ፡, 36, 40, 41, 43, 44, 85, 236, 238, 239, 241, 249, 250
ወለተ፡ ሥላሴ፡ ሐረጉ፡, 242
ወለተ፡ ሥላሴ፡ ዝማነሺ፡, 94
ወለተ፡ ሩፋኤል፡, 41, 58
ወለተ፡ ሩፋኤል፡ (አስናቀች፡), 84
ወለተ፡ ቂርቆስ፡, 96
ወለተ፡ ቂርቆስ፡ ዘሩቱ፡, 261
ወለተ፡ ቃለ፡ አብ፡, 233
ወለተ፡ ብርሃን፡, 67
ወለተ፡ ተክለ፡ ሃይማኖት፡, 29, 35, 36, 41, 43, 59, 96, 239, 241
ወለተ፡ ተክለ፡ ሃይማኖት፡ አየለች፡, 87
ወለተ፡ ተድሉ፡ መድህን፡, 233
ወለተ፡ ትንሣኢ፡, 249
ወለተ፡ ትንሣኤ፡, 253
ወለተ፡ አመተ፡ ኢየሱስ፡, 60
ወለተ፡ አረጋዊ፡, 93
ወለተ፡ አብርሃ፡, 237
ወለተ፡ አብርሃ፡ ጽዮን፡, 251
ወለተ፡ ኢየሱስ፡, 31, 42, 58, 59, 233, 245, 246, 251
ወለተ፡ ኢየሱስ፡ ስጊነ፡, 248
ወለተ፡ ኢየሱስ፡ እታዩ፡ እት፡ አዩ፡, 231
ወለተ፡ ዓቢየ፡ እግዚእ፡, 41
ወለተ፡ ዓቢየ፡ እግዚእ፡, 41
ወለተ፡ ኤሊያስ፡ ዛበች፡, 95
ወለተ፡ እግዚእ፡, 33, 230, 251
ወለተ፡ እግዚእ፡ ወለተዝጐ፡, 246
ወለተ፡ ኪዳን፡, 67, 91, 98, 231, 232, 235, 237, 243, 245
ወለተ፡ ኪዳን፡ አበበች፡, 77
ወለተ፡ ኪዳን፡ ወርት፡, 250
ወለተ፡ ኪዳን፡ ድርጌ፡, 99
ወለተ፡ ወል፡ ወለተ፡ ሃና፡ ዘነበች፡, 252
ወለተ፡ ወልደ፡, 81

ወለተ፡ ወልድ፡ (ስመኛ፡), 77
ወለተ፡ ወልድ፡ (ወርቅነሽ፡), 77
ወለተ፡ ዋህድ፡, 31
ወለተ፡ ዚደን፡ ደሰ፡, 233
ወለተ፡ ዮሐንስ፡, 59, 242
ወለተ፡ ዮሐንስ፡ ማርሸኛ፡, 238
ወለተ፡ ዮሐንስ፡ ባች፡ አምላክ፡, 79
ወለተ፡ ገብርኤል፡, 60, 228, 232, 233, 243, 246, 248
ወለተ፡ ገብርኤል፡ (ይሻረጒ፡), 83
ወለተ፡ ገብርኤል፡ ቦሰና፡, 36
ወለተ፡ ገብርኤል፡ ኪዳኔ፡, 82
ወለተ፡ ጊዮርጊስ፡, 42, 98, 229, 230, 236
ወለተ፡ ጊዮርጊስ፡ ማሚተ፡, 93
ወለተ፡ ጊዮርጊስ፡ ወልደ፡ ተከለ፡ ሃይማኖት፡, 34
ወለተ፡ ጻድቃ፡ (ጻድቃን፡) እታለሙ፡, 90
ወለተ፡ ጻድቃን፡, 42, 239, 246, 249, 251, 252
ወለተ፡ ጻድቃን፡ መብራህቲ፡, 247
ወለተ፡ ጻድቅ፡ (ቦጋለች፡), 75
ወለተ፡ ጻድቅ፡ (አሰለፈች፡), 76
ወለተ፡ ጻድቅ፡ አበበች፡, 85
ወለተ፡ ጻድቅ፡ አቻሽማነው፡, 90
ወለተ፡ ጻድቅ፡ ወርቂ፡ (ወርቅነሽ፡), 75
ወለተ፡ ሥላሴ፡ (ዝማነሽ፡), 78
ወለደ፡ ኪዳን፡, 32
ወለደ፡ ሐዋርያት፡, 235
ወለደ፡ ሚካኤል፡, 43, 92
ወለደ፡ ሚካኤል፡ አያሌው፡, 82, 83
ወለደ፡ ማርያም፡, 43, 71, 86, 98
ወለደ፡ ማርያም፡ ቤቲ፡, 86
ወለደ፡ ሰማዕት፡ ከበደ፡, 79
ወልደ፡ ሥላሴ፡, 43, 242
ወልደ፡ ተክለ፡ ሃይማኖት፡ ይንገሥ፡, 82
ወልደ፡ ትንሣኤ፡, 89, 246
ወልደ፡ አማኑኤል፡, 78
ወልደ፡ አምክ፡, 58
ወልደ፡ አረጋይ፡, 43
ወልደ፡ ኢየሱስ፡, 65, 97
ወልደ፡ እግዚአብሔር፡ ኦርዓያ፡, 30
ወልደ፡ ዮሐንስ፡, 43, 76, 250
ወልደ፡ ገራማ፡, 231, 235
ወልደ፡ ገብርኤል፡, 40, 65
ወልደ፡ ጊዮርጊስ፡, 236
ወልደ፡ ጊዮርጊስ፡ መላኩ፡, 72
ወርቂቱ፡, 232
ወርቃራሁ፡ እንተማርያም፡, 75

Index of Names of Owners in the Magic Scrolls

ወርቃፈሩሁ፡ እናተ፡ ማርያም፡, 92
ወርቅአፈሩሁ፡ እናተ፡ ማርያም፡, 87
ዋጋዬ፡, 71
ውልቅቱ፡ ጨሬ፡, 71
ውጢቱ፡ ወለተ፡ ኢየሱስ፡, 252
ዘሥላሴ፡, 47
ዘነቦች፡, 84
ዘውዲ፡, 88
ዘውዲቱ፡, 74
ዘውዲቱ፡ (ዘውዬ፡), 78
የሺ፡, 92
የሽአራግ፡ ወለተ፡ ዮሐንስ፡, 76
የብንል፡, 251
የግሌ፡ እናተ፡ ገብርኤል፡, 95
ያልጋ፡, 235
ያልጋነሽ፡, 233
ያልጋኔሽ፡, 238
ይግለጡ፡ ተክለ፡ ሥላሴ፡, 81
ዮሐንስ፡ ሐጽጉ፡, 245
ደስታ፡ ዓመተ፡ ማርያም፡, 86
ደርቤ፡ አራጋው፡, 32
ደብረ፡ ማርያም፡, 33
ደብሪቱ፡, 30
ድርብ፡ ድርብ፡, 244
ድብሪቱ፡, 81
ጆን፡ ወልዳ፡ ዮሐንስ፡ ሕናይስኪ፡, 33
ገርጉ፡, 76
ገብረ፡ እግዚአብሔር፡, 39, 58, 92
ገብረ፡ ሐና፡ ይማም፡, 91
ገብረ፡ ሕይወት፡, 31, 43, 235
ገብረ፡ ሕይወት፡ (ገብረ፡ ኃይወት፡), 250
ገብረ፡ መስቀል፡, 97, 230, 237
ገብረ፡ መድኅን፡, 33
ገብረ፡ ሚካኤል፡, 96, 240
ገብረ፡ ማርያም፡, 43, 229, 235
ገብረ፡ ማርያም፡ ወለተ፡ ሥላሴ፡, 232
ገብረ፡ ማርያም፡ ገብሬ፡, 84
ገብረ፡ ሰንበት፡ ኬሬ፡, 76

ገብረ፡ ሰንበት፡ ገብሬ፡, 90
ገብረ፡ ሥላሴ፡, 39, 65, 97
ገብረ፡ ቂርቆስ፡, 97
ገብረ፡ አናንያ፡, 59
ገብረ፡ ኢየሱስ፡, 97, 98
ገብረ፡ ኢየሱስ፡ ዳርጌ፡, 71, 72
ገብረ፡ ኤያቄም፡, 97
ገብረ፡ እግዚአብሔር፡, 39, 58, 92
ገብረ፡ ወልድ፡, 85
ገብረ፡ ወልድ፡ ሞላ፡, 80
ገብረ፡ ኢየሱስ፡ ዳርጌ፡, 71, 72
ገብረ፡ ጻድቅ፡, 89, 91, 240
ገብረ፡ ኪዳን፡ ንጉሤ፡, 78
ገብራ፡ ማርያም፡, 30
ገብቶ፡ ወለተ፡ መድኅን፡, 81
ገድለ፡ ተክለ፡ ሃይማኖት፡, 29
ጉቱ፡ ገብረ፡ ሰንበት፡, 87
ጊታንሀ፡ ገብረ፡ መድኅን፡, 81
ጌትነት፡, 73
ግብረ፡ መስቀል፡, 35
ጤጋ፡ ገብረ፡ ማርያም፡, 81
ጣሒሬ, 232, 239
ጥላሁን፡ ኃይለ፡ ሥላሴ፡, 77
ጥላሁን፡ ገብረ፡ ሥላሴ፡, 83
ጥሩነሽ፡ አስካለ፡ ማርያም፡, 73
ጸምሮ፡ ቃለ፡, 97
ጸዳለ፡ ማርያም፡ ጨዳል፡, 90
ጽጌ፡ ሐና፡, 75
ጽጌ፡ ሚካኤል፡, 230
ጽጌ፡ ማርያም፡, 30, 85, 89, 94
ጽጌ፡ ማርያም፡ አባተ፡, 82
ጸፈተ፡ ሥላሴ፡, 96
ፈለቀ፡ ወልደ፡ ሚካኤል፡, 93
ፍሥሓ፡ ጊዮርጊስ፡, 31
ፍጢማ፡, 240, 243, 244
ፓሩ፡ ወለተ፡ ሰንበት፡, 249
ፓሩዬ፡ አመተ፡ ኢየሱስ፡, 252

www.ingramcontent.com/pod-product-compliance
Lightning Source LLC
Chambersburg PA
CBHW040744020526
44114CB00048B/2902